NEWCOMER'S
HANDBOOK

FOR MOVING TO AND LIVING IN

NEW YORK CITY

Including Manhattan, Broooklyn, The Bronx,
Queens, Staten Island, and Northern New Jersey

23rd Edition

FIRST BOOKS

503-968-6777
www.firstbooks.com

Newcomer's Handbook for Moving to and Living in New York City, 23rd Edition

Newcomer's Handbook® and First Books® are registered trademarks of First Books.

Author (23rd Edition): Julie Schwietert Collazo. Previous Editions: Stewart Lee Allen, Jennifer Cecil, Jack Finnegan, and Belden Merims
Editors: Holly Tri, Linda Franklin
Cover design and layout: Erin Johnson Design and Masha Shubin
Interior neighborhood photos: Stewart Lee Allen
Cover Images: Chrysler Building, Brooklyn Bridge, Moon/Stars by Erin Johnson; Statue of Liberty © 2009 susaro (iStockPhoto.com); Bethesda Terrace by Masha Shubin
Interior design: Erin Johnson Design
Interior layout and composition: Masha Shubin
Maps provided by Scott Lockheed and Jim Miller/fennana design

Paperback: ISBN-13: 978-1-937090-59-3   ISBN-10: 1-937090-59-0
Kindle: ISBN-13: 978-1-937090-60-9   ISBN-10: 1-937090-60-4
ePub: ISBN-13: 978-1-937090-61-6   ISBN-10: 1-937090-61-2

Printed in the USA on recycled paper.

Published by First Books®, 503-968-6777, www.firstbooks.com.

What readers are saying about *Newcomer's Handbooks*:

I recently moved to Atlanta from San Francisco, and LOVE the ***Newcomer's Handbook for Atlanta***. It has been an invaluable resource—it's helped me find everything from a neighborhood in which to live to the local hardware store. I look something up in it everyday, and know I will continue to use it to find things long after I'm no longer a newcomer. And if I ever decide to move again, your book will be the first thing I buy for my next destination.

– Courtney R.
Atlanta, Georgia

I recently got a copy of your ***Newcomer's Handbook for Chicago,*** and wanted to let you know how invaluable it was for my move. I must have consulted it a dozen times a day preparing for my move. It helped me find my way around town, find a place to live, and so many other things. Thanks.

– Mike L.
Chicago, Illinois

Excellent reading (***Newcomer's Handbook for San Francisco and the Bay Area***) ... balanced and trustworthy. One of the very best guides if you are considering moving/relocation. Way above the usual tourist crap.

– Gunnar E.
Stockholm, Sweden

I was very impressed with the latest edition of the ***Newcomer's Handbook for Los Angeles***. It is well organized, concise and up-to-date. I would recommend this book to anyone considering a move to Los Angeles.

– Jannette L.
Attorney Recruiting Administrator for a large Los Angeles law firm

In looking to move to the Boston area, a potential employer in that area gave me a copy of the ***Newcomer's Handbook for Boston***. It's a great book that's very comprehensive, outlining good and bad points about each neighborhood in the Boston area. Very helpful in helping me decide where to move.

– no name given (online submit form)

TABLE OF CONTENTS

THIS BOOK IS DEDICATED TO THE PROPOSITION THAT LIVING IN NEW York City is something extraordinary and wonderful. However, the transition from newcomer to New Yorker isn't necessarily achieved without some discomfort. To minimize the difficulties involved in moving to the Big Apple, we have written the *Newcomer's Handbook® for Moving to and Living in New York City*, which has been continually updated since its 1980 inception, in order to keep up with change in this fastest-paced of cities. These pages will help you navigate this magnificent city and set you on the path to becoming a New Yorker yourself. Whether you are looking for the right neighborhood, the right health club, the right synagogue, or simply a quiet, green oasis, these chapters will guide you in your search.

In addition to regular updating, this 23rd edition includes new information on finding a home to rent or buy in the **Finding a Place to Live** chapter, as well as new activities for the active in **Sports and Recreation**, some direction for those seeking a brief respite from the city in **Quick Getaways**, and the most current information on everything from phone lines to satellite radio in **Getting Settled**. The chapter **Green Living** is devoted to greening your home, finding environmentally friendly services and products, using greener transportation, and identifying green resources. Throughout the book, wherever available, we've included websites for institutions and establishments that are mentioned. There is information on getting around the city by subway, bus, bike, and by car in the **Transportation** chapter. For the outdoorsy and nature loving, you'll find the **Greenspaces** chapter helpful, and for the erudite and inquisitive, see the **Cultural Life** chapter.

As usual, we welcome readers' suggestions and comments on the tear-out page at the back of the book.

We hope that the information presented on the following pages will help you establish a New York City residence smoothly and speedily. We also hope that once you select your neighborhood and settle in, the book will help you get on with the pleasure part: enjoyment of the city's myriad and unrivaled resources. Should you have any city-specific queries, from questions about parking, trash pickup, or upcoming neighborhood festivals, dial the city's call center at 311 (outside New York City, 212-639-9675). Operators are on duty 24/7 and will work to answer your questions or direct you to the appropriate New York City agency. You can also visit the city's official website: www.nyc.gov.

F ROM THE WIND-WHIPPED CORNER OF EAST END AVENUE ON AN ICY January evening, Greenwich Village seems as accessible as Alaska. So you cancel plans to meet a Village acquaintance downtown, call a friend on East 67th, and get together at an Upper East Side bistro instead. Clearly, the neighborhood in which you live affects what you do and whom you see in New York City. It takes time, exploration, and a certain street-honed sophistication to feel at home in any new area, but the fact that New York is a walking city will benefit you tremendously as you get to know it. Unless money is no object, today's rental market often requires compromises, not only in the way you live but also in the neighborhood you choose. But wherever you settle, once established, you're likely to become rooted in your own part of town.

More than just an address or a source of necessary services, neighborhoods provide residents with identification and a sense of belonging, which in turn provides sufficient sustenance and heart for daily confrontations with the city's size and pace. Most New Yorkers feel fairly chauvinistic about their area and delight in extolling its virtues—and detailing its faults. As large as New York City is, individual neighborhoods are often as tight-knit as small towns.

In the following profiles, Manhattan neighborhoods are listed clockwise (picture an exceedingly elongated clock) starting with Yorkville, continuing south along the East River, downtown, around the tip of the island, and then uptown along the Hudson, ending with Washington Heights/Inwood. Descriptions of communities in The Bronx, Brooklyn, Queens, and Staten Island—as well as five in New Jersey—follow Manhattan. No description, however, can substitute for your own experience. You are strongly encouraged to visit the neighborhoods that interest you and talk to residents before signing a lease. (Among other things, it is an excellent way to get leads on apartments that might otherwise escape your attention.) Resources and city services within each neighborhood are included in order to facilitate orientation once you're settled.

For newcomers who might wish to look farther afield, to the suburbs for example, we have listed additional communities worth investigating in Brooklyn, Queens, and Staten Island, as well as suburban towns in New Jersey, Connecticut, Westchester County, NY, and Long Island, none more than an hour's commute from Manhattan. Your choice of location will depend largely on where you will be working, your life situation (single, married, family, gay, etc.), your economic situation, what you enjoy doing, and what neighborhood ambiance appeals to you. Suggestions on how to go about finding an apartment or house and how best to enjoy the city come after **Neighborhoods**, in **Finding a Place to Live** and in other sections.

FORMULAS FOR FINDING STREET AND AVENUE ADDRESSES ABOVE 14TH Street are described below. Crosstown street numbers follow a more-or-less set pattern; not so for avenue street numbers. In a town where 950 Amsterdam Avenue is at 107th Street, 950 Broadway at 23rd, 950 Fifth at 76th, and 950 Third at 57th, the somewhat elaborate system used to discover the location of an avenue address is worth knowing.

EAST AND WEST SIDE AVENUES

To determine the cross street for an address on an avenue, proceed as follows: first, take off the last digit of the building number; second, divide the remainder by two; third, add or subtract the number given in the column below.*

Avenues A, B, C, D . . . . + 3
1st Ave . . . . +3
2nd Ave . . . . +3
3rd Ave . . . . +10
4th Ave . . . . +8
5th Ave
    Up to 200 . . . . *+13*
    Up to 400 . . . . *+16*
    Up to 600 . . . . *+18*
    Up to 775 . . . . *+20*
    From 775 to 1286
    (cancel last figure) . . . . *-18*
6th Ave
    (Ave of the Americas) . . . . *-12*
7th Ave
    Below 110th St. . . . . *+12*
    Above 110th St. . . . . *+20*
8th Ave . . . . +10
9th Ave . . . . +13
10th Ave . . . . +14
Amsterdam Ave . . . . +60
Broadway
    Above 23rd St. . . . . *-30*
Columbus Ave . . . . +60
Convent Ave . . . . +127
Lenox Ave . . . . +110

Lexington Ave . . . . +22
Madison Ave . . . . +26
Manhattan Ave . . . . +100
Park Ave . . . . +35
West End Ave . . . . +60

EAST SIDE CROSSTOWN STREETS

5th to Madison & Park 1-99
Park to Lexington 100-139
Lexington to 3rd 140-199
3rd to 2nd .200-299
2nd to 1st .300-399
1st to York .400-499

WEST SIDE CROSSTOWN BELOW 58TH

5th to Ave of Americas 1-99
Ave of Americas to 7th 100-199
7th to 8th .200-299
8th to 9th .300-399
9th to 10th .400-499
10th to 11th 5 00-599

WEST SIDE CROSSTOWN ABOVE 58TH

Central Park West to Columbus .100-199
Columbus to Amsterdam 200-299
Amsterdam to West End 300-399
West End to Riverside 400-499

*Central Park West and Riverside Drive do not fit into this formula. Divide the house number by 10 and add 60 to find the cross street on Central Park West; for Riverside Drive, divide the house number by 10 and add 72.

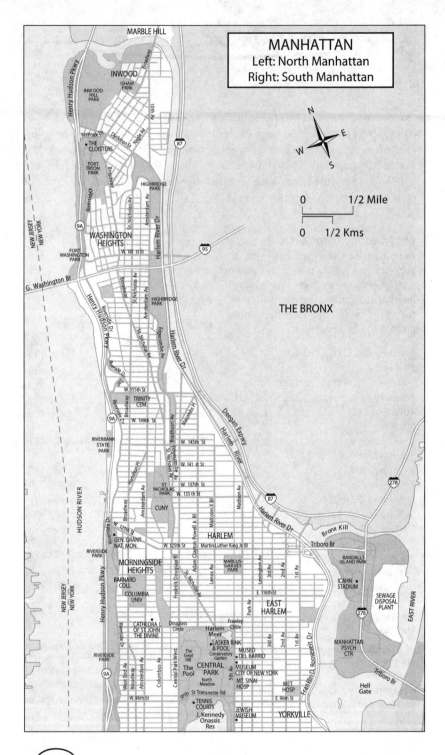

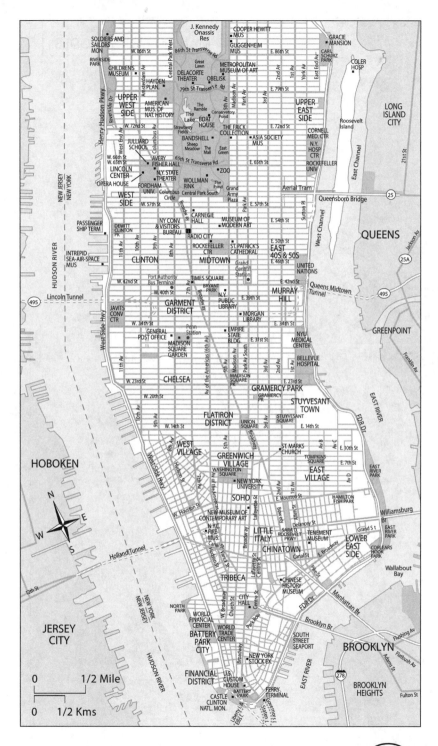

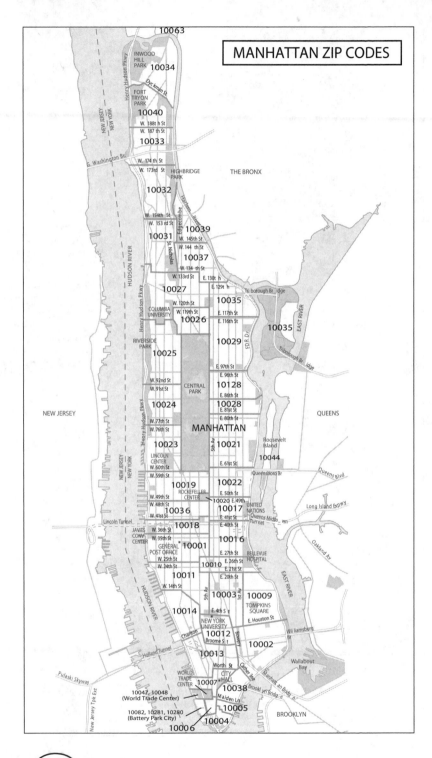

MANHATTAN ZIP CODES

MANHATTAN

"New York, New York, it's a wonderful town, The Bronx is up and the Battery's down," goes the song. That'll do for a start. Like the rest of the world, when New Yorkers say New York they generally mean Manhattan. And from Manhattan, The Bronx is up (north), and the Battery is the southern-most tip of this long, skinny island. To navigate Manhattan you need to know that the island is plotted out in a grid, with crosstown streets running east and west, and avenues stretching north and south, except below 14th Street, where much of the street pattern becomes irregular. Fifth Avenue bisects most of this grid, with cross streets designated east or west. For example, West 25th Street runs west of Fifth Avenue; East 25th stretches east from Fifth. Building numbers begin at Fifth, so 15 West 25th Street is on the first block west of Fifth Avenue and 15 East 25th Street is on the block east of Fifth Avenue. North to south there are 20 city blocks to a mile; crosstown blocks are longer, but not uniformly. The longest avenue in Manhattan, and the oldest, Broadway follows an old Indian trail from the Battery up north through the top of the island into The Bronx. Unlike the other avenues, it crosses from the east side to the west side as it winds its way along.

YORKVILLE

Boundaries and Contiguous Areas: North: East 96th Street and East Harlem; **East**: East River; **South**: East 79th Street and Upper East Side; **West**: Lexington Avenue and Upper East Side

What once distinguished **Yorkville** from its Upper East Side surroundings was the character imbued by immigrants from Germany and Eastern Europe. Now, however, you'll find more co-op signs and health clubs than residents of Hungarian or Czech ancestry. In the 1980s, a co-op, condo, and rental apartment boom finished off what World War II started: the erosion of Yorkville's old-world ethnicity. Although you will still find some old walk-ups on cross streets in the east 80s, most of these pre-war buildings were leveled, beginning in the late 1940s, to make way for new apartment buildings attractive to professionals who, once drawn to the neighborhood, began replacing the immigrants in the remaining railroad flats. Only traces of Yorkville's European heritage remain, and while Yorkville is still the most accessible part of the Upper East Side, what began as a scattering of stolid brick apartment buildings in mid-century is now an area chockablock with high-price high-rises.

Eighty-sixth Street, from Lexington to First avenues, has been attempting to redefine itself into a pricier shopping strip for nearly a decade; however, most of the shopping choices along the well-traveled 86th Street are currently of the chain store variety, with well-known fast food eateries and popular electronics retailers turning the area into a kind of open-air mall. Several cinemas are also found here, as is a mega-branch of Barnes & Noble and an East Side outpost of Fairway, the quintessential New York City grocery store. If you're looking for smaller mom-and-pop shops, head to York Avenue, where you'll find hold-outs like the much-loved Ottomanelli Butcher Shop and a handful of Hungarian bakeries.

Yorkville was a pleasant rural community when the first wave of German and Irish immigrants arrived on these shores in the 1850s. Tranquil pastures surrounded river estates owned by wealthy merchants, many of whom were of German origin. In the 1880s the completion of the Second and Third Avenue elevated lines opened the area to settlement, and German immigrants, many attracted by jobs in the developing breweries, moved north from the Lower East Side. Irish immigrants followed and then, as they grew more prosperous, Hungarians, Czechs, and Slovaks. Today their descendants are more likely to be found in Queens and Westchester than in Yorkville, and it is a dwindling, elderly Middle European population that patronizes the few remaining ethnic bakeries, butcher shops, and restaurants. Not that these stores are empty; customer ranks have been swelled by appreciative young professionals who now dominate the area.

The inviting mix of old and new buildings that characterizes Yorkville, as well as the community's relatively low crime rate, upper-middle-class status, and good public schools, make it an attractive option for the determined apartment seeker. Housing construction is active in this neighborhood, with luxury rentals rising between East 86th and 96th Streets; 13 new buildings have been constructed since 2007, and at least three more are in planning or early building phases. Variations in housing pricing have traditionally been determined by proximity to the Lexington Avenue subway line; the closer you were, the higher your rent was likely to be. This formula no longer applies, however. Although Second Avenue apartments used to offer more attractive rents because they weren't as close to the subway, the construction of the long-awaited Second Avenue subway line, underway since 2007 and scheduled for partial completion in the last quarter of 2016, is expected to be a game-changer. While you may still find a deal in apartment buildings next to active construction zones, median rents are rising more quickly than in most other Manhattan neighborhoods.

For a refreshing pause, explore Carl Schurz Park bordering the East River at 86th Street and East End Avenue, where you can also spy the mayor's residence, graceful Gracie Mansion, built in 1799. Jutting over FDR Drive, this relatively green oasis recalls Yorkville of yore and affords a spectacular view of the East River, its islands, boats, and barges. The charm of this park is that other than neighborhood residents, many New Yorkers don't know it's there, allowing for more elbow room in an often-crowded city. Astors, Rhinelanders, and Schermerhorns once had their estates here, and this quiet neighborhood is still Yorkville's most coveted roost.

While the new, upscale apartment towers continue to attract a tide of young professionals to the upper northeast reaches of Yorkville, many of the older, six-story redbrick buildings and the more affordable tall towers are now also attracting families. It's not uncommon to see parents or nannies pushing strollers and kids pointing to the child-inspired goods displayed in store windows. Three of the city's best private girls' schools (Brearley on E 83rd Street, Spence on E 91st Street, and Chapin on East End Avenue) are institutions in the neighborhood, and the Asphalt Green sports/community center is a Yorkville amenity. The gentrification of so many other parts of the city combined with the vast number of buildings that have been built here over the past twenty years has made it considerably easier to find apartments in Yorkville and the adjacent Upper East Side. Just be prepared to pay handsomely if you want to occupy one of them.

Website: www.nyc.gov
Area Codes: 212, 646, 917
Post Offices: Yorkville Station, 1617 Third Ave; Gracie Station, 229 E 85th St; Cherokee Station, 1483 York Ave
Zip Codes: 10021, 10028, 10128
Police Precinct: Nineteenth, 153 E 67th St, 212-452-0600, www.nyc.gov/nypd
Emergency Hospitals: Mt. Sinai Hospital, 1190 Fifth Ave, 212-241-8000, www. mountsinai.org; Metropolitan Hospital Center, 1901 First Ave, 212-423-6262, www.nyc.gov/mhc
Libraries: 96th St Branch, 112 E 96th St, 212-289-0908; Yorkville Branch, 222 E 79th St, 212-744-5824; www.nypl.org
Public School Education: School District #2 in region 9 at 333 Seventh Ave, 12th floor, 212-356-3700, www.www.schools.nyc.gov
Community Resources: 92nd St Y, 1395 Lexington Ave, 212-415-5500, www.92y.org
Transportation—Subway: #6: 77 St, 86 St, 96 St; #4/#5 (Express): 86 St; www. mta.info
Transportation—Bus: Crosstown 96th St (M96); Crosstown 86th St (M86); Crosstown 79th St (M79); Uptown First Ave – Downtown Second Ave (M15); Uptown Third Ave – Downtown Lexington Ave (M98, M101, M102, M103); www.mta.info

UPPER EAST SIDE

Boundaries and Contiguous Areas: North: East 96th Street; **East**: the East River; **South**: 59th Street; **West**: Fifth Avenue

The affluent heart of the **Upper East Side**—that quadrant between Fifth, 79th, Lexington, and 59th Street and the panhandle stretching from 79th along Fifth to 96th Street—has landmark status. But this does not mean Manhattan's most popular neighborhood for the wealthy and the upwardly mobile is completely homogeneous. Each avenue traversing the area, from Fifth east to York, has a distinctive character.

Fifth Avenue, flanking Central Park, glitters with some of the city's most magnificent museums, most exclusive cooperatives, and some of its most glamorous relics, those wonderfully ornate mansions that so clearly reflect the tastes and fortunes of our turn-of-the-20th-century millionaires. Fricks, Dukes, Carnegies, Whitneys—their versions of palaces, châteaux, and Gothic castles established the avenue as highly fashionable. Dominating Fifth physically and artistically in the East 80s is the Metropolitan Museum of Art ("The Met" for short), also the site of a lively street scene. Its sprawling stone steps, while providing access to the museum, offer seats and a meeting place from which to watch mimes, musicians, and street vendors who use the sidewalk around the entrance as performing space and open-air art boutique.

Madison Avenue between 60th and 86th streets is a nearly continuous line of classy international boutiques and fine arts galleries. This solid wall of chic starts at Barneys on 60th Street and parades north past Hermès, Valentino, Lanvin, and many more. You'll also find luxe gourmet food purveyors, including Laduree (famed for their macarons), stationers, boutique pharmacies, and other store-fronts replete with carefully displayed fine goods. Around 81st Street and P.S. 6 (Public School #6), the premier elementary school on the Upper East Side, a number of trendy designers have set up shop. Above 86th Street, where Andrew Carnegie built the elaborate mansion that now houses the Cooper-Hewitt

Museum, most of the other palatial Beaux-Arts residences constructed in the early 1900s have been acquired by schools, consulates, and cultural institutions. Today these grand buildings, interspersed with bow-fronted, brick Georgian homes and solid pre-World War II apartment buildings, form an exceedingly harmonious neighborhood.

On Park, the handsome center strip of year-round greenery and seasonal plantings makes the stately square cooperative buildings that proceed shoulder to elegant shoulder up the avenue more gracious still. These plazas, collectively referred to as The Park Avenue Malls, also exhibit sculptures made by accomplished artists; the exhibits, which change regularly, make the avenue even more pleasant.

Lexington Avenue has largely taken over from Madison as purveyor of quality produce to Upper East Siders. Immaculate and imaginative shops harboring fishmongers and florists, greengrocers and bakers, are crowded into the ruddy, rustic brick buildings that line the street.

The area from Third Avenue east to the river, once the province of the "el" train and tenements, has been "Trumped up" with sleek glass and granite shafts interspersed with postwar brick apartment blocks that loom over the once characteristic, and now disappearing, five-story walk-ups. Popular eateries featuring ethnic fare—Chinese, Thai, Greek, Italian, Indian—line the avenues, and turn-of-the-20th-century buildings once aimed at young professional singles are now home to many young professional parents. The multitude of strollers and busy youngsters cramming into St. Catherine's Park (a playground), between 67th and 68th Streets on First Avenue, is testimony to the Upper East Side's ongoing baby boom. The proliferation of apartments and gentrification of other neighborhoods, plus an increase in what are considered "safe" parts of town, have made living in this area more accessible than in previous years. As realtors explain it, the Upper East Side is still a terrific neighborhood and has not changed much in the past two decades. However, unlike 20 years ago, there are now other excellent neighborhoods to be found throughout Manhattan, so the waiting lists to get into apartments in the Upper East Side have shortened. That said, however, the Upper East Side's luxury co-ops and condominiums don't come cheap. According to Trulia.com, in 2014 the average price for one square foot of Upper East Side real estate was just under $1,500. Co-ops average $1.25 million dollars. There are less expensive options, to be sure, but a strong relationship with a trusted broker is the best means of finding it.

Websites: www.uppereast.com, www.cb8m.com, www.friends-ues.org, www.nyc.gov, www.madisonavenuebid.org

Area Codes: 212, 646, 917

Post Offices: Lenox Hill Station, 217 E 70th St; Gracie Station, 229 E 85th St; Cherokee Station, 1483 York Ave

Zip Codes:10021, 10022, 10028, 10128

Police Precinct: Nineteenth, 153 E 67th St, 212-452-0613, www.nyc.gov/nypd

Emergency Hospitals: Lenox Hill Hospital, 100 E 77th St, 212-434-2000, www.lenoxhillhospital.org; New York Presbyterian Hospital/Weill Cornell Medical Center, 525 E 68th St, 212-746-5454, www.nyp.org/facilities/weillcornell.html; Manhattan Eye, Ear and Throat Hospital (part of Lenox Hill Hospital), 210 E 64th St, 212-434-2000, www.lenoxhillhospital.org; nearby: Mt. Sinai Hospital, 1190 Fifth Ave, 212-241-8000

Libraries: 96th St Branch, 112 E 96th St, 212-289-0908; Webster Branch, 1465 York Ave, 212-288-5049; 67th St Branch, 328 E 67th St, 212-734-1717; www.nypl.org; The New York Society Library, 53 E 79th St, 212-288-6900, www.nysoclib.org, a private institution, with membership dues of $275 per year and 250,000 volumes, is an outstanding resource; its reference room is open to non-members.

Public School Education: School District #2 in region 9 at 333 Seventh Ave, 12th floor, 212-356-3700, www.www.schools.nyc.gov

Adult Education: Marymount Manhattan College, 221 E 71st St, 212-517-0400, www.mmm.edu; Hunter College, 695 Park Ave, 212-772-4000, www.hunter.cuny.edu

Community Resources: 92nd St Y, 1395 Lexington Ave, 212-415-5500, www.92y.org; Cooper-Hewitt Museum, 2 E 91st St, 212-849-8400, www.cooperhewitt.org; The Jewish Museum, 1109 Fifth Ave, 212-423-3200, www.thewjewishmuseum.org; Solomon R. Guggenheim Museum, 1071 Fifth Ave, 212-423-3500, www.guggenheim.org; Whitney Museum of American Art, 945 Madison Ave, 212-570-3600, www.whitney.org; Metropolitan Museum of Art, 1000 Fifth Ave, 212-535-7710, www.metmuseum.org; Frick Collection, 1 E 70th St, 212-288-0700, www.frick.org; Asia Society, 725 Park Ave, 212-288-6400, www.asiasociety.org; China Institute, 125 E 65th St, 212-744-8181, www.chinainstitute.org; Society of Illustrators, 128 E 63rd St, 212-838-2560, www.societyillustrators.org; Mount Vernon Hotel Museum & Garden, 421 E 61st St, 212-838-6878, www.mvhm.org; Neue Galerie, 1048 5th Ave, 212-628-6200, neuegalerie.org; and numerous other societies, museums, galleries, and auction houses.

Transportation—Subway: #6: 96 St, 86 St, 77 St, 68 St, 59 St/Lexington Ave; #4/#5 (Express): 86 St, 59 St/Lexington Ave; F: 63 St at Lexington Ave; N/Q/R/: 59 St/Lexington Ave; www.mta.info

Transportation—Bus: Crosstown 96th St (M96); Crosstown 86th St (M86); Crosstown 79th St (M79); Crosstown 72nd St (M72); Crosstown 66th/67th St (M66); Crosstown 57th St (M57); Crosstown 57th & 72nd (M30); Crosstown 57th & Uptown/Downtown on York Ave (M31), Uptown Madison Ave – Downtown Fifth Ave (M1, M2, M3, M4); www.mta.info

ROOSEVELT ISLAND

Location: off of 59th Street in the East River

Roosevelt Islanders have always had an unusual commute: a silent aerial ride to and from 59th Street and Second Avenue in Manhattan (every 7 to 15 minutes for $2.50) up and over the East River with the city's skyline first at eye level and then, incredibly, beneath your feet. Small wonder that the tram finds favor with tourists and day-trippers too. Residents used to be reduced to taking cabs or a roundabout bus ride through Queens to Manhattan when the tram occasionally faltered, but since 1989, the F train has connected the island with Queens (at 21st Street and 41st Avenue) and Manhattan (at 63rd and Lexington Avenue).

An appealing small-town quality pervades this island community of under 15,000, with its modern apartment buildings and schools that go up to the eighth grade. It's quiet. There's far less car traffic here than in other parts of the city, and a red bus provides regular service between the tram terminal and high-rises lining relatively spotless streets where strolls with baby carriages and street corner chats are ritual—a sort of zip back in time. There's even a fortnightly publication called *The Main Street WIRE*. Several spacious parks, six historical landmarks, a waterfront promenade, Four Freedoms Park, and unparalleled views of the Manhattan skyline highlight life on this 147-acre island. Roosevelt Island has extensive recreational facilities and shops that supply basic needs, if not exotic or ethnic ones. Built by early farmers in 1796, the Manor House is preserved at the foot of Main Street and the Renwick Lighthouse is restored, though not open to the public. Another historic site, the mid-19th-century Smallpox Hospital, is currently undergoing restoration.

Inauguration of the long-awaited subway line in 1989 was accompanied by Manhattan Park's five-building development on an eight-acre site, which added 1,100 units to the housing stock and some 2,500 inhabitants to the island's population. Manhattan Park, which has no studio apartments, attracts upper-middle-class families with stunning views and concierge service at prices below comparable Manhattan apartments. These residences, along with a rash of residential buildings constructed over the past decade, have drawn a growing number of young professionals, many with families, to consider living on the island. Buildings like The Octagon (which was constructed around the historic Octagon Lighthouse) have raised the bar—and the rent—with LEED certification, trendy design, and an array of amenities worthy of the toniest Manhattan apartments, such as free happy hour parties for tenants, a waterside pool, on-site daycare, and express shuttles to the tram and subway.

All of these come at a price, however. Apartments in The Octagon—starting at $2,225 for a studio and as much as $6,000 for a three-bedroom—are certainly on the upper end, but they're no longer considered anomalous. These kinds of price tags are increasingly normative as new buildings rise up on the island. You may find a better deal, however, if you're in the market to buy, as a smattering of condos and co-ops hover just under the million-dollar mark. Most of the city's major real estate agencies now include Roosevelt Island in their listings (even Sotheby's!), so start by familiarizing yourself with the main residences, their addresses, and their amenities, and then schedule visits or tours of

the ones that interest you. Contact the Roosevelt Island Development Corporation for more information (212-832-4540, www.rioc.com) about these and other
apartment complexes on the island. While residents enjoy the peaceful, low-crime
character of this narrow two-and-a-half-mile island, some are concerned that the
island is beginning to get too crowded. Drawbacks? Despite the marvelous views
of Manhattan, which sits just a stone's throw away, there is still limited access
when commuting back and forth. And not everyone finds the groomed ambiance
to their liking.

There is a long-standing rumor that dogs are not permitted on Roosevelt
Island, and this is simply not true. Dogs are perfectly welcome; it's finding a lease
that allows your companion to come inside that is virtually impossible.

Websites: www.rioc.com, www.cb8m.com, www.mainstreetwire.com, www.nyc.
gov

Area Codes: 212, 646, 917

Post Office: Roosevelt Island Post Office, 694 Main St

Zip Code: 10044

Police Precinct: One Hundred and Fourteenth, 34-16 Astoria Blvd, Queens, 718-
626-9311, www.nyc.gov/nypd

Emergency Hospital: NYU Langone Medical Center, 550 First Ave (Manhattan),
212-263-7300, www.med.nyu.edu

Library: Roosevelt Island Library, 524 Main St, 212-308-6243; www.nypl.org

Public School Education: School District #2 in region 9, 333 Seventh Ave, 12th
floor, 212-356-3700, www.www.schools.nyc.gov

Community Resources: Roosevelt Island Youth Program, 506 Main St, 212-935-
3645, www.rooseveltislandyouthprogram.com, offers various classes for
children; Main St Theatre & Dance Alliance, 548 Main St, 212-371-4449, www.
mstda.org features performances and offers classes in theater, dance, yoga,
and aerobics for kids and adults.

Transportation—Tramway: 59th St and Second Ave in Manhattan

Transportation—Subway: Roosevelt Island (F); www.mta.info

Transportation—Bus: Manhattan-Queens (Q101, 60, 32); Queens (Q102); Red
Bus, Main St; www.mta.info

EAST FORTIES AND FIFTIES

Boundaries and Contiguous Areas: North: 59th Street and the Upper East Side;
East: East River; **South**: 42nd Street and Murray Hill; **West**: Lexington Avenue

In 1763, when James Beekman built a summer home called Mount Pleasant on the
rural landscape that is now the bustling corner of 51st Street and First Avenue, it's
unlikely he could have imagined the value this property would eventually command. With steady growth and development, by the late 18th century this urbane

neighborhood was known as Turtle Bay Farm. The mid-19th century brought industrialization and the "el," or elevated subway trains, rumbling over tenements built along the East River. A construction boom in the 1920s left the heart of Turtle Bay much as you see it today: handsome, tree-shaded blocks of carefully maintained brownstones interspersed with relatively small apartment buildings. But not until the 1940s, when the squalid slaughterhouses that had replaced the riverside slums were razed to make room for the United Nations, and the 1950s, when the "el" came tumbling down, did Turtle Bay become eminently respectable from Lexington Avenue clear to the East River. Today the neighborhood remains full of coveted addresses and is a self-assured place with charming culs-de-sac, such as Amster Yard on 49th Street, Greenacre Park on 51st, and Turtle Bay Gardens, the private, somewhat secret, garden enclosed by twenty Italianate townhouses in which Katharine Hepburn and E. B. White once lived.

Apartment prices, as befits a neighborhood embracing exclusive Sutton Place, Beekman Place, United Nations Plaza, and a Trump Tower, are among the highest around. For the least rarefied rates, look along First and Second Avenues and the side streets in between. The 3,000-unit Tudor City (which lies on what used to be called Goat Hill (for its slaughterhouses)) is just southwest of Sutton Place. Bounded by 40th and 43rd Streets, this huge complex of Tudor-style buildings between First and Second Avenues was built to revitalize a slum area and includes a hotel, church, and private parking area. Unfortunately for would-be tenants, 10 of the buildings are cooperatives.

The neighborhood is remarkable for other architectural points of interest too. The extraordinary Guastavino tile-vaulted hall beneath the Queensboro Bridge at 59th Street, between First and York Avenues, is among them. Designed originally in 1914 as an open-sided marketplace but left dormant for many years, the 24- to 44-foot-high domed ceilings now house a market-style food emporium, restaurants, and retail shops. Home Depot has a store in the neighborhood, at 980 Third Avenue, near 59th Street, offering a virtually endless array of do-it-yourself options, hardware selection, instructional seminars, tool rental, and home decorating supplies.

Websites: www.nyc.gov, www.tudorcity.com
Area Codes: 212, 646, 917

Post Offices: Tudor City Station, 5 Tudor City Place; FDR Station, 909 Third Ave; Dag Hammarskjold Station, 884 Second Ave;
Zip Codes: 10016, 10017, 10022
Police Precinct: Seventeenth, 167 E 51st St, 212-826-3211, www.nyc.gov/nypd
Emergency Hospitals: New York Presbyterian Hospital/Weill Cornell Medical Center, 525 E 68th St, 212-746-5454, www.nyp.org/facilities/weillcornell.html; NYU Langone Medical Center, 550 First Ave (Manhattan), 212-263-7300, www.med.nyu.edu
Libraries (nearest): 58th St Branch, 127 E 58th St, 212-759-7358; Mid-Manhattan, 455 Fifth Ave, 212-340-0863; Terence Cardinal Cooke-Cathedral, 560 Lexington Ave, 212-752-3824; www.nypl.org
Public School Education: School District #2 in region 9 at 333 Seventh Ave, 12th floor, 212-356-3700, www.www.schools.nyc.gov
Adult Education: Turtle Bay Music School, 244 E 52nd St, 212-753-8811, www.tbms.org
Community Resources: YMCA of Greater New York, Vanderbilt Branch, 224 E 47th St, 212-912-2500, www.ymcanyc.org/vanderbilt; YWCA of the City of New York, 50 Broadway, 212-755-4500, www.ywcanyc.org; Japan Society, 333 E 47th St, 212-832-1115, www.japansociety.org
Transportation—Subway: #6: 59 St/Lexington Ave, 51 St, 42 St/Grand Central; #4/#5 (Express): 59 St/Lexington Ave, 42 St/Grand Central; N/Q/R 59 St/Lexington Ave; E/V: 53 St/Lexington Ave, 53 St/Fifth Ave; S (Crosstown shuttle)/#7 (Crosstown to Queens): 42 St/Grand Central; www.mta.info
Transportation—Bus: Crosstown 49th/50th Sts (M27, M50); Crosstown 42nd St (M42); Crosstown 42nd St – Downtown Broadway (M104); Uptown Madison Ave – Downtown 5th Ave (M1, M2, M3, M4); Uptown Third Ave – Downtown Lexington Ave (M98, M101, M102, M103); Uptown First Ave – Downtown Second Ave (M15); www.mta.info

MURRAY HILL

Boundaries and Contiguous Areas: North: 42nd Street and the East Forties and Fifties; **East**: East River; **South**: 34th Street and the Gramercy Park Area; **West**: Fifth Avenue

Murray Hill is the kind of neighborhood where you can walk into a compact, ground-floor apartment, open a back door, and have access to a garden larger than the flat. Time was when the great mansions of Fifth and Madison Avenues—lastingly elegant buildings such as J. P. Morgan's magnificent McKim, Mead, and White-designed library—conferred social status on the houses highest on the hill. Below these were the stables and carriage houses serving them, and in the shadow of the old Third Avenue "el" tenements. The tenements are gone now, and as Fifth Avenue became more commercial, residential Murray Hill shifted east and the carriage houses proved to be fashionable—indeed, charming—homes.

The streets are a mix of tranquil landmarks, such as Sniffen Court, a private mews at 150-158 East 36th Street; nondescript brick apartment buildings; postmodern fantasies, such as the undulating, 50+ story Corinthian; and brownstones: solid and unpretentious turn-of-the-20th-century buildings that are nonetheless elegant and lend a particularly substantial quality to city life.

The neighborhood takes its name from a Quaker merchant, Robert Murray, who built a farmhouse at what is now the corner of 37th Street and Park Avenue. Grand Central Terminal stands on what was his cornfield. Murray's wife and daugh-

ters played a minor role in the Revolutionary War by detaining General Howe and his officers at tea while Washington and his troops escaped their pursuit. Among the historic buildings in the area is the slender brownstone at 125 East 36th Street where Franklin and Eleanor Roosevelt first lived. An active neighborhood association guards the quiet residential character of Murray Hill.

NYU and Bellevue Hospitals and related medical facilities are a major presence just to the south, and the casual, inviting shops and restaurants crowding Second and Third Avenues play to a youthful audience, where the bar scene can get quite raucous on a weekend. Housing possibilities include proliferating highrises on the flatlands east of Third, as well as brownstones and carriage houses on Murray Hill itself.

Websites: www.murrayhillnyc.org, www.nyc.gov
Area Codes: 212, 646, 917
Post Offices: Murray Hill Finance Station, 115 E 34th St; Murray Hill Annex, 205 E 36th St
Zip Code: 10016
Police Precinct: Seventeenth, 167 E 51st St, 212-826-3211, www.nyc.gov/nypd
Emergency Hospitals (nearest): NYU Langone Medical Center, 550 First Ave (Manhattan), 212-263-7300, www.med.nyu.edu; Bellevue Hospital Center, 462 First Ave, 212-562-4141, www.nyc.gov/bellevue

Libraries: Kips Bay Branch, 446 Third Ave, 212-683-2520, www.nypl.org; New York Public Library's Science, Industry, and Business Library (SIBL), 188 Madison Ave, 917-275-6975; The Morgan Library and Museum, 225 Madison Ave, 212-685-0008, www.morganlibrary.org, an exquisite edifice housing an extraordinary collection of rare books, including three Gutenberg Bibles, manuscripts, and works of art

Public School Education: School District #2 in region 9 at 333 Seventh Ave, 12th floor, 212-356-3700, www.www.schools.nyc.gov

Adult Education: American Academy of Dramatic Arts, 120 Madison Ave, 800-463-8890, www.aada.org; Stern College for Women, Yeshiva University, 245 Lexington Ave, 646-592-4150, www.yu.edu/stern

Community Resources: Murray Hill Neighborhood Association, 212-886-5867, www.murrayhillnyc.org

Transportation—Subway: S (Crosstown shuttle): 42 St/Grand Central; #7 (Crosstown to Queens): Fifth Ave, 42 St/Grand Central; #6: 33 St, 42 St/Grand Central; #4/#5 (Express): 42 St/Grand Central; www.mta.info

Transportation—Bus: Crosstown 34th St (M16, M34); Uptown Madison Ave – Downtown Fifth Ave (M1, M2, M3, M4); Uptown Third Ave – Downtown Lexington Ave (M98, M101, M102); Uptown First Ave – Downtown Second Ave (M15); www.mta.info

GRAMERCY PARK AREA

Boundaries and Contiguous Areas: North: 34th Street and Murray Hill; **East**: First Avenue and Stuyvesant Area; **South**: East 14th Street; **West**: Park Avenue South/Chelsea and the Flatiron District

The actual park (and namesake of the neighborhood), **Gramercy Park**, is a verdant, block-square, fenced, and locked enclave to which only residents of the surrounding buildings hold keys. With its lovely old trees, squirrels, flowering spring plantings, and the occasional nanny, the park is reminiscent of a quiet

London square. But it wasn't the work of a homesick Brit; a real estate developer wanting to increase the value of his 66 lots laid out the private park in 1831. That this strategy was successful is evidenced by the quality of the ornate, later-19th-century buildings that still surround the square—elaborate structures such as The Players Club (Edwin Booth's former home) and the National Arts Club (designed in a Gothic Revival style by Calvert Vaux).

The air of dignified elegance that permeates Gramercy Park and sets such a pleasant tone for the neighborhood as a whole is reinforced by historic Stuyvesant Square (located four blocks to the southeast at 15th Street), with its lovely brick Friends Meeting House and brownstone St. George's Church, where J. P. Morgan worshiped. In general, this is an enclave of small townhouses and rows of trim brick fronts interspersed with renovated tenements, modest apartment houses, and an occasional high-rise.

North of the park, the Kips Bay neighborhood, stretching from Lexington Avenue to the East River, houses a fairly middle- and upper-middle-class populace, including medical personnel from the hospitals along First Avenue, in corner high-rises and side street brownstones. Large developments in the neighborhood include Waterside Plaza, between 23rd and 28th Streets, home to many United Nations employees because of its location, and the subsidized complex Henry Phipps Plaza, along Second Avenue in the 20s.

To the west, Lexington Avenue in the 20s, redolent with the spices of the Indian restaurant strip known locally as "Curry Hill" (a play on adjacent Murray Hill), is recently gentrified. Apartment buildings there have been upgraded, making the area worth a look. Convenient takeout is a bonus.

The beautiful—and popular—Madison Square Park and Union Square Park are hubs of activity, especially during the day and evening, and Park Avenue South is one of Manhattan's top commercial market and dining destinations. With the number of fashion and publishing businesses in this neighborhood, housing here attracts a smart set of residents, and developers are tripping over themselves to build new condos replete with upscale amenities. Union Square Park is home to what may be the city's most popular Greenmarket, which takes place in the park on Mondays, Wednesdays, Fridays, and Saturdays.

As this area continues to grow in popularity, available apartments will become scarcer. The most desirable, overlooking Gramercy Park, are expensive and vacancies are rare. You will have a better chance in one of the newer high-rises in the east 20s, including those lining 23rd Street. In any event, the Gramercy area is neighborly, although busy, with a healthy community presence. Area safety is assisted by the presence of young police cadets in training and by the police station itself on 21st Street. As is the case throughout the city, it's a good idea to walk through the community talking with doormen, building superintendents, and if possible, residents when searching for an apartment here.

Website: www.nyc.gov

Area Codes: 212, 646, 917
Post Offices: Murray Hill Finance Station, 115 E 34th St; Madison Square Station, 149 E 23rd St
Zip Codes: 10003, 10010, 10016
Police Precincts: Seventeenth (above 30th St), 167 E 51st St, 212-826-3211; Thirteenth, 230 E 21st St, 212-477-7411, www.nyc.gov/nypd
Emergency Hospitals: (nearest): NYU Langone Medical Center, 550 First Ave (Manhattan), 212-263-7300, www.med.nyu.edu; Bellevue Hospital Center, 462 First Ave, 212-562-4141, www.nyc.gov/bellevue; Beth Israel Medical Center, 16th St at First Ave, 212-420-2000, www.bethisraelny.org
Libraries: Kips Bay Branch, 446 Third Ave, 212-683-2520; Epiphany Branch, 228 E 23rd St, 212-679-2645; www.nypl.org
Public School Education: School District #2 in region 9 at 333 Seventh Ave, 12th floor, 212-356-3700, www.www.schools.nyc.gov
Adult Education: School of Visual Arts, 209 E 23rd St, 212-592-2000, www.sva.edu; Baruch College of Adult and Continuing and Professional Studies, 55 Lexington Ave, 646-312-1000, www.baruch.cuny.edu
Community Resources: Theodore Roosevelt Birthplace, 28 E 20th St, 212-260-1616, www.nps.gov/thrb; Roosevelt's exuberantly Victorian birthplace contains letters, books, and objects collected from his many trips contained in this two-house gallery and museum.
Transportation—Subway: L (Crosstown to Brooklyn): 14 St/Union Sq, Third Ave, First Ave; #6: 33 St, 28 St, 23 St, 14th St/Union Sq; N/Q/R/#4/#5 (Express): 14 St/Union Sq; www.mta.info
Transportation—Bus: Crosstown 34th St (M16, M34); Crosstown 23rd St (M23); Crosstown 14th St (M14); Uptown Madison Ave – Downtown Fifth Ave (M1, M2, M3, M4); Uptown Third Ave – Downtown Lexington Ave (M101, M102); Uptown First Ave – Downtown Second Ave (M15); www.mta.info

STUYVESANT TOWN AND PETER COOPER VILLAGE

Boundaries and Contiguous Areas: North: 23rd Street; **East**: FDR Drive; **South**: 14th Street and the East Village; **West**: First Avenue and Gramercy Park Area

From the outside, it might be easy to take the rather plain buildings that comprise **Stuyvesant Town**, 14th to 20th Streets, and its little brother, **Peter Cooper Village**, 20th to 23rd Streets, as city housing projects; the exteriors aren't much to write home about and some of the adjacent real estate is on the scruffier side, including the VA Hospital on 23rd Street. All this being said, though, apartment buildings, like books, shouldn't be judged by surface appearances. On the inside of these nondescript buildings are apartments that tend toward the larger end of what middle- and upper-middle-class Manhattanites can afford. This, coupled with some useful amenities, such as a 24-hour security force and an abundance of play areas for kids, make these twin complexes worth a look, especially for families. On the other hand, the complex has been embroiled for a good bit of its nearly 70 year history in ownership disputes, and the 2010 default on the mortgage by Tishman Speyer Properties is among the most recent. Should you be interested in looking into the possibility of a home here, you're best advised to do so with a real estate broker who specializes in the complex.

The community surrounding Peter Cooper and Stuyvesant includes luxury buildings, as well as owner-occupied brownstones and upgraded tenements. When scouting the area (First Avenue west to Lexington), try the side streets. The

neighborhood is a comparison shopper's dream, with major supermarkets and many ethnic food stores (especially south on First Avenue), clothing shops, and decorating showrooms along First and Second Avenues vying for your dollars. The nearby 14th Street and Union Square area covers you for electronics, books, and groceries (Whole Foods, Trader Joe's, and the Union Square Greenmarket). There are large, quiet, tree-shaded parks for breaks between apartment visits, and in warm weather, the public swimming pool at 23rd Street and Asser Levy Place is available for a few cooling laps. (In fact, look for this turn-of-the-20th-century stone Roman bath even if you can't swim; it's a beauty.) And if you are, like so many people, concerned about available health care, this neighborhood, with five top hospitals within walking distance, merits serious consideration.

Websites: www.nyc.gov, www.pcvstliving.com, www.town-village.com
Area Codes: 212, 646, 917
Post Offices: Madison Square Station, 149 E 23rd St
Zip Codes: 10009, 10010
Police Precinct: Thirteenth, 230 E 21st St, 212-477-7411, www.nyc.gov/nypd
Emergency Hospitals: NYU Langone Medical Center, 550 First Ave (Manhattan), 212-263-7300, www.med.nyu.edu; Bellevue Hospital Center, 462 First Ave, 212-562-4141, www.nyc.gov/bellevue; Beth Israel Medical Center, 16th St at First Ave, 212-420-2000, www.bethisraelny.org

Libraries: Epiphany Branch, 228 E 23rd St, 212-679-2645; Kips Bay Branch, 446 Third Ave, 212-683-2520; www.nypl.org

Public School Education: School District #2 in region 9 at 333 Seventh Ave, 12th floor, 212-356-3700, www.www.schools.nyc.gov

Adult Education: School of Visual Arts, 209 E 23rd St, 212-592-2000, www.sva. edu; Baruch College of Adult and Continuing and Professional Studies, 55 Lexington Ave, 646-312-1000, www.baruch.cuny.edu

Transportation—Subway: L (Crosstown to Brooklyn): 14 St/Union Sq, Third Ave, First Ave; #6: 23 St, 14 St/Union Sq; N/Q/R/#4/#5: 14 St/Union Sq; www.mta.info

Transportation—Bus: Crosstown 34th St (M16) goes across 34th St and down Second Ave, then east across 23rd St and uptown to 34th St along FDR Drive; Crosstown 23rd St (M23); Crosstown 14th St – Downtown Avenue A/Avenue D(M14A/M14D); Uptown First Ave – Downtown Second Ave (M15); Uptown/ Downtown Avenue C – Crosstown Houston St (M21); www.mta.info

EAST VILLAGE

Boundaries and Contiguous Areas: North: 14th Street and the Stuyvesant Town area; **East**: East River; **South**: Houston Street and the Lower East Side; **West**: Broadway and Greenwich Village

More than most Manhattan neighborhoods, the **East Village** has been a reliable mirror for the social changes that have occurred in New York since the mid-20th century. Once a Puerto Rican and Ukrainian enclave, it became the epicenter of

the beatnik/hippie movement in the 1950s and '60s, only to decline into the infamous homeless and drug wars of the 1980s. While remnants of each of these eras enrich the area and give it an unusually nuanced social fabric, the East Village today is dominated by younger professionals and upmarket alternative types who throng its bars, cafés, health food stores, boutiques, and restaurants late into the night. The latest wave of immigrants has arrived in baby strollers, with a noticeable number of young families moving into the area (or perhaps they're just the artists and thespians of yore growing up).

The most obvious gentrification is happening west of First Avenue. Old-school grunge-punk cafés have added playrooms and public schools have set up innovative teaching programs. P.S. 363, at 121 East 3rd Street, places an emphasis on learning in a non-competitive environment (the Insideschools website says about P.S. 363, "In at least one classroom, children wear slippers," and, "Instead of report cards, parents receive letters twice a year describing their children's progress."), and P.S. 364 at 600 East 6th Street, known as the Earth School, is similarly child-centered, with a curriculum emphasizing an ecological bent. Rents in this area can be as high as almost anywhere in the city. Cheaper digs can be found for the moment in the Puerto Rican/young singles area east of First Avenue, known as Alphabet City (so named because that's where the numbered avenues give way to alphabetized ones). But until the endlessly delayed Second Avenue subway line is finished, Alphabet City remains cut off from any convenient mass transit.

There are two distinct centers to the East Village. The eastern part is focused on Tompkins Square Park, where the notorious homeless camp of the 1980s now features dog runs, fairs, farmers' markets, and shaded benches. On the western edge the tone is set by the distinctly urban Astor Place, with its metal sculpture popularly known as the "Cube." This spinning steel cube sculpture by Tony Rosenthal continues to be the hangout for adolescent punks and skaters, but the wave of the future is the green glass tower behind it—it'll cost you $2 million for any of 40 apartments in the ultra-modern "Sculpture for Living." This high-rise is typical of the buildings transforming the area's traditional low-rise, brick-and-leaf ambiance, from the controversial "Blue Building" on Delancey to the glass cube of the private arts school Cooper Union has erected on Astor Place. The area to the south, between the Bowery and Broadway (called NoHo for North of Houston), remains notable for its elegant old loft buildings, recalling the era of the millionaire Astor.

Housing comes in two main forms: old walk-ups and converted lofts. Many walk-ups are rent stabilized. If you think you're being offered a rent-stabilized apartment at market price, you can find out at the New York State Department of Homes and Community Renewal (DHCR), www.nyshcr.org. In addition, much of NoHo is legally reserved for certified artists. Check with the City Loft Board, www.nyc.gov/loftboard, to determine a building's eligibility and to see if it is in compliance with city loft laws.

Since much of East Village housing consists of minimally rehabbed tenements, you should be prepared for the lack of elevators. Start your apartment search by studying ads in the *Village Voice*, check Cooper Union and NYU bulletin boards, or walk the streets and talk to people who live there. Numerous websites will also be helpful, among them craigslist.com and rent.com. Finding reasonable rent is a challenge and many people find a permanent apartment by first subletting—check out sublet.com if this idea appeals to you.

Websites: www.nyc.gov, www.bedfordandbowery.com/tag/east-village/
Area Codes: 212, 646, 917
Post Offices: Cooper Station, 93 Fourth Ave; Tompkins Square Station, 244 E 3rd St

Zip Codes: 10003, 10009

Police Precinct: Ninth, 130 Ave C, 212-477-7811,www.nyc.gov/nypd

Emergency Hospitals: Beth Israel Medical Center, 16th St at First Ave, 212-420-2000, www.bethisraelny.org; New York Eye and Ear Infirmary of Mt. Sinai, 310 E 14th St, 212-979-4000, www.nyee.edu

Libraries: Ottendorfer Branch, 135 Second Ave, 212-674-0947; Tompkins Square Branch, 331 E 10th St, 212-228-4747; www.nypl.org

Public School Education: School District #1 in region 9 at 333 Seventh Ave, 12th floor, 212-356-3700, www.www.schools.nyc.gov

Adult Education: New York University's School of Continuing and Professional Studies, 7 E 12th St, 212-998-7100, scps.nyu.edu, offers a huge range of classes; Third Street Music School Settlement, 235 E 11th St, 212-777-3240, www.thirdstreetmusicschool.org; The Cooper Union for the Advancement of Science and Art, 30 Cooper Sq, 212-353-4100, www.cooper.edu

Community Resources: La Mama Experimental Theater Club, 66 4th St, 646-430-5374, www.lamama.org, on the cutting edge of avant-garde theater for over two decades; PS 122, 150 First Ave, 212-477-5829, www.ps122.org, is a reclaimed public school turned cutting edge performance space (hence its PS pun); The Nuyorican Poets Café, 236 E 3rd St, 212-505-8183, nuyorican.org, has been home to bilingual NYC Puerto Rican poets, writers, musicians, and performers since 1973; Joseph Papp Public Theater, 425 Lafayette St, 212-539-8500, www.publictheater.org, founded in 1954, is home to plays, musicals, and Shakespeare; Classic Stage Company has been successfully producing classics since 1967 at 136 E 13th St, 212-677-4210, www.classicstage.org; Third Street Music School (see above) offers concerts and recitals; Cooper Union, 30 Cooper Sq, 212-353-4100, www.cooper.edu, has frequent exhibits, concerts, and lectures.

Transportation—Subway: L (Crosstown to Brooklyn): 14th St/Union Sq, Third Ave, First Ave; N/R/Q: 14 St/Union Sq, 8th St/NYU; #4/#5: 14th St/Union Sq; #6: 14 St/Union Sq, Astor Pl, Bleecker St; B/D: Broadway-Lafayette; F/V: Broadway-Lafayette, Second Ave; www.mta.info

Transportation—Bus: Crosstown 14th St (M14); Crosstown East – West 8th/9th Sts (M8); Uptown Third Ave/Lexington – Downtown Lexington/Third Ave (M101, M102); Uptown First Ave – Downtown Second Ave (M15); Crosstown East – West Houston St (M21); Downtown Bowery – City Hall (M103); Union Sq – Battery Park via Ave B (M9); www.mta.info

LOWER EAST SIDE, LITTLE ITALY, CHINATOWN

Boundaries and Contiguous Areas: North: Houston Street and the East Village; **East**: East River; **South**: Downtown; **West**: Broadway and SoHo

"Give me your tired, your poor ..." wrote Emma Lazarus, and when they arrived, many of them settled on the **Lower East Side**. Between 1870 and 1920, wave upon wave of immigrants from Italy, China, and the ghettos of Eastern Europe poured into the warren of then fetid tenements on Mulberry, Elizabeth, Hester, and Division Streets. Here, many lived and worked until able to move up and out to the suburbs or more spacious quarters in other boroughs, leaving room for the next wave. Others remained, and many generations have grown up in this neighborhood that defined what coming to America was all about.

Public housing, especially along the easternmost strip of the Lower East Side, alleviated some of the crowding and let in some light and air, and along Grand Street, from Essex Street to the East River, 28 co-op buildings provided affordable housing for the middle class. The Grand Street co-ops now sell at market rates their previous owners could not have imagined. Renewal began along the fringes,

where the young and impecunious—artists, students, and the like—established beachheads. Formerly vacant tenements have been renovated, attracting a more affluent crowd. Along East Houston (pronounced "how-ston") and grungy Ludlow Street, clubs, trendy restaurants, and boutiques have gentrified the area and have skewed the population toward a younger set. The area still has lots of appeal, but regular complaints from long-term residents about noise levels, along with the number of bars, represent unmistakable signs of questionable progression. Nonetheless, an old-fashioned community spirit pervades the Lower East Side, and many long-time tenants still pay much lower rents than newcomers to this area.

There are actually a number of Lower East Side neighborhoods, each very distinctive, but all characterized by scarce parking and narrow streets crowded with shops and restaurants. To the east is the old Jewish Lower East Side, now largely Latino and Chinese; Chinatown is in the southwest portion, which continues to expand inexorably northward into the third area, Little Italy, whose Italian character seems to diminish a bit each year. Colorful Orchard Street still has a few Yiddish-speaking shopkeepers, many of them Hasidim, but much of the once vibrant Jewish community is gone, and forlorn old synagogues have been converted into churches, are abandoned, or are used for other purposes. Some of the buildings above the shops, formerly vacant, now house young professionals in $3,000-a-month studios, and antique shops and young designer boutiques have crept in among the dusty menswear shops and fabric stores.

A wave of recent arrivals has burst **Chinatown**'s traditional seams past East Broadway into the old Jewish enclave and north over Canal Street into Little Italy, which is now predominantly Asian. Housing is impossibly crowded, and sweatshops can still be found, though they likely won't be obvious to you at first sight. Walking the almost impassable sidewalks of Chinatown on a Saturday, one would think this area existed solely to satisfy the city's insatiable appetite for Chinese food. The northern edge of Chinatown east of Bowery has recently been "discovered" by younger professionals, making for an interesting mix with the older Chinese residents, as well as the potential for an area that seems likely to be become the next Nolita (for North of Little Italy) or some other imaginative name.

Little Italy, between Canal and Houston streets, has a vanishing Italian population, but the selection of Italian restaurants and cafés manages to hold steady, thanks, in part, to tourists, who still show up here hoping for a glimpse of the Little Italy of yore. Along Mulberry Street on a warm spring evening, the combined hisses of uncountable cappuccino machines sound like a locomotive gathering steam. Although frozen dim sum take the place of frozen ravioli in innumerable small stores, a bit of the old Southern Italian character remains, as does the community's reputation as a don't-mess-with-us, low-crime neighborhood with strong ethnic ties around the old, original St. Patrick's on Mulberry Street. On the northern edge of Little Italy, galleries, boutiques, and cafés have filled once-vacant storefronts, and the neighborhood has acquired the name Nolita.

Infiltration of the Lower East Side by the middle class is no longer news. Construction remains active on The Bowery; the New Museum is now up and running and surrounded by high-rise luxury condos working their way down the strip from the Village and uptown from SoHo, as well as overdesigned boutique hotels and restaurants featuring pricey plates whose provenance is listed in excruciating detail on the menu. CBGB's, the legendary punk club, is now gone and in its place (if not literally) is the 712-unit mixed-use residential and commercial complex called Avalon Chrystie Place, which features a three-story Whole Foods with a food court level, a cheese cellar, a specialty beer shop, and lots of space for groups to meet.

Those considering a rental here would do best to talk to someone who lives in the neighborhood and to walk around, looking block by block, as one can be quite different from the next in tone and character. Real estate websites tend to have more broker listings than no-fee listings for this area.

Website: www.nyc.gov
Area Codes: 212, 646, 917
Post Offices: Knickerbocker Station, 128 E Broadway; Pitt Post Office 185 Clinton St; Chinatown Station, 6 Doyers St

Zip Codes: 10002, 10012, 10013
Police Precincts: Fifth, 19 Elizabeth St, 212-334-0711; Seventh, 19½ Pitt St, 212-477-7311, www.nyc.gov/nypd
Emergency Hospital (nearest): New York-Presbyterian Lower Manhattan Hospital, Hospital, 170 William St, 212-312-5000, www.nyp.org/lowermanhattan
Libraries: Hamilton Fish Park Branch, 415 E Houston St, 212-673-2290; Seward Park Branch, 192 E Broadway, 212-477-6770; www.nypl.org
Public School Education: School District #2 in region 9 at 333 Seventh Ave, 12th floor, 212-356-3700, www.schools.nyc.gov
Community Resources: The Henry Street Settlement offers a variety of resources, including its Abrons Arts Center at 265 Henry St, 212-766-9200, www.henrystreet.org. The New Federal Theatre, at 292 Henry St, 212-353-1176, www.newfederaltheatre.com, specializes in minority dramas and has been a staple of the neighborhood since 1975. The Lower East Side Tenement Museum, 103 Orchard St, 877-975-3786, www.tenement.org, includes exhibits in three buildings (one of which has been "unrestored" to illustrate life as it was), as well as neighborhood walking tours. The Museum of Chinese in America, 215 Centre St, 212-619-4785, www.mocanyc.org, offers historical walking tours as well as exhibits and video documentaries.
Transportation—Subway: F: Broadway-Lafayette, Second Ave, Delancey-Essex St, East Broadway; V: Broadway-Lafayette, Second Ave; B/D: Broadway-Lafayette, Second Ave; #6: Bleecker St, Spring St, Canal St; N/R/Q: Prince St, Canal St; J/M/Z: Chambers St, Canal St, Bowery, Delancey-Essex St; www.mta.info
Transportation—Bus: Crosstown Houston St (M21); Uptown First Ave – Downtown Second Ave (M15); Uptown Bowery/Third Ave – Downtown Third Ave/Bowery M103); Crosstown Delancey St (M39); Uptown Grand St/Essex St/Avenue A – Crosstown 14th St to Union Sq (M14A); www.mta.info

DOWNTOWN

Boundaries and Contiguous Areas: North: Chambers Street and Tribeca; **East**: East River; **South**: Upper New York Bay; **West**: Hudson River

The southernmost reaches of Manhattan, "**Downtown**" (also referred to as "Lower Manhattan"), have always been a curious place when it comes to living. By day, the streets are elbow-to-elbow with busy people moving at a brisk pace, most, presumably, headed to their offices or the trading floor to keep the nation's—and the world's—financial machine humming. They are joined by tourists kitted out in "I LOVE NY" t-shirts, with cameras around their necks and slightly dazed expressions on their faces: What should they do next? Take a picture with the famous Wall Street bull? Shop till they drop at mega-store Century 21? Visit the free National Museum of the American Indian? Hop on a ferry bound for the Statue of Liberty or Ellis Island? Or pay tribute to the victims of the September 11 terrorist attacks at the memorial built in the footprints of the Twin Towers? As they decide, their heads are turned skyward to take in some of the most diverse architecture in the city—the centuries old Trinity Church, with its cemetery, on the one hand and the

undulating, ultra-contemporary, Frank Gehry-designed apartment tower that soars up 76 stories at 8 Spruce Street on the other, with plenty of 19th- and 20th-century eye candy (including City Hall, the courthouses, and the Woolworth Building) in between.

But visit this neighborhood after 5 p.m. and you'll see a scene that looks and feels quite different. Gone are the men and women in suits and the touts selling New York souvenirs. Gone are the tourists, who have headed uptown for their evening entertainment. Gone, it seems, is everyone; the streets have rolled up. Restaurants are closed for the day. You're not even likely to see a dog walker, such a ubiquitous early evening sight in nearly every other neighborhood.

In fact, it wasn't until fairly recently that Downtown could even really be considered a neighborhood, at least a residential one. Though people *have* always lived here, there's never been the same kind of cohesive cultural or social history among residents to give this neighborhood a particular stamp of identity. Furthermore, the population density here just didn't reach the same kinds of levels typical of more popular neighborhoods like Chelsea or the Upper East Side. That began to change a bit, however, after the terrorist attacks of September 11. That might seem a bit paradoxical—why would anyone want to move to what was effectively a crime scene and a graveyard?— but part of the city's plan to revitalize and rebuild the devastated part of Lower Manhattan after 9/11 was to root the renewal efforts in a sort of rebranding initiative, restoring confidence and interest in Downtown by drawing people there to live. In the years immediately following 9/11, the city implemented a variety of incentives to draw New Yorkers downtown to live, and a number of residential complexes popped up, including the Gehry building, which is, at least as of this writing, America's tallest residential building. Along with the increased apartment inventory and attractive pricing (relatively speaking), services that had long been lacking in the neighborhood—such as grocery stores—were established, making residential real estate deals somewhat easier to seal.

Though it is unlikely this neighborhood will ever have the kind of feel that any other New York neighborhood has, that does not mean it's without its charms or conveniences. For one thing, it is very well serviced by public transportation and, in fact, transportation of all types, from several subway lines to ferries and water taxis playing the Hudson and East Rivers. It enjoys the green and recreational spaces of several parks. And its cultural institutions, while often overlooked by the majority of New Yorkers, are first-rate, among them the aforementioned National Museum of the American Indian and Poets House, as well as the year-round roster of performances and exhibits at Brookfield Place, formerly known as (and still often referred to as) Winter Garden, in the World Financial Center. There's also lots of history to be learned here; after all, Downtown was *the* original residential neighborhood of New York, and many of its earliest buildings and storied episodes of history are preserved and still accessible to the public.

Does the shadow of 9/11 haunt the people who have colonized this neighborhood? In a word, no. After nearly a decade of in-fighting and feet-dragging, the pace of construction on the new World Trade Center accelerated exponentially in 2012 and the building opened in November 2014. The memorial and museum, while predictably (and appropriately) somber, have been integrated into the neighborhood and, specifically, the site of the tragedy, in a meaningful way. Nearly 15 years after the terrorist attacks, Downtown is finally beginning to settle and be resettled. And while "deal" is a word that hardly ever applies to real estate in *any* New York City neighborhood, the range of rental prices here seems less fixed than in other parts of the city. In other words, there's room to negotiate. Ample space, river and Statue of Liberty views, and proximity to public transportation, as well as the relative newness of a building and its particular clutch of amenities will all influence the price of a Downtown pad, so keep these factors in mind as you look around.

Finally, one word to the wise: the 2012 hurricane known as Superstorm Sandy exposed what many New Yorkers suspected but had previously chosen to selectively ignore: the lower lying areas of the city are incredibly vulnerable to flooding and its effects. Large swaths of lower Manhattan were damaged severely by the storm, among them major portions of South Street Seaport, raising questions for city government officials and for urban planners about retrofitting for floods and other climate and weather events that might contribute to rising waters. What does this mean for you? You may want to ask as you're searching the area about a building's particular vulnerabilities—is it in one of the city's flood zones?—and research whether you might need insurance to protect your home in the event of a flood or similar event. The flood zone map of the city can be accessed here: www.nyc.gov/html/oem/html/hazards/storms_evaczones.shtml.

Websites: www.cb1.org, www.downtownny.com, www.batteryparkcity.org, www. brookfieldplaceny.com, www.nyc.gov, www.downtownexpress.com, www. renewnyc.com

Area Codes: 212, 646, 917

Post Offices: John Street Station, 114 John St; Federal Plaza Station, 26 Federal Plaza, Bldg 1; Church Street Station, 90 Church St

Zip Codes: 10004, 10005, 10006, 10007, 10038, 10041, 10280, 10281, 10282

Police Precinct: First, 16 Ericsson Place, 212-334-0611, www.nyc.gov/nypd

Emergency Hospital: New York-Presbyterian Lower Manhattan Hospital, 170 William St, 212-312-5110, www.nyp.org/lowermanhattan

Library: New Amsterdam Branch, 9 Murray St, 212-732- 8186; www.nypl.org

Public School Education: School District #2 in region 9 at 333 Seventh Ave, 12th floor, 212-356-3700, www.www.schools.nyc.gov

Adult Education: Pace University, 1 Pace Plaza, 212-346-1200, www.pace.edu; Borough of Manhattan Community College, 199 Chambers St, 212-220-8000, www.bmcc.cuny.edu

Community Resources: South Street Seaport, 19 Fulton St, 212-732-8257, www.southstreetseaport.com; South Street Seaport Museum, 12 Fulton St at Water St, 212-748-8600, www.southstreetseaportmuseum.org; Federal Reserve Bank, 33 Liberty St, 212-720-6130, www.newyorkfed.org; American Numismatic Society, 75 Varick St, 212-571-4470, www.numismatics.org; Museum of Jewish Heritage, 36 Battery Ple, 646-437-4200, www.mjhnyc.org; Trinity Church, Broadway at Trinity Place, 212-602-0800, www.trinitywallstreet.org, houses a museum and offers frequent concerts, as does St. Paul's Chapel, Broadway at Fulton St, 212-233-4164, www.saintpaulschapel.org; One Bowling Green is the address of the Alexander Hamilton US Customs House, which is also home to the National Museum of the American Indian, 212-514-3700, www.nmai.si.edu; Brookfield Place (complex of shops and restaurants and a venue for free cultural events, formerly known as Winter Garden at World Financial Center), 200 Vesey St, 212-417-7000, www.brookfieldplaceny.com

Transportation—Subway: #1: Chambers St, Rector St, South Ferry; #2/#3 (Express): Chambers St, Park Pl, Fulton-Broadway-Nassau, Wall St; E: World Trade Center; A/C: Chambers St, Fulton-Broadway-Nassau; N/R: City Hall, Rector St, Whitehall-South Ferry; #6: Brooklyn Bridge-City Hall; #4/#5: Brooklyn Bridge-City Hall, Fulton-Broadway-Nassau, Wall St, Bowling Green; J/M/Z: Chambers St, Fulton-Broadway-Nassau, Broad St; PATH: Station beneath World Trade Center site, connections to Hoboken, Jersey City, and Newark; www.mta.info

Transportation—Bus: Crosstown Chambers/West/Vesey/Park Row to Madison St (M22); Uptown Church/Centre/Lafayette – Downtown Broadway (M1); Uptown Church/Sixth Ave – Downtown Broadway (M6); Battery Park to LES/Alphabet City/Union Sq (M9); Wall St to Uptown First Ave – Downtown Second Ave (M15); Uptown and Downtown Grand Central Terminal – Wall St Express (M25x) weekdays only; Uptown Lincoln Center – Downtown Battery Park City (M20); www.mta.info

TRIBECA

Boundaries and Contiguous Areas: North: Canal Street and SoHo; **East**: Broadway; **South**: Chambers Street and Downtown; **West**: Hudson River

South of Canal Street, where the island of Manhattan narrows toward its tip, Greenwich Street angles toward West Broadway, leaving in its wake not only the loft district dubbed TriBeCa (**Tri**angle **Be**low **Ca**nal, but no one ever capitalizes the initials anymore) but triangular blocks and crossroad parks unique in the city. Felicitous little Duane Park, the most charming of the lot, breathes into an area composed of 19th-century brick and cast iron structures, sprawling warehouses, and commercial space. For all its artsy trendiness, it retains an air of peace and tranquility that is rare in the Big Apple.

Before becoming "Tribeca-fied," the area consisted of a warren of scruffy walk-ups that housed the city's wholesale fruit, vegetable, and flower district, the Washington Market, as well as the butter and egg district. Most of the market was razed and sent packing to The Bronx in the late 1960s, to be replaced in part by the luxury residential development Independence Plaza, at 40 Harrison Street, but a few vestiges of the produce district remain, including a row of Federal houses tucked under Independence Plaza's angular wing and the two-block Staple Street—an alley actually. There are no staples there.

Tribeca is also home to a number of elegantly sculptural cast-iron buildings—the first built not far from Duane Park by James Bogardus in 1849. The noticeably cleaner of the arched and colonnaded facades front residential lofts and cooperatives skillfully adapted from commercial space, as well as the gal-

leries and offices of the avant-garde establishment (the pioneering fringe has moved across the East River into the Brooklyn neighborhoods of Greenpoint and Williamsburg and the Queens neighborhoods of Astoria and Long Island City). Loft living with amenities is now an accepted urban lifestyle, and Tribeca has changed radically from the quiet backwater it remained throughout the 1970s. It is a prime destination for those who like their buildings wide and their spaces open. Catering to such tastes, antique and design stores cluster along Franklin and Duane streets.

The vaunted, often vaulted, warehouses just south of the Holland Tunnel

housed the clubs responsible for Tribeca's once-famous nightlife scene. Restaurants that the area's early disco devotees haunted now feed a more staid clientele. Tribeca hosts a kaleidoscopic range of dining with its 300 restaurants—including some of the best three- and four-star restaurants in Manhattan—frequented by the hip, the chic, and the up-and-coming; midday, these eateries nourish Wall Street suits and the rumpled denizens of City Hall. In 2006 the neighborhood had the dubious distinction of being ranked the 12th most expensive ZIP code in the US by *Forbes*. The neighborhood remains one of the priciest in the city. Marketing directors, who monitor rental trends across the city, average rents in Tribeca during the first quarter of 2014 were just over $9,500. And if you're thinking of buying, your pockets should be deep, very deep. Loft sales easily reach seven digits.

Among the attractions of living in Tribeca are a growing population of families where singles and childless couples once ruled the roost, an attractive neighborhood school (P.S. 234), and a local newspaper, the *Tribeca Trib*, along with unimpeded bike riding on weekends, the architecture, nightlife, and (for some renters and buyers) celebrity neighbors. Drawbacks? Few grocery stores.

Websites: www.cb1.org, www.nyc.gov, www.tribecatrib.com

Area Codes: 212, 646, 917

Post Offices: Canal St Station, 350 Canal St; Federal Plaza, 26 Federal Plz

Zip Code: 10013

Police Precinct: First, 16 Ericsson Place, 212-334-0611, www.nyc.gov/nypd

Emergency Hospitals (nearest): New York-Presbyterian Lower Manhattan Hospital, 170 William St, 212-312-5110, www.nyp.org/lowermanhattan

Library (nearest): New Amsterdam Branch, 9 Murray St, 212-732-8186; www.nypl.org

Public School Education: School District #2 in region 9 at 333 Seventh Ave, 12th floor, 212-356-3700, www.www.schools.nyc.gov

Adult Education: Borough of Manhattan Community College, Office of Continuing Education, 212-346-8420, www.bmcc.cuny.edu/ce, offers a variety of inexpensive evening and weekend courses, ranging from computer to business to self-improvement.

Community Resources: Hudson River Park from Battery City is undeniably one of the most attractive amenities of life in Tribeca. Visit the park's website, www.hudsonriverpark.org, for maps, facility listings, and information about current events (in summer, concerts, movies, and al fresco dancing are all featured). Tribeca is also home to alternative spaces displaying works for and by the avant-garde, much as upper Madison Avenue houses deluxe galleries catering to the establishment. One such gallery is the Artists Space at 38 Greene St, 3rd Floor, 212-226-3970, www.artistsspace.org, but most galleries come and go. Finally, movie fans flock to the neighborhood each year for the annual Tribeca Film Festival, www.tribecafilmfestival.org.

Transportation—Subway: #1: Canal St, Franklin St, Chambers St; #2/#3 (Express): Chambers St; A/C: Canal St, Chambers St; E: Canal St; J/M/N/Q/R//Z/#6: Canal St; www.mta.info

Transportation—Bus: Crosstown Madison & Chambers St/West St & Grand St (M22); Uptown Hudson St/Eighth Ave – Downtown Seventh Ave/Varick St (M20); Uptown Sixth Ave – Downtown Seventh Ave/Broadway (M6); Uptown and Downtown Grand Central Terminal – Wall St Express (X25) weekdays only; www.mta.info

SOHO

Boundaries and Contiguous Areas: North: West Houston Street and Greenwich Village; **East:** Broadway and Lower East Side; **South:** Canal Street and Tribeca; **West:** Sixth Avenue

SoHo's cast iron buildings are justifiably famous and a visual delight. Look up to appreciate the beauty of the patterns—columnar shapes, Greek Revival capitals, and other architectural embellishments—pressed into the cast iron facades. Windowsill house plants, paintings, and some of the city's most colorful walls reveal the loft residences, which now occupy most of what was once manufacturing space. The structures are based on a technique perfected by James Bogardus around 1850. Forerunners of today's "curtain wall" skyscrapers, these cast iron buildings are supported by interior columns, obviating the need for thick walls and allowing the use of much more glass than was previously possible. As a result, the graceful windows, many of them arched, nicely complement the strong, solid buildings, and the whole is extremely harmonious.

The buildings remain exceedingly attractive to the city's artists, ever on the lookout for good light and space, though the deals that were attainable here in the 1960s are no more.

With the discovery of SoHo by the affluent, high prices have driven many of the original artists to less costly neighborhoods, although laws help protect some of the older artist residents. Despite inflated rents and tony retail neighbors, the neighborhood retains an artsy feel, thanks to art galleries and boutiques that continue to populate the area.

The popularity of SoHo has in no way diminished. On the contrary, monied arrivistes commingle with painters and sculptors on the upper floors of the converted cast iron structures while at street level, hard-edged, minimalist (whatever the fashion-of-the-moment) showrooms spread their plate glass windows far and wide. "An international marketplace for style and design," *The New York Times* calls it, attracting shoppers from Jersey to Germany. "This feels like the world's greatest shopping mall," exclaims a merchant of upscale linens. Just so. You can buy the latest in wearable art, Japanese designer clothes, French prêt-à-porter, exquisite antique blouses and accessories, plus antique or art deco furniture and more. Take a shopping break in a chic eatery along West Broadway's restaurant row. Bring money. And if you live here, don't venture out on the weekend. It's packed.

While loft living is legal in many buildings, and you need not necessarily qualify as an artist to rent or sublet SoHo space, caution is advised in taking over a lease or paying key money for a loft or apartment. Check with the New York City Loft Board (311, www.nyc.gov/loftboard) for the status of legal rents and living situations (see **Lofts** in **Finding a Place to Live**). Many artists sublet when they go on sabbatical or receive grants that take them out of town. If you're not in the market for a condo in one of controversial high-rises going up on Soho's western edge, the best line on housing availability down here is by word of mouth (and conversation is lively at the local art galleries and show openings, which anyone can attend) and by browsing community bulletin boards.

Websites: www.artseensoho.com, www.sohonyc.com, www.nyc.gov
Area Codes: 212, 646, 917
Post Offices: Village Station, 201 Varick St; Canal Street Station, 350 Canal St
Zip Codes: 10012, 10013
Police Precinct: First, 16 Ericsson Place, 212-334-0611, www.nyc.gov/nypd
Emergency Hospital (nearest): New York-Presbyterian Lower Manhattan Hospital, 170 William St, 212-312-5110, www.nyp.org/lowermanhattan
Libraries (nearest): Jefferson Market Branch, 425 Sixth Ave, 212-243-4334; Hudson Park Branch, 66 Leroy St, 212-243-6876,www.nypl.org.
Public School Education: School District #2 in region 9 at 333 Seventh Ave, 12th floor, 212-356-3700, www.www.schools.nyc.gov
Adult Education: International Culinary Center (formerly The French Culinary Institute), 462 Broadway, 888-324-2433, www.internationalculinarycenter.com; offers a variety of professional and non-professional cooking courses (lunch and dinner too, at their restaurant, L'Ecole; dial 212-219-3300 for reservations or visit www.lecolenyc.com).

Community Resources: New Museum of Contemporary Art, 235 Bowery, 212-219-1222, www.newmuseum.org; the Museum of Comic and Cartoon Art, 594 Broadway, near Prince St, 212-254-3511, www.moccany.org; New York City Fire Museum, 278 Spring St, 212-691-1303, www.nycfiremuseum.org. The district is crammed with great and small gallery spaces—investigate them at leisure. Most are closed Sunday and Monday. A scan of *Gallery Guide*, available in galleries throughout the city, gives a total picture of the area's resources and current shows. For weekly guides to arts events in SoHo see the *Village Voice*, the "Arts and Leisure" section of the *New York Times*, *Time Out New York*, and the *New Yorker*'s "Goings on About Town" section. Nearby Tribeca also offers opportunities to explore the more avant-garde side of the arts, as does the East Village.

Transportation—Subway: B/D/F/V: Broadway-Lafayette; A: Canal St; C/E: Spring St, Canal St; N/R: Prince St, Canal St; J/M/Q/Z: Canal St; #6: Canal St, Bleecker St; #1: Houston St, Canal St; www.mta.info

Transportation—Bus: Crosstown Houston St (M21); Downtown Fifth Ave – Uptown Sixth Ave (M5); Downtown Seventh Ave/Broadway (M20); Uptown Sixth Ave – Downtown Seventh Ave/Broadway (M6); www.mta.info

GREENWICH/WEST VILLAGE

Boundaries and Contiguous Areas: North: 14th Street, Chelsea, and Flatiron District; **East**: Broadway and the East Village; **South**: West Houston Street and SoHo; **West**: Hudson River

Greenwich Village is the kind of community where neighbors look after each other's plants and pets and where people call the police or fire department if they notice something amiss. Consistent with its bohemian history, residents here still tend to be arts-oriented, and more liberal and politically active than other city dwellers, particularly when it comes to incursions, real or threatened, on the neighborhood's cherished landmarks and its signature style. It was the Village's great good fortune to have its 18th-century farm lane streets in place before city planners superimposed the grid pattern on most of Manhattan. The crooked streets that intersect major arteries at skew angles have a certain charm, although navigating the streets may take time and determination.

Since the 19th century, the brick, Federal-style structures along these crooked streets have housed more than their share of the city's talented and creative. Writers came first: Edgar Allan Poe in 1837, followed later by Mark Twain, Henry James, and Walt Whitman. Artists and intellectuals followed. A handful of people and institutions played key roles in the evolution of the Village as a magnet for those in the vanguard of the arts and letters. Gertrude Vanderbilt Whitney opened her first studio here, exhibiting and encouraging the artists who subsequently became the nucleus of the "Ashcan school" of social realist painters. Mabel

Dodge's famed literary salon was on Washington Square, and the Provincetown Players established an early experimental theater on MacDougal Street in 1916. New York University was founded on Washington Square in the 1830s, the New School on West 12th Street in the 1920s. By then the local populace included John Dos Passos, e.e. cummings, Willa Cather, Henry Miller, and Eda St. Vincent Millay, making Greenwich Village the avant-garde capital of the nation.

After World War II, abstract expressionists, method actors, controversial novelists, and muckraking journalists all coexisted here, bringing creative vitality to the area. The written word was set to music in the fifties and sixties as folk legends performed anti-war hymns in small coffeehouses. Hippies, yippies, and the latest in fashionable cultural trends and lifestyles have always been part of the Village's attraction; it was only when rents began to spiral upwards during the 1970s that the neighborhood's accessibility for artists and writers diminished. These days, there are probably more art collectors around than artists, but the charm of the Village, with its pleasing proportions and special kind of peacefulness, remains. An annual art show on the streets around Washington Square Park and the city's foremost (and most outrageous, or at least gargantuan) Halloween Parade are among the festivities that make this neighborhood special, though the latter nearly disappeared in 2013 after its 40-year run due to the expense of its production. The park itself, with its famed arch gleaming, feels fresh and safe after a renovation and clean-up campaign.

Greenwich Village contains a balanced mix of high-rise elevator buildings, older, rent-stabilized apartments, lofts, renovated tenements, and brownstones. Since the late 1990s, new "luxury" buildings have soared up around the neighborhood, causing consternation among many long-time residents, some of whom complain not only about the sore-thumb aesthetics of these glittery jewel boxes, but also their propensity to lose their shiny glass windows, which occasionally rain glittery, splintery shards down onto Village sidewalks. Many of these new buildings can be found on Eighth Avenue around 14th Street and farther to the west along the side streets between 14th and 23rd, as well as lining the West Side Highway between those same cross streets.

The Meatpacking District in the far-West Village, south of 14th Street, has experienced a complete makeover since the late 1990s, with film studios, trendy restaurants, nightclubs, galleries, upscale clothing stores, boutique hotels, and luxury apartment buildings completely overtaking the old transvestite hooker hangouts and butcher shops. The evening crowds here are huge, particularly in the summer, when The High Line, the city's "park in the sky," built on disused elevated subway rails, is open late. It offers a breezy, flowery respite from New York's sticky humidity and features a number of artisanal food vendors selling everything from pulled pork to popsicles. The park is one of the neighborhood's best attractions, which is saying a lot, given the number of galleries, restaurants, and shops that still stake a claim to the kind of independent spirit that is quickly being sucked away by spiraling rents.

Because the area is essentially an assembly of small communities—the central **Washington Square** neighborhood, and the **West Village**, bounded by Seventh Avenue and the Hudson River—searching for rentals is best done on foot and through reliable real estate agents.

Websites: www.nycgv.com, www.nyc.gov, www.villagealliance.org
Area Codes: 212, 646, 917
Post Offices: West Village Station, 527 Hudson St; Cooper Station, 93 Fourth Ave; Village Station, 201 Varick St
Zip Codes: 10003, 10011, 10012, 10014
Police Precinct: Sixth, 233 W 10th St, 212-741-4811, www.nyc.gov/nypd
Emergency Hospital: New York-Presbyterian Lower Manhattan Hospital, 170 William St, 212-312-5110, www.nyp.org/lowermanhattan
Libraries: Jefferson Market Branch, 425 Sixth Ave, 212-243-4334; Hudson Park Branch, 66 Leroy St, 212-243-6876; www.nypl.org
Public School Education: School District #2 in region 9 at 333 Seventh Ave, 12th floor, 212-356-3700, www.www.schools.nyc.gov.
Adult Education: Parsons School of Design, 66 Fifth Ave, 212-229-8900, www.newschool.edu/parsons; New School University, 66 W 12th St, 212-229-5150, www.newschool.edu; The Cooper Union for the Advancement of Science and Art, 30 Cooper Sq, 212-353-4100, www.cooper.edu; Greenwich House Music, 46 Barrow St, 212-242-4770, www.greenwichhouse.org; Greenwich House Pottery, 16 Jones St, 212-242-4106, www.greenwichhousepottery.org; New York University, 50 W 4th St, 212-998-1212, www.nyu.edu; Pratt Manhattan, the local branch of Brooklyn's Pratt Institute, 144 W 14th St, 718-636-3600, www.pratt.edu, has extensive evening and weekend course offerings in the arts and professional areas.
Community Resources: Yeshiva University Museum, 15 W 16th St, 212-294-8330, www.yumuseum.org; Cherry Lane Theatre, 38 Commerce St, 212-989-2020, www.cherrylanetheatre.org; Lesbian, Gay, Bisexual and Transgender Community Center, 208 W. 13th St, 212-620-7310, wwwgaycenter.org

Transportation—Subway: L (Crosstown to Brooklyn): Eighth Ave, Sixth Ave, 14 St/Union Sq; A/C/E: 14 St, W 4 St; #1: 14 St, Christopher St, Houston St; #2/#3 (Express): 14 St; F/V: 14 St, W 4 St; N/R/Q: 14 St/Union Sq, 8 St/NYU; #4/#5/#6: 14 St/Union Sq; www.mta.info

Transportation—Bus: Crosstown 14th St (M14A/M14D); Crosstown 8th/9th Sts (M8); Crosstown Houston to Ave C (M21); Uptown Greenwich St/Tenth Ave – Downtown Ninth Ave/Hudson St (M11); Uptown Hudson St/Eighth Ave – Downtown Seventh Ave (M20); Uptown Sixth Ave – Downtown Fifth Ave (M5); Uptown Sixth Ave – Downtown Broadway (M6); Uptown University Place/Madison Ave – Downtown Fifth Ave (M2, M3); www.mta.info

FLATIRON DISTRICT/UNION SQUARE

Boundaries and Contiguous Areas: North: 23rd Street and Madison Square; **East**: Park Avenue South and Gramercy Park Area; **South**: 14th Street; **West**: Sixth Avenue and Chelsea

Thanks to the famous wintry photograph by Edward Steichen, the thrusting nose of the Flatiron Building is familiar, even to out-of-towners. The triangular structure at the convergence of Broadway and Fifth Avenue at 23rd Street was a wonder, a skyscraper, when completed in 1902. The 21-story, steel-frame edifice was also at the apex of Ladies' Mile, New York's elegant shopping district. Macy's, Tiffany & Co., Lord & Taylor, and other now forgotten luxurious emporiums cut a fashionable swath down Broadway, Fifth, and Sixth Avenues in the late 19th century.

But just as the rumbling Sixth Avenue elevated subway had stimulated the development of the Ladies' Mile, so the city's booming economy caused the great stores to move uptown. The buildings with elegant cast iron fronts, elaborate mansard roofs, Byzantine columns, and Gothic finials were abandoned to a dim and sooty half-life as manufacturing lofts and warehouses, and it wasn't until the1990s that a reawakening began to occur south of 23rd Street. When it did, the wedge-shaped Flatiron Building lent its name to a neighborhood that is now among the most desirable in the city.

Andy Warhol was, perhaps, among the first to make a mark in the **Flatiron District** when he established his notorious Factory on **Union Square**. Professional photographers began moving bed-and-tripod into the neighborhood's vast manufacturing lofts in the 1970s. Photo supply houses and model agencies came next, followed by publishing houses, advertising agencies, and most recently, Internet and new media startups. A large Whole Foods and a host of clothing stores have opened at one end, with a four-story Barnes & Noble at the other. At the northern end of this neighborhood you'll find Madison Square Park, popular for the al fresco Shake Shack and its public art installations, as well as free Wi-Fi and, above all, the Mario Batali gastro-temple, Eataly, just across the street. The nearly 50,000-square foot food emporium features a fresh market and cheese, charcuterie, bread, and seafood departments, as well as multiple restaurants, two cafés, and a gelato stand. The country's only museum devoted to the subject of math sits on the northern end of Madison Square Park, and on the southeastern side, the handsome clock-faced building is being transformed into a hotel that's slated to have at least a portion of its square footage reserved for luxury residences. The combination hotel-residence trend is becoming increasingly popular in this and other parts of the city.

Nearby, on lower Fifth Avenue, fashion heavyweights have taken root and the abandoned palaces of the Ladies' Mile on Sixth Avenue have reopened as megastores selling books, housewares, office supplies, and clothes. On Broadway, home furnishing stores cluster around the feet of ABC Carpet and Home. The shop Fishs Eddy is particularly fun, with its affordable restaurant and diner remainders and overstock, and plenty of New York City-themed goods for the kitchen and home.

Finding a rental here is a challenge; a good bit of the housing stock, especially on the Union Square end of the neighborhood, is designated for NYU students. Check side streets, especially on the west side of Madison Square Park, for rentals; even 23rd Street is upping the number of available rentals, what with a clutch of recently constructed buildings, among them the slightly out of place One Madison, where famous neighbors include mega-media magnate Rupert Murdoch and mega-model Gisele Bündchen. More typical of the Flatiron District, however, are the elegant, converted living lofts hidden away in the stolid manufacturing buildings. Consult a real estate broker for the occasional sublet that comes on the market. Besides a prime location with good public transportation, you'll have the graceful, green breathing spaces of the two parks and the four-day-a-week greenmarket (see **Greenmarkets** in the **Shopping for the Home** chapter). Manhattanites trek year-round to the northwest corner at East 16th and Broadway for fresh produce, fish, sausages, cheese, pretzels, breads, honey—oh, endless edibles—and colorful armloads of cut flowers. Don't be surprised if you spot a star chef procuring what's local, seasonal, and fresh if you take an early morning turn through the market.

Websites: www.cb1.org, www.unionsquarenyc.org, www.nyc.gov, www.cenyc.
   org, www.madisonsquarepark.org, www.madparknews.com
Area Codes: 212, 646, 917

Post Offices (nearest): Cooper Station, 93 Fourth Ave; Madison Square Station, 149 E 23rd St; Old Chelsea Station, 217 W 18th St
Zip Codes: 10003, 10010, 10011
Police Precinct: Thirteenth, 230 E 21st St, 212-477-7411, www.nyc.gov/nypd
Emergency Hospital (nearest): New York-Presbyterian Lower Manhattan Hospital, 170 William St, 212-312-5110, www.nyp.org/lowermanhattan
Libraries (nearest): Muhlenberg Library, 209 W 23rd St, 212-924-1585; Andrew Heiskell Braille & Talking Book Library, 40 W 20th St, 212-206-5400, TTY 212-206-5458, a full-service library with large circulating collections of special format materials, audio playback equipment, and a variety of electronic reading aids; www.nypl.org
Public School Education: School District #2 in region 9, 333 Seventh Ave, 12th floor, 212-356-3700, www.www.schools.nyc.gov
Adult Education: School of Visual Arts, 209 E 23rd St, 212-592-2000, www.sva.edu; Baruch College of Continuing and Professional Studies, 55 Lexington Ave, Room B1-116, 646-312-5000, www.baruch.edu
Community Resources: Tibet House, 22 W 15th St, www.tibethouse.org, 212-807-0563; Theodore Roosevelt Birthplace, 28 E 20th St, 212-260-1616, www.nps.gov/thrb; Roosevelt's exuberantly Victorian birthplace, a two-house gallery and museum, contains letters, books, and objects collected from his many trips. Rubin Museum of Art, 150 W 17th Street, 212-620-5000, www.rubinmuseum.org has an exceptional collection of Himalayan art. Its quiet café features an interesting assortment of live Eastern music on the weekend.
Transportation—Subway: L (Crosstown to Brooklyn): Sixth Ave, 14 St/Union Sq; #6: 23 St, 14 St/Union Sq; N/R/Q: 23 St, 14 St/Union Sq; #4/#5: 14 St/Union Sq; F/V: 23 St, 14 St; #1: 23 St, 18 St, 14 St; #2/#3 (Express): 14 St; www.mta.info
Transportation—Bus: Crosstown 23rd St (M23); Crosstown 14th St (M14A/M14D); Uptown Madison Ave – Downtown Fifth Ave South (M1, M2, M3); Uptown Sixth Ave – Downtown Fifth Ave (M5); Uptown Sixth Ave – Downtown Broadway (M6); Uptown Sixth Ave – Downtown Seventh Ave (M7); Uptown Eighth Ave – Downtown Seventh Ave (M20); www.mta.info

CHELSEA

Boundaries and Contiguous Areas: North: 34th Street and Clinton; **East**: Sixth Avenue and Flatiron District; **South**: 14th Street and Greenwich Village; **West**: Hudson River

Residential **Chelsea** is a sunny community renowned for peace, quiet, and four- and five-story brownstone row houses, congruent with its origins, which date to 1750, when Captain Thomas Clarke's farm encompassed the area. In the 1830s, Clarke's grandson, Clement Clarke Moore, began developing Chelsea as a highly desirable suburb. Moore donated land for the block-square General Theological

Seminary just down the street from the Gothic Revival style St. Peter's Episcopal Church, where he read his "A Visit from Saint Nicholas" to family and parishioners. The tree-shaded Seminary Close is still a neighborhood oasis.

To the west, the Hudson River Railroad attracted slaughterhouses, breweries, and shanties, and in 1871, Chelsea was darkened by the city's first elevated railroad, on Ninth Avenue. Successive decades saw the brief emergence of West 23rd Street as the city's theater district; the raising of vast cast iron structures on Sixth Avenue to house fashionable emporiums such as the original B. Altman's; and in the 1920s and 1930s, a thriving vice district; the beginning of the nation's movie industry; and the opening of one of the city's first cooperative apartment houses, now the Hotel Chelsea (aka the Chelsea Hotel), home over the years to artists and writers. Urban renewal in the 1950s and 1960s spurred the restoration of many fine townhouses and made way for two low-income housing projects and the middle-income International Ladies Garment Workers cooperative between Eighth and Ninth Avenues.

Sharing the side streets with restored one- and two-family houses is the occasional apartment house and tenement, not to mention formidable **London Terrace**, 405 West 23rd Street, with 14 buildings. The lofts in the photography, flower, fur, and fashion districts (roughly 15th to 30th Streets between Fifth and Eighth Avenues, which includes the Flatiron District) were discovered by artists in the 1950s and some now attract young families and professionals.

In 1982 the down-at-the-heels Elgin, a 1930s movie house on Eighth Avenue, was transformed into the exuberantly art deco Joyce Theater, the first theater in the dance capital of the world to be specifically designed for small- and medium-sized dance troupes. Since then, Chelsea has become something of a dance and performance district. Way west, nightclubs offer do-it-yourself dance in-between auto-repair shops and factories, which are rapidly disappearing, replaced by art galleries, hotels, and upscale apartment buildings, all developments spurred on by the success and popularity of The High Line, the park built on the old elevated subway tracks.

Eighth Avenue, between 14th and 23rd Streets, is Chelsea's equivalent of Main Street. With a lively restaurant scene and boutiques punctuating the relatively unobtrusive condos and co-ops, the once predominantly gay Eighth

Avenue strip is becoming a bit more sedate and taken over by chain retailers, banks, and drugstores. Chelsea-ites and Villagers shop for quality foods in the imaginatively recycled Nabisco factories on Ninth Avenue and 15th Street called Chelsea Market (which has some of the best fish and produce in the city, as well as baked goods, wine, spices, and more). The block-long Whole Foods Market on 24th Street and Seventh Avenue features 30,000 square feet of organic foods, fine cheeses, and free-range meats. Along with great food shopping, the other feature drawing people to Chelsea is the neighborhood's art scene: more than 100 trendy galleries cluster near 22nd Street and along the western corridor between 17th and 27th Streets. Ninth and Tenth Avenue eateries feed the gallery crowd. Artistically named apartment complexes, such as The Tate, attract singles, couples, and families alike. They are drawn not only for the upscale residences, but also the neighborhood's cultural and recreational amenities.

Simultaneously anchoring the western edge of Chelsea is the extraordinary 1.7-million-square-foot Chelsea Piers Sports and Entertainment complex in four piers over the Hudson River, stretching between 17th and 23rd Streets. The movie industry returned to Chelsea in the new film and television studios housed in the pier-head, through which once streamed passengers from some of the world's great ocean liners. In fact, in 1912, this was to be the destination of the ill-fated Titanic. In the handsome complex stretched out behind the studios, workout devotees strain and sweat on state-of-the-art equipment, while others (especially youngsters from all over the city) run; ice skate; in-line pirouette; play league hockey, soccer, and basketball; scale a climbing wall; bowl; refine gymnastic skills; or drive balls to target greens on a 200-foot Astroturf fairway under night lights. Others watch and hang out at one of several restaurants. For those who enjoy watching sports, you can take in the pros at Madison Square Garden, which draws crowds to the west 30s to see the Knicks (basketball), Rangers (hockey), and The Liberty (women's basketball), along with the circus and other events.

North of the piers and looming over the Hudson, the vast industrial Starrett-Lehigh Building, long semi-vacant, attracts high-profile tenants now, including art galleries, film studios, and new media groups. Many of its neighbors, former industrial buildings, too, are now luxury lofts or are in the process of being converted to such properties. Chelsea is the new SoHo, and its proximity to the every-year-more-amazing Hudson River Park makes it even better than its neighbor to the south.

Chelsea's hot; housing here is expensive and much in demand, and living spaces are often small. The new frontier, less attractive but accessible, is Sixth, Seventh, and Eighth Avenues, from 23rd to 31st Streets, where a zoning change now allows construction of apartment buildings in a previously industrial zone. Tenth Avenue has become home to a number of clubs, bars, and galleries, and a growing number of desirable apartments are colonizing this area, once considered the too-far, too-gritty west. Home Depot opened its flagship Manhattan store at 40 West 23rd Street in 2005 and offers a virtually endless array of do-it-yourself options, hardware selection, instructional seminars, tool rental, and home decorating supplies. All this gentrification, however, has a price, which you'll notice just as soon as you start apartment hunting here. This neighborhood is best considered with the help of a real estate agent who specializes in Chelsea rentals.

Websites: www.chelseamarket.com, www.nyc.gov, www.hudsonriverpark.org

Area Codes: 212, 646, 917

Post Offices: General Post Office, James Farley Station, 421 Eighth Ave, open 24 hours; London Terrace Station, 234 Tenth Ave; Old Chelsea Station, 217 W 18th St

Zip Codes: 10001, 10011

Police Precincts: Midtown South, 357 W 35th St, 212-239-9811; Tenth, 230 W 20th St, 212-741-8211, www.nyc.gov/nypd

Emergency Hospitals (nearest): Beth Israel Medical Center, 16th St at First Ave, 212-420-2000, www.bethisraelny.org; Mt. Sinai-Roosevelt, 1000 10th Ave, 212-523-4000, www.roosevelthospitalnyc.org

Libraries: Muhlenberg Branch, 209 W 23rd St, 212-924-1585; Andrew Heiskell Braille & Talking Book Library, 40 W 20th St, 212-206-5400; www.nypl.org

Public School Education: School District #2 in region 9, 333 Seventh Ave, 12th floor, 212-356-3700, www.www.schools.nyc.gov

Adult Education: Fashion Institute of Technology (FIT), 227 W 27th St, 212-217-7999, classes plus art gallery open to the public, www.fitnyc.edu

Community Resources: McBurney YMCA, 125 W 14th St, 212-912-2300, www.ymcanyc.org/mcburney; The Joyce Theater, 175 Eighth Ave, 212-691-9740, www.joyce.org; The Kitchen, 512 W 19th St, 212-255-5793, www.thekitchen.org; Dia Art Foundation, 535 W 22nd St, 212-989-5566, www.diaart.org; Atlantic Theater Company, 336 W 20th St and 330 W 16th St, 212-691-5919, www.atlantictheater.org; Hudson River Park, www.hudsonriverpark.org

Transportation—Subway: L (Crosstown to Brooklyn): Eighth Ave, Sixth Ave; A: 34 St/Penn Station, 14 St; C/E: 34 St/Penn Station, 23 St, 14 St; #1: 34 St/Penn Station, 28 St, 23 St, 18 St, 14 St; #2/#3 (Express): 34 St/Penn Station, 14 St; B/D: 34 St/Herald Sq; F/V: 34 St/Herald Sq, 23 St, 14 St; N/Q/R/: 34 St/Herald Sq; www.mta.info

Transportation—Bus: Crosstown 34th St/Ninth Ave (M16) Twelfth Ave (M34); Crosstown 23rd St (M23); Crosstown 14th St (M14) also down Ave A and Ave D; Uptown Tenth Ave – Downtown Ninth Ave (M11); Uptown Eighth Ave – Downtown Seventh Ave (M20); www.mta.info

MIDTOWN/GARMENT DISTRICT

Boundaries and Contiguous Areas: North: 59th Street (Central Park South) and Central Park; **East:** Lexington Avenue and East 40s and 50s, Fifth Avenue (south of 42nd Street) and Murray Hill; **South:** 34th Street and Chelsea; **West:** Eighth Avenue and Clinton

For all that it contains within its bounds and despite vigorous efforts by developers to rebrand the area as the hot new place to live, Midtown's Garment District is not really considered a neighborhood. Some 700,000 people work here, but few call it home. Not since the mansions of the mighty—the Rockefellers, the Havemeyers, the Vanderbilts—were left to the wrecking ball and commercial development around the turn of the 20th century has **Midtown** felt like a neighborhood. This core of the core of the city throbs and bustles daily with industry in the **Garment District**, commerce between Lexington and Sixth Avenue (or Avenue of the Americas, its official name rarely used by New Yorkers), with shoppers from Macy's to Bergdorf Goodman to Bloomingdale's, and tourists everywhere. Except for the Theater District, and the 40s and 50s west of Sixth Avenue, Midtown is quiet at night, all but deserted in some areas.

There are few supermarkets here, no appealing playgrounds, and only one city park, the elegant and much-loved Bryant Park behind the New York Public Library at 42nd Street, with its ice skating rink in winter, movie series in summer, year-round children's carousel, and a variety of restaurants and cafés in and around its rectangle of green. What *is* here is almost all of the city's legitimate

theater, ballet at City Center Theater, music at Carnegie Hall, and smaller venues, museums, restaurants of every conceivable persuasion, Rockefeller Center, major art galleries along 57th Street, and shopping until you're dropping. Not to mention that perhaps your job is here.

Despite its lack of residential character, you *can* live in Midtown. On the high side—and, of course, for a high price—you can live in the Trump or one of the other glassy towers along Fifth and Park Avenues and Central Park South, in some fine pre-war (World War II, that is) apartment buildings between Sixth and Eighth Avenues in the 50s, or just a bit more modestly in modern doorman buildings. The occasional brownstone is a side street surprise west of Fifth. Newer builds, such as The Orion on 42nd, may look appealing at first glance, but despite their sheen and their amenities, they are not for families with children, as the nearby transit hubs, especially the Port Authority, tend to have a seedy, grimy vibe. Explore the area first—preferably at various times of day and in the evening—and talk to residents in order to be sure about location. The neighborhood's character is by no means uniform, and a block can make a big difference in one's quality of life here. Also, big developments—namely, the Manhattan West development—are in the works, so this neighborhood is likely to continue changing considerably in the next five to ten years. Keep in mind, this is a busy, often noisy area and no place for a car. If you're working in the area, or if you enjoy nightlife, theater, and dining out, this may be a good neighborhood for you. If you like a more residential feel or if you're moving with kids in tow, you should probably look elsewhere, at least for now.

The search here is best made with the help of reliable real estate agents. Watch the ads in the Sunday *Times* to find agents handling properties in the area.

Websites: www.nyc.gov, www.timessquare.com, www.timessquarenyc.org, www. fashioncenter.com

Area Codes: 212, 646, 917

Post Offices: Grand Central Station, 450 Lexington Ave; Midtown Station, 223 W 38th St; Rockefeller Center Station, 610 Fifth Ave; Bryant Station, 23 W 43rd St; Murray Hill Station, 115 E 34th St; Times Square Station, 340 W 42nd St

Zip Codes: 10016, 10017, 10018, 10019, 10020, 10022, 10036

Police Precincts: Midtown North, 306 W 54th St, 212-767-8447; Midtown South, 357 W 35th St, 212-239-9811; www.nyc.gov/nypd

Emergency Hospital: Mt. Sinai-Roosevelt, 1000 10th Ave, 212-523-4000, www. roosevelthospitalnyc.org

Libraries: General Society Library, 20 W 44th St, 212-921-1767, www.generalsociety.org, a membership library; Fifty-Eighth St Branch, 127 E 58th St, 212-759-7358; Mid-Manhattan Branch, 455 Fifth Ave, 212-340-0863; New York Public Library Stephen A. Schwarzman Building (non-circulating research library; children's section, downstairs, is circulating), Fifth Ave and 42nd St, 917-275-6975; www.nypl.org; the Science, Industry and Business Branch (SIBL), 188 Madison Ave, 917-275-6975

Public School Education: School District #2 in region 9 at 333 Seventh Ave, 12th floor, 212-356-3700, www.www.schools.nyc.gov

Adult Education: The Graduate Center, City University of New York (CUNY), 365 Fifth Ave, 212-817-7000, www.gc.cuny.edu

Community Resources: International Center of Photography (ICP), 1133 Sixth Ave, 212-857-0000, www.icp.org; Museum of Modern Art, 11 W 53rd St, 212-708-9400, www.moma.org; Paley Center for Media, 25 W 52nd St, 212-621-6600, www.paleycenter.org; Museum of Arts & Design, 2 Columbus Circle, 212-299-7777, www.madmuseum.org; New York City Center, 131 W 55th St, 212-581-1212, www.nycitycenter.org; Carnegie Hall, 154 W 57th St, 212-247-7800, www.carnegiehall.org; NYC's Official Visitor Information Center, 810 Seventh Ave, 212-484-1200, www.nycvisit.com

Transportation—Subway: S (Crosstown shuttle): 42 St/Times Sq, 42 St/Grand Central; #1: 59 St/Columbus Circle, 50 St, 42 St/Times Sq, 34 St/Penn Station; #2/#3: 42 St/Times Sq; B/D: 59 St/Columbus Circle, Seventh Ave, 47–50 Sts

Rockefeller Center, 42 St, 34 St/Herald Sq; F: 57 St, 47–50 Sts/Rockefeller Center, 42 St, 34 St/Herald Sq; V: 53 St/Fifth Ave, 47–50 Sts/Rockefeller Center, 42 St, 34 St/Herald Sq; N/R/Q: 59 St/Lexington Ave, 59 St/Fifth Ave, 57 St, 49 St, 42 St/Times Sq, 34 St/Herald Sq; Q: 57 St, 42 St/Times Sq, 34 St/Herald Sq; A: 59 St/ Columbus Circle, 42 St/Port Authority, 34 St/Penn Station; C: 59 St/Columbus Circle, 50 St, 42 St/Port Authority, 34 St/Penn Station; E: 53 St/Lexington Ave, 53 St/Fifth Ave, Seventh Ave, 50 St, 42 St/Port Authority, 34 St/Penn Station; #7 (Crosstown to Queens): 42 St/Times Sq, Fifth Ave, 42 St/Grand Central; #6: 59 St/Lexington Ave, 51 St, 42 St/Grand Central, 33 St; #4/#5 (Express): 59 St/ Lexington Ave, 42 St/Grand Central; www.mta.info

Transportation—Bus: Crosstown 34th St (M34); Crosstown 42nd St (M42) Downtown Broadway – Crosstown 42nd St, (M104); Crosstown 49/50th Sts (M27, M50); Crosstown 57th St (M31, M57) Crosstown 57th St – Uptown York Ave (M31); Uptown Eighth Ave – Downtown Seventh Ave (MI0); Uptown Sixth Ave – Downtown Fifth Ave (M5); Uptown Sixth Ave – Downtown/Seventh Ave and Broadway (M6, M7); Uptown Madison Ave – Downtown Fifth Ave (M1, M2, M3, M4); Uptown Lexington Ave – Downtown Third Ave (M98, M101, M102, M103); www.mta.info

CLINTON/HELL'S KITCHEN

Boundaries and Contiguous Areas: North: 59th Street and Lincoln Center; **East**: Eighth Avenue and the Theater District; **South**: 34th Street and Chelsea; **West**: Hudson River

Despite efforts by the city and local residents to refer to the neighborhood as "**Clinton**," most people still call this area "**Hell's Kitchen**." The neighborhood— which produced gangster Owney Madden and inspired *West Side Story*—was for a long time a poor, workingman's district with often-squalid tenements and rooming houses; it is still home to some rough and tumble types and has some raunchy blocks catering to transients. But the spillover from Times Square, which continues, remarkably, to out-Times-Square itself, is bleeding into this area.

Upgrading began in the 1970s when Manhattan Plaza, 400 West 43rd Street, with its two towers, pool, and tennis courts, was built. People with enough money to pay the high rents originally charged for the apartments were disinclined to live here because of the neighborhood, so the buildings were converted to subsidized housing for the long-time residents who were displaced by the complex and for people in the performing arts. This new population helped found and now supports the thriving Off-Broadway Theater Row on the south side of 42nd Street, a bonanza for New York's theater-going public, not to mention the theater world. The new respectability is firmly anchored on far-west 42nd Street by 1 River Place, a vast luxury rental building zigzagging across a whole block on the city's western edge. Now in an area once characterized by sleaze and depression, there are good restaurants, theaters featuring more "cutting edge" Off-Broadway shows, blocks of spiffed-up townhouses, and handsome co-op renovations, such as the Piano Factory. Clinton's new frontier is Tenth Avenue, where The Foundry, a 222-apartment, mixed-income rental complex, rose over a parking lot and taxi garage in 2000. The transformation of **West 42nd Street** from the tawdry "Deuce" that it once was to a safer, family-oriented entertainment/business center continues.

One Worldwide Plaza, a 49-story tower capped by a nouveau mansard roof, is both a symbol and a powerful instrument of change in Clinton. Prestigious law firms and ad agencies now occupy space at Eighth Avenue and 50th Street, where

the shabby old Madison Square Garden once squatted, and winos, hookers, and drug pushers roamed. A plaza separates the office spire in the mixed-use Zeckendorf development from the residential area, which is located to the west in the block-square complex. Public seating is available year-round on the open plaza, a pleasant respite from the noise that surrounds. Live bands often play near the fountain on the plaza in the summer, and five Off-Broadway theaters are tucked underneath in a space originally planned as a subterranean parking garage. Eighth Avenue is showing robust signs of growth, with condominiums beginning to replace long-standing dives and disused distribution warehouses, and Ninth Avenue and its adjoining side streets are starting to move up as well. Remnants of the bad old days remain in the form of rundown theaters and several adult video stores—and yes, there is still a shady element found on some of the streets after dark. Perhaps the biggest concern when considering this neighborhood is congestion— too many buildings, too many residents, and too many visitors, not to mention traffic heading for the tunnel to New Jersey. However, for the young trendsetter, theatergoer, or thespian, this may be the "hottest" place to settle. For a family with kids or those seeking a quiet refuge, Clinton would be an unlikely option.

One mammoth presence that has profoundly affected Clinton is the Jacob K. Javits Convention Center, 655 West 34th Street. Now, where there had been a nondescript patch of garages, warehouses, and parking lots, a mini-neighborhood springs forth. A few artists, designers, architects, and others have carved homes out of these industrial buildings. The ethnic food shops and tantalizing fruits and vegetables along Ninth Avenue feed them. The massive convention center, which attracts everything from the annual New York Auto Show to Book Expo America, will soon be even easier to reach, as the #7 subway line is being extended west practically to its front door. This transportation development isn't the only aspect of the neighborhood's radical transformation. If you're solidly in the middle class and looking for affordable housing through the city's 80/20 program, keep your eye on the new residential buildings rising here. Many of them are being built on former brownfield sites and will prove a boon to bargain seekers (again, keeping in mind that the term "bargain" is utterly relative in New York). Because of these changes, apartment hunting here should be done block by block, on foot, and at different hours of the day. Besides the possibility of lucking into a reasonable rental, it will give you a good idea about the feel of an area and if it changes at night.

Websites: www.clintoncommunitygarden.org, www.nyc.gov

Area Codes: 212, 646, 917

Post Offices: Midtown Station, 223 W 38th St; Times Square Station, 340 W 42nd St; Radio City Station, 322 W 52nd St

Zip Codes: 10018, 10019, 10036

Police Precincts: Midtown North, 306 W 54th St, 212-767-8300; Midtown South, 357 W 35th St, 212-239-9811, www.nyc.gov/nypd

Emergency Hospital: Mt. Sinai-Roosevelt, 1000 10th Ave, 212-523-4000, www.roosevelthospitalnyc.org

Library: Columbus Branch, 742 10th Ave, 212-586-5098, www.nypl.org

Public School Education: School District #2 in region 9 at 333 Seventh Ave, 12th floor, 212-356-3700, www.www.schools.nyc.gov

Adult Education: John Jay College of Criminal Justice, 899 10th Ave, 212-663-7867, www.jjay.cuny.edu

Community Resources: Alvin Ailey American Dance Theater, 405 W 55th St, 212-405-9000, www.alvinailey.org; St. Clement's Episcopal Church, 423 W 46th St, 212-246-7277, www.stclementsnyc.org, has a special mission to the arts community, and its services are as likely to consist of theatrical performances as liturgy; New World Stages, 340 W 50th St 2646-871-1730, www.newworldstages.com; Intrepid Sea, Air and Space Museum, Pier 86 at W 46th St and 12th Ave, 212-245-0072, www.intrepidmuseum.org

Transportation—Subway: A: 59 St/Columbus Circle; E: Seventh Ave; C/E: 50 St, 42 St/Port Authority, 34 St/Penn Station; #1: 59 St/Columbus Circle, 50 St, 42 St/Times Sq; #2/#3: 42 St Times Sq; N/R/Q: 57 St/Seventh Ave, 49 St, 42 St/Times Sq; Q: 57 St, 42 St/Times Sq; B/D: 59 St/Columbus Circle, Seventh Ave; #7/S (Crosstown shuttles): 42 St/Times Sq; www.mta.info

Transportation—Bus: Crosstown 57th St (M57, M31); Crosstown 49th/50th Sts (M27, M50); Crosstown 42nd St (M42); Crosstown 34th St (M16, M34); Uptown Tenth Ave – Downtown Ninth Ave (M11); Uptown Eighth Ave – Downtown Seventh Ave (M10, M20); Downtown Broadway (M104) to 42nd St and then crossing to the East Side along 42nd St; www.mta.info

LINCOLN CENTER AREA

Boundaries and Contiguous Areas: North: 72nd Street and the Upper West Side; **East**: Central Park West; **South**: 59th Street and Clinton; **West**: Hudson River

This neighborhood, dubbed **Lincoln Square**, is a prime example of how a major cultural facility can improve a marginal New York location. Construction in 1960 of the glass and travertine Lincoln Center complex, with theaters, opera and ballet houses, concert halls, the performing arts branch of the New York Public Library, and The Juilliard School, transformed a dreary stretch of rundown tenements and warehouses into an area of architectural and cultural interest. Limousines now queue up where once trucks double-parked, and it seems as if every other pedestrian carries a musical instrument or moves with the marked grace of a ballet dancer.

Lincoln Square received a new boost in 2010, when officials unveiled another renovation, this time of the Center's plaza and public spaces. The addition of ample

greenspace, a circular fountain, and an upscale restaurant with some al fresco dining made the space welcoming even for visitors not arriving at the complex for a performance. It also made the plaza, which plays host to numerous free and ticketed outdoor concerts and dances during summer months, still more attractive.

Just south of Lincoln Center, at Columbus Circle (where 59th Street meets Broadway), a subway transportation hub deposits thousands of people at the entrance of Central Park, the Museum of Arts and Design, any number of pricey cafés and restaurants, including tony seafood spot, Marea, and the Time Warner Center, a two-tower complex that is home to a number of clothing and home goods retailers, a Whole Foods, and the Jazz at Lincoln Center concert hall. Time Warner is also home to some of the most expensive restaurants in the U.S., among them Per Se, whose tasting menu is $310 (drinks not included). See www.shopsatcolumbuscircle.com for details.

Columnar apartment and office buildings rise above the cafés, restaurants, and boutiques lining Broadway, Columbus, and Amsterdam Avenues. Fordham University's West Side Campus and the TV station ABC are also firmly planted in the neighborhood, adding a boost to the renaissance of Columbus and Amsterdam Avenues, which cater to the food, drink, and clothing needs of West Side residents.

Condo spires and columns have shot up south and west of the culture complex, even on barren Tenth Avenue, which may be the new frontier of Lincoln Square. Tall, white-brick luxury buildings compose most of Lincoln Square's housing. Breaking that mold, 35-story twin towers on a stone base, designed to appeal to families with dogs, opened to renters on West End Avenue between 64th and 65th streets in 2000. The builder was quoted in the *Times* as saying he chose that neighborhood because "it's young, vibrant, and cultural, blends the old New York with the new … and appeals to a broad range of people."

There's also **Trump Place**, a cluster of luxury apartment buildings constructed atop defunct railroad yards fronting the Hudson River between 59th and 72nd Streets. Despite vigorous opposition from area residents, who resented "The Donald's" incursion on their turf, the deep-pocketed Don managed to build a virtual city of his own, albeit one that isn't exactly convenient. While that part of the neighborhood may not entice, do keep an eye on possibilities surrounding Lincoln Center. It remains a vibrant location, wonderful for walking or sitting outside in warm weather at one of the many cafés. A wide range of popular stores can be found, and best of all, it's near Central Park and, of course, Lincoln Center.

Websites: www.nyc.gov, www.lincolncenter.org

Area Codes: 212, 646, 917

Post Offices: Columbus Circle Station, 27 W 60th St; Ansonia Station, 178 Columbus Ave

Zip Codes: 10019, 10023

Police Precincts: Midtown North, 306 W 54th St, 212-767-8400; Twentieth, 120 W 82nd St, 212-580-6411, www.nyc.gov/nypd

Emergency Hospital (nearest): Mt. Sinai-Roosevelt, 1000 10th Ave, 212-523-4000, www.roosevelthospitalnyc.org

Libraries: Library of the Performing Arts at Lincoln Center, 40 Lincoln Center Plaza, 917-275-6975; Riverside Branch, 127 Amsterdam Ave at 65th St, 212-870-1810; www.nypl.org

Public School Education: School District #3, 88 W 125th St, 212-342-8300; Committee on Special Education, 52 Chambers St, 212-374-6085; www.www.schools.nyc.gov

Adult Education: Fordham University, 113 W 60th St, 212-636-6000, www.fordham.edu; The Juilliard School, 60 Lincoln Center Plaza, 212-799-5000, www.juilliard.edu; Art Students League of New York, 215 W 57th St, 212-247-4510, www.theartstudentsleague.org; The Elaine Kaufman Cultural Arts Center at the Goodman House, 129 W 67th St, 212-501-3303, www.kaufman-center.org, offers courses in music, dance, art, and the theater

Community Resources: For the plethora of cultural events, theaters, library, shops, restaurants, exhibits, and tours at Lincoln Center, call their customer service department at 212-875-5456 or go to www.lincolncenter.org; Merkin Concert Hall at the Elaine Kaufman Cultural Arts Center, 129 W 67th St, 212-501-3330, www.kaufman-center.org, presents a variety of concerts, primarily ethnic and chamber music; American Folk Art Museum, 2 Lincoln Square, 212-595-9533, www.folkartmuseum.org

Transportation—Subway: #1: 72 St, 66 St, 59 St/Columbus Circle; #2/#3 (Express): 72 St; A: 59 St/Columbus Circle; B/C: 72 St, 59 St/Columbus Circle; D: 59 St/Columbus Circle; www.mta.info

Transportation—Bus: Crosstown 72nd St (M72); Crosstown 66th/67th Sts (M66); Crosstown 57th St (M57, M31); Uptown Tenth/Amsterdam Ave – Downtown Ninth/Columbus Ave (M11); Uptown Eighth Ave – Downtown Central Park West/Seventh Ave (M10); www.mta.info

UPPER WEST SIDE

Boundaries and Contiguous Areas: North: 110th Street and Morningside Heights; **East:** Central Park West; **South:** 72nd Street and Lincoln Center; **West:** Hudson River

For decades, large sprawling apartments and an active community life have been luring writers, musicians, intellectuals—in general, those seeking an alternative to the Upper East Side's more buttoned-up lifestyle—to the **West Side**. Indeed, the city's first large apartment buildings, with lofty ceilings, thick walls, and space to waste, were built here around the turn of the 20th century. Grand structures rose first along Central Park West (note the famed Dakota at 72nd Street), claimed by some aficionados to be the most architecturally elegant avenue in New York; next on Broadway (the neoclassical Ansonia between 73rd and 74th Streets and the block-square Apthorp between 78th and 79th are particularly grand), which was to be Park Avenue West but isn't; and then on West End Avenue and Riverside Drive. Many of these historic apartment buildings have been converted to condos or are in the conversion process.

Most buildings along the apartment-lined avenues managed to remain sufficiently attractive to hold the middle class. But the rows of brick, limestone, and brownstone townhouses built for the newly affluent on the cross streets during the early 1900s declined into squalid tenements and SRO (single room occupancy) rooming houses for people down on their luck. Not until the late 1960s, when an ambitious urban renewal plan spurred building and renovation, did this veritable architectural museum again become an address for affluent achievers. Today the typical brownstone houses the owner's family on the garden or parlor floors and tenants on the original bedroom floors above. Ranks of condo towers have shot up along Columbus and Amsterdam between 87th and 99th Streets—just outside the boundaries of the Central Park West Historic District. These svelte and pricey condominiums provide residents with plenty of play space: health clubs, pools, rooftop gardens, and party rooms are standard. Meanwhile, **Upper Broadway** is being transformed as high-rises are slotted among the wearier old-timers between 97th Street and Columbia University. A short-term rental in one of these buildings offers the undecided newcomer an opportunity to try out the neighborhood before making a long-term commitment.

Most of the handsome pre-war stone buildings fronting Central Park—the San Remo, the Beresford, and the Majestic, among others—are cooperatives now, and as sought after and as pricey as those on Fifth Avenue across the park. Just south of 96th Street, a few condos and rentals are to be found, and north of 96th to 110th, in the area known as **Manhattan Valley**, a mix of condos, co-ops, and rentals makes Central Park West slightly more accessible for those with some-what slimmer pocketbooks. The vast apartment co-ops lining West End Avenue and curving along Riverside Drive have enduring appeal and enduringly high price tags. Pioneers stake their claims in Manhattan Valley east of Broadway in the upper 90s and 100s and west of Broadway between 96th and 110th Streets. For the less adventurous and thicker of purse, existing rental apartments are well

worth pursuing, if only to live between Manhattan's greenest playgrounds, Central and Riverside Parks, and near one of its cultural stalwarts, the mas-sive Museum of Natural History, which devotes almost 25 acres of floor space to some of the finest scientific collec-tions in the world.

Residents of the Upper West Side enjoy Central Park, the city's premier playground, as their front yard; River-side Drive, which stretches quietly from 72nd Street to 165th Street, looking west over Riverside Park; the Hudson River; and stunning sunsets over the Jersey Palisades. Market rate rental apartments are mostly between 92nd and 96th Streets, the rest being largely co-ops whose boards tend to be less snobbish than in some other neighbor-hoods. Broadway is two blocks away, with its gourmet food markets. It is Riverside Park, however, that gives the neighborhood its sense of community. Residents raise their children there, walk their dogs, play, and dream there. Says one, "With its many levels it is a wonderful place to walk and stroll, sit and read, and have a sandwich—even in the colder months."

Website: www.nyc.gov

Area Codes: 212, 646, 917

Post Offices: Cathedral Station, 215 W 104th St; Planetarium Station, 127 W 83rd St; Ansonia Station, 178 Columbus Ave;

Zip Codes: 10023, 10024, 10025

Police Precincts: Twenty-fourth, 151 W 100th St, 212-678-1811; Twentieth, 120 W 82nd St, 212-580-6411, www.nyc.gov/nypd

Emergency Hospitals (nearest): Mt. Sinai-Roosevelt, 1000 10th Ave, 212-523-4000, www.roosevelthospitalnyc.org; Mt. Sinai-St. Luke's Hospital, 1111 Amsterdam Ave 212-523-4000, www.stlukeshospitalnyc.org

Libraries: Bloomingdale Branch, 150 W 100th St, 212-222-8030; St. Agnes Branch, 444 Amsterdam Ave, 212-621-0619; Riverside Branch, 127 Amsterdam Ave, 212-870-1810; www.nypl.org

Public School Education: School District #3 in region 10 at 388 W 125th St, 212-342-8300, www.www.schools.nyc.gov

Adult Education: Bank Street College of Education, 610 W 112th St, 212-875-4400, www.bankstreet.edu

Community Resources: Central Park, stretching from 59th St over 840 acres up to 110th St is the city's playground, rich with athletic activities, playgrounds, sunbathing sections, a zoo, restaurants and food vendors, street entertainers, a skating rink, summer concert series, and more; www.centralparknyc.org. The Beacon Theatre, 2124 Broadway, 212-465-6625, www.beacontheatre.com; American Museum of Natural History and the Rose Center for Earth and Space, Central Park West from 79th St to 81st St, museum information: 212-769-5100, www.amnh.org; the Bard Graduate Center for Studies in the Decorative Arts, 38 W 86th St, 212-501-3000, www.bgc.bard.edu; Children's Museum of Manhattan, 212 W 83rd St, 212-721-1223, www.cmom.org; Nicholas Roerich Museum, 319 W 107th St, 212-864-7752, www.roerich.org

Transportation—Subway: #1: 110 St/Cathedral Pkwy, 103 St, 96 St, 86 St, 79 St, 82 St; #2/#3 (Express): 96 St, 72 St; B/C: 110 St/Cathedral Pkwy, 103 St, 96 St, 86 St, 81 St, 72 St; www.mta.info

Transportation—Bus: Crosstown 96th St (M96); Crosstown 96th/106th Sts (M106) Crosstown 86th St (M86); Crosstown 79th St (M79); Crosstown 72nd St (M72); Crosstown 66th/67th Sts (M66) ending at Central Park West and 72nd St; Uptown Riverside Drive – Downtown Riverside Drive (M5); Uptown Amsterdam (Ninth) Ave – Downtown Columbus (Tenth) Ave (M7, M11); Uptown Broadway – Downtown Broadway (M104); www.mta.info

MORNINGSIDE HEIGHTS

Boundaries and Contiguous Areas: North: 125th Street and Harlem; **East**: Morningside Drive; **South**: 110th Street and Upper West Side; **West**: Hudson River

In a cityscape that changes constantly, it's hard to attach the superlative of "most changed" to a single neighborhood, but Morningside Heights is definitely in the running for the distinction. Just a few years ago, the area was a curious, often incongruent mix of spectacular university and religious buildings leading up to a zone of gritty, non-descript warehouses, its residents an equally disparate group of ivory tower academics, students, and recent grads, and working class laborers. The neighborhood is still in transition, but change has been occurring at an accelerated pace, due, in large part, to land and building acquisitions made by Columbia University, which is ever in need of space in a city where square footage is always in short and competitive supply.

Those acquisitions have been controversial; long-time residents and business owners feel squeezed, financially and otherwise, by the effects of Columbia's expansion. On the other hand, Columbia, one of the nation's oldest, richest, and

largest educational institutions, has always lent this neighborhood a definite intellectual air and a cultural life enjoyed by anyone who has cared to take advantage of it. Add neighboring Barnard College, as well as two important religious seminaries, the Manhattan School of Music, a large teaching hospital, two major churches, and the pastoral parcels of Riverside and Morningside parks, and you'd be hard-pressed to find a neighborhood more inclined to nourishing the mind, body, and soul.

Work on its massive towers remains halted indefinitely, but if they are ever completed, the Episcopal Cathedral Church of St. John the Divine will literally tower over the community; now spire-less, the world's largest Gothic cathedral just looms. (The tall Gothic church tower you do see rising northwest of Columbia belongs to Riverside Church, the Rockefellers' non-denominational gift to the city.) St. John's caters to cultural as well as spiritual needs, sponsoring a particularly rich and wide-ranging series of concerts from chamber music through liturgical works to jazz and other events, including poetry readings, craft fairs, and dance programs. Broadway, Morningside Heights' main street, showcases bookstores, coffee shops, all-night fruit stands, student bars/jazz joints, boutiques, and restaurants, ranging from cheap, takeout fast food that's ideal for a college student's budget to ethnic and elegant. The lively street life that continues late at night makes the neighborhood relatively safe and certainly interesting.

Housing in this neighborhood presents an interesting challenge for apartment seekers. For one thing, the range of building types is so diverse: from newer luxury buildings to non-descript, pre-war walk-ups, and of course, the less-affordable beauties of Riverside Drive. This range of stock makes for diverse pricing, too, especially since a substantial percentage of apartments here are essentially reserved for college students. Thanks to them, the demand here will always be likely to outpace supply. While you may find working with a broker to be the fastest route to finding your new apartment, this neighborhood is still one place where you're just as likely to discover your next home by calling a number found on a flyer at a bus shelter around the university, especially if you're single, younger, and looking for an apartment share.

Websites: www.morningside-heights.net, www.nyc.gov, www.morningsidepark. org

Area Codes: 212, 646, 917

Post Office: Columbia University Station, 534 W 112th St; Morningside Station, 232 W 116th St

Zip Codes: 10025, 10026, 10027

Police Precinct: Twenty-sixth, 520 W 126th St, 212-678-1311, www.nyc.gov/nypd

Emergency Hospital: Mt. Sinai-St. Luke's-Hospital Center 1111 Amsterdam Ave, 212-523-4000, www.stlukeshospitalnyc.org

Libraries: 115th St Branch, 203 W 115th St, 212-666-9393; Morningside Heights Library, 2900 Broadway, 212-864-2530; George Bruce Library, 518 W 125th St, 212-662-9727; www.nypl.org

Public School Education: School District #3 in region 10, 88 W 125th St, 212-342-8300, http://schools.nyc.gov

Adult Education: Barnard College, 3009 Broadway, 212-854-5262, www.barnard. edu; Columbia University, 2960 Broadway at 116th St, 212-854-1754, www. columbia.edu; Union Theological Seminary, 3041 Broadway 212-662-7100, www.utsnyc.edu; Bank Street College of Education, 610 W 112th St, 212-875-4400, www.bankstreet.edu; Jewish Theological Seminary, 3080 Broadway, 212-678-8000, www.jtsa.edu; Manhattan School of Music, 120 Claremont Ave, 212-749-2802, www.msmnyc.edu

Community Resources: Cathedral Church of St. John the Divine, 1047 Amsterdam Ave, 212-316-7540, www.stjohndivine.org, also has on its large grounds
a Biblical Garden with plantings inspired by the Old Testament; Riverside
Church, 490 Riverside Dr, 212-870-6700, www.theriversidechurchny.org, offers
educational and cultural programs in addition to religious services

Transportation—Subway: #1: 125 St, 116 St/Columbia, 110 St/Cathedral Pkwy;
B/C: 125 St, 116 St, 110 St/Cathedral Pkwy; A/D: 125 St; www.mta.info

Transportation—Bus: Crosstown 116th St (M116); Uptown Amsterdam Ave –
Downtown Columbus Ave (M7, M11); Uptown Broadway – Downtown Broadway
(M104); LaGuardia Airport via 125th St (M60); www.mta.info

THE HARLEMS

Boundaries and Contiguous Areas: *East Harlem*: **North** and **East**: Harlem River;
South: 96th Street, Upper East Side, and Yorkville; **West**: Central Park; *Harlem*:
North: 155th Street and Washington Heights; **East**: Harlem River; **West**: Hudson
River; **South**: 125th Street and Morningside Heights

"The Harlems," as we refer to them here, are actually two neighborhoods: the
Harlem you know from your high school literature class, the Harlem of Ralph
Ellison and Langston Hughes, and Spanish Harlem, also referred to as "El Barrio"
(Spanish for "The Neighborhood"), a section of upper Manhattan that since the
1940s and 1950s has been home to a large population of Puerto Ricans and, more
recently, Mexicans, Dominicans, and other Spanish-speaking immigrants. Though
they share the geographical territory indicated above, they are, in many ways,
quite different, and that's also true when it comes to apartment hunting. Let's take
a look at each of "The Harlems" in turn.

Harlem, originally settled in 1636 by Dutch tobacco farmers, blossomed into
a prosperous suburb in the 1800s. Around 1900, black New Yorkers began settling
into an abundance of apartment buildings left empty when real estate developers' plans for a white, middle-class neighborhood failed to materialize. In
addition to brand new housing stock, Harlem offered its first black residents a less
racially hostile environment than other parts of the city, though a great deal has
changed since the golden days of the Harlem Renaissance, the early 20th-century
literary and artistic movement that put this New York neighborhood on the map.
Gone are some of the most iconic cultural and social institutions of that era,
including Lenox Lounge, but thankfully, a few remain, including the Apollo Theater, which opened in 1913. In the place of those lost juke joints and social clubs,
you'll find a rich variety of newer institutions, including the Schomburg Center for
Research in Black Culture, which is a world-renowned research branch of The New
York Public Library, and The Studio Museum in Harlem, a contemporary art
museum devoted to showing works that are, in their words, "inspired and influ-
enced by black culture." And black culture—or shall we say, black cultures,

plural—is alive and well, especially on 125th Street, the main west to east corridor that cuts through this neighborhood. In addition to African-Americans, there is a large and growing African community here. In particular, there is a sizable population of West Africans, so many, in fact, that a portion of central Harlem is referred to as "Le Petit Sénégal." You'll see vendors from West Africa peddling cocoa butter, cologne, perfume, and incense from sidewalk tables along 125th and women in traditional West African print dresses sitting in chairs on the same sidewalks, quietly offering their hair braiding services.

The arrival of these large groups of immigrants has added to the diversity of the neighborhood, which has become increasingly heterogeneous over the past decade, not only racially and culturally, but also economically. This increasing heterogeneity has made for some complicated—and, occasionally, conflict-ridden—social and political dynamics in Harlem, particularly as lifelong residents experience rent increases and some of the less pleasant effects of gentrification. On the other hand, the influx of a more moneyed class has also had its benefits. Wealthier New Yorkers and transplants, many of them African-Americans, finally realized that some of the city's choicest real estate was languishing, abandoned, and unoccupied, and their investments—property purchases and

full-scale renovations—saved some historic homes, helped combat negative effects of blight, and slowly but surely, drew new business interests into Harlem. Among those interests are the restaurants of Ethiopian-Swedish chef, Marcus Samuelsson, whose Red Rooster is one of the neighborhood's liveliest eateries and a string of neighboring cafés, bars, and bistros along Lenox Avenue.

Harlem is chock-a-block with history, much of it enshrined officially vis-á-vis the designation of historic districts. There's Striver's Row, on West 138th and 139th Streets, between Seventh and Eighth Avenues, dominated by brownstones that are now part of the **St. Nicholas Historic District.** Here you'll also find Abyssinian Baptist Church, New York's oldest black church, at 132 West 138th Street. Equally appealing to professionals, and to City College professors, is the **Hamilton**

Heights area just north of the college, in particular Hamilton Terrace, with its handsome landmarked brownstones. The central area around the **Mount Morris Park Historic District**, between 116th and 125th Streets, has become a highly desirable location. The western strip along the water continues to be the site of redevelopment, though it's not the most accessible section of the neighborhood with respect to public transportation.

To the south, just above Central Park, in the area known as **West Central Harlem** or **Manhattanville**, between 110th and 116th Streets, are rentals and co-ops in a redeveloped and now popular area. Some rentals here, particularly those north of 116th Street to 125th, are priced slightly below market. City-sponsored renovation of abandoned apartment buildings has recently created affordable condos across from Morningside Park. It's worth investigating whether the city's 80/20 program has any current housing lotteries open in the neighborhood. If not—or if you don't qualify—thorough exploration and the help of a good realtor are essential. Further north, **Sugar Hill**, with its mixture of high-rise and pleasing brownstone apartments in the 140s and 150s between St. Nicholas and Edgecombe Avenues, has an enduring appeal, as does **Riverside Drive**, a racially mixed area housing professionals, as well as middle- and low-income residents.

Cultural and educational institutions and welcoming greenspaces abound in Harlem. In its heart, at Lenox Avenue (Malcolm X Boulevard) and West 135th Street, is the Schomburg Center for Research in Black Culture, which houses the world's largest collection of black history. On West 135th Street is the facility's outdoor sculpture garden; the outdoor amphitheater is on West 136th. Another neighborhood treasure is the splendid Riverbank State Park—28 acres of landscaped greenery with spectacular sunset views over the Hudson at 145th Street. Completed in 1993 atop a waste treatment plant, the recreational complex comprises indoor and outdoor swimming pools, a gym and fitness room, softball fields, basketball, tennis and handball courts outdoors, an indoor theater and amphitheater, and an ice and roller skating rink. Admission is free, open daily from 6 a.m. to 11 p.m., with a fee for the use of tennis courts and a nominal fee for the pool (see **Sports and Recreation**). In the long-term, a big change is coming to the more industrial area between West 129th and West 133rd, west of Broadway, with Columbia University now being given the go-ahead (via eminent domain in some cases) to create a huge new and controversial campus over the next 25 years. Acquisition of existing businesses and property has already occurred, and in parts of the neighborhood, construction on the expanded campus has begun.

Harlem's east side is known as **Spanish Harlem** or **El Barrio**. Here, you'll find mostly tenements and housing projects, though a handful of new buildings have gone up in the past decade that are being marketed as luxury units. You might think realtors would find it a hard sell—literally—to move units in these buildings, but the lower price points and the appeal of being part of a neighborhood "in transition" draw younger professionals who may not have the buying power to live in the tighter downtown markets. As these buildings have filled up, new businesses, such as the charming bookstore La Casa Azul, have joined institutions like Taller Boricua (a Puerto Rican art gallery and multidisciplinary cultural center) and El Museo del Barrio, a museum dedicated to Latin American art, as well as locally-owned and operated businesses like La Marqueta, an indoor produce and meat market on 116th and Park.

With all these developments then, "The Harlems" are in a moment of transition, and it is a good time to take advantage of rents that are still low compared to other parts of the city. This is especially true since services and attractions have expanded. If the good life is defined by jazz clubs, all-night dancing, authentic soul food, urban poetry, and flourishing arts of every genre, then Harlem is indeed providing all the necessary elements. The highly touted Dance Theatre of Harlem, productions by the award-winning Classical Theatre of Harlem, the annual Harlem Book Fair, the Urban World Film Festival, numerous jazz venues, and home purchases by African-American celebrities have generated great interest here. Visitors, who for years did not venture past 96th Street, are now beating down a path to check out this revitalized neighborhood. Even former president Bill Clinton has an office on 125th Street.

Websites: www.nyc.gov, www.harlembespoke.blogspot.com, www.welcometo-harlem.wordpress.com,

Area Codes: 212, 646, 917

Post Offices: Hamilton Grange Station, 521 W 146th St; Manhattanville Station, 365 W 125th St; Hellgate Station, 153 E 110th St; Triborough Station, 167 E 124th St; College Station, 217 W 140th St; Lincolnton Station, 2266 Fifth Ave

Zip Codes: 10026, 10027, 10029, 10030, 10035, 10039

Police Precincts: Twenty-third, 162 E 102nd St, 212-860-6411; Twenty-fifth, 120 E 119th St, 212-860-6511; Twenty-eighth, 2271 Eighth Ave, 212-678-1611; Thirtieth, 451 W 151st St, 212-690-8811; Thirty-second, 250 W 135th St, 212-690-6311; www.nyc.gov/nypd

Emergency Hospitals: Harlem Hospital Center, 506 Lenox Ave, 212-939-1000, www.nyc.gov/hhc/harlem; Mount Sinai Medical Center, 1468 Madison Ave, 212-241-6500, www.mountsinai.org

Libraries: 125th St Library, 224 E 125th St, 212-534-5050; Countee Cullen Branch, 104 W 136th St, 212-491-2070; George Bruce Library, 518 W 125th St, 212-662-9727; Hamilton Grange Branch, 503 W 145th St, 212-926-2147; Harlem Library, 9 W 124th St, 212-348-5620; www.nypl.org; Schomburg Center for Research in Black Culture, 515 Malcolm X Boulevard, 917-275-6975, houses the city's African-American archives and presents local artists' works

Public School Education: East Harlem schools fall in district 2, region 9, 333 7th Ave, 212-356-7500, www.www.schools.nyc.gov

Adult Education: City College, City University of New York (CUNY), 160 Convent Ave, 212-650-7000, www.ccny.cuny.edu; Boricua College, a private Hispanic liberal arts college, 3755 Broadway, 212-694-1000, www.boricuacollege.edu

Community Resources: Harlem celebrates its past and present history each summer by hosting a season-long series of events, called Harlem Week (though the celebration runs longer than a week), www.harlemweek.com; Apollo Theater, 253 W 125th St, 212-531-5300, an institution and the hub for Harlem-based entertainment since 1913, www.apollotheater.org; The Studio Museum in Harlem, 144 W 125th St, 212-864-4500, www.studiomuseum.org; The Museum of the City of New York, 1220 Fifth Ave, 212-534-1672, www.mcny.org; El Museo del Barrio, 1230 Fifth Ave, 212-831-7272, www.elmuseo.org; Dance Theatre of Harlem, 466 W 152nd St, 212-690-2800, www.dancetheatreofharlem.com; Harlem School of the Arts, 645 St. Nicholas Ave, 212-926-4100, www.hsanyc.org; The Classical Theatre of Harlem, 566 W 159th St, 347-688-6304, www.cthnyc.org

Transportation—Subway: #1: 157 St, 137 St, 125 St; #3: 148 St, 145 St; #2/#3: 135 St, 125 St, 116 St, 110 St/Central Park North; A: 145 St, 125 St; B/C: 155 St, 145 St, 135 St, 125 St, 116 St, 110 St/Cathedral Pkwy; D: 155 St, 145 St, 125 St; #4/#5/#6: 125 St; #6: 116 St, 110 St, 103 St, 96 St; www.mta.info

Transportation—Bus: Crosstown 96th St (M96); Crosstown 116th St (M116); Uptown/Downtown Riverside Dr (M5); Uptown/Downtown Broadway (M100, M104, M4); Uptown/Downtown Powell Ave (M2) Uptown/Downtown St. Nicholas Ave (M3); Uptown/Downtown Third, Lexington, Amsterdam Ave (M101, M100); Third, Lexington, Lennox Ave (M98, M102, M103); www.mta.info

WASHINGTON HEIGHTS-INWOOD

Boundaries and Contiguous Areas: North: Harlem River and Riverdale; **East**: Harlem River; **South**: 155th Street and Harlem; **West**: Hudson River

Up here, where outcroppings from the Hudson riverbed rise to form Manhattan's highest ground, the tawny stone arches rhythmically lining the central courtyard at The Cloisters are echoed by the exceptionally graceful curve of the steel suspension cables of the silvery, two-level George Washington Bridge. Long before John D. Rockefeller, Jr., gave the city the magnificent medieval Cloisters Museum, as well as Fort Tryon Park, George Washington headquartered Revolutionary forces on the strategic terrain now called Washington Heights. In fact, Morris-Jumel Mansion, which Washington used as his headquarters during the fall of 1776, still sits proudly on a hill in the neighborhood and is open to the public.

Six hundred acres of parkland, almost all of it in Fort Tryon Park and rocky, wooded Inwood Hill Park, refresh and beautify one of the most densely populated, and narrowest, sections of New York. On the map, the top of Manhattan looks like a knobby finger pointing across the Harlem River at The Bronx from the elongated fist of Manhattan. Washington Heights and Inwood are all "West Side" on both sides of the island as the Harlem River lops off the "East Side" at 138th Street. It was here in 1776 that the new American Army built Fort Washington, only to suffer a whopping defeat and have 3,000 men killed or taken prisoner by the British. The progress of the battle is commemorated in plaques down Broadway.

Narrow as it is, this finger of Manhattan contains many neighborhoods, only two of which, along the western edge, we describe here. Commercial Broadway cuts through the area on a north-south bias, dividing the almost solidly Hispanic, mostly low-income Harlem River (eastern) half from the more middle-income (western) half overlooking the Hudson River. The western section contains the most coveted housing—solidly constructed pre-World War II one- and two-bedroom apartments, many with marvelous pleasing river views—situated in square, five- to ten-story buildings. The clusters of yellow, buff, and occasionally red brick art deco buildings clumped along a rocky spine above the river in the Hudson Heights section of Washington Heights have special appeal. Two of the most desirable complexes, half-timbered Hudson View Gardens, between 183rd and 185th Streets on Pinehurst Avenue, and Castle Village, with its gardens and panoramic Hudson River views nearby, are cooperatives, as are many of the neighborhood buildings. Sublets, where you can get them, are still priced well below rentals farther Downtown, as are the co-ops.

In previous years, a violent drug trade made parts of **Washington Heights**, the West 150s and 160s in particular, a dicey neighborhood despite its solidly middle-class population and the presence of prestigious New York Presbyterian Hospital. Most recently, however, crime is way down, and though rentals and co-op prices are up, they are significantly less than what comparable properties cost below 96th Street brownstones, and large apartments in pre-war buildings are well worth a look, especially along Riverside Drive West, Fort Washington Avenue, and the connecting streets, including those west of Fort Washington Avenue.

For another dimension, travel up to **Inwood** and stroll the grassy fields of Inwood Hill Park near 218th Street and Indian Road. Ahead of you, to the north, Harlem River sweeps under Henry Hudson Bridge, beyond which you can see the Jersey Palisades. To your immediate right are Columbia University's Robert K. Kraft Field at Lawrence A. Wien Stadium, the only college stadium in Manhattan, and

the college boathouse and tennis bubble, all part of the university's Baker Athletic Complex. Inwood Hill Park is one of the city's loveliest and least-known parks, with wetlands, rolling greens, and six miles of footpaths rising into rocky woods, where there are Indian caves to be seen. It's quiet, except for an astonishing variety of birds. The man jogging past is as likely to be an opera singer or an artist as he is to be a broker or a police officer. A farmers' market, Inwood Greenmarket, takes place on Isham Street on Saturdays, year-round.

If you find the friendly unassuming neighborhood attractive, plan to search, and search hard, on foot, questioning supers and building managers. Inwood is a small neighborhood of pleasing pre-war brick apartment buildings located between the park and Broadway, north of 207th Street, Broadway and 207th the two main streets. There are no trendy restaurants, lively after-hours clubs, or art film houses here. But the cost of a sunny one-bedroom (or two or three) on the park, if you can find one to rent, will likely pique your interest, especially if you've been looking Downtown. But prices are on the rise. With developments like the $3 million condo Noma 175 popping up (its 12 units sold for between $345,000 and $396,000 each, according to the real estate blog, *Curbed*), Inwood's village-type ambiance might soon be changing, and along with it, prices. Get in while the getting is still good and consult a reputable local real estate agent when pursuing housing here, especially if you're hoping to find an apartment in one of those beautiful river-view co-ops.

Websites: www.nyc.gov, www.uptowncollective.com
Area Codes: 212, 646, 917
Post Offices: Audubon Station, 511 W 165th St; Fort George Station, 4558 Broadway; Inwood Station, 90 Vermilyea Ave; Fort Washington Station, 556 W 158th St
Zip Codes: 10031, 10032, 10033, 10034, 10040
Police Precincts: Thirty-fourth, 4295 Broadway, 212-927-9711; Thirty-third, 2207 Amsterdam Ave, 212-927-3200, www.nyc.gov/nypd
Emergency Hospital: New York-Presbyterian Hospital, 650 W 168th St, 212-305-7367, www.nyp.org
Libraries: Fort Washington Branch, 535 W 179th St, 212-927-3533; Washington Heights Branch, 1000 St. Nicholas Ave, 212-923-6054; Inwood Branch, 4790 Broadway, 212-942-2445; www.nypl.org
Public School Education: School District #6 in region 10, 388 W. 125th St, 212-342-8300, www.www.schools.nyc.gov
Adult Education: Yeshiva University, 500 W 185th St, 212-960-5400, www.yu.edu
Community Resources: The Cloisters, division of the Metropolitan Museum of Art, Fort Tryon Park (193rd St and Fort Washington Ave), 212-923-3700, www.metmuseum.org, devoted to the art and architecture of Medieval Europe; Audubon Terrace Museum complex, Broadway between W 155th and 156th Sts, including the American Academy of Arts and Letters, 633 W 155th St, 212-368-5900, www.artsandletters.org, and The Hispanic Society of America, 613

W 155th St, 212-926-2234, www.hispanicsociety.org, includes a library and museum; Inwood Community Services, 651 Academy St, 212-942-0043, www. inwoodcommunityservices.org; Morris-Jumel Mansion and Museum, 65 Jumel Terrace, 212-923-8008, www.morrisjumel.org; Dyckman Farmhouse Museum, 4881 Broadway, 212-304-9422, www.dyckmanfarmhouse.org

Transportation—Subway: A: 207 St, Dyckman St, 190 St, 181 St, 175 St, 168 St; C: 168 St, 163 St, 155 St; #1: 215 St, 207 St, Dyckman St, 191 St, 181 St, 168 St, 157 St; B/D: 155 St; www.mta.info

Transportation—Bus: Crosstown 181st St (Bx3, Bx11, Bx13, Bx36); Uptown/ Downtown Fort Washington Ave – Broadway (M4); Uptown/Downtown Broadway (Bx7, M100); Uptown/Downtown St. Nicholas Ave (M3); Uptown/ Downtown Lexington Ave to 193rd St (M101); Uptown/Downtown Third Ave, Adam Clayton Powell Blvd. (M102); Washington Heights/Midtown – limited service between 179 St and 34th St, via Harlem River Dr and Third Ave (M 98); www.mta.info

THE BRONX

When Swedish sailor Jonas Bronck purchased 500 acres of farmland north of Manhattan in the seventeenth century, he staked a claim to the Aquahung River, which bordered his property to the east. The river became known as the Bronck's River, and his farm known simply as the Bronck's. Thus began the modern development of what is now the fourth most populous of New York's five boroughs.

In spite of containing some of New York City's loveliest greenspaces, among them Wave Hill and the New York Botanical Garden, The Bronx has a tarnished reputation. Urban sprawl practically ruined the borough in the 1960s, when Robert Moses bisected the borough with the Cross-Bronx Expressway; simultaneously, a wave of crime and unemployment ravaged many of the low- to middle-income neighborhoods. A widespread pandemic of landlord arson destroyed much of the south Bronx in the '70s and early '80s and made the phrase "The Bronx is burning!" synonymous with urban decay. And as if all that wasn't enough, the crack and cocaine upsurge of the 1980s hit The Bronx especially hard, as did the consequences of the 1973 passage of the Rockefeller drug laws, which imprisoned an unprecedented number of people on drug-related charges. And then there were the gangs, immortalized in movies like *The Warriors*.

It's little wonder, then, that overcoming this reputation has been—and remains—a challenge. But we'll let you in on a secret: the intrepid souls who are willing to venture—and possibly live—this far north of the city's action will be rewarded with considerably lower rents and, in many cases, considerably larger apartments. Besides the appeal of these two factors, there are plenty of historical and cultural reasons to consider moving to **The Bronx**. First, you'd be joining a

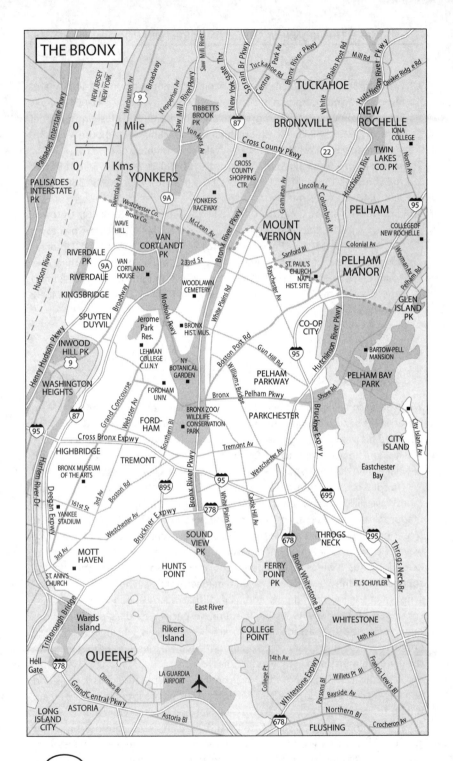

THE BRONX

0   1 Mile

0   1 Kms

TUCKAHOE

BRONXVILLE

NEW ROCHELLE

IONA COLLEGE

TWIN LAKES CO. PK

YONKERS

CROSS COUNTY SHOPPING CTR.

PELHAM

COLLEGE OF NEW ROCHELLE

PALISADES INTERSTATE PK

YONKERS RACEWAY

MOUNT VERNON

PELHAM MANOR

RIVERDALE PK

VAN CORTLANDT PK

WAVE HILL

VAN CORTLAND HOUSE

WOODLAWN CEMETERY

ST. PAUL'S CHURCH NAT'L HIST. SITE

GLEN ISLAND PK

RIVERDALE

KINGSBRIDGE

SPUYTEN DUYVIL

Jerome Park Res.

BRONX HIST. MUS.

CO-OP CITY

BARTOW-PELL MANSION

INWOOD HILL PK

LEHMAN COLLEGE C.U.N.Y

NY BOTANICAL GARDEN

PELHAM PARKWAY

PELHAM BAY PARK

WASHINGTON HEIGHTS

FORDHAM UNIV.

BRONX ZOO/ WILDLIFE CONSERVATION PARK

PARKCHESTER

CITY ISLAND

FORD-HAM

Cross Bronx Expwy

HIGHBRIDGE

TREMONT

Tremont Av

Eastchester Bay

BRONX MUSEUM OF THE ARTS

YANKEE STADIUM

MOTT HAVEN

SOUND VIEW PK

THROGS NECK

ST. ANN'S CHURCH

HUNTS POINT

FERRY POINT PK

FT. SCHUYLER

East River

Wards Island

Rikers Island

COLLEGE POINT

WHITESTONE

QUEENS

Hell Gate

LA GUARDIA AIRPORT

LONG ISLAND CITY

ASTORIA

FLUSHING

long and illustrious list of former residents, among them Edgar Allan Poe (whose cottage still sits on the Grand Concourse, the borough's main avenue) and Mark Twain. The borough is also home to some contemporary superstars of the athletic variety: the beloved New York Yankees, whose new stadium, across the street from the original, opened in 2009. The neighborhood where the Yankees play may be one of the most maligned, but it shouldn't be (not anymore, anyway), and some fine apartments are to be found in pre-war buildings on the cross streets between Jerome Avenue (which runs under the elevated train line) and the Grand Concourse, as well as in the art deco buildings on the Concourse itself. Though they're a shadow of their former glorious selves, the apartments in the Concourse beauties are certainly larger than their counterparts in comparable Manhattan buildings. Word of mouth, flyers, and especially, chatting up building supers (bonus points if you speak Spanish) are still the best ways to find an apartment in this South Bronx neighborhood, which gets a cultural boost from The Bronx Museum of the Arts. This neighborhood is also an excellent choice because it sits neatly between two major subway lines. Just don't expect upscale grocery stores and hip cafés. Corner bodegas, fast food, and fried chicken chains still rule the roost here.

A wealth of public land is probably The Bronx's greatest asset; parkland accounts for almost a quarter of the 43-square-mile borough. Partially forested Van Cortlandt Park, a playground for cross-country skiers in the winter, is the spot for soccer, rugby, and football in the summer. You'll also find the city's oldest public golf course there. Even larger Pelham Bay Park, from which little City Island dangles, harbors Orchard Beach along its sandy shore. But the star is Bronx Park, with 500 acres about equally divided between two of the city's most enjoyable institutions: the Bronx Zoo (officially the New York Zoological Society's International Wildlife Conservation Park) and the New York Botanical Garden. The Enid Haupt Conservatory, a sparkling crystal greenhouse complex, displays thousands of plant varieties in natural micro-climates and must be seen. Kids of all ages, naturalists, and explorers too, frequent the zoo.

Other reasons to consider The Bronx? Four of the city's finest high schools are found here: the prestigious public Bronx High School of Science, from which many Intel Science Award winners graduate, as well as the private Fieldston, Horace Mann, and Riverdale Country schools. Eight universities and colleges enhance the borough's scholastic character.

Then there's the bucolic escape of City Island, which floats rather quaintly in placid Long Island Sound, providing a New England-esque escape from city life and the finest seafood around. It may seem a world away, but it actually belongs to The Bronx. And over on the Hudson's shore, Riverdale shelters some estates and sylvan lanes worthy of suburban Scarsdale, although more densely packed. In-between these two neighborhoods, it's worth looking at some of the apartment buildings along Mosholu and Pelham Parkways, as well as in The Bronx's Little Italy neighborhood, a compact area around Arthur Avenue. If environmental consciousness influences your choice of living space, check out some of the new developments focused on green living, including the ambitious Bronx Commons (www.whedco.org/Green-Homes/). When finished, this affordable housing project will include a rooftop farm with a hydroponic greenhouse. Finally, don't neglect the southernmost swath of The Bronx, the part leading up to the Third Avenue Bridge. Here, old factories are being converted into residences and new affordable housing projects are attempting to attract Manhattan refugees who can no longer pay that borough's astronomical rents.

Other than good old-fashioned pound-the-pavement efforts and chatting up supers, how do you go about finding an apartment in The Bronx? Web-based listing services, such as craigslist.com and rent.com, make a strong showing here, but the champion of Bronx rentals can be found at www.goldfarbproperties.com, with photos and no-fee listings as a priority. Below, a couple of stand-out neighborhoods for your consideration.

RIVERDALE

Boundaries and Contiguous Areas: North: 263rd Street and Yonkers; **East**: Broadway and Van Cortlandt Park; **South**: West 239th Street and West 242nd Street, Spuyten Duyvil and Kingsbridge; **West**: Hudson River

Riverdale seems more like Westchester than New York and is certainly a departure from the rest of The Bronx. Call it a suburb in the city. It was mostly farmland, in fact, until the mid-19th century, when a few wealthy souls fled Manhattan's cholera epidemics and carved out impressive estates overlooking the river. Among these was Wave Hill (see below). In 1853, with the completion of a railroad bridge across Spuyten Duyvil Creek (now known as the Harlem River), Riverdale soon became a prosperous suburb, desirable for possessing the best of both rural and urban life. When Riverdale was appended to New York City in 1874, it took the objections of Frederick Law Olmsted, co-designer of Central Park, to prevent the re-mapping of the winding, wooded roads that make Riverdale so beguiling today. But no one could prevent Robert Moses from bisecting both Riverdale and Spuyten Duyvil with a clean slash of the Henry Hudson Parkway in the 1930s.

Many of the original mansions survive along the winding roads, often invisible behind ivy-covered stone fences. Prospective purchasers can sometimes buy part of one, as many have been "condoed." Posh private schools attract kids who drive in from New Jersey and the suburbs, as well as those who arrive by subway and bus from the boroughs. Shops are discreetly confined to a few zones of mom-and-pop businesses; supermarket complexes are built elsewhere. Riverdale's low, tree-shaded profile appeals to both affluent New York professionals and resident foreigners.

Tall, red-brick apartment towers cluster in clumps along the potholed lanes in south Riverdale, built mostly in the 1960s and '70s, and now almost all are co-ops and condos. Spacious apartments, many with enviable views, can occasionally be had at prices slightly below Manhattan standards, but are increasingly harder to find, as the area has become dense with ex-Manhattanites.

In north Riverdale, along the Yonkers border, brick and stucco houses on smallish lots can be had in a quiet neighborhood, but again, prices are rising. There are plenty of mini-mansions in Riverdale, but there is a recent new explo-

sion of less expensive high-rise condos in the southern area near the exclusive (and landmarked) community of **Fieldston**. The urban grid and bustle so typical of New York is found on the flats below in **Kingsbridge**.

For a great day in this neighborhood, visit Wave Hill, West 249th Street and Independence Avenue (call 718-549-3200 or go to www.wavehill.org for directions). The Hudson-side complex at 249th Street and Independence Avenue consists of two stone manor houses offering occasional chamber music, a café, a greenhouse, and 28 acres of perfectly gorgeous gardens, wherein summer outdoor sculpture exhibits compete for your attention with lovely river views.

Websites: www.ilovethebronx.com, www.bronx.com, www.ssbx.org, www.riverdalepress.com, www.nyc.gov

Area Codes: 718, 347

Post Offices: Riverdale Station, 5951 Riverdale Ave; Fieldston Station, 444 W 238th St; Kingsbridge Station, 5517 Broadway

Zip Codes: 10463, 10471

Police Precinct: Fiftieth, 3450 Kingsbridge Ave, 718-543-5700

Emergency Hospital (nearest): Montefiore Medical Center West Campus, 112 E 210th St, 718-920-4321. In addition to four adult Emergency Departments, Montefiore has a Pediatric Emergency Department at The Children's Hospital at Montefiore, 3415 Bainbridge Ave, 718-741-2150

Library: Riverdale Public Library, 5540 Mosholu Ave at 256th St, 718-549-1212, www.nypl.org. For a full listing of NYPL branches in The Bronx, please visit www.nypl.org/locations#bronx-list

Public School Education: School District #10 in region 1, 1 Fordham Plaza, 718-741-5852/718-741-7644

Adult Education: Manhattan College, 4513 Manhattan College Pkwy, 718-862-8000, www.manhattan.edu; College of Mt. St. Vincent, 6301 Riverdale Ave, 718-405-3267, www.cmsv.edu; Bronx Community College, 2155 University Ave, 718-289-5100, www.bcc.cuny.edu

Community Resources: Wave Hill, 67W 249th St and Independence Ave, 718-549-3200, www.wavehill.org; Riverdale YM-YWHA, 5625 Arlington Ave, 718-548-8200, www.riverdaley.org

Transportation—Subway: #1 at 242nd and 238th streets (in Kingsbridge); www.mta.info

Transportation—Bus: Commuters in Fieldston and Riverdale tend to use MTA buses, 718-652-8400, express buses to mid-Manhattan and Wall Street, 45 minutes, $6 one way. Local buses include the BX7 or BX10. Get a Bronx bus map for local MTA routes or go to www.mta.info.

Transportation—Train: Metro-North Hudson line, 212-532-4900, Riverdale Station at 200 W 254th St by the Hudson River, 25 minutes from Grand Central. Note: tickets cost significantly more if you buy them on the train. Purchase tickets at station ticket windows or online at www.mta.info.

SPUYTEN DUYVIL

Boundaries and Contiguous Areas: North: 239th Street and 242nd Street and Riverdale; **East**: Waldo and Johnson Avenues and Kingsbridge; **South**: Harlem River and Washington Heights-Inwood; **West**: Hudson River

Henry Hudson gazes off at his river from atop a 100-foot Doric column in Henry Hudson Memorial Park. Spuyten Duyvil (pronounced SPY-ten DIE-vul, supposedly from "Spitting Devil") has a southward pitch, so it seems to look back at

Manhattan, but if you live here, you're sure to look west to the spectacular sunsets, which blaze and bleed over the river.

There's little to distinguish Spuyten Duyvil from Riverdale, which abuts it to the north. Both are bisected by the Henry Hudson Parkway and they share a rocky perch high over the Hudson River. But little Spuyten Duyvil, which has its own zip code and post office, feels like a village, despite being sliced and dotted with co-ops and condos. Perhaps it's charming little Edgehill Church, a country church, or the 19th-century wood frame houses on a winding street below in the shadow of the Henry Hudson Bridge. The narrow streets are all jammed and tangled down here, wiggling around Spuyten Duyvil Shorefront Park, where strollers meander along a path that wanders down to the railroad station. Back up the hill, joggers run along scenic Palisade Avenue above Riverdale Park and the Metro-North tracks.

Housing here is mostly in apartments, though there are houses occasionally on the market, especially east of the parkway. Both rentals and co-ops are below Manhattan price levels, with the most expensive being those west of the highway with river views. Shopping is available along Johnson Avenue, east of the parkway from 235th to 236th Streets, and along Riverdale Avenue between 235th and 238th Streets. There's also a shopping area conveniently located around the 231st Street subway stop.

Website: www.nyc.gov
Area Codes: 718, 347
Post Office: Spuyten Duyvil Station, 562 Kappock St
Zip Code: 10463
Police Precinct: Fiftieth, 3450 Kingsbridge Ave, 718-543-5700
Emergency Hospital (nearest): Montefiore Medical Center West Campus, 112 E 210th St, 718-920-4321. In addition to four adult Emergency Departments, Montefiore has a Pediatric Emergency Department at The Children's Hospital at Montefiore, 3415 Bainbridge Ave, 718-741-2150.
Libraries: Spuyten Duyvil Branch, 650 W 235th St, 718-796-1202; Kingsbridge Branch, 291 W 231st St, 718-548-5656; www.nypl.org. For a full list of NYPL branches in The Bronx, please visit www.nypl.org/locations#bronx-list.visit.
Public School Education: See Riverdale
Adult Education: See Riverdale
Community Resources: See Riverdale
Transportation—Subway: #1 at 238th, 231st and 225th streets (all in Kingsbridge); www.mta.info
Transportation—Bus: Commuters tend to use MTA buses, 718-652-8400, www.mta.info, for express bus service to mid-Manhattan and Wall Street. For local bus routes, use an MTA map or look at www.mta.info.
Transportation—Train: Metro-North Hudson Line, 212-532-4900, same pricing as Riverdale (see above); www.mta.info

YOU MIGHT ALSO WANT TO CONSIDER ...

- **City Island (www.cityisland.com);** no, it's not Nantucket, but this unselfconscious little island dangling off Pelham Bay Park provides boat fanciers and aquaphiles with salty air, Technicolor sunsets, and the scruffy charm of a watery small town ... not to mention fresh seafood. It's fairly inexpensive, though not altogether convenient living here, but you can park your sailboat out back. Housing on this tiny island is limited.

- **Crotona Park East (AKA East Morrisania);** once the background for Jimmy Carter's pronouncement that The Bronx was America's "worst slum," little Crotona Park East has become what realtors call a "transition neighborhood." There's still lots of graffiti, but crime has dropped almost 100% in the last decade, and housing values are climbing—but still very affordable, considering it's only a 35-minute commute to Midtown.

- **Mott Haven/Port Morris;** the southernmost neighborhood in the storied South Bronx has begun to show signs of new life, with artists and young professionals moving into newly refurbished tenements and historic brownstones and the chic new loft dwellings in The Clock Tower. New restaurants are opening, and an antiques district has cropped up along Bruckner Boulevard. Low prices, around a dollar a square foot per month, and the proximity to Manhattan are the biggest draws, and realtors are optimistically calling the area SoBro, but surrounding areas are still rather dicey and clusters of housing projects are a stone's throw away.

- **Pelham Parkway/Bay;** straddling the leafy parkway that stretches between Bronx Park and Pelham Bay Park in the central Bronx, this area's ethnically and economically diverse populace lives in shady streets with lots of older two-story houses that go for around $500,000 (one-room co-ops go for under $100,000). Count on an hour to get to Downtown Manhattan, but at least you don't have to change lines. "If you can't afford Riverdale, then you buy here," says one realtor.

BROOKLYN

"I too lived—Brooklyn, of ample hills, was mine," so wrote Walt Whitman, and so too can you live. New York is frequently described as a vertical city, but that sort of top-down crowding is not the domain in expansive Brooklyn. Though inextricably tied with neighboring Manhattan, **Brooklyn** is very much a city of its own. It has a strong spirit, a unique character, an autonomous sense of community, and rich too is its history. There is no city like New York, and no borough quite like Brooklyn.

Formerly home to *The Honeymooners* and *The Cosbys* and to the Dodgers at Ebbets Field, and still home to Coney Island's infamous roller coaster, the Cyclone, Brooklyn has played no small hand in defining America's cultural landscape. It

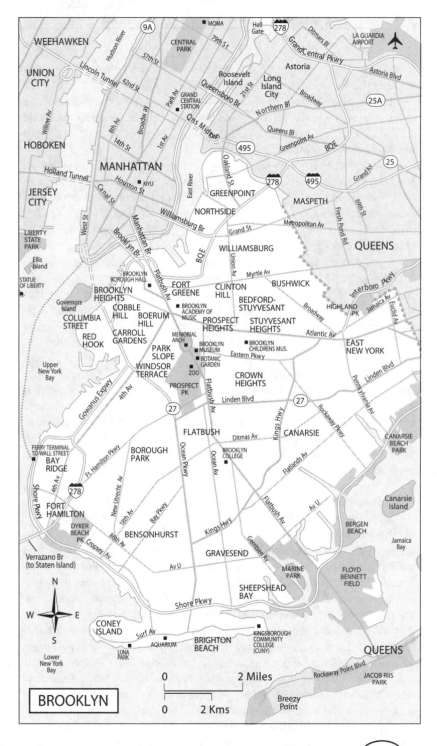

BROOKLYN

is also one of the nation's ten most populous communities. Brooklyn remains a viable option for anyone looking to move to New York City.

Boosters boast about excellent subway transportation, the quality of the public schools in District 15, and the lively cultural climate engendered by the culture scene's "big three": the Brooklyn Museum, Brooklyn Botanic Garden, and Brooklyn Academy of Music (BAM). Brooklyn, it is said, is a state of mind.

The borough has been humming with change for several years now. As Manhattan's real estate market has swollen, artists, commuters, and the middle class have made their way to Brooklyn's pleasant neighborhoods. Immigrants, most recently from Asia and especially China, have flocked to Brooklyn, which is increasingly perceived as the chic alternative to crowded, expensive Manhattan. Major developments are making their marks along the waterfront, and a steady gentrification has taken hold of many formerly underdeveloped neighborhoods.

The year 1987 marked the beginning of the long-overdue commercial revitalization of downtown; part of MetroTech Center, a 7.6-million-square-foot commercial and academic complex in the heart of downtown Brooklyn, 1 Pierrepont Plaza opened first, housing Morgan Stanley operations. A suburban-type mall with megastores along Flatbush Avenue at Atlantic Avenue marked the completion of the first phase of the Atlantic Center, with housing and office buildings added afterward. Within Atlantic Center is Atlantic Terminal, which houses both subway and Long Island Rail Road stations. The convenience of the trains, plus a big parking garage for people with cars, made this shopping hub particularly attractive, especially when a Target was added. Then, in late 2012, Barclays Center, a state-of-the-art, multipurpose arena, opened and gave the area yet another boost. Barclays is home to the Brooklyn (formerly New Jersey) Nets and has hosted some of the hottest names in music and the performing arts.

A development project of a different nature, but one received with perhaps even more enthusiasm, is Brooklyn Bridge Park (www.brooklynbridgepark.org), the borough's answer to Manhattan's Hudson River Park. The 85-acre waterfront park begins at the Manhattan Bridge and runs south past Brooklyn Bridge; along the way, you'll find water parks, kayak launches, picnic and recreation areas, and much more. Views include unobstructed panoramas of lower Manhattan and the Statue of Liberty, as well as the Williamsburg, Brooklyn, and Manhattan Bridges.

Other parts of Brooklyn's shores are undergoing their own transformations. The riverfront area of **Greenpoint** has been spiffed up, not the least reason being that it is marketed as an amenity for the numerous high-rise apartment buildings that have sprung up like mushrooms in the neighborhood. From Greenpoint southward to Williamsburg, the shoreline has changed dramatically over the past decade, thanks to these new apartment buildings, many of which are also now accessible via the East River Ferry, which makes multiple stops along the Brooklyn shoreline. Soon, one of the last vestiges of Brooklyn's industrial past will disappear when the Domino Sugar refinery, once the largest in the world, is converted into a residential complex right on the waterfront. The project, which has not yet broken ground, has been controversial, not only because of nostalgia and the landmark status of parts of the Domino building, but because the percentage of the project designated for affordable housing has changed several times since plans were announced. In a neighborhood where rents have skyrocketed in recent years, the need for affordable housing is certainly acute.

While some neighborhoods remain in need of revitalization, gentrification has been hard at work in many sections of Brooklyn over the past two decades. Plenty of neighborhoods are family friendly and remain—at least for now—more affordable than Manhattan, though with the influx of newcomers and developments to the borough, "affordable" is becoming a relative term.

Names of Brooklyn realtors can be found under **Apartment Hunting** in the **Finding a Place to Live** chapter. Craigslist.com, rent.com, and many other sites carry extensive listings for the entire borough and are a first stop for as many realtors as potential tenants.

BROOKLYN HEIGHTS

Boundaries and Contiguous Areas: North: Fulton Ferry Landing and Cadman Plaza West; **East**: Cadman Plaza and Court Street; **South**: Atlantic Avenue and Cobble Hill; **West**: The Esplanade overlooking the East River and Brooklyn-Queens Expressway (BQE)

A *New York Times* article described two young lawyers walking home along Henry Street in the Heights one summer evening discussing cooperative apart-

ments they had just bought. Not only did they estimate the purchase prices to be about 20% lower than comparable real estate in Manhattan, but they also believed the location couldn't be topped professionally. And as generalizations go, that is a fair one. A large percentage of Heights residents have arrived, are established, and will continue to lead the good life in carefully restored 19th- and early-20th-century townhouses built by earlier generations of successful Manhattan professionals.

Robert Fulton's steamboat ferry service, inaugurated in 1814, spurred the development of the rural Brooklyn settlement. Newly accessible to lower Manhattan, and cooled by East River breezes, the Heights attracted

merchants and lawyers, who built the substantial homes and noteworthy churches that characterize the community today. Brooklyn Heights boasts 684 pre-Civil War-era houses alone, and more than a dozen mostly-Gothic Revival churches.

The opening of the Brooklyn Bridge in 1883 brought the Heights that much closer to Wall Street and provided its most spectacular landmark, the gossamer span flung from Gothic tower to Gothic tower over the busy East River. Wealth crossed the bridge to Brooklyn Heights and created one of the richest communities in the nation by the turn of the century. But the Depression wiped out many residents, the bankers and businessmen who worked on Wall Street, and blight came to the Heights.

In the 1950s and early 1960s, Brooklyn's first "brownstoners," attracted by the innate quality of the rundown housing stock, discovered Brooklyn Heights. These pioneers began a wave of renovation that, in the ensuing decades, has swept over row upon row of dilapidated Brooklyn townhouses. Today the Heights' relatively cohesive population resides in stolid pre-war apartment buildings and lovingly restored brownstones, as well as in striking warehouse conversions down at Fulton Ferry Landing. Besides the obvious—a five-minute subway zip to Manhattan—other commuting modes include the feet: hearty residents stride briskly along the soaring raised center walkway of the Brooklyn Bridge to their jobs in Lower Manhattan.

From the start, accessibility to Wall Street attracted residents to the Heights, and the exceptional view of Manhattan and the harbor kept them there. The magnificent panorama of the sweeping East River beneath the soaring bridges and lower Manhattan beyond brings a steady stream of day-trippers. Strolling the wide and gracious Esplanade and visiting the quiet, historic district with its informal restaurants and pleasant shops are popular pastimes.

From the north end of the Esplanade, continue down the hill past the pristine Watchtower complex to the foot of the hill and the great stone base of the Brooklyn Bridge. There, along the water to the underbelly of the Manhattan Bridge, you are in one of Brooklyn's hippest neighborhoods, **DUMBO** (for **D**own **U**nder **M**anhattan **B**ridge **O**verpass). Artists, ever in search of affordable space, started moving into the then spooky industrial area in the 1970s, despite the lack of services or other people. In the years since then, it has become more like SoHo, but better, thanks to its proximity to the water. There are lots of open greenspaces, restaurants, retail shops, art galleries, and performance spaces in an area now occupied by an old warehouse. There are excellent local art events on a constant basis, but as happened in SoHo, rents have already managed to become inaccessible for creatives, and the artists themselves are being crowded out of the area and replaced with well-heeled Wall Street types.

Websites: www.southbrooklyn.com, www.ibrooklyn.com, www.dumbonyc.com, www.nyc.gov
Area Codes: 718, 347

Post Offices: General Post Office, 271 Cadman Plaza East; Municipal Building Station, Municipal Bldg, 210 Joralemon St
Zip Code: 11201
Police Precinct: Eighty-fourth, 301 Gold St between Tillary St and Johnson St, 718-875-6811
Emergency Hospital (nearest): Mount Sinai Doctors Brooklyn Heights, (Note: This site has an urgent care center but does NOT have an emergency room): 300 Cadman Plaza W, 929-210-6000, www.mountsinai.org/brooklyn-heights
Libraries: The Business and Career Library, 718-623-7000, www.biz.brooklynpubliclibrary.org and the Brooklyn Heights Branch of the Brooklyn Public Library, 718-623-7100, www.brooklynpubliclibrary.org, share the same address: 280 Cadman Plaza West.
Public School Education: School District #13, 335 Park Place, 718-935-3234, www.schools.nyc.gov
Adult Education: Long Island University, 1 University Plaza, 718-488-1011, www.liu.edu/Home/Brooklyn; New York City College of Technology ("City Tech"), 300 Jay St, 718-260-5500, www.citytech.cuny.edu; St. Francis College, 180 Remsen St, 718-522-2300, www.sfc.edu
Community Resources: Arts at St. Ann's, 29 Jay St, 718-254-8779, www.artsatstanns.org, sponsors numerous concerts and other cultural events; the Brooklyn Arts Council, 55 Washington St, Suite 218, 718-625-0080, coordinates and supports the efforts of a wide range of cultural programs within the borough—call or go to the website to review an events calendar, www.brooklynartscouncil.org; New York Transit Museum (located in a former subway station), Boerum Pl and Schermerhorn St, 718-694-1600
Transportation—Subway: #2/#3, Clark St, Borough Hall; #4/#5, Borough Hall; A/C High St/Brooklyn Bridge; N/M/R at Court St; www.mta.info
Transportation—Bus: For a Brooklyn bus map and schedule call 718-330-3322, Monday through Friday from 9 a.m. to 5 p.m., or go to www.mta.info.

COBBLE HILL

Boundaries and Contiguous Areas: North: Atlantic Avenue and Brooklyn Heights; **East:** Court Street and Boerum Hill; **South:** DeGraw Street and Carroll Gardens; **West:** Hicks Street

If it were possible to walk across the Mediterranean, a stroll starting at Atlantic Avenue down Court, Cobble Hill's main shopping street, to Carroll Gardens could be compared to a walk from the Middle East to Italy. Atlantic's famed Near East and Middle Eastern spice and grocery stores and restaurants filter along Court south for a couple of blocks before meeting up with the pizzerias, Neapolitan bakeries, and shops selling Italian housewares, near the heavily Italian Carroll Gardens on Cobble Hill's southern boundary. This intriguing ethnic mix results in top-notch food sources that attract shoppers from all over Brooklyn.

The row upon row of landmarked brownstones that cluster around the main streets of Court and Smith are less expensive and not quite as grand as those in Brooklyn Heights but beautifully shaded by large, leafy trees (note particularly the sycamore trees that completely cover Clinton Street as it crosses Baltic, Veranda, and Congress Streets on the way to the Heights). They attract a young professional crowd and **Cobble Hill** is probably the most homogeneous of all the Brooklyn brownstone communities. Award-winning Cobble Hill Park is a monument to neighborhood cohesiveness here. Apartment buildings and converted industrial properties have been established in Cobble Hill, notably the Henry Street Mews condos and One Tiffany Place, just west of the Brooklyn-Queens Expressway. Other conversions include Cobble

Hill Towers, the city's first low-income housing project when it was built in 1878, and the P.S. 78 condominiums, lodged in a late-19th-century public school on Pacific Street.

It is not necessary to leave the neighborhood to find a good movie, a chic new sweater, or a bistro meal. The Cobble Hill Cinemas boasts five screens. And along Smith Street, where it moves down into Carroll Gardens, boutiques and restaurants cater to a young and prosperous clientele from the neighborhood and beyond. Local P.S. 29 is said to have the most extracurricular activities of any public school in NYC.

Websites: www.southbrooklyn.com, www.brooklyncb6.org,www.nyc.gov

Area Codes: 718, 347

Post Office: Municipal Building Station, Municipal Bldg, 210 Joralemon St

Zip Codes: 11201, 11231

Police Precinct: Seventy-sixth, 191 Union St between Hicks St and Henry St, 718-834-3211

Emergency Hospital: Mount Sinai Doctors Brooklyn Heights, (Note: This site has an urgent care center but does NOT have an emergency room): 300 Cadman Plaza W, 929- 210-6000, www.mountsinai.org/brooklyn-heights

Library (nearest): Carroll Gardens Branch, 396 Clinton St, 718-596-6972, www.brooklynpubliclibrary.org

Public School Education: School District #15 in region 8, 131 Livingston St., 718-935-4317, www.schools.nyc.gov

Adult Education: See Brooklyn Heights and Boerum Hill
Community Resources: See Brooklyn Heights and Boerum Hill
Transportation—Subway: #2/#3/#4/#5, Borough Hall; F/G, Bergen St; www.mta. info
Transportation—Bus: For a Brooklyn bus map and schedule, call 718-330-3322, Monday through Friday from 9 a.m. to 5 p.m., or go to www.mta.info.

CARROLL GARDENS

Boundaries and Contiguous Areas: North: DeGraw Street and Cobble Hill; **East:** Gowanus Canal; **South:** Hamilton Avenue; **West:** Brooklyn-Queens Expressway

In **Carroll Gardens**, singularly deep and lushly planted gardens front the four- and five-story row houses so characteristic of Brooklyn's brownstone neighborhoods. These splendid yards, with trees as tall as the high-stooped town-houses, form part of an eleven-block tract laid out in the 1850s. Verdant block fronts are, however, only part of the reason urban homesteaders began moving to Carroll Gardens in the 1970s. This predominantly Italian community has a lower crime rate than many other areas in Brooklyn. And furthermore, just like Cobble Hill, another "tight" neighborhood to the north, Carroll Gardens boasts better-than-average public elementary and secondary schools.

Other pluses? Great food shopping. You'll find plenty of vegetable stands lining Court Street, where bulbous pecorino cheeses, salamis, and whole prosciuttos hang from grocery store ceilings. And subway transportation to Manhattan by F train is fast and direct.

Less expensive and less gentrified than the Heights and Cobble Hill, Carroll Gardens has long had limited housing stock, although there are more and less expensive units in the southern section, where conversions in industrial buildings have become the norm. On the eastern edge, an area in revival, the former St. Agnes School has become the School House in Carroll Gardens, a 90-unit middle-income rental on DeGraw Street. The occasional low-rise condo appears.

Walk along Court and you'll still hear Italian spoken. Bocce remains the game of choice among the senior set in sweet little Carroll Park, where handsome brownstones on the park's north side and graceful old trees make it feel like Washington Square in Greenwich Village. Heading north along Smith Street you can buy designer clothes in chic boutiques and eat Vietnamese, French, or nouveau Italian in smart eateries. Use a real estate agent to find an apartment here if, after a stroll on the park-like streets, you find it appealing.

Another area to consider is the more affordable Columbia Street Waterfront District, adjacent to but separated from Carroll Gardens and Cobble Hill by the Gowanus Expressway. Its modest brick row houses were once the homes of the longshoremen who worked the docks here, but the neighborhood declined when the expressway isolated it from its loftier neighbors. Revival began in the 1980s with the construction of the Columbia Terrace condominiums and the conversion of a former Tiffany lamp factory into condos on cobblestoned Tiffany Place. There are no subway stations here, and other services are limited, but on-street parking is easy and the view from its quiet streets across Buttermilk Channel to the Statue of Liberty and Lower Manhattan is stunning. For the truly adventuresome, there is the possibility of houseboats on Gowanus Canal. Long celebrated for its stench and as a dumping ground for mob hits—the book *Motherless Brooklyn* calls it "the only body of water in the world that is 90 percent guns"—recent improvement has led to a few houseboat dwellers during the winter. There's also kayaking trips regularly made by Gowanus Dredgers Canoe Club (www.gowanuscanal.org).

Websites: www.southbrooklyn.com, www.brooklyncb6.org, www.nyc.gov
Area Codes: 718, 347
Post Office: Red Hook Station, 615 Clinton St
Zip Code: 11231
Police Precinct: Seventy-sixth, 191 Union St, 718-834-3211
Emergency Hospitals: Mount Sinai Doctors Brooklyn Heights, (Note: This site has an urgent care center but does NOT have an emergency room): 300 Cadman Plaza W, 929- 210-6000, www.mountsinai.org/brooklyn-heights
Library: Carroll Gardens Branch, 396 Clinton St at Union St, 718-596-6972, www. brooklynpubliclibrary.org
Public School Education: School District #15 in region 8, 131 Livingston St., 718-935-4317, www.schools.nyc.gov
Adult Education: See Brooklyn Heights and Boerum Hill
Community Resources: See Brooklyn Heights and Boerum Hill
Transportation—Subway: F, Carroll St, Smith St; G, Carroll St, Smith St; www.mta. info
Transportation—Bus: For a Brooklyn bus map and schedule call 718-330-3322, Monday through Friday from 9 a.m. to 5 p.m., or go to www.mta.info.

BOERUM HILL

Boundaries and Contiguous Areas: North: State Street; **East**: Third Avenue; **South**: Degraw Street; **West**: Court

East and slightly downhill from sedate Cobble Hill and just south of bustling downtown Brooklyn, **Boerum Hill** seems lighter and more spacious along its blocks of three- and four-story brick and brownstone homes. Stately sycamores shade quiet streets such as Bergen, where children play untended on sidewalks that line the flowering yards fronting set-back row houses. Ethnically more heterogeneous than its neighbors to the west, it is a community of families, who shop along commercial Smith and Court Streets. Smith has also been dubbed "restaurant row," featuring French bistro-esque cafés. Nearby, Atlantic Avenue is home to antique stores and Middle Eastern restaurants.

The Boerum Hill Historic District, bounded roughly by Hoyt and Nevins, Pacific and Wyckoff Streets, contains an outstanding assemblage of pre–Civil War Italianate and Greek Revival row houses, which constituted a fashionable district in the mid-19th century; the stretch of State Street between Hoyt and Smith has national landmark status. The neighborhood declined in later years, and today it is a monument to the efforts of new homeowners, who, in the early 1960s, fought off a city effort to tear down the then-dispirited rooming houses to make way for urban renewal. Boerum Hill's turnaround—from near-slum to tight residential community—was achieved by a dedicated band of pioneers with enough foresight to see the area's potential. The neighborhood has a strong sense of community, and many keep close tabs on proposed development.

It was the construction of the Gowanus Canal and the draining of the swamps south of Warren Street beginning in 1845 that prompted the development of what are now Cobble Hill and Boerum Hill.

Rentals (when they can be found) in the handsome townhouses here are relatively affordable by New York City standards. Co-ops and condos can also be found. House prices are approaching the cost of comparable homes in Brooklyn Heights.

Slicing across Boerum Hill from the waterfront, noisy Atlantic Avenue is somewhat blighted by the presence of the grim Brooklyn House of

Detention and its surroundings, but from Hoyt Street eastward, its concentration of inviting antique and Victorian bric-a-brac shops attracts shoppers from all over the city.

Websites: www.southbrooklyn.com, www.nyc.gov
Area Codes: 718, 347
Post Office: Times Plaza, 542 Atlantic Ave
Zip Code: 11217
Police Precinct: Seventy-sixth, 191 Union St between Hicks St and Henry St, 718-834-3211
Emergency Hospitals: Mount Sinai Doctors Brooklyn Heights, (Note: This site has an urgent care center but does NOT have an emergency room): 300 Cadman Plaza W, 929- 210-6000, www.mountsinai.org/brooklyn-heights; The Brooklyn Hospital Center, 121 DeKalb Ave, 718-250-8000, www.tbh.org
Library: Pacific Branch, 25 Fourth Ave, 718-638-1531, www.brooklynpubliclibrary. org
Public School Education: School District #15 in region 8, 131 Livingston St, 718-935-4317, www.schools.nyc.gov
Adult Education: Brooklyn YWCA, 30 Third Ave, 718-875-1190, www.ywcabklyn. org, offers a health program plus a variety of adult classes
Transportation—Subway: #2/#3, Hoyt St, Nevins St; #4/#5 Nevins St; F, Bergen St; G, Bergen St, Hoyt/Schermerhorn Sts; A to Hoyt/Schermerhorn Sts; www. mta.info
Transportation—Bus: For a Brooklyn bus map and schedule call 718-330-3322, Monday through Friday from 9 a.m. to 5 p.m., or go to www.mta.info.

PARK SLOPE

Boundaries and Contiguous Areas: North: Flatbush Avenue; **East**: Prospect Park West; **South**: Windsor Place; **West**: Fifth Avenue

The mere mention of Park Slope to most New Yorkers conjures up images of armies of granola-eating, breastfeeding moms pushing their strollers about and trampling anyone inconsiderate to get in their way. But it still remains one of the most heterogeneous—and handsome—of the gentrified Brooklyn neighbor-hoods, as well as the largest. Don't expect big deals here; real estate is expensive, with rentals averaging $3,000 to $4,000 a month for a two-bedroom (and there are plenty of outliers at higher price points, too). The one thing that hasn't changed is the 526-acre Prospect Park, designed by Central Park architects Frederick Law Olmsted and Calvert Vaux, and Park Slope's proximity to three of Brooklyn's cul-tural bastions: the Brooklyn Museum, the Central Library at Grand Army Plaza, and the Brooklyn Botanic Garden. One of the many attractions of Prospect

Park—especially for the stroller set—is the Wildlife Conservation Center, a state-of-the-art children's zoo with a restored 1912 carousel.

Park Slope's development paralleled that of Prospect Park in the 1880s. Sites with a park view were most highly prized, and small Victorian mansions line Prospect Park West. Proximity to the park and Grand Army Plaza determined the quality of the Victorian bow-fronted townhouses that march row upon stolid row down the west-sloping streets. North Slope, nearest Prospect Park West and the Plaza, is considered the classiest part of the neighborhood. South Slope, below 9th Street, is the less expensive, still-developing section. Old industrial properties, such as the Ansonia Clock factory complex on 12th Street (once the country's largest clock works and now deluxe condominiums) have been converted to apartments and co-ops. Seventh Avenue, the principal shopping street and scene of a hugely successful fair each spring, reflects neighborhood needs: boutiques, card shops, unisex hair cutters, twee gift shops, and restaurants are everywhere. Think Berkeley, California,  with an East Coast twist—there's even a popular food co-op (Park Slope Food Co-op, 782 Union Street, 718-622-0560, www.foodcoop.com), which provides fresh organic foods and household supplies at low prices to members who volunteer to work there. Since members do not have to be residents of Park Slope to join, folks come from all over Brooklyn.

Without qualification, Park Slope, together with Brooklyn Heights, is a suitable address for middle-class professionals, especially those with families. P.S. 321, District 15's progressive, well-regarded elementary school, has served as an additional attraction to young families. But don't go looking for bargains; in real estate parlance, the neighborhood is "hot" (and has been for a while), especially along the park. Prices are lower down the slope and in adjoining **Windsor Terrace** and **Prospect Heights**, two communities nicely situated near Prospect Park. (For more on these, see the section at the end of the chapter.) Down the slope west of Fifth Avenue around the Gowanus Canal, artists and crafters have established homes and studios in a neighborhood known now simply as **Gowanus**. Cleaned up, if not yet pristine, the canal twists through a somewhat gritty area, where, as mentioned, some have even set up houseboats. Also, investigate the **Sunset Park/Green-Wood Cemetery** area, bounded by 65th Street on the south and Prospect Expressway on the north. This ethnically mixed community offers less expensive rentals and fun neighborhood shopping and dining along Fifth Avenue. In the northeast corner is the hilly and inviting Green-Wood Cemetery (see **Greenspace and Beaches**).

Websites: www.southbrooklyn.com, www.brooklyncb6.org, www.nyc.gov

Area Codes: 718, 347

Post Offices: Van Brunt Station, 275 Ninth St; Park Slope Station, 198 Seventh Ave; Prospect Park West Station, 225 Prospect Park West

Zip Codes: 11215, 11217

Police Precinct: Seventy-eighth, 65 Sixth Ave between Sixth St and Bergen St, 718-636-6411

Emergency Hospital: Methodist Hospital, 506 Sixth St, 718 -780-3000, www.nym. org

Libraries: Brooklyn Central Library, 10 Grand Army Plaza, 718-230-2100; Park Slope Branch, 431 Sixth Ave, S 718-832-1853, www.brooklynpubliclibrary.org

Public School Education: School Districts #13 and #15 in region 8, 131 Livingston St., 718-935-4317, or for District 13, 335 Park Place, 718-935-3234, www. schools.nyc.gov

Adult Education: Brooklyn Museum Art School, 200 Eastern Pkwy, 718-638-5000, www.brooklynmuseum.org; Brooklyn Botanic Garden, 1000 Washington Ave, 718-623-7200, www.bbg.org, holds classes for plant enthusiasts; Brooklyn Conservatory of Music, 58 Seventh Ave, 718-622-3300, www.bqcm.org

Community Resources: Brooklyn Museum, 200 Eastern Pkwy, 718-638-5000, www.brooklynmuseum.org; behind the six Ionic columns of McKim, Mead, and White's famed building are housed a number of exemplary collections, as well as facilities for the cultural and educational programs sponsored daily by the museum; lectures and special programs are also offered; Brooklyn Arts Exchange, 421 Fifth Ave, 718-832-0018, www.bax.org; St. John's Recreation Center, 1251 Prospect Pl, 718-771-2787, www.nycgovparks.org/facilities/recreationcenters/B245

Transportation—Subway: With the exception of the A and C trains, subways stop near one part of Park Slope or the other. #2/#3/#4/#5 trains stop at Grand Army Plaza; F stops at Fourth Ave, Seventh Ave and 15th St; D stops at Seventh Ave and Atlantic Ave; B/M/N/R stop along Fourth Ave at Pacific St, Union St, 9th St, and Prospect Ave; www.mta.info

Transportation—Bus: For a Brooklyn bus map and schedule call 718-330-3322, Monday through Friday from 9 a.m. to 5 p.m., or go to www.mta.info.

FORT GREENE/CLINTON HILL

Boundaries and Contiguous Areas: North: Myrtle Avenue; **East:** Classon Avenue; **South:** Atlantic Avenue; **West:** Flatbush Avenue and Boerum Hill

"... Brooklyn's other fine residential district, the Hill ... abounded in churches and middle-class houses, the majority of whose owners worked in New York." So wrote a Brooklyn historian of late 19th century Fort Greene and Clinton Hill. Despite a decline in the intervening years, that description is valid once again, except for the fringe areas to the north and east. What occasioned the turnabout? Historic designation and the brownstone revival, mainly.

Revival came late, in the 1970s, to **Fort Greene**. Even the once-elegant brownstones on the choice streets nearest Fort Greene Park had become dilapidated wino rows. But beneath the grime and neglect, the original detailing remained, awaiting the attention of determined urban pioneers. Now perfectly restored Anglo-Italianate brownstones line Washington Park, South Oxford Street, and South Portland Avenue. And sweeping 33-acre Fort Greene Park, the community's centerpiece designed by Olmsted and Vaux, has been restored to its rather English graciousness.

Once something of an Irish enclave (it was nicknamed "Young Dublin," not a compliment in the 1800s), Fort Greene is now integrated, both racially and socio-economically, and determined to stay that way. The throbbing cultural presence of the Brooklyn Academy of Music (BAM) helped stimulate the growth of a substantial community of African-American artists in Fort Greene. The area around BAM continues to grow as a cultural enclave with dance troupes and artists moving into the neighborhood. The excellent Brooklyn Flea Market ("Brooklyn Flea" for short) has a Fort Greene location at Lafayette and Clermont (www.brooklynflea.com) and for artists and entrepreneurs the nearby Navy Yards is an excellent

resource for working spaces (the streets nearer the Yards are also where cheaper apartments can sometimes be found).

Clinton Hill, like Fort Greene, which it borders, contains an astonishing treasury of late-19th-century urban architecture. The key name in this neighborhood is Pratt. Kerosene magnate Charles Pratt built several handsome mansions on

Clinton Avenue, including the present residence of the Bishop of Brooklyn, and also founded, built, and until his death in 1891, ran Pratt Institute, the focal point and cultural center of the community. Now the students, grads, and faculty of Pratt (art, design, architecture, engineering, computers, and library sciences) fill the streets and much of the local housing.

Clinton Hill has a few high-rises and lots of newish quasi-industrial quasi-artist loft buildings going up, and therefore, a greater variety of housing than Fort Greene. But Clinton Hill has only one subway line, the sporadic G train, which means a transfer to reach Manhattan. Many find the five-minute bus ride to downtown Brooklyn with a free transfer to a variety of trains or a quick bike ride more convenient. Fort Greene, on the other hand, is well tended by the subway system (see below). Both neighborhoods offer easy, on-street parking.

Both the MetroTech commercial development to the west on Flatbush Avenue and the Atlantic Center mixed-use development on the southeast edge of Fort Greene have boosted the value and the cost of housing on the hill. Apartment hunting here is best done through a knowledgeable real estate agent.

Websites: www.historicfortgreene.org, www.nyc.gov
Area Codes: 718, 347
Post Office: General Post Office, 271 Cadman Plaza East
Zip Codes: 11201, 11205, 11217, 11238
Police Precinct: Eighty-eighth, 298 Classon Ave, 718-636-6511
Emergency Hospital: Brooklyn Hospital Center, 121 DeKalb Ave, 718-250-8000, www.tbh.org; Interfaith Medical Center 1545 Atlantic Ave, 718-613-4000, www.interfaithmedical.com
Libraries: Clinton Hill Branch, 380 Washington Ave, 718-398-8713; Walt Whitman Branch, 93 St Edwards St, 718-935-0244; Bedford Branch, 496 Franklin Ave, 718-623-0012; www.brooklynpubliclibrary.org
Public School Education: School District #13 in region 8, 335 Park Place, 718-935-3234, www.schools.nyc.gov
Adult Education: Pratt Institute, Continuing Education, 200 Willoughby Ave, 718-636-3779, www.pratt.edu; Medgar Evers Community College, 1650 Bedford Ave, 718-270-4900, www.mec.cuny.edu; St. Joseph's College, 245 Clinton Ave, 718-940-5300, www.sjcny.edu; Long Island University, 1 University Plaza, Flatbush Ave at DeKalb Ave, 718-488-1011, www.liu.edu/Home/Brooklyn
Community Resources: Brooklyn Academy of Music (BAM), 30 Lafayette Ave, 718-636-4100, www.bam.org; Brooklyn Children's Museum, 145 Brooklyn Ave, Crown Heights, 718-735-4400, www.brooklynkids.org; Fort Greene Park, Brooklyn's first, 30 acres designed by Prospect Park and Central Park's Olmsted and Vaux, www.fortgreenepark.org; Clinton Hill Community Supported Agriculture, a nonprofit, volunteer-run organization that brings fresh, locally grown, organic produce to its members, 347-603-0359, www.clintonhillcsa.

org; Museum of Contemporary African Diasporan Arts, contemporary art by black artists living in Brooklyn, 80 Hanson Pl, 718-230-0492, www.mocada.org

Transportation—Subway: A/C, Lafayette Ave; B/D at DeKalb Ave; M/N/Q/R, DeKalb Ave; #2/#3/#4/#5 at Nevins St; G at Fulton St, Clinton/Washington Aves; www.mta.info

Transportation—Bus: For a Brooklyn bus map and schedule call 718-330-3322, Monday through Friday from 9 a.m. to 5 p.m., or go to www.mta.info.

GREENPOINT

Boundaries and Contiguous Areas: North: Newtown Creek and Queens; **East**: Newtown Creek and the Brooklyn-Queens Expressway (BQE); **South**: North 12th Street and Williamsburg; **West**: East River

Set right next to the urban partyland of Williamsburg, Greenpoint—once known as "Little Poland"—can seem a world apart. Streets of colorfully sided tenements are lined with trees, and the housewives in aprons chatting on the stoops are more likely to be speaking Polish than English. The northernmost tip, which borders Queens, is so cut off it feels like a country town—until you notice the Manhattan skyline across the river peeking over the rooftops.

The main commercial drag is the two-lane Manhattan Avenue. Dollar stores predominate and garlands of *kielbasa* sausages hang in most of the butcher shop windows. At least a half-dozen restaurants have Polish-language menus with specials like *pierogi* and *kasha*. But alongside these Old World institutions,

Thai and Jamaican restaurants are popping up, as are artisanal butchers and bakers, and the local health food store now offers everything from soy milk to tofu burgers. The neighborhood east of Manhattan Avenue, which borders a large industrial area, remains almost exclusively working-class Polish, but the Greenpoint Historic District to the west, littered with the mansions of coffee and spice merchants of yore, has seen a flood of upscale professionals.

And more are on the way—20,000 new units have gone up in riverfront high-rises in what seems like a matter of days. While some moan about the loss of character, the buildings will finally make the riverfront, recently lined with abandoned warehouses, accessible to everyone. These riverfront parks, plus beautiful Monsignor McGolrick Park and McCarren Park, with their running tracks and baseball diamonds, make the whole area extremely family friendly.

Two features, however, may serve to help keep rents from spiraling ever upward. The northern area of Greenpoint is only served by the erratic G subway line and the buses aren't much better (especially on weekends). In addition, the area is environmentally fragile, though major recovery efforts in recent years have produced significant results. Greenpoint sits on one the largest oil spills in U.S. history. An estimated 17 to 30 million gallons of petroleum products were spilled near Newtown Creek in the 1940s and much of the oil remains trapped beneath the neighborhood. Although Greenpoint's drinking water is perfectly safe (it is piped in from upstate New York), the spill has been the subject of litigation for years, and residents raise recurrent concerns over health hazards posed by fumes rising from the soil. There's also a large sewage treatment facility in Greenpoint's northeastern corner that, while perfectly harmless, can get quite ripe when it rains. That being said, the treatment facility has attempted to ingratiate itself with the neighborhood by turning part of its grounds into a surprisingly pleasant and little-known park (www.nyc.gov/html/dep/html/environmental_education/new-town.shtml).

Greenpoint is small enough to explore on foot, and a day wandering about to get a feel for it is an excellent idea. Visit the local real estate offices you see, most of which have been in the area for decades (speaking Polish helps).

Websites: www.hellobrooklyn.com, www.brooklyn-usa.org,www.freewilliamsburg. com, www.nyc.gov. For more info on the oil spill, visit riverkeeper.org.

Area Codes: 718, 347

Post Offices: Greenpoint Station, 66 Meserole Ave; CPU 368, 94 Nassau Ave; Williamsburg Station, 263 South 4th St; CPU 369, 442 Lorimer St

Zip Code: 11222

Police Precinct: Ninety-fourth, 100 Meserole Ave, 718-383-3879

Emergency Hospitals (nearest): Woodhull Medical and Mental Health Center, 760 Broadway, 718-963-8000, http://www.nyc.gov/html/hhc/woodhull/html/home/home.shtml; Brooklyn Hospital Center, 121 DeKalb Ave, 718-250-8000, www.tbh.org

Library: Greenpoint Branch, 107 Norman Ave, 718-349-8504; Leonard Branch, 81 Devoe St, 718-486-3365; Williamsburgh Branch, 240 Division Ave, 718-302-3485; www.brooklynpubliclibrary.org

Public School Education: School District #14 in region 8, 131 Livingston St, 718-935-4299, www.nycenet.edu

Transportation— Subway: G, Greenpoint Ave, Nassau Ave; www.mta.info

Transportation—Bus: Red Hook/Queens, via Manhattan Ave (B61); Williamsburg/Eastern Greenpoint via Nassau Ave (B48). For a complete Brooklyn bus map and schedule call 718-330-3322, Monday through Friday from 9 a.m. to 5 p.m., or go to www.mta.info.

WILLIAMSBURG/EAST WILLIAMSBURG

Boundaries and Contiguous Areas: *Williamsburg*: **North**: North Twelfth Street and McCarren Park; **East**: Manhattan Avenue/Flushing Avenue and East Williamsburg; **South**: Kent Avenue and Clinton Hill; **West**: East River; *East Williamsburg*: **North**: Ridgewood/Maspeth (Queens); **East**: Bushwick; **South**: Broadway/Bedford-Stuyvesant; **West**: Maspeth Avenue/Manhattan Avenue and Williamsburg

Common lore has it that Williamsburg has more artists per capita than any other neighborhood in the United States. True or not, this former industrial wasteland, once one of the worst neighborhoods around, has undergone one of the most radical and fast-moving transformations in the city, with many of its most recent newcomers arriving from Western Europe. Williamsburg itself is considered an umbrella term describing four distinct neighborhoods. There is **Northside**, which lies northwest of the Brooklyn-Queens Expressway, with a fading Polish population; **Italian Williamsburg**, southeast of the same; there is **Southside**, south of Grand Street, with a heavier Puerto Rican population; and finally, the actual **Williamsburg**, a heavily concentrated Hasidic community near the Marcy and Hewes train stations. To the dismay of the families that have been living quietly here for generations, as well as the pioneering artists of the '90s, this entire area has exploded over the past decade, and shows no sign of slowing.

Once inexpensive and just a quick stop out of Manhattan on the L train, which is loved and loathed in equal measure by its riders, in the mid-1990s Williamsburg became an annex to the boho East Village crowd, who loved its large industrial spaces and cheap rents. As vacancies in Williamsburg dried up and prices began to rise, the "second stop" and "third stop" out of Manhattan became the next best thing, and East Williamsburg began to absorb some of the growth. At this point, the first stop (Bedford Avenue) area has rents comparable to those in Lower Manhattan and the crowds on any day or night (especially late night) can resemble the hipster mobs that fill the Lower East Side bar scene. The most intense

manifestation of this is on Bedford, between McCarren Park and Metropolitan Avenue. It's a remarkably lively neighborhood, if lacking the gracious buildings and trees of other parts of Brooklyn: performance artists doing their thing on corners, impromptu sculptures, roving art exhibits, and craft shows—even performance art snack trucks—are everyday events here.

It's been said you can walk from Warsaw to Puerto Rico to Israel if you traverse the 20-block-long stretch of this part of Bedford Avenue, and it's almost true. The Puerto Rican Southside is slowly gentrifying, with an interesting rich man's gulley along Broadway anchored by the luxury high-rise Schaefer Landing development. Beyond that is an area mixing Dominican and Hasidic residents, which at Division gives way to a completely Hasidic neighborhood. Rents are cheaper here but usually inaccessible to anyone who is not Hasidic. As you go farther inland, things get rougher (particularly after the third Graham stop), with prices declining the farther you get from the L line.

The old meatpacking district near the waterfront is now full of restaurants serving sushi and other favorites, along with the Music Hall of Williamsburg and the bright yellow Brooklyn Brewery, complete with tours and a space for parties; much of this industrial area is currently being redeveloped, with whole blocks razed to become quasi-loft living and waterfront high-rises. Still, there's an edgy, industrial feel here, part of it maintained quite purposefully by hipster residents.

Numbered streets—declining from North 15th to Grand—cross Bedford Avenue, Northside's main street. To the east, traffic roars along the elevated Brooklyn-Queens Expressway.

After a $4.8 million restoration highlighting its rather Andalusian glory, the Metropolitan Pool and Bathhouse at Bedford and Metropolitan Avenues is a fabulous neighborhood amenity. Accessible to the disabled, the pool and recreation center are operated by the Parks Department. A few blocks north, the 35 acres of McCarren Park have been given a huge uplift to match the new millionaire high-rises surrounding one side of it, including new ball fields, tennis courts, a running track, and a fitness course. The McCarren Pool, long abandoned and used for concerts, has also been restored, and reopened in 2012. There are a few mini-parks along the river (slated to be joined into one long esplanade as development occurs), as well as a so-called "hipsters park" where North 11th meets the water.

The Brooklyn Film Festival is centered in Williamsburg, with stated aims to discover, expose, and promote independent filmmakers while drawing worldwide attention to Brooklyn (www.brooklynfilmfestival.org). Italian Williamsburg is host to the annual Festa del Giglio, a two-week (!) celebration of Italian culture, honoring St. Paulinus of Nola, www.olmcfeast.com.

Websites: www.freewilliamsburg.com, www.nyc.gov
Area Codes: 718, 347
Post Office: Williamsburg Station, 263 S 4th St; CPU 369, 442 Lorimer St
Zip Codes: 11206, 11211

Police Precinct: Ninety-fourth, 100 Meserole Ave, 718-383-3879
Emergency Hospitals (nearest): Brooklyn Hospital Center, 121 DeKalb Ave, 718-250-8000, www.tbh.org; Interfaith Medical Center, 1545 Atlantic Ave, 718-613-4000, www.interfaithmedical.com; Wyckoff Heights Medical Center, 374 Stockholm St, 718-963-7272, www.wyckoffhospital.org
Libraries: Leonard Branch, 81 Devoe St, 718-486-3365; Williamsburgh Branch, 240 Division Ave, 718-302-3485; www.brooklynpubliclibrary.org
Public School Education: School District #14 in region 8, 215 Heyward St, 718-302-7600, www.schools.nyc.gov
Community Resources: McCarren Park, which forms a chunk of the boundary between Williamsburg and neighboring Greenpoint, has several ball fields and a recently resurfaced jogging track. It also contains the McCarren Park Pool, an enormous facility that reopened in 2012.
Transportation—Subway: L, Bedford Ave, Lorimer St, Grand Ave, Grant St, Montrose Ave, Morgan Ave; G, Nassau Ave, Metropolitan Ave, Broadway; J/M/Z, Marcy Ave, Hewes St, Lorimer St, Flushing Ave, Myrtle Ave; www.mta.info
Transportation—Bus: For a Brooklyn bus map and schedule call 718-330-3322, Monday through Friday from 9 a.m. to 5 p.m., or go to www.mta.info.

YOU MIGHT ALSO WANT TO CONSIDER ...

- **Bay Ridge**, way out by the Verrazano-Narrows Bridge and overlooking the Narrows, is studded with parks and restaurants. This conservative community with a Scandinavian and Italian heritage is 50 minutes by subway from Manhattan. (www.bayridge.com)
- **Bushwick**, an inland area that adjoins Williamsburg, has been relabeled Williamsburg by hopeful real estate agents. In a sense, it is, albeit Williamsburg of the mid-1990s. The neighborhoods are rougher and the trendy mobs invisible, but there are growing pockets of younger artist types moving out here, and the rents are definitely lower.
- **Flatbush**, fairly vast and varied, is geographically and psychologically the heart of Brooklyn. Its most appealing neighborhoods are Prospect Park South and Ditmas Park, both of which feature lovely old Victorian homes along stately, tree-lined streets, and strong community spirit. Prices are moderate, and the area is showing signs of new growth.
- **Fort Hamilton**, just beyond Bay Ridge around the base of the Verrazano-Narrows Bridge, has more co-ops and condos among its one-family houses, with a similar perch on the Narrows. It's about an hour by subway to Manhattan.
- **Prospect Heights** is located uphill, but downscale in price, from Park Slope, Prospect Park, Brooklyn's major cultural institutions, and accessible transportation. Its handsome brownstones, greystones, and co-op apartments have attracted young, professional arrivals in recent years and developers. A number

of luxury condos and building conversions have pushed rents upward over the past five years.

- **Red Hook**, south of the Columbia Street Waterfront District on Upper New York Bay, is still for pioneers, but not for long. The transportation situation remains difficult, and although Ikea opened its first NYC outpost here and there's a robust hipster contingent, it still remains off the beaten path for a lot of folks. Rows of small houses intersperse the industrial landscape; the area features stunning views, a vast sky, and water edged by historic stone warehouses.
- **Ridgewood**; arguably in Queens, this very quiet, traditionally German neighborhood has always considered itself part of Brooklyn, and people still argue about it today. It's farther out on the L line, but a number of Williamsburg refugees have started exploring the area, with its untouched 19th-century streets and tree-lined avenues. See also the entry on page 109.
- **Stuyvesant Heights**, 12 landmarked blocks of exceptional brownstones along stately, tree-lined streets on the southern edge of Bedford-Stuyvesant, is home to a largely African-American professional community. Twenty-five subway minutes from Manhattan.
- **Windsor Terrace** is a safe, old-fashioned community of small, detached houses, row houses, and apartments nicely sandwiched between Prospect Park and beautiful, park-like Green-Wood Cemetery. Quiet, except for the birds.

QUEENS

"Queens is not New York!" exclaims a character in the film *Quiz Show*. And that is exactly what residents and lovers of Queens would have you believe. Being overlooked and underappreciated has protected Queens for decades from the madness of Manhattan that sent them (or keeps them) there in the first place.

Among the five boroughs, **Queens** is the acknowledged bastion of New York's middle class, even as gentrification begins, finally, to wield its brush on the borough. As skyscrapers identify Manhattan and brownstones Brooklyn, so solid brick buildings—free-standing, Tudor-inspired houses, semi-detached, two-, three-, and four-family dwellings, and six-story apartment blocks—define a good part of the largest borough (in terms of land) in the city. And middle-class does not mean white by any means—according to Census data, Queens is the most diverse community in the entire country. Indeed, more than 150 languages are spoken in the borough.

Until 1909 and the completion of the Queensborough Bridge, semi-rural Queens was a backwater connected to Manhattan only by ferry boat across the East River. But the bridge, followed almost immediately by train and then by subway service through new tunnels under the East River, opened the way for commuters and commerce. Developers snapped up great parcels of land, and 1908 saw the

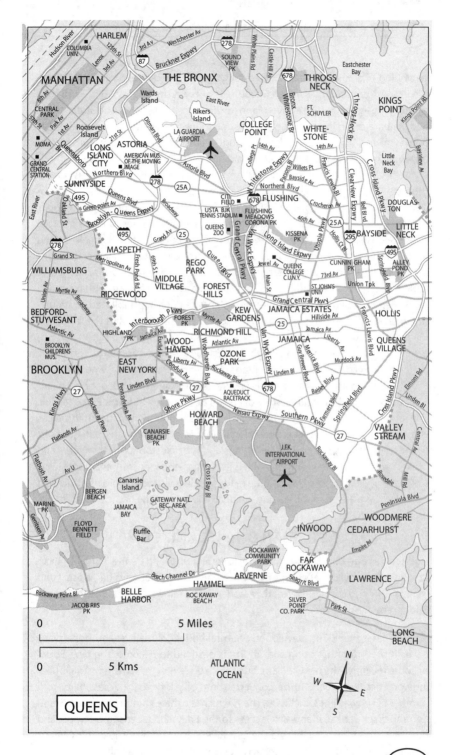

beginning of a building spree that continued, with few pauses, until World War II. While some communities are architecturally noteworthy—Forest Hills Gardens, a carefully designed 1909 enclave planned down to its English rustic street signs, and Malba, a charming mélange of lawns, leafy lanes, and handsome, mostly 1920s homes nestled under the Whitestone Bridge—most of the housing is sturdy, unremarkable pre-World War II stock often laid out, suburban-style, in tracts.

While many Queens neighborhoods are identified with various ethnic groups—Greeks gravitate to Astoria, Latin Americans to Jackson Heights, Russians to Rego Park, Asians to Flushing—an international mix of businesspeople, engineers, and other professionals and their families continues to move into the area. Long Island City, just across the East River from Manhattan, is finally seeing its long-awaited development pick up steam. Astoria, situated north/northwest of Long Island City and Sunnyside, both equally accessible to Manhattan, has seen a rapid rise in rent as the middle class gets priced out of Manhattan. Within subway reach, Rego Park, Forest Hills, and Kew Gardens are popular established communities where one- and even two-bedroom apartments rent for about the same as a Manhattan studio. Farther east, condominium units crowd every nook and cranny of Bayside with an endless sea of high-rises. Bayside has great appeal for those who prefer its quiet congestion to Manhattan's noise and immensity and who don't find the trip to Manhattan by express bus or Long Island Railroad too daunting.

Information about real estate brokers can be found in **Finding a Place to Live.** The local publication, the *Queens Chronicle* (718-205-8000, www.queenschronicle. com), provides real estate tips plus some insight into the borough itself. Craigslist (www.craigslist.com) has extensive listings and is a first stop for both owners and brokers with listings. Remember that it is also a first stop for nearly everybody else, so refresh your browser constantly, be ready to call or visit as you browse, and read carefully: there are often misleading headers, and there is the occasional scam.

ASTORIA/LONG ISLAND CITY

Boundaries and Contiguous Areas: *Astoria*: **North**: Grand Central Parkway; **East**: Brooklyn-Queens Expressway; **South**: 35th Avenue and Sunnyside; **West**: Long Island City; *Long Island City*: **North**: Astoria; **East**: Steinway Street; **South**: Pulaski Bridge; **West**: East River

Since at least the 1970s, developers, cultural critics, journalists, and bohemians have all predicted that **Long Island City** is destined to become "the next SoHo" or, more recently, "the next Williamsburg." With dozens of massive industrial buildings practically begging to be converted into airy lofts; easy accessibility to a number of subway lines, including the 7, which is a three-minute ride from Grand Central; quick vehicular and bike access to the Ed Koch/Queensboro Bridge; and river transportation available via the East River Ferry and Water Taxi, this Queens neighborhood, and its sister, Astoria, is closer to Manhattan than all of the popular

Brooklyn neighborhoods that have successfully transitioned from neglect to gentrification in the past few decades.

In a way, the prediction has come to fruition. A number of those former industrial spaces *have* been converted into light-filled lofts, some with exceptional, unobstructed views of the East River and Manhattan skyline, and they've been joined by a ballooning number of new residential and mixed-use skyscrapers. Services that were once in limited supply here, namely grocery stores, good restaurants, and schools, have popped up as more families locate in Long Island City, especially in the waterfront section of the neighborhood that spans 46th to 50th Avenues along Center Boulevard. Playgrounds and recreational spaces are increasing in number too.

The seedy side of Long Island City, with its numerous "gentleman's clubs" clustered underneath the Queensboro Bridge, has been spiffed up since 2012, when the city transformed Queensboro Plaza with a new traffic pattern, the addition of a bike path, and plenty of landscaping and seating. New, trendy restaurants and retailers have begun forcing the strip clubs to retreat, and residents have celebrated the arrival of hip bars. A growing artistic community, whose members host plenty of performances and exhibits, means LIC residents don't necessarily need to hop on the train and head to "the city" for their culture fix. MoMA's

(Museum of Modern Art) PS1 is the anchor of this artistic community, but it's joined by theater, dance, and other performance collectives, as well as a number of galleries and experimental art spaces. Working artists host regular open studio events, often in collaboration with Long Island City restauranteurs and independent businesses, who open their doors for curious culture vultures.

The neighborhood's proximity to Manhattan and zoning laws favoring hotel developers have made the neighborhood a magnet for hoteliers too. Rooms cost a fraction of those in Midtown and are often considerably more spacious. And there are plenty of recreational opportunities in the neighborhood. Long Island City sits along the East River, and there are several put-in points for kayaks, as well as programs offering free use of the watercraft; parks, playgrounds, and a riparian bike path all provide the chance to stay active. The 2013 opening of The Cliffs at Long Island City, billed as the largest indoor rock climbing gym in the Northeast US, helps locals stay fit year-round.

Despite all these positive developments, the neighborhood has yet to exert the same kind of cachet as, say, SoHo or Williamsburg, though rents don't reflect that. Apartment prices have been soaring since 2010 and currently sit just around $3,000 a month for a one-bedroom unit in a newly- or recently-constructed "luxury" building. The price is right—if barely—for many young families, who flock to the luxury buildings along the neighborhood's southern end for East River views, 7 train access, and the newly-opened public and charter schools.

A number of big-name realty firms have set up offices in Long Island City, among them heavy-hitters like The Corcoran Group and Douglas Elliman. If you're interested in relocating to Long Island City, check the listings in their offices, which you'll find along the stretch of Vernon Boulevard between 46th and 48th Avenues. This part of Vernon is also home to a growing number of cute home design and gift boutiques, as well as excellent restaurants reflecting the borough's cultural diversity.

There's room for debate—and debate people do, endlessly—about where Long Island City ends and Astoria begins, but it's generally agreed, at least by addresses established by the post office, that avenues north of 36th Avenue fall squarely in Astoria. Increasingly, the distinct characters of each neighborhood are being asserted. If LIC is shiny, hip, and sleek post-industrial, **Astoria** is quirky, indie, and as one local blogger puts it, proud to be ugly. While there is a growing number of newly built apartment buildings and condos, they tend to lack the design consciousness of the new builds in Long Island City, merely adding to the rag-tag patchwork of architectural styles that characterize Astoria. And that's just fine with most residents, who like the hodgepodge fabric of their neighborhood and all it represents.

Astoria has traditionally been a stronghold of the Greeks, and you'll still find plenty of excellent Greek restaurants and cafés here, especially along Broadway and on 30th Avenue, both just off the N/Q train stops. And you'll still find plenty of Greeks too, often discussing politics and news from the homeland over frappés at favorite spots like Omonia, which gained fame for making the wedding cake in the popular movie *My Big Fat Greek Wedding*. Increasingly, the Greeks are being joined by numerous other immigrant groups, especially Pakistanis and Bangladeshis, and Manhattan expats, particularly actors and other creatives, who've been priced out of the borough. The diversity is visible in the neighborhood's abundance of grocery stores and specialty food markets that cater to an international clientele, and the growing number of independently owned businesses that serve needs and wants residents once had to go to Manhattan to satisfy.

Housing stock in Astoria is, for the most part, found in walk-ups, and walking the street, talking with supers and residents, is one of the best ways to find an apartment here. Craigslist.com is another good source.

Websites: www.licpartnership.org, www.nyc.gov, www.licarts.org, www.astorial-ic.org, www.astoriaugly.tumblr.com

Area Codes: 718, 347

Post Offices: Astoria Station, 27-40 21st St, Astoria; Steinway Station, 43-04 Broadway, Astoria; Woolsey Station, 22-68 31st St, Astoria; Broadway Station, 21-17 Broadway, Astoria; Main Branch, 46-02 21st St, Long Island City; Plaza Station, 24-18 Queens Plaza South, Long Island City

Zip Codes: 11101, 11102, 11103, 11105, 11106

Police Precinct: One Hundred Fourteenth, 34-16 Astoria Blvd at 35th St, Astoria, 718-626-9311

Emergency Hospitals: Mt. Sinai Hospital of Queens, 25-10 30th Ave, Long Island City, 718-932-1000, www.mshq.org; Elmhurst Hospital Center, 79-01 Broadway, Elmhurst, 718-334-4000, www.nyc.gov/elmhurst hospital

Libraries: Astoria Branch, 14-01 Astoria Blvd, Astoria, 718-278-2220; Steinway Branch, 21-45 31st St, Long Island City, 718-728-1965; Broadway Branch, 40-20 Broadway, Long Island City, 718-721-2462; www.queenslibrary.org

Public School Education: School District #30 in region 4, 28-11 Queens Plaza, 718-391-8323, www.www.schools.nyc.gov

Community Resources: Queens Chamber of Commerce, www.queenschamber.org; The Isamu Noguchi Museum and Sculpture Garden, 9-01 33rd Rd, 718-204-7088, www.noguchi.org; Socrates Sculpture Park, 32-01 Vernon Blvd, Long Island City, 718-956-1819, www.socratessculpturepark.org; Museum of the Moving Image, 36-01 35th Ave, Astoria, 718-784-0077 www.movingimage.us; MoMA PS1 (formerly P.S.1 Contemporary Art Center), 22-25 Jackson Ave, Long Island City, 718-784-2084, www.ps1.org; The Sculpture Center, 44-19 Purves Street, 718-361-1750. www.sculpture-center.org

Transportation—Subway: N/Q, Queensboro Plaza, 39th Ave, 36th Ave, Broadway, 30th Ave, Astoria Blvd-Hoyt Ave, Ditmars Blvd; E/G/V, 23rd St, Queens Plaza; G/R/V/E, Queens Plaza, 36th St, Steinway St and 46th St; F, 21st St/Queensbridge; www.mta.info

Transportation—Bus: For a Queens bus map and schedule, stop by the College Point Bus Depot, 128-15 28th Ave, Flushing, or call 718-330-1234, or go to www.mta.info. The MTA also offers express service on several routes to midtown Manhattan for $6.

SUNNYSIDE

Boundaries and Contiguous Areas: North: Barnett Avenue and the Sunnyside Conrail Yards; **East**: 52nd Street and New Calvary Cemetery; **South**: Long Island Expressway; **West**: 36th Street and Long Island City

This traditionally blue-collar community bounded by railroad yards, industrial tracts, cemeteries, and the legendary LIE (the Long Island Expressway, also known as the world's longest parking lot) won't be the next "in" New York neighborhood. But the sensible, mostly brick homes and apartments lining **Sunnyside**'s residential streets, ten minutes by train from Manhattan, do attract young professionals, as well as immigrants, offering more space for lower-than-Manhattan rents.

Newcomers are especially drawn to **Sunnyside Gardens**. "The Gardens," the first US development to be modeled on the English garden community, occupies 55 leafy acres north of bustling Queens Boulevard. Towering London plane trees shade the 650 one-, two-, and three-family brick townhouses, which enclose long communal gardens. The effect is English village, with shrub-lined walks penetrating the landmarked blocks. "Like Greenwich Village and far more than Brooklyn Heights, it was a mixed community, in which one might mingle without undue intimacy with one's neighbors," recalls urban critic/historian Lewis Mumford, who lived in The Gardens from their inception in 1924 until 1936. They seem little changed and are likely to remain so, considering they were given landmark status in 2007.

There are private homes and rentals in greater Sunnyside as well, but most of the brick apartment blocks are non-rentable co-ops. The three main shopping thoroughfares are small-town Skillman Avenue at The Gardens' southern edge, Queens Boulevard in the shadow of the elevated IRT Flushing Line, and running diagonally southwest from the Boulevard, Greenpoint Avenue, which leads directly into neighboring Brooklyn. There and on the side streets you can rent Korean movies; buy Irish imports; eat Italian, Middle European, or Chinese; or lift a pint at Moriarty's Pub Restaurant. The city's longest-established Spanish language theater, the Thalia on Greenpoint Avenue, plays to sellout crowds on weekends. There's a large and growing Orthodox Jewish community here as well. Sunnyside is an appealingly cohesive community, for all its ethnic diversity.

Websites: www.nyc.gov, www.sunnyside-chamber.org
Area Codes: 718, 347

Post Office: Sunnyside Station, 45-15 44th St, 718-729-7806

Zip Code: 11104

Police Precinct: One Hundred Eighth, 5-47 50th Ave, Long Island City, 718-784-5411

Emergency Hospital (nearest): Elmhurst Hospital Center, 79-01 Broadway, Elmhurst, 718-334-4000, www.nyc.gov/elmhurst hospital

Library: Sunnyside Branch, 43-06 Greenpoint Ave, 718-784-3033, www.queenslibrary.org

Public School Education: School District #24 in region 4, 98-50 50th Ave, 718-592-3357, www.schools.nyc.gov

Community Resources: Sunnyside Chamber of Commerce, 718-784-7700, www.sunnyside-chamber.org

Transportation—Subway: #7 to Manhattan, 40th St, 46th St, 52nd St; www.mta.info

Transportation—Bus: For a Queens bus map and schedule, stop by the College Point Bus Depot, 128-15 28th Ave, Flushing, or call 718-330-1234, or go to www.mta.info. The MTA also offers express service on several routes to midtown Manhattan for $5.

Transportation—LIRR: Woodside Station, Roosevelt Ave and 61st St; www.mta.info

REGO PARK

Boundaries and Contiguous Areas: North: Queens Boulevard; **East:** Yellowstone Boulevard and Forest Hills; **Southwest:** Woodhaven Boulevard

Until 1920 only one thoroughfare wound through this vegetable farmland of western Long Island, and that was a cow path. Within five years, the Real Good Construction Company had purchased three of the farms and prudently named the area for itself as Rego Park. A branch of the Long Island Railroad extended near the area, and development followed quickly; houses were purchased as soon as they were built, and sometimes before they were finished.

Rego Park has long had a strong Jewish community, with a growing presence of Russian and Iranian families. Recent years have seen a rapid influx of Asians, particularly South Koreans, and these and other cultures mingle well in this middle- to upper-class swath of land beside Forest Hills. Three subway lines and several express buses to and from Manhattan help keep this diverse, low-crime neighborhood accessible. Also convenient are the numerous businesses and shops in the area, both along 63rd Drive—that former cow path—as well as quick access to the Queens Center (www.shopqueenscenter.com), a mammoth shopping complex anchored by Macy's, JC Penney, and H&M. Many of the independent businesses along 63rd Drive stand in the original buildings constructed in the twenties and thirties.

Running parallel to Queens Boulevard, the LIRR divides the commercial and residential interests in the area. Nearly two-thirds of the homes in Rego Park are rentals, but real estate prices have risen dramatically, although they still remain about 25% less than most of Queens.

Website: www.nyc.gov
Area Codes: 718, 347
Post Office: Rego Park Station, 92-24 Queens Blvd
Zip Code: 11374
Police Precinct: One Hundred and Twelfth, 68-40 Austin St, Forest Hills, 718-520-9311
Emergency Hospital: Elmhurst Hospital Center, 79-01 Broadway, Elmhurst, 718-334-4000, www.nyc.gov/elmhurst hospital

Library: Rego Park Branch, 91-41 63rd Dr, 718-459-5140, www.queenslibrary.org
Public School Education: School District #28 in region 3 (see **Forest Hills**)
Adult Education: Queens College (see **Flushing**); St. John's University (see **Forest Hills**)
Community Resource: Queens Chamber of Commerce, 718-898-8500, www.queenschamber.org
Transportation—Subway: R/G, and V at 63rd Dr and 67th Ave; www.mta.info
Transportation—Bus: For a Queens bus map and schedule, stop by the College Point Bus Depot, 128-15 28th Ave, Flushing, or call 718-330-1234, or go to www.mta.info. The MTA also offers express service on several routes to midtown Manhattan for $5.
Transportation—LIRR: Forest Hills Station, Austin St and 71st (Continental) Ave; www.mta.info

FOREST HILLS

Boundaries and Contiguous Areas: North: Long Island Expressway; **East:** Grand Central Parkway and Corona Park; **South:** Union Turnpike and Kew Gardens; **West:** Yellowstone Boulevard and Rego Park

Practical Queens Boulevard, a major shopping thoroughfare that sensibly separates curbside businesses from through traffic with narrow concrete dividers, belies the charm of Forest Hills as it cuts through the heart of the neighborhood. To the north, larger apartment buildings dominate. South, a block just off Austin, considered one of the most enticing shopping streets in Queens, lies "The Gardens." Forest Hills Gardens, designed in the eclectic tradition by an architect of the Beaux-Arts school, has few peers in the half-timbered world of Victorian Tudor. Brick-fronted Cotswoldian houses face curving drives and landscaped plots originally planned by Frederick Law Olmsted, Jr. The walled Gardens area is distinctively exclusive, being both gated and with private security. Shopping and noshing opportunities also add allure to the somewhat crowded Forest Hills neighborhood, as do the schools that perform on average about 30% better than most NYC schools. In addition to the attractive Austin Street spots, appealing cafés and craft and antique stores have cropped up on Metropolitan Avenue.

Old and established, **Forest Hills** is becoming increasingly cosmopolitan. (A local real estate agent reports a map of Forest Hills on sale in Tokyo bookstores.) And increasingly, its brick apartment buildings have gone co-op. The six- to ten-story, mostly red brick rental buildings congregating on either side of Queens Boulevard stretch across 108th Street and over to Forest Hills High School,

standing prominently above the Grand Central Parkway, which borders the neighborhood from nearby Flushing Meadows Park. The IND/BMT subway lines, as well as major arteries like Ascan, Metropolitan, and 108th Street, are worth pursuing for their quality pre-war construction as well as convenience to public transportation and shopping. Semi-detached apartments and units in private homes may require a slightly longer walk but offer landscaped lots and winding streets as dividends. While a great number of Forest Hills' residents have been firmly entrenched for many years, rentals and co-ops occasionally do pop up; act quickly, they won't stay on the market long. Prices are on the upswing, increasing yearly. Count on at least $2 million for a large house and about $250,000 for a studio apartment.

Rents vary considerably, ranging from about $1,900 to more than $3,000/month, depending upon the size, location, and neighborhood amenities.

Website: www.nyc.gov

Area Codes: 718, 347

Post Office: Forest Hills Station, 106-28 Queens Blvd

Zip Code: 11375

Police Precinct: One Hundred and Twelfth, 68-40 Austin St, 718-520-9311

Emergency Hospitals: Forest Hills Hospital, 102-01 66th Rd, 718-830-4000, www. northshorelij.com/hospitals/location/forest-hills

Libraries: Forest Hills Branch, 108-19 71st Ave, 718-268-7934; North Forest Park, 98-27 Metropolitan Ave, 718-261-5512; www.queenslibrary.org

Public School Education: School District #28 in region 3, 90-27 Sutphin Blvd, 718-557-2618, www.schools.nyc.gov

Adult Education: St. John's University, 8000 Utopia Pkwy, Jamaica, 718-990-2000, www.stjohns.edu

Community Resources: Queens Chamber of Commerce, 718-898-8500, www. queenschamber.org; West Side Tennis Club, 1 Tennis Place, 718-268-2300, www.foresthillstennis.com; Forest Hills Jewish Center, 106-06 Queens Blvd, 718-263-7000, www.fhjc.org

Transportation—Subway: E/F/G, and R, all to 71st (Continental) Ave; www.mta. info

Transportation—Bus: For a Queens bus map and schedule, stop by the College Point Bus Depot, 128-15 28th Ave, Flushing, or call 718-330-1234, or go to www.mta.info. The MTA also offers express service on several routes to midtown Manhattan for $5.

Transportation—LIRR: Forest Hills Station, Austin St and 71st (Continental) Ave; www.mta.info

KEW GARDENS

Boundaries and Contiguous Areas: Northeast: Queens Boulevard; **South**: Metropolitan Avenue and Forest Park; **West**: Union Turnpike and Forest Hills

Bracketed by LaGuardia Airport and John F. Kennedy International, Queens is home to thousands of airline employees. **Kew Gardens**, sitting nearly midway between the city's two prime airports, is particularly popular with flight crews, hence the nickname "Crew Gardens." Real estate agents report more rentals available and more singles residing in Kew Gardens than in Forest Hills and Rego Park.

The neighborhood's oldest section dates to 1912, when the Kew Gardens Corporation was formed. The substantial Colonial and Tudor-accented private homes built on high, comparatively hilly ground between Maple Grove Cemetery and Forest Park have cachet even today. The blocks of red brick apartment buildings that ring Kew's center, the older ones especially, represent real value, though most are co-op. Austin Street and Metropolitan Avenue together with Lefferts and Queens Boulevards make up Kew's main shopping area. There's a pleasingly small-town feel on Austin around the railroad station, and the 538-acre Forest Park (see **Greenspace and Beaches**) provides rustic peace and quiet, as well as horseback riding.

Nevertheless, with the infusion of recent immigrants, Kew Gardens has become a cosmopolitan community. Along Lefferts Boulevard you'll find an Irish bar and restaurant, a Russian grocer, an Uzbekistani Cultural Center, and a Caribbean nightclub, suggesting just a few of the ethnic components of this

neighborhood. Good schools and easy accessibility to nearly all of the borough's main roads and highways make this a viable alternative to Forest Hills.

At its southeastern-most tip, Kew Gardens hosts Queens Borough Hall just across the Van Wyck Expressway, a long bureaucratic brick and limestone structure usually filled with politicians and, occasionally, useful publications about the borough.

Websites: www.nyc.gov, www.kewgardenshistory.com
Area Codes: 718, 347
Post Office: Kew Gardens Station, 83-30 Austin St
Zip Codes: 11365, 11375, 11415
Police Precinct: One Hundred and Second, 87-34 118th St, Richmond Hill, 718-805-3200
Emergency Hospital (nearest): Forest Hills Hospital, 102-01 66th Rd, 718-830-4000, www.northshorelij.com/hospitals/location/forest-hills

Libraries: Lefferts Branch, 103-34 Lefferts Blvd, Richmond Hill, 718-843-5950; Glen Oaks Branch, 256-04 Union Turnpike, Glen Oaks, 718-831-8636; www. queenslibrary.org

Public School Education: School District #28 in region 3 (see Forest Hills)

Adult Education (nearest): Queens College, 65-30 Kissena Blvd, Flushing, 718-997-5000, www.qc.cuny.edu

Community Resources: Queens Borough Hall, 120-55 Queens Blvd, Kew Gardens, 718-520-3220; Queens Chamber of Commerce, www.queenschamber.org

Transportation—Subway: E/F, Kew Gardens/Union Turnpike

Transportation—Bus: For a Queens bus map and schedule, stop by the College Point Bus Depot, 128-15 28th Ave, Flushing, or call 718-330-1234, or go to www.mta.info. The MTA also offers express service on several routes to midtown Manhattan for $5.

Transportation—LIRR: Kew Gardens Station, Lefferts Blvd and Austin St; www. mta.info

FLUSHING

Boundaries and Contiguous Areas: North: Cross Island Parkway and Whitestone; **East**: Utopia Parkway and Francis Lewis Boulevard and Bayside; **South**: Union Turnpike; **West**: Grand Central Parkway and Forest Hills

Middle-class **Flushing** sprawls on either side of the Long Island Expressway, embraced by two great parks at the center of thriving northern Queens. The nexus of multiple bus routes, rail lines, and traffic arteries, downtown Flushing looks like the crossroads of the world. The majority of residents are now Asian-American, hence the vibrant Asian restaurant and market scene here. Flushing is New York's largest Chinatown and the largest urban center in Queens. On weekends, the colorful Chinese fish-fruit-and-vegetable vendors, Korean gift stores, Muslim butchers, and sari shops along Main Street draw people from outside the area, and religious meeting places range from Protestant to Muslim to a number of Hindu temples. Toward the Long Island Expressway and surrounding Queens College is a less ethnically diverse area, where English is predominant and residents have lived for many years, some in red brick developments like Pomonok or Electchester, which were built for members of the electrical union.

Away from commercial Main Street, Union Turnpike, and Northern Boulevard, the grid of shady residential streets has changed little, except perhaps to have become more presentable. The profusion of well-established trees, 2,000 varieties throughout Flushing, constitutes a treasure and a living remnant of the nursery industry that flourished here from pre-Revolutionary times until recently. Another survivor, its back turned to Northern Boulevard, the austere Friends' Meeting House has been a place of worship since 1694, except during the Revolutionary War, when it was a British hospital, prison, and stable. The Bowne House Historical

Society (37-01 Bowne Street), built nearby in 1661, was an earlier site of Quaker worship and of the struggle for religious freedom in what was then a Dutch settlement. Down Bowne Street, in a modest residential neighborhood, is an extraordinary Hindu temple covered with stone statues. That's Flushing.

Great tracts of green breathing space surround and bisect the neighborhood. Flushing Meadows-Corona Park contains within its 1,200 acres remnants of the 1939 and 1964 New York World's Fairs, two lakes, a marina, the Queens Zoo, a botanical garden, the Queens Museum, Theatre in the Park, the New York Hall of Science, and an indoor ice-skating rink. Adjacent is Citi Field, home of the New York Mets, and the USTA National Tennis Center, site of the annual US Open Tennis Championships. Tucked away within Flushing's borders is the more intimate and landscaped Kissena Park, which sits around a lake and contains an appealing nature center.

As might be expected, the presence of Queens College and Flushing's rich ethnic mix support an unusually vibrant cultural life: music, art, literary pursuits, and theater flourish here. The Flushing Branch of the Queens Library on Main Street, handsomely rebuilt in 1998, is the busiest branch of the busiest library system in the nation. Open daily, its holdings include books, periodicals, videos, and CDs in some 30 languages, computer WorldLinQ in Chinese, Korean, Russian, Spanish, and French, an Adult Learning Center, and a unique International Resource Center. The Main Street Flushing subway station nearby is a boon to the 100,000 commuters who use it, many of them transferring from the web of bus routes that cross here.

Besides the convenience of transportation and the physical amenities, what Flushing has to offer is more space at less-than-Manhattan rents. For luxury condos, look elsewhere, Bayside perhaps. High-rise apartments cluster near downtown Flushing. The rest is two-story brick apartment enclaves, one- and two-family houses, detached and semi-attached, all with on-street parking. Ads to sell or rent these properties are often placed in *Newsday* and *The New York Times* by their owners; consult these same pages and the list of realtors in **Finding a Place to Live** to find brokers who handle other properties.

Website: www.nyc.gov
Area Codes: 718, 347

Post Offices: Linden Hill, 29-50 Union St; Station A, 40-03 164th St; Kew Gardens Hills, 75-23 Main St

Zip Codes: 11354, 11355, 11358, 11365, 11366, 11367, 11368

Police Precincts: One Hundred and Ninth, 37-05 Union St, 718-321-2250; One Hundred and Seventh, 71-01 Parsons Blvd, 718-969-5100

Emergency Hospitals: New York Hospital Queens, 56-45 Main St, 718-670-2000, www.nyhq.org; Flushing Hospital Medical Center, 4500 Parsons Blvd, 718-670-5000, www.flushinghospital.org

Libraries: Flushing Main Branch, 41-17 Main St, 718-661-1200; Hillcrest Branch, 187-05 Union Turnpike, 718-454-2786; McGoldrick Branch, 155-06 Roosevelt Ave, 718-461-1616; Mitchell-Linden Branch, 31-32 Union St, 718-539-2330; Pomonok Branch, 158-21 Jewel Ave, 718-591-4343; www.queenslibrary.org

Public School Education: School Districts #25 and #26 in region 3, 30-48 Linden Place, 718-281-7605 and 61-15 Oceania St., 718-631-6900, www.schools.nyc.gov

Adult Education: Queens College, 65-30 Kissena Blvd, 718-997-5000, www.qc.cuny.edu

Community Resources: Queens Historical Society, Kingsland House, 143-35 37th Ave, 718-939-0647, www.queenshistoricalsociety.org; Queens Chamber of Commerce, www.queenschamber.org; The Bowne House Historical Society, 37-01 Bowne St, 718-359-0528; www.bownehouse.org; New York Hall of Science, 47-01 111th St, Flushing Meadows-Corona Park, 718-699-0005, www.nyscience.org, includes over 200 hands-on exhibits, plus a science playground for children; Queens Museum, Flushing Meadows-Corona Park, 718-592-9700, www.queensmuseum.org; Kupferberg Center for the Performing Arts, Queens College, 65-30 Kissena Blvd, 718-793-8080, www.kupferbergcenter.org; Flushing Council on Culture and the Arts at Town Hall, 137-35 Northern Blvd, 718-463-7700, www.flushingtownhall.org; Kissena Park Nature Center, Rose Ave and Parsons Blvd, 718-359-1297, www.nycgovparks.org/parks/kissenapark; Queens Botanical Garden, 43-50 Main St, 718-886-3800, www.queensbotanical.org; Queens Theatre in the Park, Flushing Meadows-Corona Park, 718-760-0064, www.queenstheatre.org

Transportation—Subway: #7, Willets PointMain St; E/F, Union Turnpike-Kew Gardens; www.mta.info

Transportation—Bus: For a Queens bus map and schedule, stop by the College Point Bus Depot, 128-15 28th Ave, Flushing, or call 718-330-1234, or go to www.mta.info. The MTA also offers express service on several routes to midtown Manhattan for $5.

Transportation—LIRR: Main Street Station, Main St & 41st Ave; www.mta.info

BAYSIDE

Boundaries and Contiguous Areas: North and **East**: Cross Island Parkway; **South**: Long Island Expressway; **West**: Francis Lewis Boulevard and Utopia Parkway

The bright, barn-red Long Island Railroad station, white-trimmed and snappy, differentiates Bayside from other Queens stops. So does the concentration of pubs and restaurants—some dim and glitzy, others homey-comfortable with fireplaces—that surround the station. These places attract singles and have a bubbling atmosphere after work and on weekends more akin to Long Island than New York. North of this Bell Boulevard and 41st Avenue junction, one- and two-family homes reestablish that urban/suburban quiet that typifies residential Queens, with gated Bayside Gables dominating the area, until you reach **Bay Terrace**. Here, newer condominiums and co-op garden apartment buildings break the mold.

Bayside has been rated among the best places to live a number of times. While the older, free-standing homes contain rental apartments, condominium rentals in the pristine **Bay Club**, among other high-rises, are probably the biggest draw. The enormous development consists of 1,036 condominiums in two three-pronged towers, a glass-domed swim club, a health club, and five tennis courts.

The **Bay Bridge** condo development nearby, with some 2,000 luxury townhouses, is a shorefront village in itself. From the Bay Club windows, and from those in the older co-ops, you can see how the community got its name—Bayside is bounded on two sides by Little Bay and Little Neck Bay. The Whitestone, Robert F. Kennedy (formerly Triborough), and Throgs Neck Bridges connect Queens to The Bronx. Tucked within the densely populated high-rises that pack many a Bayside block are several town parks (including the 655-acre Alley Pond Park and the recently opened seaside Fort Totten), plenty of shopping, and excellent schools; these features, combined with the relative regularity of the LIRR schedule and the low crime rate, have made this family area a commuter favorite for decades, especially with NYC police and firefighters.

Bayside has water views but no direct subway connection to Manhattan. Commuters have three public transportation choices: the Long Island Railroad, express buses, or Queens buses to Flushing's Main Street Station and the #7 Flushing Line subway to 42nd street in Manhattan. The LIRR is typically the fastest route.

Websites: www.baysidequeens.com, www.nyc.gov
Area Codes: 718, 347
Post Offices: Bayside Station, 212-35 42nd Ave; Bayside Annex, 41-29 216th St
Zip Codes: 11357, 11360, 11361, 11364
Police Precinct: One Hundred and Eleventh, 45-06 215th St, 718-279-5200
Emergency Hospital: St. Mary's Hospital for Children, 29-01 216th St, 718-281-8800, www.stmaryskids.org
Library: Bayside Branch, 214-20 Northern Blvd, 718-229-1834, www.queenslibrary.org
Public School Education: School District #26 in region 3, 61-15 Oceania St, Bayside, 718-631-6900, www.schools.nyc.gov
Adult Education: Queensborough Community College, 222-05 56th Ave, 718-631-6262, www.qcc.cuny.edu
Community Resources: Crocheron Park, 33rd Ave and Little Neck Parkway, 718-762-5966, www.nycgovparks.org/parks/crocheronpark, a 45-acre park; Queensborough Community College Gallery, 222-05 56th Ave, 718-631-6396, www.qcc.cuny.edu; Queens Chamber of Commerce, www.queenschamber.org
Transportation—Bus: For a Queens bus map and schedule, stop by the College Point Bus Depot, 128-15 28th Ave, Flushing, or call 718-330-1234, or go to www.mta.info. The MTA also offers express service on several routes to midtown Manhattan for $5.
Transportation—Train: regular LIRR service; www.mta.info
Transportation—LIRR: Station: 213th St and 41st Ave; www.mta.info

<u>YOU MIGHT ALSO WANT TO CONSIDER ...</u>

- **Douglaston** is an upper middle-class community at the northeastern end of Queens, bordering on Long Island, having mostly one- and two-family houses and co-ops, relatively low real estate taxes, and lower prices than upscale Great Neck (Long Island) to the east. A 25-minute commute to Manhattan on the Long Island Railroad.
- **Jamaica Estates**, with its winding roads, shady streets, Tudor houses, and English street names, is 45 minutes by the E or F train to Manhattan. Expensive homes in a small, rather exclusive community tucked away in mid- to north Queens.
- **Middle Village** is mid-Queens, middle class, and relatively affordable, with tidy one- and two-family houses and a scattering of condos housing an old-fashioned, "close-knit" community of civic-minded people and plenty of mom-and-pop stores. Amenities include Juniper Valley Park, from which the Manhattan skyline is visible, good schools, Italian specialty stores, and German bakeries.
- **Richmond Hill**, with Victorian houses, golf and tennis in Forest Park, and a variety of ethnic stores, is less expensive than neighboring Kew Gardens and Forest Hills, for the most part. An easy commute by train or subway. Check out Richmond Hill Historical Society, www.richmondhillhistory.org.

- **Ridgewood**, a half-hour from Grand Central by subway, boasts a German heritage still apparent in its shops and restaurants, solid row houses (some of them landmarked), and a strong neighborhood feeling. Especially prized are the harmonious yellow-brick houses along Stockholm Street and two blocks of 69th Avenue, between Fresh Pond Road and 60th Street. See also entry on page 92.
- **Whitestone** is between the Whitestone and Throgs Neck Bridges in northern Queens and 30 minutes on the #7 from Times Square (45 minutes by express bus). A highly residential, quiet, family neighborhood featuring some private homes, plus many co-ops and condos—few rentals. Includes exclusive Malba (see the introduction to the **Queens** profile above) and Francis Lewis Park along the riverfront.

STATEN ISLAND

Giovanni da Verrazzano discovered hillocky Staten Island in 1524, but until the dedication of his namesake bridge 440 years later, the island remained something of a backwater. Henry Hudson claimed Staaten Eylandt for the Dutch East India Company in 1609; however, Britain acquired Staten Island when its troops took over New Amsterdam in 1644. In 1687 the Duke of York offered the island as a prize in a sailing competition; the team from Manhattan won and has laid claim to the land mass ever since. By the mid-1800s, a railroad, trolley cars, and ferry service made the island's seashore and salubrious air accessible to the gentry. The fickle fashionables had moved on though by the time Staten Island became part of New York City in 1898. Too bad, because the city improved the new borough's ferry service immeasurably: by 1904 there were a number of sturdy seaworthy boats running on schedule for the first time since young Cornelius Vanderbilt instituted ferry service to Manhattan around 1810.

That ferry still runs today. For those who aren't in the know, New York's least-populated borough is simply the turn-around point for the boat, which transports up to 60,000 people a day. That's just fine with long-time area residents, who would just as soon keep their 61-square-mile island off the coast of New Jersey to themselves. Dreams of remaining far from the maddening New York frenzy were conclusively shattered when the austerely beautiful Verrazano-Narrows Bridge connecting Staten Island with Brooklyn was opened in 1964. The island's semi-rural isolation ended once and for all—save for the three public golf courses and 15 parks—as Brooklynites flocked across the longest single-span bridge in the world to take up residence in dozens of new tract developments. Population growth continues today. Not everyone agrees on the reasons or the impact; in fact, it's the cause of endless discussion and debate on the island. "Those who are coming want more to follow," says one realtor, meaning both residents and the businesses that serve them. "And those who are here want it to stop."

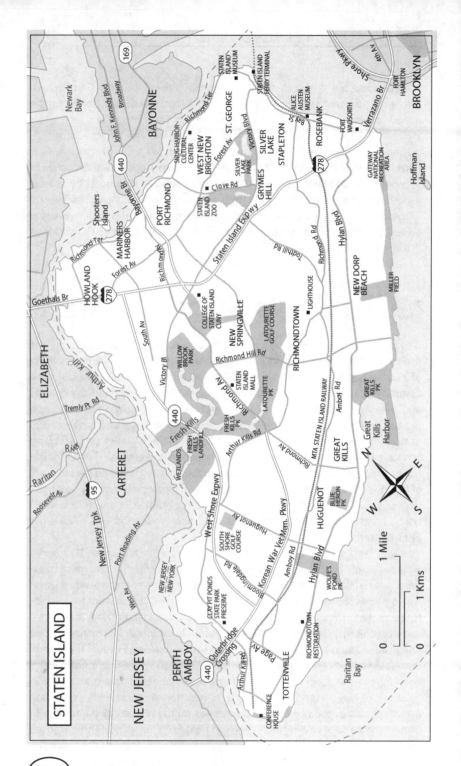

"The more things change, the more they stay the same" might be a good tag-line for the status of Staten Island today. Still staunchly conservative, particularly when compared to the other boroughs, notoriously liberal in their political bent, the island is nonetheless attracting—gasp—hipsters (!), who are drawn over by the lower rents and the sense that there's still the possibility of developing their own businesses without the instant overhead guaranteed by the other boroughs. Long-time residents either resent the influx or question what it will ultimately mean for the less expensive lifestyle they've enjoyed over the years. "Gentrification has already hit St. George," says one lifelong resident, noting the openings of Flagship Brewery, SI Makerspace, Culture Lab, the organic garden at Snug Harbor, and tech meet-ups at Borough Hall as evidence. And you'd be hard-pressed to find a native Staten Islander who's thrilled about developers' plans to build The New York Wheel, which will be the tallest observation Ferris wheel in the world, if it indeed opens in 2017 as projected. Already, housing prices in the area have been affected; in summer 2014, an apartment near Bay Street Landing sold for over a million dollars, a record. "I'm afraid of what the new apartments around the light-house museum and the Ferris wheel will cost," said the same resident.

Precipitous slopes reminiscent of San Francisco and stunning views from the craggy ridge that rises between St. George and Richmondtown characterize that portion of Staten Island nearest Manhattan, so it's not hard to see why Man-hattan refugees are headed for the hills. On leafy Todt, Emerson, and Grymes Hills, multi-million-dollar homes look over the treetops to Brooklyn and Man-hattan. Wood-frame Victorian houses, salted among the stucco mini-mansions and angular contemporary homes, are the darlings of homesteaders. You're more likely to find a rental apartment in a converted one- or two-family house than in an apartment building on Staten Island—although red brick apartment towers do exist, especially the new ones in St. George.

The Staten Island Chamber of Commerce (130 Bay Street, 718-727-1900, www.sichamber.com) sells an excellent street map and the MTA's Staten Island Bus Map (free at the Chamber) is equally useful.

ST. GEORGE

Boundaries and Contiguous Areas: North: Richmond Terrace and the Kill Van Kull; **East**: Bay Street; **South**: Victory Boulevard and Stapleton; **West**: Jersey Street and The Narrows

Flags aflutter, the beguiling limestone and brick Borough Hall caps a rise to the right of St. George's ferry terminal. To the left as you exit the terminal, a stunning structure, at once public sculpture, bridge, and lighthouse-like tower, crowns a plaza, inviting visitors to climb to its glassy top for a smashing view of the harbor and lower Manhattan beyond. The two are symbolic of St. George's struggle against blight. The downtown sector, is quaint and historic; uphill, within sight of the neo-Gothic spires of Curtis High School (between St. Mark's Place and Hamilton Avenue), you'll find restored Victorian, Tudor, and 1920s-stucco houses. Four formerly vacant apartment buildings there have been transformed into the Village on St. Marks with affordable rentals suitable for commuters to the Financial District. And the Saturday Greenmarket on St. Marks brings a village square feel to downtown St. George from May to December.

In contrast to the maple-shaded period homes, the three converted grain and coffee warehouses that comprise Bay Street Landing are certainly up-to-date. Arguably the borough's trendiest housing, these waterside condominiums located a five-minute walk east of the ferry terminal were the first stage in an ongoing harborfront revival. Initially a steal at about $1,000/month, they have recently sold for as "little" as $400,000 and as much as one million. Here, black pines and juniper separate the public marina, esplanade, and the glass-enclosed Landing Café from the access road—shades of Sausalito. New rentals, rare in Staten Island, are to be found in moderately priced waterfront midrises at Harbor View.

Come spring, fishing enthusiasts flock to the charter boats tied up at the Landing's pristine docks. The Joseph L. Lyons Pool, one of Staten Island's four municipal swimming pools, and the George Cromwell Center, an indoor recreation center with tennis courts and a track situated on a pier, are both located near The Landing's complex. The new Richmond County Bank Ballpark is the home of exciting baseball action featuring the Staten Island Yankees (statenisland.yankees.milb.com), a minor league affiliate of The Bronx Bombers.

Websites: www.statenislandusa.com, www.statenislandadvance.com, www.silive.com, www.nyc.gov

Area Codes: 718, 347

Post Offices: St. George Station, 45 Bay St; Stapleton Station, 160 Tompkins Ave; CPU 503, 1300 Clove Rd

Zip Code: 10301

Police Precinct: One Hundred Twentieth, 78 Richmond Terr, 718-876-8500

Emergency Hospitals (nearest): Staten Island University Hospital, 475 Seaview Ave, 718-226-9000, www.siuh.edu

Library: St. George Library Center, 5 Central Ave, 718-442-8560, www.nypl.org

Public School Education: School District #31 in region 7, 715 Ocean Terr, 718-556-8350, www.schools.nyc.gov

Adult Education: CUNY: College of Staten Island, 2800 Victory Blvd, 718-982-2000, www.csi.cuny.edu

Community Resources: Richmond County Bank Ballpark, 75 Richmond Terr, 718-720-9265; Snug Harbor Cultural Center, 1000 Richmond Terr, 718-448-2500, www.snug-harbor.org, is located in a clutch of handsome Greek Revival buildings on 80 tree-filled acres. Once a haven for indigent sailors, the colonnaded buildings are now the locus of Staten Island's cultural rebirth; concerts, art exhibits, and plays fill the high-ceilinged halls. Also on the grounds you'll find the Staten Island Botanical Garden, 718-273-8200, www.sibg.org, which contains the Chinese Scholar's Garden, 8 pavilions of peace and tranquility, www.sibg.org/cg; and the Staten Island Children's Museum, 718-273-2060. The nearby Staten Island Museum, 75 Stuyvesant Pl, 718-727-1135, www.statenisland-museum.org, a museum offering tours and cultural events, and the Noble Maritime Collection, 718-447-6490, www.noblemaritime.org.

Transportation—Train: The Staten Island Railway, run by the MTA, costs $2.50 one way and provides service between the St. George Ferry Terminal and Tottenville at the southern tip of the 13.9-mile-long island. The second stop, Tompkinsville Station, is used for Bay Street Landing. Call 718-330-1234 for information.

Transportation—Bus: Local buses cost $2.50 one way. Express buses to Manhattan via the Verrazano-Narrows Bridge and Brooklyn Battery Tunnel cost $6 one way. Call 718-330-1234, www.mta.info, for bus information.

Transportation—Ferry: Free passenger ferries run every 15 or 20 minutes during rush hours, every half hour at other times, every hour from 11 p.m. to 6 a.m. Service is less frequent on holidays and weekends. Car service has been suspended on the ferry since September 11th, 2001. Call 718-330-1234 or visit www.siferry.com, for information.

STAPLETON

Boundaries and Contiguous Areas: North: Victory Boulevard and St. George; **East**: Bay Street and Upper New York Bay; **South**: Canal and Broad streets; **West**: Louis Street, Van Duzer Street, and Grymes Hill

Bordering Bay Street, Stapleton boasts a batch of more-collectibles-than-antiques stores and a few somewhat upscale watering holes. These cafés, tarted up with Tiffany style lamps, polished brass, and old-fashioned bottle vases, point to the presence of newcomers in Stapleton's craggy hills, though the area still has a slightly edgy, grungy feel, a sure sign of gentrification on the way.

And with good reason: Stapleton can be summed up by "location, location, location." Just two subway stops from the ferry terminal, Stapleton tends to attract artists and young families looking for a third bedroom. More recently, it has played

its siren song for bankers and stockbrokers from Lower Manhattan who want to invest some of their hard-earned money in land they can own. There's also a considerable Sri Lankan population here, and its influence is seen (and tasted) in several restaurants and businesses around the neighborhood.

Sturdy 19th-century homes characterize housing in **Stapleton Heights** and adjacent **Ward Hill**. Asphalt shingles sheath houses down on the flats near the gourmet takeout shops, the library, and handsome Tappan Park. The Mud Lane Society, a group of community boosters, promotes Stapleton with an annual house tour. An abandoned six-acre military base on the shore is slated by the city for redevelopment into a 360-unit mix of retail and residential with a seaside walkway, although nothing has yet to materialize.

The area, still quaint and serene, has seen some modest growth on Beach and Van Duzer Streets, though owners of commercial spaces are starting to adjust market rental rates for their storefronts, so there's been considerable business turn-over here as one business loses its lease and is replaced by another daring enough to make a go of it.

Websites: www.statenislandusa.com, www.si-web.com, www.silive.com, www. preservestatenisland.org, www.prodigalborough.com, www.nyc.gov

Area Codes: 718, 347

Post Offices: Stapleton Station, 160 Tompkins Ave; Rosebank Station, 567 Tompkins Ave

Zip Code: 10301

Police Precinct: One Hundred Twentieth, 78 Richmond Terr, 718-876-8500

Emergency Hospital (nearest): Staten Island University Hospital, 475 Seaview Ave, 718-226-9000, www.siuh.edu

Library: Stapleton Branch, 132 Canal St, 718-727-0427, www.nypl.org

Public School Education: School District #31 in region 7 (see **St. George**)

Adult Education (nearby): St. John's University, 300 Howard Ave, 718-390-4500, www.stjohns.edu

Community Resources (nearby): the Jacques Marchais Center of Tibetan Art houses Tibetan monastery artifacts at 338 Lighthouse Ave in Richmondtown, 718-987-3500, www.tibetanmuseum.org; the Richmondtown Restoration, a historic village comprised of 15 buildings operated by the Staten Island Historical Society at 441 Clarke Ave, 718-351-1611, www.historicrichmondtown.org; The Conference House, a pre-Revolutionary manor house, at 298 Satterlee St, 718-984-6046, www.theconferencehouse.org; Alice Austen House Museum and Garden, 2 Hylan Blvd, 718-816-4506, www.aliceausten.org

Transportation—Bus: #74/#76/#51 travel Bay St as far as Canal; the #78 runs along Van Duzer St and St. Paul's Ave in Stapleton Heights (details under **St. George**); www.mta.info

Transportation—Train: the Stapleton Station is the third stop on the SIR train (details under **St. George**); www.mta.info

GRYMES HILL AND SILVER LAKE

Boundaries and Contiguous Areas: North: Louis Avenue; **East**: Stapleton, Van Duzer Street, and Richmond Road; **South**: Clove Road and the Staten Island Expressway; **West**: Victory Boulevard

On blustery autumn days, salty sea breezes rattle maple and birch branches, garnishing **Grymes Hill** with russet leaves. Save for the outline of Wall Street's mist-shrouded skyline, the place feels much more like Westchester. Interspersed with narrow blacktop lanes and imposing old houses, the hills of Staten Island radiate a rustic sub-urbanity.

The higher you climb any one of the island's myriad hills, the more imposing the homes become. Four-hundred-foot-high **Todt Hill**, the tallest of Staten Island's peaks, is the toniest. Grymes Hill, nearer the ferry terminal, is the most intellectual: St. John's University and Wagner College cluster its slopes; the College of Staten Island lies in an adjacent valley, and the girl-only Notre Dame Academy occupies nine acres

on the edge of town. Though 12-story Sunrise Tower is a co-op, there are 475 two-
and three-bedroom rental apartments in the Grymes Hill Apartments Complex, built
by Donald Trump's father in the 1940s. In addition, rental apartments can be found in
remodeled one-family homes and underneath it all is an old series of caves used to
make beer during the Prohibition (now, alas, sealed up by a developer).

Silver Lake combines with Clove Lakes Park to form a sylvan greenbelt. There
are tennis courts, bridle paths, an ice skating rink, and a municipal golf course laid
out around the reservoir, and between Clove Road and Broadway a small, accessible zoo with a first-rate reptile collection.

Websites: www.statenislandusa.com, www.silive.com, www.nyc.gov
Area Codes: 718, 347
Post Offices: St. George Station, 45 Bay St; Stapleton Station, 160 Tompkins Ave
Zip Codes: 10301, 10304
Police Precinct: 120th, 78 Richmond Terrace, 718-876-8500
Emergency Hospitals (nearest): Staten Island University Hospital, 475 Seaview
      Ave, 718-226-9000, www.siuh.edu
Library (nearest): Stapleton Branch, 132 Canal St, 718-727-0427, www.nypl.org
Public School Education: School District #31 in region 7 (see **St. George**)
Adult Education: College of Staten Island, 2800 Victory Blvd, 718-982-2000; St. John's
      University, 300 Howard Ave, 718-390-4500, www.stjohns.edu; Wagner College,
      1 Campus Rd, near Howard Ave, 718-390-3100, www.wagner.edu; Notre Dame
      Academy, 76 Howard Ave, 718-273-9096, www.notredameacademy.org
Community Resources: Staten Island Zoo, 614 Broadway, 718-442-3100, www.
      statenislandzoo.org (also see **Stapleton**)
Transportation—Bus: #74 traverses Van Duzer St along the base of Grymes Hill;
      the #61/#62/#66/#67 traveling Victory Blvd connect with the #60 shuttle bus
      at Clove Rd; the shuttle follows Howard Ave as far as the St. John campus (de-
      tails under **St. George**); www.mta.info
Transportation—Train: A steep climb is required to reach Grymes Hill from Staple-
      ton, the nearest stop on the SIR line (details under **St. George**); www.mta.info

LIVINGSTON

Boundaries and Contiguous Areas: North: the Kill Van Kull; **East:** the Snug
Harbor Cultural Center; **South:** Henderson Avenue; **West:** Bement Avenue

In fast-growing Staten Island, underdevelopment is a matter of some pride. This is
readily apparent in Livingston, just a few miles west of bustling St. George on the
North Shore in what is part of West New Brighton. Once an important stop on the
Underground Railroad, the town, then called Elliotsville, was home to several
prominent families, including that of Robert Gould Shaw, brought to modern-day
fame by the film *Glory* as the leader of the first black regiment in the Civil War. The

name Livingston came with the construction of a now-defunct railway station at Richmond Terrace and Bard Avenue, which was called Livingston Station, though no one knows why (no one knew then, either).

Livingston retains the wide streets and airy colonial homes of its auspicious history, and a great number of majestic elm and oak trees shade the sidewalks. The population of roughly 3,500 people is made up primarily of middle-class families that deeply appreciate the town's quiet, private feel, and take full advantage of the commercial options more readily available in nearby St. George.

Walker Park, near the north end of Bard Avenue, contains a number of tennis courts, and is home to the Staten Island Cricket Club; nearby Snug Harbor contains a wide array of activities (see **St. George**). For the privacy to be found here, prices aren't bad: single-family homes, many of them built before 1900, range between half a million and $800,000. Two-family (and less historic) homes are also available, though pricier. Rentals run about less than half the cost of Manhattan apartments, with a roomy two-bedroom costing between $1,000–2,000. A 20-minute bus ride on the S40 will place you at the ferry terminal.

- **Websites:** www.statenislandusa.com, www.silive.com, www.preservestatenisland.org, www.nyc.gov
- **Area Codes:** 718, 347
- **Post Office:** West New Brighton Station, 1015 Castleton Ave
- **Zip Code:** 10310
- **Police Precinct:** One hundred twentieth, 78 Richmond Terr, 718-876-8500
- **Emergency Hospitals (nearest):** Staten Island University Hospital, 475 Seaview Ave, 718-226-9000, www.siuh.edu mc.org
- **Library (nearest):** West New Brighton Branch, 976 Castleton Ave at North Burgher Ave, 718-442-1416, www.nypl.org
- **Public School Education:** School District #31 in region 7 (see **St. George**)
- **Adult Education:** St. John's University, 300 Howard Ave, 718-390-4545, www.stjohns.edu; Wagner College, 631 Howard Ave, 718-390-3100, www.wagner.edu

- **Community Resources:** See **St. George**
- **Transportation—Bus:** The S40 runs local along Richmond Terrace in the north and is joined by the limited-stop S90. The local S44 and limited-stop S94 run east-west along Henderson Ave. All four connect with the ferry at St. George.

YOU MIGHT ALSO WANT TO CONSIDER …

- **Port Richmond,** just south of West New Brighton on the Kill Van Kull, offers reasonably priced housing, much of it pre-war, one- and two-family homes, and a 50-minute commute by express bus or bus/ferry from Manhattan.
- **Arden Heights** is one of many South Shore neighborhoods that are being encroached upon by the rapid growth in the neighborhoods to the north. Centered on the Village Greens, one of New York's first planned urban developments, Arden Heights sports a number of homes and townhouses clustered on looped streets, which keep traffic at a minimum and ease the pain of parking suffered by other Staten Islanders. Two shopping centers, small parks, and a community center serve residents, and two Olympic-sized swimming pools lie in a 16-acre park.
- **Castleton Corners** was once called Four Corners, in reference to the intersection of Victory Boulevard and Manor Road, at the town's center. The intersection is now central to a commercial district, and the neighborhood around it, largely unaffected by the rapid growth that followed in the wake of the Verrazano-Narrows Bridge, has become upscale.
- **Grasmere** is conveniently located on the self-named stop of the Staten Island MTA line. It has an unusually bucolic feel, even for Staten Island. The key feature of this tiny community is the 15-acre Brady's Pond, said to be the only swimmable freshwater pond in New York City, complete with lifeguards, beaches, rowboats, and a bunch of irritable swans. The tiny hamlet's location near the Verrazano-Narrows Bridge makes it an excellent nest for car commuters.
- **New Dorp** is right on the express line and is filled with restaurants, yoga studios, art shops, and Victorian homes. It's also close to Cedar Grove Beach, once a private beach, now public, and sporting a brand new bike path.
- **West New Brighton** is a stable community across the Kill Van Kull from New Jersey and just southwest of the ferry. Here, Victorian houses and apartments are available alongside offerings of golf, tennis, and extensive parkland in Silver Lake Park and Clove Lakes Park, which includes the Staten Island Zoo. The Snug Harbor Cultural Center is nearby. Staten Island Chamber of Commerce, 718-727-1900, www.sichamber.com.
- **Rosebank** is located in the middle of the eastern part of the Island and claims to be where modern chewing gum was invented. This is a very quiet area with many older homes, but there are also some interesting old abandoned warehouses in the area that are in the process of being converted into residences. A cadre of hipster-friendly restaurants has emerged on Rosebank's Bay Street.

NEW JERSEY

Although the popular HBO series *The Sopranos* aired its final episode in 2007, the show's depiction of a certain kind of New Jersey lifestyle continues to exert its influence over the imaginations of people considering a move to the Garden State, as has the more recent series, *The Real Housewives of New Jersey*. Do all New Jersey women *really* have big hair? Do all Garden State residents *really* talk with that accent? And does everyone go to "The Shore" for vacation?

The realities of living in New Jersey, of course, are quite different from television, especially for the growing number of young professionals who are jumping across the Hudson River to colonize (slightly) cheaper Jersey neighborhoods, especially Hoboken, Weehawken, and Jersey City. While each of these neighborhoods, and the others we describe below, has its own attractions and identity, the Jersey side of the Hudson is typically more affordable, less frenetic, and in some ways, more family-friendly, than the New York side. You'll sacrifice certain conveniences, of course, and commuting will become a more prominent part of your daily routine, but if you want to retreat to a more residential area after spending your days in the pulsing financial and cultural capital of the world, then it's worth considering New Jersey as an option for your next address.

First, a few general tips about apartment hunting in New Jersey. Though the ever-popular craigslist does have extensive listings for North Jersey, none of the towns there yet have ranked pages of their own within the site (although there is a page for those immediately around Manhattan). Personal visits and contacting locals and brokers will yield more detailed information; many of the same brokerage firms listed in the New York City section also have listings for New Jersey. For those looking to buy, www.zillow.com is a useful resource for determining localized trends in housing costs, and for renters, www.rent.com has thorough and detailed New Jersey listings. Finally, the state government operates a 211 phone service that helps residents connect with all its departments, as well as answer questions about what services are available.

FORT LEE AND EDGEWATER

Boundaries and Contiguous Areas: North: Englewood and Englewood Cliffs; **East**: Hudson River; **South**: Cliffside Park and West New York; **West**: Leonia and Palisades Park

Apartment towers in **Fort Lee** ride the Palisades above the Hudson like so many schooner masts making their way up the river. Beneath the rocky cliffs sits the small community of Edgewater, where George Washington and his Continental Army landed in November of 1776, after the battle of Washington Heights. General Charles Lee had supervised the fortifications on the site that bears his name, and their remnants are still to be found there. Fort Lee remained a sleepy little

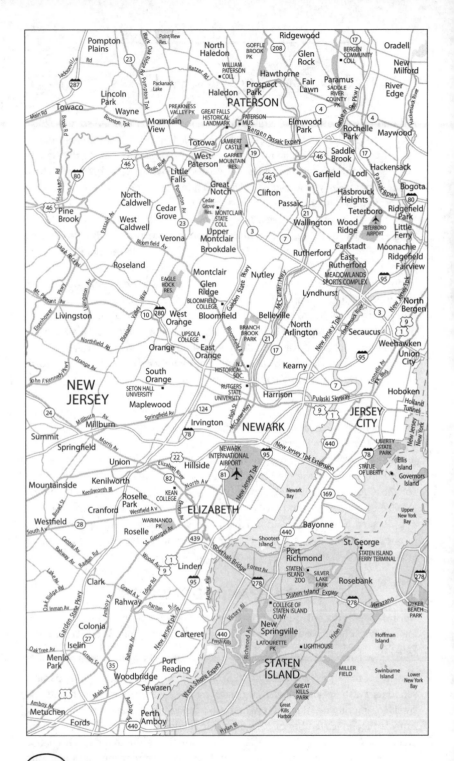

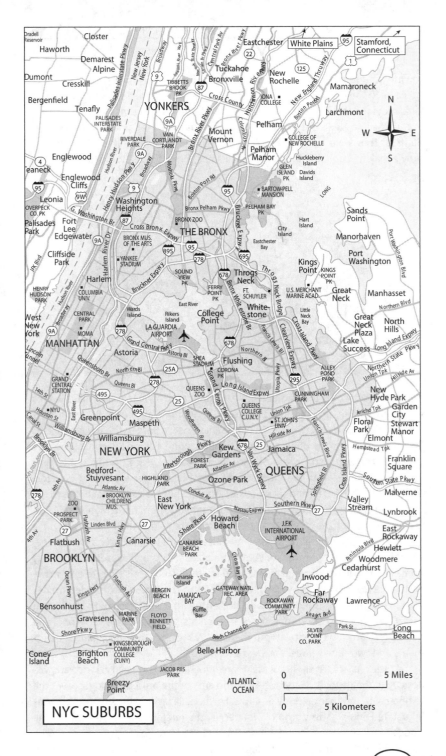

NYC SUBURBS

town with a ferry landing throughout most of the 19th century. Civil War gun-boats used the volcanically formed Palisades for target practice, and these same cliffs provided the Belgian paving stones for the streets of Manhattan.

In the late 1800s a series of resorts and amusement centers flourished on The Bluffs, as they were known, only to dwindle away and be reborn as the country's movie making capital in the 1920s. For a while, every major studio had lots here,

only to get scared by the unpredictable weather and move to California. The area went into decline until the completion of the George Washington Bridge in 1931 gave Fort Lee a suburban future. The tallest high-rise in Bergen County rose in Fort Lee in 1972 and such buildings grew rapidly along Palisade Avenue. Fort Lee straddles the approach to the bridge—which can produce horrific traffic jams during rush hours—but the most sought-after housing lies south of the bridge. An estimated 80% of its approximately 35,000 inhabitants commute to jobs in the city, largely by Jersey Transit to the Port Authority Bus Terminal in Manhattan. Fort Lee also has a large immigrant community; many of its members are Korean.

Fort Lee has maintained a small-town feel, despite its having grown faster—and taller—than it could plan for. Along the quiet streets off Palisade Avenue, tidy homes nearly fill their lovingly manicured postage-stamp lots (they're expensive, nonetheless). It's the view—Manhattan afloat on the Hudson—that determines the price of real estate and rentals. Apartments with a view fetch near-Manhattan prices, whether they are co-ops, condos, or rentals, but you use the same pool and health club at a lower rent without the view. Away from the edge, garden apart-ments and two-family houses are less expensive.

At the eastern, river end of Main Street in 33-acre Fort Lee Historic Park, vis-itors trace the Revolutionary history of the area in the museum and discover the remnants of Continental Army dugouts. The park lies within the greater Palisades Interstate Park, a narrow strip of wooded land stretching for miles between the Hudson and the Palisades Interstate Parkway, with marinas, picnic areas, and a scenic drive. Known to few outside the immediate area, the park constitutes an extraordinary recreation asset for residents of Fort Lee and Edgewater. For the extremely energetic, this is also the starting point for The Long Path, a 350+-mile hiking trail that goes all the way to Albany.

Main Street winds down the steep hill into River Road in **Edgewater**, one of the more unusual small towns in New Jersey. A blue-collar pocket only three streets wide, Edgewater hunches under the Palisades along steep, narrow streets, some of whose modest houses have recently been replaced by clutches of tidy condos. There's a somewhat funky feel to the town.

Construction of upscale, high- and low-rise condo and rental developments along the river side of River Road has brought a wave of affluent young professionals, and change, to Edgewater and the adjoining riverside towns directly to the south: North Bergen, West New York, and Weehawken (see below). Sprawling handsomely at water's edge, or suspended over it on piles, housing complexes with aquatic names such as Admiral's Walk, Mariner's Cove, and Jacob's Ferry offer all the amenities—tennis, pool, health club—and the view, at a price. Clustered about are cinemas, a supermarket, restaurants, and hotels; and Mitsuwa, a Japanese mall complete with a Japanese supermarket, restaurant, and specialty shops, attracts shoppers from throughout the tri-state area. Interspersed helter-skelter among these waterside centers are the occasional industrial site, a golf driving range, a tennis club, and marinas.

Edgewater is growing, with rental and condo projects proliferating, along with retail space and now a cineplex. Office complexes are being carved out of abandoned industrial sites. And with this critical mass, the megastores—Bed, Bath & Beyond, Barnes & Noble, Staples, etc.—have ventured in; Starbucks, too.

Although there is free commuter bus service to Edgewater Ferry Landing, a car is a necessity here in the relative isolation of Edgewater's narrow, winding River Road. It's advisable to drive around first to determine your proximity to the part of the city in which you work, as the commute to lower Manhattan can be longer than the view might suggest.

Websites: www.bergennow.com, www.fortleenj.org, www.edgewaternj.org
Area Code: 201
Post Offices: Main Branch, 229 Main St; Palisade Station, 1213 Anderson Ave, Fort Lee; Edgewater Station, 770 River Rd, Edgewater
Zip Codes: Fort Lee, 07024; Edgewater, 07020
Police Stations: Fort Lee Police Station, 1327 16th St, Fort Lee, 201-592-3700; Edgewater Police Station, 916 River Rd, Edgewater, 201-943-2200
Emergency Hospitals: Englewood Hospital and Medical Center, 350 Engle St, Englewood, 201-894-3000, www.englewoodhospital.com; Palisades Medical Center, 7600 River Rd, North Bergen, 201-854-5000, www.palisadesmedical.org
Libraries: Fort Lee Free Public Library, 320 Main St, 201-592-3615; Edgewater Free Public Library, 49 Hudson Ave, 201-224-6144; www.bccls.org

Public School Education: Fort Lee School District, 2175 Lemoine Ave, Fort Lee, 201-585-4612, www.fortlee-boe.net; Edgewater Park Township School District, 25 Washington Ave, Edgewater Park, 609-877-2124, www.edgewaterparksd.org

Transportation—Bus: Call New Jersey Transit, 800-772-2287), for routes and schedules, or pick up same at the Port Authority Bus Terminal at Eighth Ave and 41st St in Manhattan. You can also go to www.njtransit.com.

Transportation—Ferry: Commuter-hour ferries run every half-hour from the piers at 983 River Rd to W 39th in midtown, with a bus to Port Authority.

WEEHAWKEN

Boundaries and Contiguous Areas: North: West New York; **East**: Hudson River; **South**: Union City and Hoboken; **West**: Union City

Most housing secrets outside of Manhattan's madness are closely held and zealously guarded. Inevitably they are discovered and development follows, along with rising property values. Weehawken, once a tiny little town along the Hudson River, is no exception. It can be roughly divided into three areas: **Boulevard East**, up above the Palisades, where multi-million-dollar homes share spectacular sweeping

views of the Manhattan skyline, just across from midtown; **The Heights**, on the south side of the entrance to the Lincoln Tunnel (which provides rapid access to the city, when traffic is light); and the **Waterfront**, which has seen the most vigorous development.

The Dutch bought this site in the 17th century from the Lenni-Lenape Indians and modified its Indian name to suit Dutch tongues. Little had changed in 1804, when Aaron Burr killed Alexander Hamilton in a duel on a grassy plot near the shore here. Shipyards and industry along the shoreline came later, and with them, the mansions on the Heights. Frame, brick, and brownstone row houses were built along the side streets heading west from the cliffs and remain the chief source of prime housing in Weehawken. Most prized are houses in the tiny Bluffs section just south of Hamilton Park.

Rentals are primarily limited to one- and two-bedroom apartments that go for rates roughly two-thirds of comparable Manhattan spaces. Co-ops and luxury condos can easily exceed half a million dollars. Cars are owned by many residents, and parking is not good. As for nightlife, there's a constantly growing supply of restaurants and bars, but with Manhattan only a quick bus/boat/train ride away, most of the action is still heading to the city. Cabs across the river are always expensive, no matter which direction you travel.

Over the past decade or so, Weehawken's housing stock has increased by leaps and bounds, thanks to a series of massive developments along the shoreline. Among them is Henley on Hudson, a luxury condominium complex with every possible amenity and units whose price points start at $741,000. Literally right on the river and a quick walk from the ferry stop, it's a commuter's dream: private piers, riverside restaurants and gyms, immaculately manicured parks for the kids. It's also generated a fair amount of objections from long-time residents fearful of losing their river views.

Environmentally concerned residents should also be aware that much of this area was contaminated with hexavalent chromium, a carcinogen, the worst of which has been removed and the rest "capped" with topsoil and plastic sheeting.

NY Waterway offers continuous ferry service to Manhattan with connecting van service to midtown and the Wall Street area. (Two area ports also send ferries on 17-minute trips to destinations in lower and midtown Manhattan.) The Hudson-Bergen Light Rail also connects Weehawken with several other cities in North Jersey. There's also the Hudson River Walkway, which runs nearly 20 miles from Jersey's City's Exchange Place north to the George Washington Bridge. Though not all sections of the walkway are complete as of this writing, the Weehawken section is finished and is a lovely place for gentle exercise or for taking photographs and just enjoying the view (www.hudsonriverwaterfront.org).

Many Weehawken properties are handled by Hoboken real estate brokers or by their owners. Check the ads in the *Jersey Journal* (see **Jersey City**). Many of the same websites mentioned for finding rentals in Manhattan also include a section of listings for Weehawken and other New Jersey cities, including www.trulia.com.

Website: www.weehawken-nj.us

Area Codes: 201, 973

Post Office: Weehawken Substation, 4100 Park Ave, Suite 9

Zip Codes: 07086, 07087

Police Station: 400 Park Ave, 201-863-7800

Emergency Hospital (nearest): Palisades Medical Center, 7600 River Rd, North Bergen, 201-854-5000, www.palisadesmedical.org

Library: Weehawken Free Public Library, 49 Hauxhurst Ave, 201-863-7823, www.weehawken-nj.us/library.html

Public School Education: Weehawken Board of Education, 53 Liberty Pl, 201-422-6130, www.weehawken.k12.nj.us

Transportation—Bus: Mini-buses continuously troll Boulevard East for passengers to the Port Authority Bus Terminal in Manhattan weekdays, less frequently on weekends. New Jersey Transit service is also 10 minutes to the terminal; call 800-772-2287 for routes and schedules, or pick up same at the Port Authority Bus Terminal, Eighth Ave and 41st St in Manhattan. You can also go to www.njtransit.com.

Transportation—Ferry: Service by NY Waterway between Port Imperial and Lincoln Harbor to midtown and lower Manhattan runs every 15 to 30 minutes on weekdays from 6 a.m. to 10 p.m. with a slightly different hourly schedule on weekends. Free shuttle buses work the main streets during rush hour. Call 800-533-3779 for information or go to www.nywaterway.com.

HOBOKEN

Boundaries and Contiguous Areas: North: Weehawken; **East**: Hudson River; **South**: Jersey City; **West**: Croxton

At the turn of the millennium, Hoboken was reinventing itself. Most of this tidy, small (population 52,000) "Mile Square City" sandwiched between the Hudson River and Jersey bluffs was built between 1860 and 1910. By 1900, Hoboken was famous as the first American port of call for tens of thousands of immigrants, many of whom stayed close by, finding jobs in the city's numerous light manufacturing plants. Industrious working- and middle-class citizens built the simple, unadorned brownstone and brick row houses that comprise most of Hoboken's real estate. These large families pushed Hoboken's population to 70,000 at its peak.

The patrician Stevens family, who bought what was to become Hoboken soon after the Revolution, lived in relative isolation and splendor in what is now the Stevens Institute of Technology.

Laid out in a grid that encompasses several pleasant, leafy squares, much

of Hoboken retains a comfortable blue-collar feel. However, there is an increasingly massive presence of Manhattan refugees who are content to gaze back at the Big Apple's skyline visually afloat on the river, gleaming in the afternoon sun and ablaze with lights at night. It began in the early 1970s when a tide of disaffected New Yorkers, many of them singles, were attracted to this community just ten minutes from Manhattan by PATH train. Artists and rock musicians, as well as young professionals, discovered Hoboken, and the row house renovations, the cafés, interesting shops, and galleries dotting the original downtown and Washington Street neighborhoods show it. Where homesteaders pioneer, serious developers almost always follow. Certainly, the conversion to condos of tenement blocks along Monroe, Adams, and the other "presidential" streets west of Washington, as well as the Curling Club, the Hudson Tea, and Hudson Park complexes, among other luxury rental developments on once-industrial land in the northwest quadrant, bear witness to that fact. To the south, brownstone lofts and luxury single-family brownstones occupy formerly "undesirable" streets.

The latest and most valuable development is of the city's mile-long waterfront. Long an industrial site that had fallen to ruin, it is now lined with ambitious high-rises—among them, The Sovereign and The Berkshire—in The Shipyard area, or the Vanguard, with indoor and outdoor children's play areas, a fitness center, easy access to the riverfront promenade, and a five-minute PATH train ride to Manhattan. Then there's the massive W Hotel on River Street, which is topped with multiple floors of luxury condos featuring W amenities. Good luck getting a crash pad here; at present, all the residential units are sold out, even the multimillion dollar penthouse suite.

Meeting the needs of area residents, the Hoboken Ferry plies the Hudson from two Hoboken piers to Battery Park. The main terminal, which it shares with PATH and New Jersey Transit trains, is gloriously restored to its Beaux-Arts splendor, with Tiffany glass skylights, buff limestone, and ornamental plaster. Hoboken is now connected by electric trolleys along the 34-mile Hudson-Bergen Light Rail Transit System. The award-winning system provides a clean and efficient way for passengers to commute locally or to make major connections.

Check online at www.hudsonreporter.com for rental listings, which tend to run 10% or more below comparable Manhattan dwellings. Condos are a little less than two-thirds the cost of comparable Manhattan apartments, with the median price for a home hovering around $650,000.

Websites: www.hobokennj.org, www.hudsonreporter.com/pages/hoboken, www.hobokeni.com, www.hoboken411.com

Area Codes: 201, 973, 551

Post Offices: Uptown Station, 57 W 14th St

Zip Code: 07030

Police Station: #1 Police Plaza, 106 Hudson St., 201-420-2100

Emergency Hospital: Hoboken University Medical Center, 308 Willow Ave, 201-418-1900, www.carepointhealth.org

Library: Hoboken Public Library, 500 Park Ave, 201-420-2346, www.hoboken.bccls.org

Public School Education: Hoboken Board of Education, 158 Fourth St, 201-356-300, www.hoboken.k12.nj.us

Community Resources: DeBaun Center for the Performing Arts (debaun.org; 201-216-5111) has a rotating schedule of theater, music, and spoken word performances. Call the city's cultural affair coordinator at 201-420-2207 for a schedule of performances around town. Membership in the Hoboken-North Hudson YMCA, with its tiled pool, workout rooms, and movement classes, is an inexpensive alternative to the pricey gyms proliferating here: 1301 Washington St, 201-963-4100, www.njymca.org. Even cheaper is the sand beach at 12th and Sinatra, with free kayaking during the summer.

Transportation—PATH trains: 800-234-7284, shuttle between the Hoboken Station next to the Conrail Terminal and Manhattan every 5 to 10 minutes from about 6:30 a.m. to 8:30 p.m., every 15 minutes between 8:30 p.m. and 11:45 p.m. and thereafter every 30 minutes until 6:30 a.m. Weekend times vary. A direct line runs between Hoboken and West 33rd St in Manhattan, also makes stops at Christopher near Hudson St, then at 9th, 14th, and 23rd Sts, all on Sixth Ave. The fare is $2.50 one way. For more details, go to www.panynj.gov/path.

Transportation—Bus: Frequent commuter bus service on the #126 line operated by New Jersey Transit (www.njtransit.com for schedules); also provides connections from the Hoboken Terminal to Manhattan's Port Authority Bus Terminal at Eighth Ave and 42nd St.

Transportation—Ferry: Service between Hoboken station at the 14th St Pier and NJ Transit Terminal to midtown's 39th St, Pier 11 at Wall St, or the World Financial Center in Manhattan. Call 800-533-3779 for information or go to www.nywaterway.com.

JERSEY CITY

Boundaries and Contiguous Areas: North: Hoboken; **East**: Hudson River; **South**: Bayonne; **West**: Brunswick Street

Directly across the Hudson River from Lower Manhattan, New York's "sixth borough" is a small city with big-city amenities. And they all still have the sheen of the new, from the glossy financial centers to the trim apartment towers rimming the Hudson, to the high-tech trolleys gliding between them. A resurgent economy in the late 1990s accelerated the expansion of relatively inexpensive commercial office space and rapidly proliferating housing to add to the city's stock of 19th-century brick and brownstone townhouses. All this within five minutes of Manhattan. Following September 11th, 2001, nearly 20,000 displaced workers found themselves commuting to work at new locations here. Many of the relocated companies are now back in Lower Manhattan, but others have remained in Jersey City, taking advantage of local tax breaks.

New Jersey's second largest city—"settled in 1630" says the historical marker erected in **Paulus Hook**, the oldest section of town—was for the better part of three and a half centuries largely a working-class community. Like much of the area, it started slipping into decline around the turn of the 20th century and bottomed out in the 1950s and '60s, when a quarter of its now 254,000 inhabitants moved out and 10% of all jobs vanished. Then expatriate New Yorkers began buying and reclaiming townhouses in the historic districts bordering **Hamilton** and **Van Vorst Parks**. Co-ops and condominium conversions sprang up in these neighborhoods and in the adjoining Paulus Hook historic district. And once Banker's Trust leased space at the vast Harborside Financial Center, it became clear that back-office operations of large Manhattan corporations would prove a boon to the local economy.

Now, gleaming skyscrapers soar along wide boulevards that connect Harborside with **Newport Centre**, the enormous, $10-billion apartment, mall, business center, and townhouse-marina complex across the Hudson River from Manhattan's Battery Park City. Sears, JC Penney, and Macy's anchor the suburban-style shopping

mall there, which is in a special tax zone, making purchases subject to a tax of just 3% —and no tax on clothes at all. Eleven residential buildings offer luxury living on the waterfront; research current prices at www.newportrentalsnj.com. The size and energy of this project has driven development elsewhere in Jersey City.

South of Newport, the expanding **Avalon Cove** development (www.avaloncommunities.com) offers one- to four-bedroom rentals with tennis and racquetball courts, a swimming pool, and a riverfront walkway. In the historic district at the foot of **Washington Street**, the Portside offers more luxury rentals with more upscale condo palaces at Port Liberté to the south. Less expensive condo options can be found to the west at **Society Hill**.

Six wards—Greenville, West Side, Journal Square, The Heights, Downtown, and Bergen/Lafayette—each contain smaller neighborhoods like Paulus Hook. The city heart is Journal Square, a traditional business district served by a web of local buses, while electric-powered trolleys connect the river area with the ferry and PATH trains, as well as inland areas like Martin Luther King Drive and as far north as Port Imperial.

The *Jersey Journal* (www.thejerseyjournal.com) is the best source for Hoboken or Jersey City classified rental ads. In Manhattan, buy the *Journal* at newsstands at the 14th Street Downtown PATH station and outside the 33rd Street PATH station.

Website: www.cityofjerseycity.com

Area Codes: 201, 973

Post Offices: Main Branch (Downtown), 69 Montgomery St; Journal Square Station, 899 Bergen Ave; Five Corners Station, 645 Newark Ave

Zip Codes: 07302 covers the downtown area; Port Liberté, 07305; Newport, 07310

Police Station: Headquarters, 8 Erie St, 201-547-5477

Emergency Hospital: Hoboken University Medical Center, 308 Willow Ave, 201-418-1900, www.carepointhealth.org

Library: Jersey City Public Library, 472 Jersey Ave, 201-547-4526, www.jclibrary.org

Public School Education: Jersey City Board of Education, 346 Claremont Ave, Jersey City, 201-915-6000, www.jcboe.org

Adult Education: St. Peter's College, 2641 Kennedy Blvd, 201-761-6000, www.saintpeters.edu; New Jersey City University, 2039 Kennedy Blvd, 201-200-2000, www.njcu.edu; Jersey City branch of Hudson County Community College, 70 Sip Ave, 201-714-7100, www.hccc.edu

Community Resources: The Jersey City Museum, 350 Montgomery St, 201-413-0303; Liberty Science Center, 222 Jersey Center Blvd; Liberty State Park, 201-200-1000, www.lsc.org.

Transportation—PATH trains: 800-234-7284; it takes 20 minutes at most from Journal Sq or Grove St to 33rd St in Manhattan (with stops at Sixth Ave and Christopher, 9th, 14th, and 23rd streets in between); PATH trains also run to Hoboken and Newark from the Jersey City stations; go to www.panynj.gov/path for more information

Transportation—Bus: Coach USA, www.coachusa.com, operates frequent service between Jersey City and Wall St or the Port Authority Bus Terminal in Manhattan. New Jersey Transit runs multiple bus lines here (www.njtransit.com).

Transportation—Ferry: New York Waterway, 800-533-3779, www.nywaterway.com, operates passenger ferries from Paulus Hook, Liberty Harbor, and Port Liberté to midtown Manhattan, the World Financial Center and Pier 11. Check website for current fares.

ADDITIONAL SUBURBS

NEW JERSEY SUBURBS

Check www.nj.gov or www.nj.org for more about New Jersey communities.

- **Bayonne** is a working-class city of 64,000 south of Jersey City on Upper New York Bay, affordable and just 20 minutes from Jersey City and the PATH to Manhattan, thanks to the Hudson-Bergen Light Rail system; www.bayonnenj.org.
- **Cliffside Park**, on the Palisades just south of Fort Lee, is an affordable family neighborhood of 25,000 with an ethnically mixed population; www.cliffsideparknj.gov.
- **Englewood** is cosmopolitan with its ethnically diverse population and housing that ranges from low-income to redone turn-of-the-century estates. Traditionally home to affluent business executives, it features good shopping and restaurants and a 30-minute bus commute to Manhattan; www.cityofenglewood.org.
- **Franklin Township**, a 46-square-mile municipality, is only an hour from NYC and boasts the only primeval old-growth forest in the state, as well as a network of old canals, miles of country roads, an excellent public school district, and some of the lowest home prices in the area; www.franklintwpnj.org.
- **Leonia** is west of Fort Lee but less glitzy and not as high-rise; middle-class with a significant Korean population and a village-like feel. Proximity to George Washington Bridge makes it a quick commute by bus to the city; www.leonianj.gov.
- **Montclair**, cosmopolitan and affluent, enjoys a hilly perch from which Manhattan is visible at a distance to the east. Single-family housing is shaded by towering oaks. The bus commute takes about 30 minutes; www.montclairnjusa.org.
- **Ridgewood**, a 60-minute commute northwest of the city, houses a homogeneous white-collar population of families along manicured, tree-shaded streets. Schools are excellent, taxes high, and the downtown shopping district seems to have changed little in 50 years. The Paramus malls nearby make up for that; www.ridgewoodnj.net.
- **South Orange**, with its downtown railroad station, is convenient and quaint, and one of the few places with old-fashioned gas street lights. Housing ranges from modest to upscale up the hill, and 60 acres of parkland with four town pools add to the comfort level; www.southorange.org.
- **Summit** is an affluent community of handsome homes along winding, hilly streets now just 50 minutes from Manhattan on the Midtown Direct train to Penn Station; www.cityofsummit.org.
- **Teaneck**, just west of Englewood and without the estates, is similarly hilly and tree-shaded, more middle-class, and proud of its ethnic diversity; a 30-40-minute commute; www.teanecknj.gov.
- **Tenafly**, north of Englewood and a more homogeneous suburb, boasts a nice village center clustered around the railroad station and an excellent high school; also an easy commute; www.tenaflynj.org.
- **Westfield** nestles among the rolling Watchung Hills of Union County, about an hour by bus or 50 minutes by train and PATH from midtown. A strong sense of community, a quaint downtown, excellent schools, and extensive sports and recreation activities in three county-run parks make this culturally rich old town attractive to commuters; www.westfieldnj.com.

LONG ISLAND SUBURBS

- **Garden City** was once a summer resort for the Morgans and Vanderbilts, and it's still expensive, tidy, and manicured. About 18 miles east of midtown Manhattan, it's an easy 40 minutes to Penn Station; www.gardencityny.net.
- **Great Neck**, just over the Queens border on the northern part of Long Island, is one of the jewels of the island. The quiet village sports exclusive real estate and it's only a 40-minute commute to Manhattan; www.greatneckchamber.org.
- **Manhasset** residents enjoy the option of choosing between single-family homes and condos. The former are most attractively and expensively set around Manhasset Bay in Plandome to the north. Because of the department stores along Miracle Mile, real estate taxes are low here. About 35 minutes from Manhattan on the LIRR; www.manhassetny.org.
- **Old Westbury** once housed the North Shore estates of high society and still has 25 miles of horse trails and a polo club. Besides its rolling hills, the high cost of living here gets you good schools, three colleges, and Old Westbury Gardens; www.wcpchamber.com
- **Port Washington**, formerly a glamorous summer resort on a peninsula in the Long Island Sound, is still attractive to boaters and boasts harbor events like the annual HarborFest. The 40-minute train commute is a relatively easy one; www.portwashington.org.
- **Rockville Centre** boasts an arts guild, eight parks, a thriving shopping center, and a variety of housing. But it is best known for its century-old municipal power plant, which gives its residents the cheapest electricity on the island. About 35 minutes from Manhattan by the Long Island; www.rvcny.us.

WESTCHESTER COUNTY (NY) SUBURBS

- **Bronxville**, on the city's northern border and hilly, feels rather English and looks rather Tudor. There are also co-ops and condos, quite elegant ones near the railroad station. Known for its good schools and 70 acres of parkland; www.villageofbronxville.com.
- **Dobbs Ferry**, on the Hudson just to the north and about 40 minutes by Metro North's Hudson line from the city, also offers a variety of housing possibilities and a heterogeneous population. Appealing to academics and people in the arts; www.dobbsferry.com.
- **Edgemont**, often called "Scarsdale lite," is a hamlet within the town of **Greenburgh** next to Scarsdale, but more affordable. Its good schools have attracted a growing foreign-born population, especially Japanese. Houses are traditional in style; co-ops and condos are relatively plentiful and reasonable; www.edgemontnewyork.com.
- **Mamaroneck**, which includes **Larchmont**, houses a heterogeneous population just west of tony Rye on a neck of land in Long Island Sound. You'll find

co-ops, condos, and single-family homes, with few rentals. Waterfront is what it's about, with good recreational facilities, including boating and beaches on Harbor Island Park; a 35-minute commute; www.village.mamaroneck.ny.us.

- **Mt. Kisco** sports hilly terrain, good schools, a variety of restaurants, a town park, and a shopping area featuring chain favorites. Single-family homes, several condo developments, and apartment rentals can all be found in this northern Westchester hub; www.mtkisco.com.
- **New Rochelle** was mainly settled by French Huguenots in the late 17th century. Just 32 minutes from midtown on Metro North, it is a suburban city of 72,000, with an exceptional variety of housing choices, 9 miles of shoreline, and 35 parks, including one set on its own island; www.newrochelleny.com.
- **Pelham**, just over the Bronx County line and a 20-minute train ride north from the city, is cosmopolitan and relatively unknown. Fine old trees line its winding roads, and you can walk to everything, which includes beaches, a golf course, woodland hiking, and fishing. Taxes are high; www.townofpelham.com.
- **Scarsdale**, rocky, wooded, and upscale, has few rentals or co-ops, but it does have beautiful homes along winding, wooded roads and lots of open land. Its highly competitive public schools attract a diverse population into this family-friendly neighborhood. The commute to Manhattan is about 45 minutes; www.scarsdale.com.
- **Tarrytown** is part of Sleepy Hollow (yes, *that* Sleepy Hollow) near the Tappan Zee Bridge (which leads to Rockland County) and meanders above the Hudson River. This diverse white- and blue-collar town is rich with Revolutionary War history, including a number of battle sites. The commute is 45 minutes and housing runs the gamut from single-family homes to large condominium developments; www.tarrytowngov.com.
- **White Plains**, 45 minutes from the city, offers a quick commute by train or express bus, good shopping, ethnic restaurants, a variety of housing choices, and relatively low taxes. Recreational facilities include a golf course, outdoor pools, tennis, and an ice skating rink; www.cityofwhiteplains.com.

CONNECTICUT SUBURBS

- **Greenwich** (pronounced Gren'-itch), a 55-minute train commute from the city, offers genteel seclusion for the very wealthy, along with upscale shopping and eateries, and excellent schools, beaches, and recreational facilities. Less expensive—but still pricey—than the Greenwich "backcountry" is the downtown area, which includes some more moderate rentals. Nearby **Cos Cob**, **Byram**, and **Old Greenwich** are also somewhat more affordable; www.greenwichct.org.
- **Norwalk** is a diverse community and generally less expensive than surrounding towns. Partially redeveloped, south Norwalk, with its condos, galleries, and restaurants, appeals to a young crowd, many of whom work in nearby corporate offices. Boating, fishing, beaches, tennis, and paddle tennis are also a draw,

as are its famous oysters. **Silvermine** to the west and **Rowayton** on the south-western tip are more upscale; www.norwalkct.org.

- **Stamford**, 60 minutes from Grand Central on Metro North, is a city of 125,000 with a bustling downtown on the banks of the Mill River and the Long Island Sound. Upscale housing abounds here, including sprawling estates to the north. Housing styles are varied, parks and beaches plentiful; www.ci.stamford.ct.us.

- **Westport** on Long Island Sound became a colony of artists and writers in the 1930s and it is still popular with the sophisticated set, more like New York City than the rest of Connecticut. There is a summer theater, and the arts are still a presence, as are pricey boutiques and good shopping in nearby Stamford. Water and woods, a variety of single-family homes, a few rentals and condos charac-terize the town. The train to New York takes over an hour; www.westportct.gov.

NEWCOMERS' SHOCK AT HOUSING PRICES IS NEARLY UNIVERSAL; LIVING in New York City is expensive, regardless of whether you rent or buy (and for the record, the most recent Census data indicate that 67% of New Yorkers rent). Whatever you choose to do—and moreover, whatever you can *afford* to do—finding a place to call your own here is a daunting task. Fortunately, there are dozens of websites dedicated to helping you decode the New York City real estate market, and in this book, we offer you lots of insider tips, hard won through our own experience.

The first tip? While you should always keep your eyes and ears open for a deal, you should never expect to find one. Rent continues to increase in New York; even the recent global financial crisis did little to deflate individual rents, although developers and owners complained about market sluggishness. Vacancy rates are always low—it's hard to get New Yorkers out of New York—and prices are ever-increasing. And despite the promises and commitments to affordable housing articulated by nearly every candidate running for public office here, widespread expansion of such options never seems to happen, at least not at the rate or density at which it is needed.

Whatever happens in the housing market, you will likely pay more for rent in New York City than you have ever paid before in your life, and you will likely get less in return—at least in terms of square footage. Rent prices are calculated in the thousands, not in the hundreds, even for studio apartments, while sale prices are in the millions. According to the real estate website www.trulia.com, in 2014, the average list price for homes for sale in the city exceeded $3 million and the average list price for rentals was just shy of $4,000 per month. Keep in mind that there are extreme outliers in both directions, particularly if you're considering an apartment or home in one of the outer boroughs, especially The Bronx, Staten Island, and to a lesser extent, Queens. Take advantage of special deals if they exist (particularly move-in incentives), but always read the small print and always be prepared for a lot of competition. The good news is that there is an abundance of information right at your fingertips for learning about your rights, city housing, rental, and sales laws, and apartment hunting tips. One indispensable resource is the NYC Rent Guidelines site at www.nycrgb.org. It is well worth your time to study this particular site with care, especially since the city enacted new guidelines for rent-stabilized apartments and lofts in June 2014. And if you don't know what a rent-stabilized apartment even is, then it's time for you to take a crash course in the language of NYC real estate. Again, that website is a good start. Other sites to start visiting regularly include www.streeteasy.com, www.rent.com, www.trulia.com, www.curbedny.com, and the real estate sections of www.dnainfo.com.

In Manhattan's most established neighborhoods, location doesn't influence price significantly. If cost is a serious concern, expect a long, difficult hunt—consider subletting while you look—and you should seriously consider the remoter reaches of upper Manhattan, over the bridges in Brooklyn, Queens, The Bronx, or Staten Island, or in the suburbs. Another option, especially attractive at the studio and one-bedroom level, is to purchase a condo or a co-op. At this writing, it's hard to say where mortgage rates will be, but with the income-tax deduction for mortgage interest factored in, these apartments may be less expensive than renting an equivalent space, plus you build equity. Keep in mind, however, that you will likely pay a monthly maintenance fee, and in many cases, that fee may amount to the equivalent of a rent. Some areas also have tax abatements that might ease the cost. To see what's involved in buying an apartment or a house, turn to **Buying** at the end of this chapter.

It's understandable if you've read this far and suddenly feel overwhelmed. But keep in mind: millions of people have shown up here before you, many with far fewer resources, and they've made it. And be cheered: in return for the difficulty of finding housing you get all the riches the Big Apple has to offer, both tangible and intangible, including higher earnings, incomparable cultural resources, dynamic street life, incredible social diversity, and unparalleled personal opportunity.

To compare cost of living analyses of thousands of U.S. cities, visit www.bestplaces.net. Data cover quality of life, cost of living, salary, and more information.

APARTMENT HUNTING

First, renting—with fortitude and imagination, you can find an acceptable place to live in an appropriate neighborhood. Various strategies for doing so are listed below, but let's start with some general advice:

- **Start your search a couple of months before you expect to move.** Read newspapers, talk to rental agents, keep your ears open for word of mouth leads, and scour posted "apartment for rent" signs to get an idea of which areas have the greatest turnover in rental apartments. Keep up with neighborhood price trends and other real estate developments on websites like www.ny.curbed. com and www.trulia.com.

- **Be prepared for high rents.** In the long run, it may be possible to find that charming, sun-drenched apartment in the neighborhood of your dreams for a reasonable sum, but such gems take time, contacts, more contacts, and a little luck, so brace yourself.

- **Consider once-marginal neighborhoods.** Gentrification and other development trends have transformed certain neighborhoods over the past decade or two, turning former industrial zones such as Brooklyn's Greenpoint and Williamsburg neighborhoods and Long Island City in Queens into hip 'hoods. You'll find some attractive apartments in these areas, often with more square footage and at better price points than in Manhattan, but before getting too carried away, realize that not all of the areas are suitable, depending on your needs. If multiple transportation options and a quick commute are priorities, do some test runs before signing a lease. If you prefer a bustling neighborhood, visit during the day and in the evening to make sure you feel comfortable with the number of people who are out and about. Ask residents about local services and amenities, such as grocery stores, gyms, and cultural institutions.

- **Inquire about a neighborhood.** Local police precincts (see listings under **Neighborhoods**) can supply valuable safety information about a particular neighborhood, block, or street within their boundaries. Stop by the precinct for candid and well-founded opinions about the characteristics and police problems of a particular area. Also, talk to store owners and doormen. Online tools to source this information are helpful too. The city's Crime Map, for example, provides detailed information about the incidence of offenses ranging from petty theft to murder, searchable by neighborhood and even by specific address: http://maps.nyc.gov/crime/.

- **Consider subletting or sharing to start.** If you are in desperate need of a roof and have not discovered a feasible rental, seriously consider these alternatives. Subletting is a great way to get comfortable in the city while buying yourself time to find the optimum situation in the most suitable neighborhood. And, should you find a good roommate, sharing affords companionship and a more affordable start to life in the Big Apple. Sites like www.craigslist.org have sublet listings; students and recent college graduates may want to check www.crash-dwell.com as an alternative.

- **Finally, don't despair.** Don't panic. Negativity will get you nowhere. With persistence, patience, and that quintessential New York personality trait— moxie—you'll do just fine.

Generalities out of the way, here are some practical tips for finding your space ...

ONLINE LISTINGS—APARTMENT HUNTING

The world is fast, but New York continues to move a half-step or more ahead of everywhere else, and this is most certainly the case when it comes to finding a home. Real estate listings are often posted and removed on the same day from many of the online sites that provide them. Of these sites, **Craigslist** (newyork.craigslist.org) remains among the most popular. With listings searchable by neighborhood, price range, size, and more, it isn't hard to find something that meets your criteria. The trick that follows is getting your foot in the door. Have your phone at the ready, and refresh the page of your browser frequently, as listings are posted in real time. Considering that anyone can list virtually anything on these sites, be wary of scams. Send no financial information online, and as tight as the market might be, see an apartment before you book it. **Rent.com** (www.rent.com) has plentiful listings for those hunting apartments, roommates, sublets, and more, as does **NakedApartments.com**. Another site worth checking is **StreetEasy.com**, an NYC-based service that aggregates all listings in an area and places them into the context of pricing around the neighborhood—you can even find information about apartments that recently sold or rented in the same building and how much they went for.

The *New York Times* online real estate service (www.nytimes.com/pages/realestate) provides comprehensive coverage for those looking to rent, sublet, or buy an apartment in New York City and beyond. The newish online newspaper, **DNAinfo** (www.dnainfo.com), has an entire section devoted to real estate; check "Real Estate" under its "News" heading; pay particular attention to the "Open House Agenda" column, whose reporter scouts out (relatively) affordable finds each week. The same site also has a section called "Apartmentality," which reports on housing trends in the city. **New York City Realty** (www.cityrealty.com) offers detailed listings, photos, and floor plans of houses, co-ops, condos, and apartments for rent or sale in the city. They're updated hourly. You can search by location, price range, and size, with e-mail notification as properties in your categories come online. The site includes excellent, detailed neighborhood descriptions, and application forms. The computer-challenged can call 212-755-5544 for this site's information. It may also be worth your while to visit the websites of some of the major rental agencies, such as **Citi Habitats** (www.citi-habitats.com), **Corcoran** (www.corcoran.com), **Elliman** (www.elliman.com), and **Halstead Property** (www.halstead.com), as well as large owner/management firms such as **Rockrose** (www.rockrosenyc.com) and **TF Cornerstone** (www.tfc.com). These sites are virtual data banks of each firm's entire listings. See also **No-Fee Apartments Online**, below.

NEWSPAPER CLASSIFIED ADVERTISEMENTS

Newspapers do indeed still exist, and there is still housing to be found here, as well as a lot of contextual information in the Real Estate section that can give you up-to-date tips on what's happening in the market and specific neighborhoods. Not all landlords or brokers list on craigslist.com, because of the high signal-to-noise ratio, so the local papers can be good places to look for deals other people might not be seeing. Because individual landlords, and not just brokers, place ads, classifieds sometimes are a way to avoid brokerage commissions. Chances are, however, you will end up using a broker. The classifieds provide a good way of finding one and of discovering which brokers are active in a particular neighborhood.

• The **Sunday *New York Times'* Real Estate section** is printed Friday night and delivered to dealers sometime on Saturday. The *Times* actively discourages sale of the Sunday edition before the multi-sectioned paper is completed Saturday evening. However, many outlets sell the sections they have on hand (often for full newspaper price) Saturday night. While far fewer in number, daily ads in the *Times* are also worth checking. You would also do well to check the *Times'* website, www.nytimes.com, where the Sunday ads appear before 5 a.m. Saturday morning. Updates are made daily.

• The ***Village Voice*** is a good source of rental listings for Manhattan, as well as other boroughs. Newsstand deliveries are made around 5 a.m. Wednesdays; the newsstand on the island beside the Seventh Avenue Uptown Christopher Street subway entrance at Sheridan Square is one of the first places to receive delivery. Also, you can get early copies Tuesday night at the Village newsstand on Astor/Lafayette. Easier yet, the *Voice* listings are online, www.villagevoice.com, updated at 1 p.m. Tuesday, and 12:01 a.m. Wednesday–Saturday.

• The ***Wall Street Journal's*** Friday edition lists apartments for rent in the classified section.

• The ***New York Post's*** rental classifieds are best consulted on Friday. The Friday edition is printed Thursday night and delivered to all-night newsstands in the mid-Manhattan area (try stands at Grand Central Terminal or Penn Station Thursday night around midnight). The *Post* is a particularly good source for apartments in Queens, Brooklyn, and The Bronx. The *Post's* website, www.nypost.com, is updated daily.

• ***The Daily News'*** Brooklyn and Queens editions carry numerous rental classifieds for those boroughs. Listings in the Manhattan edition are negligible, as are online listings.

• ***Newsday***, published daily in Garden City, Long Island, and available in Manhattan, is the best source of listings in Queens and Long Island. On the web at www.newsday.com.

• ***New York Press***, a somewhat offbeat free weekly, is distributed each Wednesday, and is a good source for sublets and shares. Look for it in restaurants, stores, and street boxes all over town. *Press* listings are online, www.nypress.com, at 10 a.m. Tuesday.

- *Jersey Journal*, published in Jersey City Monday–Saturday, is the paper to consult for rentals in Hoboken and Jersey City. The *Journal* can be purchased at newsstands adjoining the 14th Street and 33rd Street PATH stations in Manhattan.
- New York City neighborhood newspapers—*The Villager*, *Chelsea Clinton News*, *The Spirit* (West Side), *Our Town* (East Side), *The Flatiron News*, *Tribeca Trib*, and others—occasionally carry a handful of rental ads, but are not prime sources.

REAL ESTATE BROKERS

If you haven't already figured this out, New York City's real estate scene is dynamic, and over the past decade, numerous changes have taken place in the realm of real estate brokerage. The city's classic, powerhouse broker agencies have been joined by slick newcomers who are eager to work the burgeoning luxury market, which sees a new building added to its inventory practically every week. Another development in brokerage is the merging of smaller boutique brokers with larger ones and the diversification of specializations beyond specific neighborhoods. In the past, many brokers maintained one central office and tended to specialize in a single neighborhood or two; today they are much more likely to have outpost offices in multiple neighborhoods, even in the outer boroughs, and most brokers are able to provide guidance and recommendations about any corner of the city.

A few tips: While most brokers can deal with rentals and sales, some specialize in one or the other. If you're not in the market to buy, be sure to ask for a broker who works the rental market. Second, even though most firms now cover the entire city, many may continue to have special expertise about a particular neighborhood; ask if this is the case. Be clear about what you want—or what you think you want—from the outset. A good broker will show you apartments that fulfill your criteria and may show you some possibilities you might have overlooked.

Finally, a word about fees. Broker commissions for unfurnished apartments currently run one month's rent or 15% of one year's rent, which you pay up front, but this may vary depending on the broker, landlord, neighborhood, availability, and other factors. Get some ground rules and ask how commissions work before agreeing to work with someone. Sometimes there is no commission at all.

Recommendations for finding a real estate broker:

- Ask friends, colleagues, your firm, and family for recommendations of brokers who are particularly helpful. As previously mentioned, not all capable agents with good lists advertise widely.
- Gather names from appealing classified listings.
- Do a web search for real estate brokers in your neighborhood(s) of choice.
- If your heart is set on one locale, try some of the smaller firms whose storefronts you'll notice while pounding the pavement. These firms seldom advertise but are often good sources for listings in the immediate vicinity.

NO-FEE APARTMENTS ONLINE

You may have noticed, among the newspaper listings, ads for no-fee services, and if you're determined to avoid a broker's fee, one of these may help. Here's how they work: pay a flat fee, detail your specifications online, and receive a list of no-fee apartments being offered by management companies and private owners. Updates are daily or weekly, and you do the rest of the work. However, listings can be wrong or out-of-date. You'll find new lists advertised constantly on places like craigslist.com, but buyer beware. Here, we mention several services that may be useful:

- **Apartment Source**, www.apartmentsource.com, online only, lets you search their database for apartments according to price, size, location, and amenities, in addition to which you receive daily e-mail updates with new vacancies to meet your specifications. You may also occasionally find sublets and short-term rentals. The site also offers a credit check. You must register for a membership.
- **backpage**, www.backpage.com, is styled similarly to craigslist. The site offers listings in multiple cities, with extensive New York postings. No fee.
- **Citi Rent**, www.citirent.com, is a clearinghouse of listings from management companies. Subscribers can search apartments by price and neighborhood. Price of subscription is determined by the number of buildings to which you apply, averaging 99 cents per building.
- **craigslist**, www.newyork.craigslist.org, is a national site with NYC listings; you can search vacancies provided by area landlords, or sublets, shared housing, or temporary accommodations as posted by individuals. No fee.
- **MLX**, 212-220-4663, www.mlx.com, is a Manhattan-wide database with no-fee and fee listings. For $149, the subscriber receives an account number and a personal identification number for three months. Search specifications include desired location, apartment size, whether pets are allowed, maximum rent, etc. Members receive a list, by fax or e-mail, of all the apartments in the database fitting the requested specs, with updates on request for as long as necessary. You can change specifications to receive listings in other categories: different neighborhoods or rent limits, for example. A free membership gives access to more limited services. Included among the listings, which are updated daily, are properties handled by some 200 brokerage companies—these would involve fees. Also included: co-ops, condos, and houses for sale by owners as well as brokers and photos.

NEW BUILDINGS

Renovated factories, warehouses, and other commercial buildings are continually adding new rental units to the city's housing supply, especially in formerly industrial or mixed-use neighborhoods such as Long Island City in Queens and Greenpoint in Brooklyn. Apartments in reconstructed or totally new buildings command top dollar. However, it is often possible to avoid brokers' commissions in these buildings when landlords and managers pay on-site rental agents to fill the buildings as quickly as possible. You'll need to have the inside track to get on these buildings' short lists. Be sure to check that the unit is zoned for residential space as you may be denied renter's insurance if you live in a non-residentially zoned building, and in rare cases, especially in Brooklyn, people have been evicted if the building is not kept up to code (or reasonably up to code).

DIRECT ACTION

In a city where single-minded apartment hunters have been known to read the obituary columns with as much intensity as the real estate classifieds, no one need feel self-conscious about approaching landlords, managing agents, superintendents, or local merchants in order to locate a place in a particular neighborhood or building.

Additional strategies include:

- **Call the managing agent of a building that interests you.** The firm's or agent's name is usually posted near a building's entrance. If no telephone number is given, check online. If no vacancies are available, ask if you can be notified of future openings, whether by phone or email.
- **Speak with the superintendent directly.** To find him, check the building directory, buzzer listings, or in the case of the smaller brownstones with shared part-time supers, your man could be the person sweeping the steps or putting garbage cans out on the sidewalk. If an apartment is available, the super or manager will sometimes send you to a broker to gain access. If a vacant apartment is found through independent efforts, you are not liable for the broker's fee. However, since reasonable apartments are in short supply, need usually overrides the fine points of the legal situation; most people prefer to pay the commission rather than go without the apartment. Once secure in your nest, if you want redress, you can file a complaint with the Division of Licenses, New York Department of State, 123 Williams St, 19th Floor, NYC 10007, 212-417-5747, www.dos.ny.gov/licensing/. This might eventually result in a settlement.
- **Pavement pounding**, accompanied by incessant querying of merchants, stoop sitters, dog walkers, letter carriers—indeed, anyone who looks like a resident of the neighborhood—can also yield results. Some hunters go building to building and strike up conversations with doormen.
- **Driving around** in the boroughs can give you the feel of a neighborhood (in Manhattan, walking is easier). You will likely see some rental signs on buildings. Take down phone numbers even if it is not a building or an area you are interested in. You never know what other buildings that rental agent or landlord can recommend.

WORD OF MOUTH

The grapevine approach—broadcasting your need through a network of local friends—is often an effective means to a desired apartment and certainly to a sublet or share that may get you into town and buy you several more months of happy hunting. However, when you're new to town the chances of having such a network are usually slim. Nonetheless, use any contacts available. Parents can call old college chums; who knows, their son or daughter may be leaving a desirable place? In any case, personal contacts are often a shot at the type of high-demand apartment that never makes it as far as the *Times* or a broker's office. In sublet situations, check to make sure the lease allows the tenant to sublet.

BULLETIN BOARDS AND BUS SHELTERS

Keep your eyes open for bulletin boards at independent bookstores, cafés, the occasional supermarket, the library, and the community and campus life centers in and around college and university campuses; though these are dwindling in the digital age, they can still yield some useful leads during your apartment search. You'll also find flyers advertising apartment vacancies on bus shelters near university campuses, especially on the Upper West Side near Columbia, where sublets will be promoted amidst flyers for language learning partners, dog walkers, and clinical research trial volunteers. Make note of the ad's details and follow up by phone or email, as indicated on the flyer.

INTERNAL COMMUNICATIONS

Many corporations and organizations publish newsletters, magazines, or e-mail bulletins for their personnel that print employee advertisements. Sublets and the occasional rental turn up in these columns, and it is worth asking friends who work for these entities to check the in-house publication for leads.

COLLEGE-RELATED ASSOCIATIONS

Some New York alumni associations try to address the difficulty graduates have settling or relocating in the city. Contact your alumni office or local group to see if they can help. Some university clubs also offer advice and an occasional lead. Alumni magazines and newsletters and Internet academic discussion groups may also offer sublet opportunities.

EMPLOYERS AND RELOCATION FIRMS

Frequently, large companies pay for the services of relocation firms to find suitable long- and short-term apartment rentals for their mid- and upper-level hires and to help solve the various problems associated with moving and settling in. The fortunate employee is saved money and headaches in the bargain. Presumably, the company you are working for will inform you if it is prepared to offer help with your search for living quarters; of course, it never hurts to ask what relocation benefits will or can be provided. Sometimes, you will be given a relocation stipend; in other situations, you may pay your expenses up-front and then be reimbursed. Either way, be sure to keep receipts of all moving-related expenses.

SUBLETS AND SHORT-TERM FURNISHED RENTALS

The majority of sublets are posted online. Craigslist (www.craigslist.org) dominates, but there are other major sites; refer to the ones listed at the beginning of our neighborhood descriptions—many have classified sections. Numerous brokers also offer long-term sublets, furnished and unfurnished, and advertise them, together with regular rentals, in local newspapers and online; expect to pay a broker's fee. You may also find an un-brokered sublet offered among the classifieds by the owner or lessee. In recent years, ads have proliferated for short-term furnished rentals without broker fees but at higher rental rates; these are not sublets, but are specifically marketed as short-term furnished rentals. Consider either of these useful interim measures, providing the time needed to discover the optimum rental apartment. Note: leaseholders of rent-stabilized or exceptionally reasonable apartments have been known to ask for fixture fees or key money in a sublet situation. While some people do pour money and energy into rehabilitating an inexpensive rental apartment and may deserve compensation for their efforts when they move, fixture fees that reflect no real value are tantamount to key money, which is illegal.

Prime sources for sublets and short-term furnished rentals include:

- **craigslist**, www.craigslist.org, is typically the first site consulted for sublets and short-term furnished rentals. Check out the sublet/shared housing section for all manner of offers. Move quickly, though—it's a popular site, and even 24 hours after a posting may be too late.
- The **New York Times**, which lists sublets under "Apartments—Furnished" and "Apartments—Unfurnished," www.nytimes.com.
- **Brokers**: a number of sublet specialists advertise in *The New York Times*. Typically, commissions on furnished rentals run between one-half and one whole month's rent for periods of less than nine months. Most agencies charge 15% for longer sublets. Here are some brokers and services currently specializing in sublets:
  - » **Apartment Placement Services**, 575 Lexington Ave, 4th Flr, 212-572-9609, specializes in short-term furnished sublets and unfurnished prime lease rentals for a fee; also places young professionals in shared apartments throughout the city. Call for an appointment.

- » **New York Habitat**, 307 Seventh Ave, Ste, 306, 212-255-8018, www.nyhabitat. com; specializes in sublets, short-term and long-term rentals, a no-fee service.
- » **Douglas Elliman Rental and Relocation Division**, 212-645-4040, www. elliman.com.
- **Bulletin boards** in large buildings, bars, or other neighborhood locations. Large apartment complexes have waiting lists for rental apartments the proverbial block long. However, leaseholders arrange sublets directly and occasionally post notices on community bulletin boards. Check with the management of these big units to see if they have a central sublet source.
- **In-house publications** tend to be a better source of sublets than of rentals.

SHARING

One of the best solutions to high housing costs, particularly for young, single people, is an apartment-share. But if you are just arriving in the city and don't know anyone, you may not have anyone to share with. If networking with old college buddies fails to turn up anything, your best bet is probably the newspapers or a roommate-finding service.

The majority of shares are offered online. Definitely refer to the sites listed at the beginning of our neighborhood descriptions—many have classified sections. You should also check the *Times* ads under "Apartments to Share." Some leaseholders prefer to have roommates pre-screened and list with agencies that arrange apartment shares for a flat fee up front. Reputations ebb and flow; we can't guarantee satisfaction. But if you want to investigate this option, you might try:

- **New York Habitat**, 212-255-8018, www.nyhabitat.com; this firm, which also handles sublets and rentals, charges the renter only when he/she agrees to rent an apartment share. The fee, a minimum of 30% of one month's rent, maximum of 15% of one year's rent, is based on length of stay.

Extremely popular is the national service, craigslist, which features a wide range of roommate listings for numerous cities. The New York section includes a wealth of room shares with price and location. Click on the individual listing for more details. Then, through e-mail or in some cases by phone, you'll contact the individual. Craigslist also has extensive listings of apartments for rent. Keep in mind that anyone can post on craigslist (meaning ads are not screened, only categorized), so use caution when following up on leads. It's always a good idea to first meet with a prospective roommate or the person you will be subletting from in a public space, and bring along a friend to view the apartment.

Other, newer online roommate sharing and matching services include Crashdwell, www.crashdwell.com, and Spareroom, www.spareroom.com.

CHECKING IT OUT

You've found what appears to be the perfect, sunny apartment in a pleasant neighborhood, and best of all, you're the first person to see it! You want to shout, "I'll take it," but you should restrain yourself and spend a few minutes looking it over first. We suggest you bring a checklist of your musts and must-nots. In addition, you should make a quick inspection to make sure the apartment's beauty is not just skin deep. A little time and a few questions asked now can save you a lot of time, money, and headache later. Specifically, you may want to look for the following:

- Are the kitchen appliances clean and in working order? Do the stove's burners work? What about the oven? Is there enough counter and shelf space? Does it smell funny in the kitchen space—or anywhere else? Does the refrigerator work?
- Do the windows open, close, and lock? Do they open onto a noisy or potentially dangerous area?
- Are there enough closets and sufficient storage space?
- Are there enough electrical outlets for all your needs? Do the outlets work?
- Are laundry facilities in the building or nearby?
- When was the apartment last painted? Was the paint lead-free? In the event you will stay longer than a year, who is responsible for painting the apartment?
- Do the bathroom fixtures work? Look for leaks under pipes.
- Is there a bug problem in the building? Look in the kitchen cabinets.
- Is the building wired for cable TV service? If not, what, if any, reception is there without cable, and can you have direct or satellite television installed?
- Is the superintendent easily accessible? Ask neighbors about the building staff. Are they helpful, trustworthy, competent, available?
- What about building security and cleanliness: check the building entry, lobby, and public areas.
- If you own a car, what is the parking situation like? Is there a long waiting list for garage space? What fee is charged for parking, or is it included as an amenity?
- Do you feel comfortable in the area? Will you feel safe here at night?
- Are public transportation and shopping nearby?
- How close are the nearest emergency hospital and police precinct?

Also, try to visit apartments during non-business hours when more people are home to get a feel for how noisy a unit will be. This will also give you a feel for the comings and goings of the building, specifically: is the front entrance locked, and is there a 24-hour doorman? Many New York apartments have astonishingly thin walls and floors so that even reasonable neighbors can be a real presence. If this might bother you, ask what the floors are made of—if it's just wood and sheet metal you should expect to hear everything your neighbors are up to. NYC government sites are excellent resources that provide information allowing you to get a sense of the neighborhood and particular building. The site http://maps. nyc.gov/doitt/nycitymap/ gives extremely detailed and up-to-date info on any building, ranging from the number of noise complaints filed by its residents, to rodent infestations to gang activity, as well as general information on nearby food programs and special education facilities. If you're drawn to an apartment because of its light and surrounding space, you might want to visit www.nyc.gov/ html/dof/html/jump/acris.shtml to find out the last time that vacant lot next to the window changed hands—there's nothing like moving into a new place and spending the next year listening to construction ten feet away.

If it all passes muster, be prepared to stake your claim without delay.

STAKING A CLAIM

It may seem to newcomers that securing an apartment, after having found one suitable, can be as difficult as gaining membership in an exclusive club. In a tight market, that's not far off the mark. You have to be found acceptable. For starters, arrive on time and be presentably dressed for appointments. Even in this city of "attitude," a little politeness goes a long way. Also, be sure to come armed with as many proofs of income as humanly possible, including the following:

- A certified check, bank check, or money order to cover a deposit equivalent to one to two months' rent. Without this, none of the rest will matter.
- Most recent W-2 form.
- Letter from current employer verifying your employment status; lacking that, your employer's business telephone number.
- Pay stubs showing a yearly income(s) equivalent to 40 to 50 times the monthly rent.
- A credit report or money to cover the fee for having a credit check done. Ask prior to your appointment what that fee is; it can range considerably. If you wish to know your own credit score, or to see what your brokers will be seeing, you may obtain your credit report for free once a year. Visit www.annualcreditreport. com for statements from the Big Three: Equifax, TransUnion, and Experian.
- Reference letters (sometimes necessary), business and personal, and one from your current landlord stating you are prompt with rent payments.
- Recent statements from checking, savings, and investment accounts. Generally, management firms will want to see the past three-six months' worth of statements.
- A complete list of any other collateral you might own, as well as its value.
- A guarantor—parents, for example, in the case of youthful renters—with documents showing an income 80 to 100 times the monthly rent, if you do not have an income adequate to satisfy the landlord.
- Have the documents neatly arranged in a special folder—this gives the impression that you're organized and a low-maintenance tenant.

Having successfully navigated these shoals and been accepted, you are ready to sign a lease. First, a word of caution: there are fraudulent real estate and rental agents who take advantage of eager and unwary apartment seekers. To avoid them, meet real estate and rental agents only in an office, not on the street. Ask for a Department of State identification card and a photo ID. Give a deposit only to the landlord, and be wary of agents who can be reached only by cell phones.

TENANT/LANDLORD RELATIONSHIPS, LEASES, SECURITY DEPOSITS

TENANT/LANDLORD OBLIGATIONS

Whether you are renting or subletting, it's a good idea to investigate tenant/landlord obligations and rental restrictions before you sign a lease. Specifics can be found at the **NYC Rent Guidelines Board** website, www.nycrgb.org. The **New York Attorney General**'s Office, 212-416-8000, has a comprehensive website that addresses tenant rights, ordinances, and lease information: www.ag.ny.gov. The state **Department of Homes and Community Renewal**'s rent information line, 718-739-6400, can also provide information; its office is also online at www.nyshcr.org. A membership group called the **New Jersey Tenants Organization (NJTO)**, www.njto.org, provides tenant-related information in that state; they can also be reached by phone at 201-342-3775. It assists with organizing local tenant associations in New Jersey, offers legal guidance to its members, and works for pro-tenant legislation. Individual membership is $25 a year. Also in New Jersey, the **New Jersey Department of Community Affairs, Office of Landlord Tenant Information**, 101 S Broad St, Trenton, NJ 08625, 609-292-6420, www.state.nj.us/dca, sets regulations for renters and landlords. Their "Truth in Renting" booklet is a good, free resource that can be downloaded from www.state.nj.us/dca/divisions/codes/publications/pdf_lti/t_i_r.pdf. Finally, online you can go to the national site, www.rentlaw.com, which provides renters with information regarding landlord/tenant law by state.

Additional resources include:

- **Metropolitan Council on Housing,** 212-979-0611, www.metcouncil.net, tenants union
- **New York City Rent Guidelines Board,** 212-385-2934
- **Rent Stabilization Association,** representing landlords and agents, 212-214-9200, www.rsanyc.org
- **TenantNet,** a website dealing with tenants' rights, www.tenant.net

DEPOSITS

The first written check undoubtedly will be a deposit held by the broker or landlord while credit references are being researched. Some landlords require certified check or bank check rather than personal check, so inquire in advance. The first person to put down a deposit (customarily one month's rent) stands the best chance of signing the lease. The credit investigation should take no more than a couple of days if you have supplied the documentation outlined above. Once you are pronounced credit-worthy, the deposit check should be accepted as your first month's rent (some landlords require two months' rent in advance, and some buildings require even more than that; it is not unheard of to pay a deposit of six months). The interest-earning security deposit, also generally one month's rent, will be refunded at the end of your lease, provided the apartment is left in the same condition in which it was found. (Now is the time to walk through with the landlord to record any existing damage.) If a real estate broker is involved, your third payment will be the broker's fee, which currently averages about 15% of the first year's rent. In some cases, the owner will pay all or part of the fee.

LEASES

Read the lease carefully *before* signing it or giving a security deposit. Married couples should have both names on the lease, especially if they go by different last names; unmarried couples should try to get both names on the lease, though the landlord is not legally obliged to do so. A standard form is customary. Be familiar with the content of the entire lease, but pay special attention to the end of the form where the qualifying clauses are printed. The document should specify any special arrangements made with the landlord about alterations, repairs, painting, and new appliances. Before signing is the time to ask questions or have uncertain terms clarified. Terms in leases can sometimes be negotiated, but be sure to get any such alterations in writing and initialed by the landlord. Ask about making alterations within the apartment, notification of moving, "quiet enjoyment" clauses, if pets are allowed, responsibility for repairs, and what, if any, responsibilities you have for public areas. Also, make sure to inquire about any extra fees, such as application fees for condo or co-op subleases or move-in/move-out deposits. Determine how the building is heated and who pays the bills. If the landlord is responsible, there must be a clause in the lease to this effect. Traditionally, especially in the pre-war buildings, landlords pay for steam heat and hot water so you only pay for gas (for cooking) and electricity. In newer buildings without boilers, tenants customarily pay for the more costly electrical heat. They may also pay for water.

Since 1982, smoke detectors, essentially one per sleeping area, have been mandatory in New York apartments. Tenants are responsible for the repair and maintenance of these alarms. Apartments with children are required by law to have window guards. And as of November 1, 2004, carbon monoxide alarms became legally required in all New York residences.

Your landlord is legally responsible for ridding your apartment of cockroaches. Some provide routine exterminator services; others simply take care of the matter as it crops up. Obviously, the ounce of prevention method is preferable and you should know in advance if regular service is included in your lease.

Check for a sublet clause. Subletting is allowed "with the landlord's permission." This means he/she can say no. To avoid permission being withheld capriciously, the clause should mention that the apartment can be sublet with written permission from the landlord and that "permission shall not be unreasonably withheld."

Conversely, if you are subletting an apartment from the original lessee, determine whether you have a legal right to be there. To address this and other questions, **Tenants & Neighbors,** 212-608-4320, 236 West 27th Street, 4th floor (www.tenantsandneighbors.org), offers useful information on your rights on their website and in publications. Call for information about membership ($35 per year, $10 for low-income). The **New York State Rent Guidelines** website, www.nycrgb.org is useful and includes an online guide to renting. If you have questions about the propriety of a sub-tenancy and the apartment falls under city- or state-enforced guidelines, try calling one of the organizations listed below under **Additional Resources** (Rent Guidelines Board, the New York Loft Board, or the Office of the DHCR) with your concerns.

Subletting a cooperative apartment can be daunting. Not only is it necessary to prove yourself to the landlord, but you must also pass the scrutiny of the building's board of directors. Unfortunately, the traditionally restrictive subletting practices of many cooperative buildings are still in effect. If you are very fortunate, you will meet with a rare co-op board that focuses on realistic concerns for their building and will consider a sublet situation. Keep in mind that if you sublet a co-op without the board's approval, you could be evicted. Individually-owned condominium apartments can typically be sublet at the owner's discretion.

Finally, for a comprehensive guide to the ins and outs of renting in the city, including housing laws, a list of agencies and resources for tenants, recent articles, and links to related sites, go to TenantNet, www.tenant.net.

RENT STABILIZATION AND RENT CONTROL

While municipal rent controls have been eliminated in most of the country, they have survived in New York City. Few if any of the **rent-controlled** apartments ever reach the market; they are either passed among qualifying members of one family like heirlooms or, once vacant, automatically become **rent stabilized** (apartments in large buildings) or decontrolled (apartments in buildings with five units or fewer). The Office of Rent Administration's website states: "In New York City, rent control tenants are generally in buildings built before February 1, 1947, where the tenant is in continuous occupancy prior to July 1, 1971. Tenants who took occupancy after June 30, 1971, in buildings of six or more units built before January 1, 1974, are generally rent stabilized." Rents in condominiums and cooperative apartments are left to market forces. Under rent control guidelines, apartments in buildings with six or more units could only see limited increases (in 2008, rents increased 4.5% for one-year leases and 8.5% for two-year leases). After the $2,000 mark, apartments no longer qualify as rent-controlled units and can be rented by the landlord at the market rate. To speed up this process, landlords are renovating many of the remaining low-rent apartments to push their value above $2,000, which allows these units to be taken off the rent control market. In short, rent control is becoming a thing of the past in New York City. The **Rent Stabilization Association** (the landlord group), 123 William Street, will answer questions about tenants' rights under rent stabilization. Call 212-214-9200 or go to www. rsanyc.org. If your apartment is rent controlled or rent stabilized, call the **Office of Rent Administration, State Department of Homes and Community Renewal (DHCR)** in your borough with any questions or problems: Upper Manhattan, above 110th Street, 163 West 125th Street, 212-961-8930; Lower Manhattan, below 110th Street, 25 Beaver Street, Fifth Floor, 212-480-6238; The Bronx, 1 Fordham Plaza, 718-563-5678; Brooklyn, 55 Hanson Place, Room 702, Brooklyn, 718-722-4778; Queens, 92-31 Union Hall Street, Jamaica, 718-739-6400; Staten Island, 60 Bay Street, Seventh Floor, Staten Island, 718-816-0278; website, www.dhcr.state.ny.us.

LOFTS

During the 1960s, the trickle of hardy artists working and living illegally in industrial lofts located in manufacturing districts became a stream. Living in a vast, often high-ceilinged space *à la bohème* became a desirable alternative lifestyle. Add a few partitions, a restaurant gas stove, some antiques—instant chic.

Illegal loft tenancies proliferated throughout the 1970s, but an amendment to the state's Multiple Dwelling Law legalized loft living in manufacturing buildings (buildings with no residential Certificates of Occupancy) containing three or more rental units. Some areas of the city were exempted, but in Chelsea and lower Manhattan, in the Fulton Ferry area of Brooklyn, and Long Island City in Queens, loft dwellers breathed a legal sigh of relief.

The loft law did not, however, create complete order out of chaos, and the legality of some loft-living situations is still in doubt. Anyone considering renting or subletting a loft is well advised to check with the **New York City Loft Board**, 280 Broadway, 3rd Floor, NYC 10007, 311, www.nyc.gov/loftboard, before signing the lease. This is the city agency charged with overseeing the legalization of residential lofts.

Look for a Certificate of Occupancy for the building and check to see if you're signing a commercial or residential lease. Be sure to use the government sites listed in **Checking It Out** to see what kind of complaints and problems have been registered for the address. Converted industrial buildings are notorious for building and safety violations, so you might want to pop over to the New York Department of Buildings website, www.nyc.gov/html/dob, where you can view any address's history going back at least 15 years.

ADDITIONAL RESOURCES—RENTERS

- **Gas or Electric** service shutoff hotline, 311
- **Housing Authority**, 250 Broadway, 311 or 212-306-3000, www.nyc.gov/nycha

- **Housing Discrimination for New York (and New Jersey)**, Fair Housing Hub, U.S. Department of Housing and Urban Development, 26 Federal Plaza, Rm 3541, 212-542-7109; housing discrimination hotline, 800-669-9777 or www. hud.gov/complaints
- **Loft Board**, 280 Broadway, 3rd Floor, 311, www.nyc.gov/html/loft
- **New York City Rent Guidelines Board**, 51 Chambers St, Suite 202, 311, www. nycrgb.org
- **NYC Heat Hotline,** 311
- **NYC Urban League**, 204 W 136th St, 212-926-8000, www.nyul.org
- **Office of Rent Administration**, New York State Homes and Community Renewal (DHCR): Upper Manhattan, above 110th St, 163 W 125th St, 212-961-8930; Lower Manhattan, below 110th St, 25 Beaver St, Fifth Floor, (see website for additional borough listings), www.nyshcr.org
- **Rent Stabilization Association** (the landlord group), 123 William St, 14th floor, 212-214-9200 or go to www.rsanyc.net

If you're settling in the Lower East Side of Manhattan or the East Village, **GOLES** (stands for **Good Old Lower East Side**) is the tenant association, and is one of the best-run tenant groups in the city: 171 Avenue B, 212-533-2541, www.goles.org.

RENTER'S/HOMEOWNER'S INSURANCE

Your neighbor upstairs has a grease fire in his kitchen, which gets out of hand. There is no fire damage to your apartment, but smoke and water damage from extinguishing the fire have rendered your furniture unusable, your walls in need of new paint, and your television and computer are out of commission. The cost of replacing all this stuff is covered by the owner's building insurance, right? Wrong. Your damages are out of pocket, unless you have renter's insurance.

While events such as this are relatively rare, they can be financially devastating when they occur. If your possessions are few, it may be worth the gamble to skip the insurance. However, your possessions can be insured against fire, water damage, and theft. Rates vary from company to company; be sure to shop around. It's a good idea to pay the additional cost for replacement coverage, and be sure your premiums provide personal liability coverage, protecting you and your family against lawsuits resulting from injuries to others, on or off the premises. If you own a dog, be sure the personal liability covers dog bites as well. Insurance is even more important for apartment owners, who will also need to be covered for structural improvements or alterations, as well as loss of personal possessions in the event of a disaster. Some co-ops and condo buildings require such coverage. When seeking insurance from an insurance agent (Yellow Pages under "Insurance" or online under keywords "Renters Insurance" or at www.insure.com), it's a good idea to get quotes from at least three providers. One company will be more competitive than another in a specific neighborhood, or in rentals, say, than in condos. If you want to check

your insurance record, contact LexisNexis Personal Reports (888-497-0011, www.
personalreports.lexisnexis.com) to order your CLUE (Comprehensive Loss Under-
writing Exchange) report. This national database of consumers' automobile and
property insurance claims is used by insurers when determining rates or denying
coverage. Contact the company if you find any errors.

Some companies that sell renters/homeowners insurance in the metropolitan area:

• **Allstate**, 800-255-7828, www.allstate.com
• **Chubb**, 866-324- 8222, www.chubb.com
• **The Hartford**, 888-413-8970, www.thehartford.com
• **Liberty Mutual Group**, 800-837-5254, www.libertymutual.com
• **Prudential** (homeowners insurance), www.prudential.com
• **Travelers**, 888-695-4625, www.travelers.com

For more information, or if you have a problem with your insurer, contact
the **New York State Department of Financial Services**, www.dfs.ny.gov; in New
Jersey go to www.state.nj.us/dobi.

BUYING

In a city of renters, why buy? Real estate values have risen sharply since the late
1990s, but so have rents. When you factor in the income tax exemption for mortgage interest, which is highest in the early years of the mortgage, the cost of
renting now can approach or even exceed the cost of buying, especially in the
studio and one-bedroom apartment category. For many, the idea of having home
equity, as opposed to paying rent to someone else, has a strong appeal. For others,
it's the satisfaction and security of home ownership. Keep in mind, however, home
ownership in New York City is quite different when compared to much of the U.S.
The $800,000 that might buy a four-bedroom, three-bathroom house with plenty
of greenery in parts of the U.S., in NYC may buy you a studio apartment with an
alcove—if you're lucky.

That said, the newcomer to New York City would be well advised to rent or
sublet for a year at least before buying: become comfortable in the city, familiar
with some of its neighborhoods, and develop a sense of how you use the city.
Furthermore, the case can be made that, given the expenses incidental to buying
(described below) and the fact that real estate values tend to rise and fall in
roughly ten-year cycles, it makes sense to buy only if you expect to spend at least
ten years in the city. Even if the market goes soft for a while, New York real estate
values will eventually rise again. New Yorkers whose parents bought brownstones
in the 1940s or '50s for several thousand dollars can attest to that from their now
inherited multimillion-dollar homes.

As with renting, the search for a condo, a co-op, or a house generally begins online or in the classified ads in the *New York Times* or the *Wall Street Journals*. The ads lead the seeker to realtor websites where one can browse through apartment images and specs. Websites offering national real estate listings proliferate, many with virtual tours. Below, a few that may be useful:

- **Homes.com**, www.homes.com
- **HomeGain**, www.homegain.com, free service that will help you locate a realtor, find the value of a home, find homes for sale, or calculate a mortgage
- **Owners.com**, www.owners.com, a "For Sale by Owners" site, excluding brokers, with area listings in New York, New Jersey, and Connecticut
- **Move.com** and **realtor.com** are affiliated sites controlled by the National Association of Realtors, a huge nationwide database of listings
- **RealtyGuide**, www.xmission.com/~realtor1, with links to broker websites, lenders, and for-sale-by-owner directories
- **Zillow,** www.zillow.com, a nationwide site that finds and compares value estimates of homes, provides maps, and shows housing trends in neighborhoods
- **ZipRealty**, www.ziprealty.com, a national site that combines Internet service with the personal attention of an agent; no cost to register to view listings

Those looking online to buy a co-op, condo, or house in the city will probably be more successful at a city-specific site, which should provide neighborhood profiles, comparative prices, and mortgage information:

- **New York City Real Estate Exchange,** www.cityrealty.com, with condos, co-ops, and houses in all boroughs

Most of the brokers who maintain apartment rental listings also have lists of homes for sale.

For those who are contemplating buying, a few considerations, which apply whether you are looking for a house, a co-op, or a condo. First, what can you afford to pay? The rule of thumb, and one that lenders use: it is safe to pay three or four times the buyer's yearly income, depending on a variety of factors. The required down payment will generally be 20% of the purchase price; it may go as low as 10%, in which case origination fees (points) to the bank will probably be higher. Be prepared for a thorough examination of your finances, your credit record, and your employment status. This, of course, assumes the buyer is not paying cash but will be obtaining a mortgage from a bank.

Know that the transaction you are about to make is going to cost more than the agreed-upon price. How much more? Generally, in New York, closing costs run 5% to 8% of the purchase price. This includes points, attorney's fees, title insurance, a title search, inspection and survey, recording tax, various fees, and the deposit of some real estate tax payments and homeowner's insurance premiums in escrow. The lender (bank or mortgage company) is required to give a good faith estimate of closing costs. In New York, the seller pays the broker's fee.

Whatever and wherever you are looking to buy, you'll need a good broker who listens to you, knows the neighborhoods, and can put you in touch with potential lenders and mortgage brokers. (See **Recommendations for finding a real estate broker**, above.) A buyer's broker, who represents only the buyer, is becoming common, particularly in the suburbs. It's a good idea to get pre-approved for a mortgage before looking; in today's market it can make the difference in your bid winning out against competing bids for a property. And in popular neighborhoods, you may need to act fast. Without being pre-approved, you can lose out on the apartment you want. You must also have a good real estate lawyer, whom you can find through the recommendations of friends, your own lawyer, or your broker. If you have no idea where to find an attorney who handles real estate transactions, call legal referral, 212-626-7373, at the **Association of the Bar of the City of New York**, 42 West 44th St, www.nycbar.org.

If you are buying a **house**, you will do well to hire a building engineer to check the structure of the house, the heating and plumbing systems, fireplaces, etc.; a thorough inspection may save you thousands of dollars or prevent you from making a disastrous purchase. In New York City, the seller must fill out lead paint disclosure forms. In the case of a co-op, or condominium, it is important to check out the financial stability of the board of directors. In all buying scenarios, it is in the best interest of the buyer to have everything reviewed by a competent real estate attorney.

When you buy a **co-op** (cooperative apartment) you are buying shares in the ownership of a building, the other shareholders of which must approve your purchase through their board. And should you choose to sell or rent your apartment later, the same approval process must be repeated, which can be a problem. In the most desirable buildings, approval may be more difficult than getting a mortgage, as shareholders attempt to guarantee the financial reliability and the "social acceptability" of their new partner. Your finances will be scrutinized, and your lifestyle may be considered. Try to get an idea about governing attitudes of the co-op board and check recent board decisions regarding upkeep and repair of the co-op before committing to an apartment. The wrong co-op board, with a list of onerous rules and regulations, can make life less than pleasant. Also, get a prospectus, minutes of the last meeting of the board, board/building rules, and a financial statement from the cooperative, and go over them with your broker and your lawyer. If your purchase is rejected, expect no explanation. Be aware that co-op size may affect your ability to get a mortgage; in co-ops with fewer than 12 units, lenders may be more likely to reject a mortgage application because the relatively small number of shareholders in such buildings raises the collective risk of default. Also, keep in mind that co-op maintenance fees (the cost of upkeep for everything outside the walls of your apartment) can be more than your mortgage, depending on the building, and only some of the maintenance fee (the portion of the fee that is allocated for property tax payments) is tax deductible. Forty to fifty percent is a ballpark figure.

In New York you will also run into low-income co-op arrangements, bearing in mind that low-income here might not be what you think. Run very much like a traditional co-op, these are designed to help people buy their own apartment by requiring, at times, little or nothing up front. You will need to prove your income (although some boards are very flexible in terms of what documentation they will accept) and you are usually restricted in terms of your reselling price, i.e., you won't be able to resell for market value. The same caveats apply here as do to the more traditional co-ops.

The purchase of a **condo** involves fewer hurdles, though some condo management organizations request letters of recommendation from prospective buyers. Here, you are buying an apartment outright, with the right to rent or resell when and as you choose. Of course, this means neither you nor the other residents have any control over who your neighbors are. In making this purchase you will also want your lawyer to examine a prospectus and financial statement on the building to avoid buying into a financially unstable property.

In either situation, condo or co-op, if you're the kind of person who likes to be left alone or has trouble getting along in a group with strict rules, purchasing a condominium or co-op could be a mistake. If such possible limitations are not an issue, then take the plunge.

Questions to ask about a co-op or condo:

- What percentage of the units are owner-occupied?
- How much are the association dues and projected assessments?
- What are the rules and regulations?
- Who manages the property?
- Have there been any lawsuits involving the association in the past five years?

Finally, a word about **mortgage brokers**. In the competition to win new clients, banks offer a confusing array of loans. Mortgage broker to the rescue! They function as a financial advisor who helps his/her client get a suitable mortgage. At no charge to you, he/she will examine your financial situation (age, income, assets, debt load, etc.) and the type of property you want to buy, and then recommend the most likely lender and the best type of mortgage for your needs. Given the mortgage broker's relationship with various banks, he/she can ease your way through the process, especially on co-op loans. If you're the ruggedly independent sort, keep in mind that in New York City your chances of getting a good mortgage are much higher with a qualified mortgage broker than without.

ADDITIONAL RESOURCES—HOMEBUYERS

Quasi-governmental agency **Fannie Mae** (800-732-6643, www.fanniemae.com) provides credit counseling, assistance with finding low-cost mortgages, and advice for low-income and first-time buyers. If you're a New York City tenant who needs to make a housing complaint, contact the **Central Complaint Bureau** of the **New York City Department of Housing and Preservation**, 100 Gold Street, NYC 10038, by dialing 311 or by visiting www.nyc.gov/hpd.

Several books and resources you may find useful include:

- *100 Questions Every First Time Homebuyer Should Ask: With Answers from Top Brokers From Around the Country*, 3rd edition (Three Rivers Press) by Ilyce R. Glink
- "Opening the Door to a Home of Your Own," a free pamphlet by the Fannie Mae Foundation, 800-834-3377. Can also be downloaded online for free at www.ctcu.org/Pdfs/home1.pdf.
- *The Ultimate Guide to Buying and Selling Co-ops and Condos in New York City*, 4th edition (Environmental Law Institute) by Neil J. Binder

The New York Public Library has a wealth of resources available in its branches and online. Go to www.nypl.org.

H AVING FOUND AND SECURED A PLACE TO LIVE, YOU NOW HAVE THE
task of getting your stuff there and perhaps storing some of it because a
New York apartment is not as big as it looks on TV.

TRUCK RENTALS

The first question you need to answer: Am I going to move myself or will I have
someone else do it for me? If you're used to doing everything yourself, you can
rent a vehicle, load it up, and hit the road. Call some of the major moving companies (listed below) to comparison shop their services and prices; also ask about
any specials. (You can also check under "Automobile Rental" or "Truck Rental," or
try looking for "truck rental" on the Internet.) Below we list four national truck
rental companies and their toll-free numbers and websites. For the best information, you should call a local office. Note: most truck rental companies now offer
one-way rentals, as well as packing accessories and storage facilities. Of course,
these extras are not free and if you're cost-conscious you may want to scavenge
boxes in advance of your move and make sure you have a place to store your
belongings upon arrival (see **Storage** below). Also, if you're planning to move
during the peak moving months (May through September), call well in advance,
at least a month ahead, of when you think you'll need the vehicle.

Once you're on the road, keep in mind that your rental truck may be a tempting
target for thieves. If you must park it overnight or for an extended period (more
than a couple of hours), try to find a safe place, preferably somewhere well-lit and
easily observable by you, and do your best not to leave anything of particular value
in the cab. Make sure you lock up and if possible use a steering wheel lock or other
easy-to-purchase safety device. The back door of the truck should be padlocked.

Four national self-moving companies to consider:

- **Budget**, 800-455-1332, www.budgettruck.com

- **Penske**, 888-996-5415, www.pensketruckrental.com
- **Ryder**, 800-345-9282, www.ryder.com
- **U-Haul**, 800-789-3638, www.uhaul.com/trucks

If you've decided to rent a truck and move yourself, be sure to consult the city's traffic rules (http://www.nyc.gov/html/dot/downloads/pdf/trafrule.pdf). You'll want to avoid double parking the truck (no small feat), but check for up-to-date rules about other do's and don'ts related to parking a U-Haul or similar vehicle on the street. Also, be sure to ask your building's management if they have specific rules about the days and times when you can move in; many do. If your apartment is in a newer building, ask whether they have a loading dock where you can pull the truck in to offload your furniture and boxes, and whether there are any other regulations, considerations, or management services you should know about on move-in day.

Not sure if you want to drive the truck yourself? Commercial freight carriers, such as UPack, 877-453-7274, www.upack.com, offer an in-between service; they deliver a trailer or smaller pod to your home and you have a set number of days to pack and load as much of it as you need, and they drive the vehicle to your destination (often with some other freight filling the remaining space), and then you have another set number of days to unpack. Keep in mind though, if you have to share truck space with another customer you may arrive far ahead of your boxes—and bed. The company's ReloCubes are dropped off as a separate metal shipping container holding about one room's worth of furnishings (these can also be stored at a remote location for as long as you need and fit into most parking spaces). Try to estimate your needs beforehand and ask for your load's expected arrival date. You can get an online estimate from some shippers, so take time to do some comparison shopping. You may also want to check the Better Business Bureau listings for moving companies, which are notorious for damaging goods and/or operating without the proper licensing. If you aren't moving an entire house and can't estimate how much truck space you will need, keep in mind this general guideline: two to three furnished rooms equal a 15-foot truck; four to five rooms, a 20-foot truck. Due to New York's narrow streets and overnight parking restrictions, self-moves may be best suited to those moving outside Manhattan.

MOVERS

INTERSTATE

First, the good news: moving can be affordable and problem-free. The bad news: if you're hiring a mover, the chances of it being so are much less. One of the best ways to find a mover is by personal recommendation. Absent a friend or relative who can recommend a trusted moving company, you can turn to the Internet: just type in "movers" on a search engine and you'll be directed to hundreds of more or less helpful moving-related sites.

You might ask a local realtor, who may be able to steer you toward a good mover or at least tell you which ones to avoid. Members of the American Automobile Association have a valuable resource at hand in AAA's Consumer Relocation Services, which will assign the member a personal consultant to handle every detail of the move free of charge and which offers discounts with premier moving companies. Call 800-839-MOVE, www.consumersrelocation.com.

But beware! Since 1995, when the federal government eliminated the Interstate Commerce Commission, the interstate moving business has degenerated into a wild and mostly unregulated industry with thousands of unhappy, ripped-off customers annually. (There are so many reports of unscrupulous carriers that we no longer list movers in this book.) Since states do not have the authority to regulate interstate movers and the federal government has been slow to respond, you are pretty much on your own when it comes to finding an honest, hassle-free mover. That's why we can't emphasize enough the importance of carefully researching and choosing who will move you.

To aid your search for an honest and hassle-free interstate mover, we offer a few general recommendations. First, get the names of a half-dozen movers and check to make sure they are licensed by the US Department of Transportation's Federal Motor Carrier Safety Administration (FMCSA), which has an excellent website with comprehensive moving resources intended to inform and protect consumers, www.protectyourmove.gov. With the mover's Motor Carrier (MC) numbers in hand, call 888-368-7238 or go online to www.li-public.fmcsa.dot.gov, to see if the carrier is licensed and insured. If the company you're considering is federally licensed, your next step should be to check with the Better Business Bureau, www.bbb.org, in the state where the moving company is licensed, as well as with that state's consumer protection board (in New York call 800-697-1220 or go to www.dos.ny.gov/consumerprotection/), or attorney general. Assuming there is no negative information, you can move on to the next step: asking for references. Particularly important are references from customers who did moves similar to yours. If a moving company is unable or unwilling to provide references or tells you they can't because their customers are all in the Federal Witness Protection Program, eliminate them from your list. Unscrupulous movers have even been known to give phony references that will falsely sing the mover's praises—so talk to more than one reference and ask questions. If something feels fishy, it probably is. One way to learn more about a prospective mover: ask if they have a local office (they should) and then walk in and check it out.

Once you have at least three movers you feel reasonably comfortable with, it's time to ask for price quotes. These are always free, so if you are charged for a quote, you can immediately look elsewhere. Best is a binding "not-to-exceed" quote, of course in writing. This will require an on-site visual inspection of what you are shipping. If you have any doubts about a prospective mover, drop them from your list before you invite a stranger into your home to catalog your belongings.

Recent regulations by FMCSA require movers to supply five documents to consumers before executing a contract. These include a brochure called "Your Rights and Responsibilities When You Move"; a concise and accurate written estimate of charges; a summary of the mover's arbitration program; the mover's customer complaint and inquiry handling procedure; and the mover's tariff, containing rates, rules, regulations, classifications, etc. For more about FMCSA's role in the handling of household goods, you can go to their consumer page at www.protectyourmove.gov.

ADDITIONAL MOVING RECOMMENDATIONS:

- If someone recommends a mover to you, get names (the salesperson or estimator, the drivers, the loaders). To paraphrase the NRA, moving companies don't move people, people do. Likewise, if someone tells you he/she had a bad moving experience, note the name of the company and try to avoid it.
- Remember that price, while important, isn't everything, especially when you're entrusting all of your worldly possessions to strangers.
- Ask about handling on the other end—subcontracting increases the chances that something could go wrong.
- Demand for moving equipment and services tends to be highest at the beginning, dead center, and end of each month.
- In general, ask questions, and if you're concerned about something, ask for an explanation in writing. If you change your mind about a mover after you've signed on the dotted line, write them a letter explaining that you've changed your mind and that you won't be using their services. Better safe than sorry.
- Ask about insurance; the "basic" (and, it's worth noting, maximum) 60 cents per pound industry standard coverage is not enough. If you have homeowner's or renter's insurance, check to see if it will cover your belongings during transit. If not, ask your insurer if you can add that coverage for your move. Otherwise, consider purchasing "full replacement" or "full value" coverage from the carrier for the estimated value of your shipment. Though it's the most expensive type of coverage offered, it's probably worth it. Trucks get into accidents, they catch fire, they get stolen—if such insurance seems pricey to you, ask about a $250 or $500 deductible. This can reduce your cost substantially while still giving you much better protection in case of a catastrophic loss.
- Whatever you do, do not mislead a salesperson/estimator about how much and what you are moving. And make sure you tell a prospective mover about how far they'll have to transport your stuff to and from the truck as well as any stairs, driveways, obstacles or difficult vegetation, long paths or sidewalks, etc. Movers are particularly prickly about stairs and narrow hallway turns, a specialty of New York apartments. The clearer you are with your mover, the better he/she will be able to serve you.
- Think about packing. If you plan to pack yourself, you can save some money, but if something is damaged because of your packing, you may not be able to

file a claim for it. On the other hand, if you hire the movers to do the packing, they may not treat your belongings as well as you will. They will certainly do it faster, that's for sure. Depending on the size of your move and whether you are packing yourself, you may need a lot of boxes, tape, and packing material. Mover boxes, while not cheap, are usually sturdy and the right size. Sometimes a mover will give a customer used boxes free of charge. It doesn't hurt to ask. Also, don't wait to pack until the last minute. If you're doing the packing, give yourself at least a week to do the job; two or more are better. Be sure to ask the mover about any weight or size restrictions on boxes.

- You should personally transport all irreplaceable items, such as jewelry, photographs, or key work documents. Do not put them in the moving van! For less precious items that you do not want to put in the moving truck, consider sending them via the US Postal Service or UPS.

- Ask your mover what is not permitted in the truck: usually anything flammable or combustible, as well as certain types of valuables.

- Although movers will put numbered labels on your possessions, you should make a numbered list of every box and item that is going in the truck. Detail box contents and photograph anything of particular value. Once the truck arrives on the other end, you can check off every piece and know for sure what did (or did not) make it. In case of claims, this list can be invaluable. Even after the move, keep the list; it can be surprisingly useful.

- Movers are required to issue you a "bill of lading"; do not hire a mover who does not use them.

- Consider keeping a log of every expense you incur for your move, e.g., phone calls, trips to New York, etc. In some instances, the IRS allows you to claim these types of expenses on your income taxes (see **Taxes** below.)

- Be aware that during the busy season (May through September), demand can exceed supply and moving may be more difficult and more expensive than during the rest of the year. If you must relocate during the peak moving months, call and book service well in advance (a month at least) of when you plan on moving. If you can reserve service way in advance, say four to six months early, you may be able to lock in a lower winter rate for your summer move.

- Listen to what the movers say; they are professionals and can give you expert advice about packing and preparing. Also, be ready for the truck on both ends—don't make them wait. Not only will it irritate your movers, but it may cost you. Understand, too, that things can happen on the road that are beyond a carrier's control (weather, accidents, etc.) and your belongings may not get to you at the time or on the day promised.

- Treat your movers well, especially the ones loading your stuff on and off the truck. Offer to buy them lunch, and tip them if they do a good job.

- Before moving pets, attach a tag to your pet's collar with your new address and phone number in case your furry friend accidentally wanders off in the confusion of moving. Your pet should travel with you and you should never plan on moving a pet inside a moving van. *The Pet-Moving Handbook*, published by **First Books** (www.firstbooks.com), also offers a wealth of practical information to help with pet relocation.

- Be prepared to pay the full moving bill upon delivery. Cash or bank/cashier's check may be required. Some carriers will take credit cards, but it is a good idea to get it in writing that you will be permitted to pay with a credit card since the delivering driver may not be aware of this and may demand cash. Unless you routinely keep thousands in greenbacks on you, you could have a problem getting your stuff off the truck. The State of New York allows movers to charge a fuel surcharge fee whenever fuel goes over a specific price; these surcharges change regularly based on current fuel prices. Check the fuel surcharge section of the state's Department of Transportation website for current rates, www.dot. ny.gov/divisions/operating/osss/truck/fuelsurcharge.

INTRASTATE AND LOCAL MOVERS

According to Section 191 of the New York State Transportation Law, all companies involved in the moving business must be insured and hold a license that permits them to provide intrastate moving services within New York State. Licenses are issued by the **New York State Department of Transportation (DOT)**, www.dot. ny.gov. To verify certification of your chosen mover, call 800-786-5368 and punch in the state license number listed on the mover's literature. Consumers can also call this number if they wish to file a complaint. New York's Better Business Bureau also accepts complaints about movers; visit the city's BBB website to file a complaint if you have one, www.bbb.org/new-york-city.

CONSUMER COMPLAINTS—MOVERS

If a **move goes badly** and you blame the moving company, you should first file a written claim with the mover for loss or damage. If this doesn't work and it's an intrastate move, contact the **New York State DOT Carrier Certification Unit**, 47-40 21st St, Long Island City, 11101, 718-482-4810; also, New York State's **Motor Carrier Compliance Bureau**, 518-457-6512, can inform you of a mover's certification and field complaints. Still not satisfied? Contact the **New York State Attorney General's Office**, locally at 55 Hansen Place, Brooklyn, 11217, 718-722-3949, or the **New York State Division of Consumer Protection**, 518-474-8583, www.dos. ny.gov/consumerprotection, and you can call the Governor's **consumer hotline**, 800-697-1220. For other questions within New York City, dial 311 to be directed to the appropriate office. Remember, for moves within the state of New York, the DOT can provide assistance only when you have used a licensed mover. Hire an unlicensed firm and you're on your own in case of damage or loss.

If your grievance is with an interstate carrier, your choices are limited. Interstate moves are regulated by the Federal Motor Carriers Safety Administration

(FMCSA), www.fmcsa.dot.gov, an agency under the Department of Transportation, with whom you can file a complaint against a carrier. While their role in the regulation of interstate carriers historically has been concerned with safety issues rather than consumer issues, in response to the upsurge in unscrupulous movers and unhappy consumers, they issued set of rules "specifying how interstate household goods (HHG) carriers (movers) and brokers must assist their individual customers shipping household goods." According to their consumer page, carriers in violation of said rules can be fined, and repeat offenders may be barred from doing business. In terms of loss, however, "FMCSA does not have statutory authority to resolve loss and damage of consumer complaints, settle disputes against a mover, or obtain reimbursement for consumers seeking payment for specific charges. Consumers are responsible for resolving disputes involving these household goods matters." They are not able to represent you in an arbitration dispute to recover damages for lost or destroyed property, nor enforce a court judgment. If you have a grievance, your best bet is to file a complaint against a mover with FMCSA (call 888-DOT-SAFT or go online to www.nccdb.fmcsa.dot.gov) and with the Better Business Bureau, www.bbb.org, in the state where the moving company is licensed, as well as with that state's attorney general or consumer protection office. To seek redress, hire an attorney.

STORAGE WAREHOUSES AND SELF-STORAGE

The ability to rent anything from 3' x 3' lockers to small storage rooms is a great boon to urban dwellers. Collectors, people with old clothes they can't bear to give away and those with possessions that won't fit in a sublet or shared apartment all find mini-warehouses a solution to too-small living spaces.

Rates for space in Manhattan self-storage facilities are competitive: expect to pay at least $79 a month for a locker 4' x 4' x 7'and as much as $3,000 a month for an 8' x 10' x 8' space. Some offer free pick-up; otherwise, you or your mover delivers the goods. If you're looking for lower rates, check the prices for storage units located in the suburbs and boroughs other than Manhattan.

As you shop around, you may want to check the facility for cleanliness and security. Does the building have sprinklers in case of fire? Do they have carts and hand trucks for moving in and out? Do they bill monthly, or will they automatically charge the bill to your credit card? Access should be 24-hours or nearly so, and some are air conditioned, an asset if you plan to visit your locker in the summer.

Finally, a word of warning: unless you no longer want your stored belongings, pay your storage bill and pay it on time. Storage companies may auction the contents of delinquent customers' lockers.

Here are a few area self-storage companies with multiple locations across the city:

- **Chelsea Mini Storage**, 626 W 28th St, Manhattan, 212-564-7735, www.chelsea-mini-storage.com; also offers moving services.

- **ExtraSpace Storage**, 855-871-9321, www.extraspace.com; most facilities are in The Bronx.
- **Manhattan Mini Storage**, 646-586-2322, www.manhattanministorage.com. You'll soon come to recognize this storage facility by its clever—and often controversial—advertisements. As its name suggests, its storage units are in Manhattan; at least eight different neighborhoods have one of these warehouses.
- **Moishe's**, 800-266-8387, www.moishes.com, has warehousing in Brooklyn and in Queens, for goods hauled by their trucks and those of others.
- **Public Storage**, 800-688-8057, www.publicstorage.com, has storage units in Brooklyn, The Bronx, Queens, and Hoboken, New Jersey.
- **Storage Deluxe**, 877-989-7867, www.storagedeluxe.com; locations in Brooklyn, The Bronx, and Queens.
- **Tuck it Away,** 866-549-4740, www.tuckitaway.com, has a handful of locations in Manhattan, Brooklyn, and Queens.
- **U-Haul Moving and Storage,** 800-468-4285, www.uhaul.com, has a limited number of storage facilities in Manhattan and Brooklyn.

The **New York City Department of Consumer Affairs** licenses storage—but not self-storage—warehouses. Dissatisfied? Call New York's Citizen's Service Center number, 311.

CHILDREN

Family and friends—especially those who have never lived in or visited New York—may think you're crazy to pack up your kids and move to the Big Apple, but despite some definite challenges (namely, expenses, space, and jockeying for a spot in a local school), New York City is an incredible place to raise children. With dozens of institutions and attractions designed especially for toddlers, kids, tweens, and teens—and even babies—and an embarrassment of riches with respect to recreational spaces, plenty of bloggers who give parents the inside dish on what kid-friendly activities are on the calendar right now, and parents just like you eager to organize play dates, you and your kids will never lack for things to do.

That being said, a move can be hard on kids, especially if they haven't been exposed to urban life before. To the extent that it's age-appropriate, involve them in the process of moving and make sure you set aside time to listen to and answer their questions.

- Be honest but positive. Listen to their concerns. Spend some time doing pre-moving research about activities so you can dive right in when you get to town, and have your children help out—they might even get positively enthusiastic for the move.
- Make sure children have their favorite possessions with them on the trip; don't pack "blankie" in the moving van.

- Make sure you have some social life planned on the other end. Your children may feel lonely in your new home, and such activities can ease the transition. If you move during the summer you might find a local camp (check with the local YMCAA) for which they can sign up for a couple of weeks in August to make some new friends. Visit sites like www.mommypoppins.com or the kid activities/groups section of *Time Out,* www.timeout.com/new-york-kids.
- Keep in touch with family and loved ones as much as possible. Photos and phone calls are important ways of maintaining links to loved ones you have left behind.
- If your children are school age, take the time to involve yourself in their new school and in their academic life. Don't let them fall through the cracks.
- Try to schedule a move during the summer so they can start the new school year at the beginning of the term.
- If possible, spend some time in the area prior to the move doing fun things, such visiting a local playground or playing ball in a local park or checking out the neighborhood stores with teenagers. With any luck, they will meet some other kids their own age.

First Books (www.firstbooks.com) offers two helpful resources for children. For children ages 6–11, *The Moving Book: A Kids' Survival Guide* by Gabriel Davis is a wonderful gift, and younger children will appreciate *Max's Moving Adventure: A Coloring Book for Kids on the Move* by Danelle Till.

TAXES

If your move is work-related, some or all of your moving expenses may be tax-deductible—so keep relevant receipts. Though eligibility varies, depending, for example, on whether you have a job or are self-employed, generally, the cost of moving yourself, your family, and your belongings is tax deductible, even if you don't itemize. The criteria: in order to take the deduction, your move must be employment-related, your new job must be more than 50 miles away from your current residence, and you must be at your new home for at least 39 weeks during the first 12 months after your arrival. If you take the deduction and then fail to meet the requirements, you will have to pay the IRS back, unless you were laid off through no fault of your own or transferred again by your employer. It's probably a good idea to consult a tax expert regarding IRS rules related to moving. However, if you're a confident soul, get a copy of IRS Form 3903 (www.irs.gov) and do it yourself!

ADDITIONAL RELOCATION AND MOVING INFORMATION

- **www.firstbooks.com**: relocation resources and information on moving to Atlanta; Austin; Boston; Chicago; Dallas–Fort Worth; Houston; Los Angeles; Minneapolis–St. Paul; Portland, Oregon; San Francisco; Seattle; Washington, D.C.;

plus a book for newcomers to the USA. International destinations include China and London.

- **USA Today** offers articles with an assortment of moving tips from how-to packing guide to tips for relocating a family. Visit http://traveltips.usatoday.com
- **www.erc.org**, the Employee Relocation Council, a professional organization, offers members specialized reports on the relocation and moving industries.
- **www.usps.com**, relocation information from the United States Postal Service.

A FTER FINDING YOUR NEW PLACE OF RESIDENCE, YOUR FIRST ORDER OF business probably will be opening a bank account. The following information about personal savings and checking accounts, credit unions, and credit cards and credit resources should make the task less daunting. We've also included information about federal, state, and city income tax procedures, as well as details for those wanting to start or move a business.

BANK ACCOUNTS AND SERVICES

While most people tend to choose their bank for its location and days and hours of operation (some banks in New York are open seven days a week), other important determinants can be services, interest rates, and minimum balance requirements. If the services a bank offers are more important to you than location, particularly now that ATMs provide easy access to cash and account information outside the branch, be sure to shop around for the best deals for your banking needs. Two of the city's largest retail banks, Citibank and Chase, operate more than 100 branches in Manhattan alone, plus more in the outer boroughs, and a growing number of their ATMs are available in drug stores and supermarkets too. Fees at large interstate banks like these two can be significantly higher than at smaller banks, however. Below, we list eight banks with multiple branches:

- **Apple Bank**, 914-902-2775, www.applebank.com
- **Bank of America**, 800-432-1000, www.bankofamerica.com
- **Capital One**, 800-464-3473, www.capitalone.com
- **Citibank**, 800-745-1534, www.citibank.com
- **HSBC**, 800-975-4722, www.us.hsbc.com
- **JP Morgan Chase & Co.**, 877-242-7372, www.chase.com
- **TD Bank**, 888-751-9000, www.tdbank.com
- **Wells Fargo**, 800-869-3557, www.wellsfargo.com

Technology has transformed banking and continues to do so. All banks offer the option of banking via your home computer, and smart phone apps and online bank accounts offer even more flexibility. For these reasons, it's important that you do some comparison shopping to see which institution and which among their personal banking service options fits your needs best.

Services offered by financial institutions include, but are not limited to, the following:

- **Checking**: Take a completed application—two references are often required, usually the name of your current bank and that of your employer—to the branch where you intend to bank, together with two signed pieces of identification: passport, driver's license, credit card, student ID with photo. One ID must have a photo. Most banks require a minimum start-up deposit; the amount varies considerably from one bank to another and based on the level of service you desire. Your account can be opened immediately, but checks and deposit slips won't be issued until your signature is verified. "Regular" non-interest-bearing personal checking accounts typically carry no charges as long as a minimum daily balance is maintained. A certificate of deposit, money market, or savings account linked to your regular checking account may also get you free checking. Institutions offering interest-earning NOW checking accounts charge a fee if the accounts fall below required minimum balances. **Debit cards** are issued automatically to new customers; most carry a MasterCard or VISA imprint and can be used to make withdrawals at any ATMs, as well as to pay for goods and services at retail outlets. You can arrange to have your paycheck go straight to your checking account via direct deposit. Be sure to inquire about fees and shop around before opening a checking account. If your address is uncertain or has problems receiving mail you can have checks and ATM cards mailed to your branch bank office.
- **Savings**: Follow the procedures detailed above for checking accounts to apply for a "statement" savings account, which provides monthly statements of all transactions and can be linked to your checking account. Many banks require an average minimum balance of at least $1,500 to avoid maintenance charges. Again, inquire about fees.
- **Online banking**: Just as ATMs did not eliminate bank tellers, Internet banking will not replace the brick-and-mortar branch. But the low operating costs and convenience of online banking render the Internet an optimal financial conduit. Capital One's 360 accounts (www.capitalone360.com), formerly ING Direct, are the leader in this area, but almost all banks offer online services, and some banks exist exclusively online. Conventional services such as transfers and balance inquiries are standard, while some banks offer applications for loans and credit lines. Larger banks have tie-ins to investment accounts, and some sites even offer financial management tips and strategies. Some institutions offer incentives to those who make transactions online, ranging from waived fees to rewards on a point system. While banks will protect your information, you must

also be attentive with your online account. Change your password regularly, and don't share it with anyone.

• **Banking by phone**: A touch-tone telephone gives access to all the banking services performed by an ATM, except deposits and cash withdrawals: you can check account balances and make transfers between accounts. For a small monthly charge (or free with a minimum combined balance of, say, $10,000) the bank will make scheduled bill payments such as rent, mortgage, or car payments, as well as payments on request to designated payees such as stores, credit card companies, and utilities. A year-end annual statement may be provided on request. Again, inquire about the latest refinements and fees, if any.

CREDIT UNIONS

According to the **National Credit Union Administration (NCUA)**, "A federal credit union is a nonprofit, cooperative financial institution owned and run by its members." Organized to serve, democratically-controlled credit unions provide their members with a safe place to save and borrow at reasonable rates. Members pool their funds to make loans to one another. The volunteer board that runs each credit union is elected by the members. According to *American Banker*'s annual survey, credit unions continually rank high in customer satisfaction. Because credit unions limit membership based on set criteria, you'll need to investigate a few for a match. Organizations such as employers, unions, professional associations, churches, and schools (alumni associations) typically provide membership. A few, such as the **Lower East Side Peoples' Federal Credit Union**, 37 Avenue B, 212-529-8197, www.lespeoples.org, have community charters enabling them to serve anyone who works or lives in that community. And some, such as the **Progressive Credit Union** at 133 West 33 Street, 7th floor, 212-695-8900, www. progressivecu.org, might contact your employer with an offer of free credit union services for company employees, which would qualify you. Credit unions lack the convenience of multiple branches but offer considerable financial benefit in exchange. For a complete list of local credit unions or information about them, you can visit the **National Association of Credit Union Service Organizations**, www.nacuso.org, or the **NCUA**, www.ncua.gov.

CONSUMER COMPLAINTS—BANKING

Federal and state governments regulate bank policies on discrimination, credit, anti-redlining, truth-in-lending, and other issues. If you have a problem, you should first attempt to resolve the issue directly with the bank. Should you need to **file a formal complaint** against your financial institution, you can do so through the Board of Governors of the **Federal Reserve System, Division of Consumer and Community Affairs**. For specifics, call 888-851-1920 or go to www.federalreserve-consumerhelp.gov. You can also pursue the issue with the following agencies:

- Nationally chartered commercial banks go through the **US Comptroller of the Currency**, Customer Assistance Group, 400 7th St SW, Suite 3E-218, Washington, D.C., 202-649-6800, www.occ.treas.gov.
- For federally chartered credit unions or state-chartered credit unions with federal insurance, contact the **National Credit Union Administration**, 1775 Duke St, Alexandria, VA, 703-518-6300, www.ncua.gov.

CREDIT CARDS

On the off chance that your mailbox hasn't been filled with credit card applications, you can call to request one. Many cards now offer various "rewards" as incentives to use them, the most common being frequent flyer miles. Shop around for the one that best suits your needs.

- **American Express**, 800-528-4800, www.americanexpress.com; once famous for issuing charge cards that must be paid off every month, American Express offers nearly two dozen different personal credit cards, including airline and hotel affinity cards that accumulate frequent-flyer miles or points for frequent hotel stays. With the exception of a student card, all AmEx cards have minimum income requirements, and most charge annual fees.
- **Discover**, 800-347-2683, www.discovercard.com; Discover cards offer an annual rebate based on the amount you charge, and some plans let you accumulate credit at various hotels or retail chains.
- **VISA,** 800-847-2911, www.usa.visa.com, and **MasterCard,** 800-627-8372, www.mastercard.us can be obtained from a variety of financial service organizations, usually banks. Interest rates vary, annual fees may even be waived, and many cards offer frequent flyer miles or other travel and retail incentives. It pays to shop around, especially if you don't pay off your balance every month.
- **Department store credit cards** can offer advantages over other forms of payment: advance notice of sales, mail or phone orders, no annual fee. Accounts may be approved instantly upon application. Macy's and Bloomingdale's cards are popular among New York shoppers; visit the customer service desks in your preferred department store for information and an application.

To compare rates and learn more about credit card features, visit **bankrate. com** or **nerdwallet.com**.

BANKING AND CREDIT RESOURCES

In addition to providing useful information about the comparative features of credit cards, the website www.bankrate.com features a wealth of personal finance tools related to credit cards and banking, including current interest rates, loans and savings calculators, and safety ratings of banks and credit unions.

If you're buying a car or boat, renovating your new fixer-upper, or sending the kids to college, online loan calculators can help you determine possible options based on your finances and needs. There are several loan calculators on bankrate. com but you can look at other sites as well:

- **myFICO**, www.myfico.com
- **E-loan**, www.eloan.com
- **The Motley Fool,** www.fool.com

In New York State, the banking industry is overseen by the state's Department of Financial Services. The department's "Consumer" webpage has numerous resources related to loans and other banking issues: www.dfs.ny.gov/consumer/dfs_consumers.htm

Obtain copies of your **credit report** from the three major credit bureaus at **www.annualcreditreport.com**. The national credit bureaus are:

- **Equifax**, P.O. Box 105873, Atlanta, GA 30348, 800-685-5000, www.equifax.com
- **Experian**, 475 Anton Blvd, Costa Mesa, CA, 92626, 714-830-7000, www. experian.com
- **TransUnion Corporation**, P.O. Box 105281, Atlanta, GA, 30348, 877-322-8228, www.transunion.com

INCOME TAXES

"Tax day," April 15, arrives promptly every 365 days, heralded by the sudden return of H&R Block signs and news reminders counting down the days until your returns must be filed. In New York City, the Internal Revenue Service and New York Department of Taxation and Finance provide literature and taxpayer information services via telephone. In case you did not know it before moving here, the bad news is that New York City takes a yearly income tax bite out of your earnings, along with the state and federal government. The good news is that it is not the highest taxed state in the country.

- **Federal income tax** forms can be obtained by calling 800-829-3676; they are also available in most post offices and libraries at tax time. Call 800-829-1040 to obtain explanatory literature, as well as answers to specific questions, such as which of the three tax forms—1040EZ, 1040A, or 1040—you should use. Many opt to visit the IRS's website, www.irs.gov, where you can find answers to tax questions, as well as downloadable tax forms and information on filing electronically. The staff at the Internal Revenue Service office (hours are weekdays 7:30 a.m.–4:30 p.m.) downtown at 290 Broadway provides instruction in the fine art of calculating your federal income tax but won't do it for you.
- **New York State and New York City** use a combined income tax form. If you have not received forms by mail, you can pick them up at your neighborhood post office. If you use either IRS 1040EZ or 1040A, choose the IT 100, which you

fill in and let the state tax people calculate for you, or the IT 200, which you calculate yourself. For those filing the Federal 1040 long form, you'll need the IT 201. A number of federal forms are available on the IRS website, www.irs.gov, and New York State tax forms can be downloaded from www.tax.ny.gov/forms. Your federal adjusted gross income is the tax base for state and city taxes. New York State taxable income is calculated by adding and subtracting various New York State "modifications," and then the New York City resident's income tax is based on your state taxable income. New Jersey residents can get tax information and download state tax forms from www.state.nj.us/treasury/taxation.

ONLINE FILING AND ASSISTANCE

Filing your taxes online can save you time, especially if you already keep your personal financial records using compatible software such as TurboTax, Quicken, or QuickBooks. Visit www.irs.gov/for-Tax-Pros for details, including a list of companies that make tax software. For some, it may be advisable to get assistance in calculating and preparing your tax return. The city has numerous H&R Block locations during tax season, as well as numerous independent accountants. Some may have a specialty, so be sure to ask if you're in need of a tax preparer skilled with a certain type of return (i.e., self-employment). Remember to keep all receipts, be prepared to spend some time, and don't show up on April 14th. Questions? Call the IRS helpline, 800-829-1040, to speak to an IRS representative. This is also the number to call to find out the status of your return if you have filed and have been waiting more than four weeks, or you can visit the IRS website: www.irs.gov.

If you need help with a tax problem or are suffering some hardship due to the tax law, you can contact the **Taxpayer Advocate Service**, an independent agency within the IRS designed to help taxpayers resolve tax problems; contact them at www.irs.gov/advocate.

Taxpayer assistance in filing on paper or electronically is available for simple returns at no cost at Manhattan IRS offices: 290 Broadway, 110 West 44th Street, and 2283 3rd Ave; Bronx IRS: 1200 Waters Place; Brooklyn IRS: 2 MetroTech Center, 1st floor; Queens office: 59-17 Junction Boulevard. No appointment is necessary at these sites, which are open Monday–Friday, 8:30 a.m.–4:30 p.m., but don't wait until April, unless you like standing in long lines. Assistance in preparing and filing returns, electronically at some sites, is provided by volunteers under the **VITA (Volunteer Income Tax Assistance)** program throughout the city and in New Jersey. To find the site nearest you call 800-829-1040 (customer assistance hotline).

For questions concerning New York State income tax call the **New York State Department of Taxation and Finance**, 518-457-5181.

STARTING OR MOVING A BUSINESS

Exceptionally high rents and significant local and state tax burdens are two of the biggest challenges facing business owners who want to hang their shingle in the city. But if proximity to power, money, and a diverse and deep talent pool is important to you, then New York City can't be beat as a place to locate a business.

If your business does not need to be based in Manhattan, you will find more space for your money in one of the other boroughs or in neighboring New Jersey.

You may choose to hire an attorney who is familiar with the process, but if you want to begin your research on your own, the following resources should help you get started:

- **Association of the Bar of the City of New York**, Legal Referral Service, 212-382-6600, www.nycbar.org
- **Internal Revenue Service**, 800-829-1040, with whom you will need to talk to get an employer tax ID number
- **New York City Department of Finance**, www.nyc.gov/finance
- **New York Department of State, Division of Corporations**, 99 Washington Ave, 6th floor, Albany, NY 12231, 518-473-2492, www.dos.ny.gov; in order to incorporate in New York, you must first reserve a name here (do an advance name search). You can obtain information and fee schedules regarding filing for C Corporation, S Corporation, Limited Liability Company, or Limited Partnership status. Discuss your options first with your attorney and/or accountant.
- **US Small Business Administration**, www.sba.gov; from counseling and training to start-up guidelines to SBA loans, the SBA is ideal for finding small business information.

L ET'S SEE. YOU'VE SIGNED A LEASE OR MORTGAGE PAPERS AND OPENED a bank account. Now, keys in hand, it's time to have utilities connected, telephone installed, and to choose your cable and Internet service providers. You can make yourself at home once you can cook and call, and really feel like a local once you possess a library card, are registered to vote, and have found a doctor. Here are some of the important how-tos (addresses are in Manhattan unless otherwise noted) for establishing yourself as a real New Yorker.

UTILITIES

CONSOLIDATED EDISON

Call **Consolidated Edison's** customer service to have gas and electricity turned on: 800-75-CON-ED. In New Jersey, call PSE&G (**Public Service Electric and Gas**), 800-436-7734, for service. A personal visit from either is not necessary unless the prior tenant's service was cut off for non-payment. Expect to wait at least one business day before service commences; note that PSE&G is open for new accounts Monday–Friday only. Deposits are no longer required for residential accounts unless a credit check indicates the need.

TELEPHONE

Many New Yorkers have, in recent years, foregone their landlines, opting instead to centralize their phone service through their mobile device or through voice over Internet protocol (VOIP) services such as Skype, www.skype.com, and Vonage, www.vonage.com. If you're intent on having a landline, however, you have several choices for local and long distance phone service in New York City, and many of the companies that offer local service also offer long distance. Verizon, AT&T, Sprint, and RCN Communications all offer local and long distance service and are among the many companies offering Internet, cellular, and digital service. Cable television giants also offer telephone and Internet service in the form of bundled telecommunications over their fiber optic cables. When calling to inquire about service, ask about weekday, evening, and weekend rates, specials, and the costs of installation. Whichever local phone service you choose, you will be offered numerous extra features, each carrying an extra monthly fee, among them: Call Waiting, Call Forwarding, Call Answering, Voice Dialing, Call Return, 3-Way Calling, and Caller ID. If you are looking to set up DSL service for your computer, inquire about the additional cost and ask about special deals.

In New York, widely used **long distance service providers** also provide local service. To institute new **local service** contact: **Verizon**, 800-837-4966, www.verizon.com; **AT&T**, 800-222-0300, www.att.com; **Sprint**, 866-866-7509, www.sprint.com; or **RCN**, 800-746-4726, www.rcn.com.

Verizon no longer requires a deposit from most customers; when required, the deposit accumulates interest and is refunded after a year. The set-up charges for all phone companies will vary depending on your needs. For example, if you need additional jacks, you will pay more. It is advantageous to ask the superintendent or someone who works in the building where the phone lines come into the building. This will expedite the process of getting phone service. **Bundling** is the current buzzword in communications: i.e., charging one rate on one bill for two or more services, for example, for long distance calls made from home phones and Internet or cable television service. Other service plan variables include volume discounts, monthly minimums, and overseas service. Comparison shop for the most comprehensive package at the best price.

TELEPHONE DIRECTORIES

Most New Yorkers probably haven't had a phone book at home for years, and New York's youngest residents may not even know what the yellow pages are. Telephone directories are still delivered to apartment buildings in most neighborhoods; these are often left in the lobby and are either retrieved by residents interested in having one or by supers keen to move them straight to the recycling bin. Most New Yorkers seek phone numbers online or through smart phone apps. Here are a few useful sites:

- **www.superpages.com** (Verizon's Super Pages)
- **www.anywho.com** (AT&T's site, includes searches for toll-free numbers)
- **www.switchboard.com**
- **www.yellowpages.com**

Of course, you can still dial 411 for directory assistance, though you'll likely incur a charge on your landline or mobile; prices vary. The service 800-FREE-411 provides directory assistance at no charge, but callers must listen to advertisements before receiving information. Information about city-related services is available by dialing 311 (outside New York City, 212-639-9675). Operators are ready to assist 24/7. The same 311 works for New Jersey.

AREA CODES

For years, Manhattanites prided themselves on their "212" area code, recognized around the country—and the world—as the phone number's equivalent of prime real estate. But by the late 1990s, the coveted 212 began to run out, and two new area codes—917 and 646—were introduced. Don't worry—for now, at least, outer borough area codes remain 718, though 347 has also been added. While 917 tends to precede a cell phone number, this is not always the case, and the same is true for 646 numbers, which are assigned to both landlines and mobile numbers. Meanwhile, 631 has been added to 516 on Long Island; in New Jersey, part of the 201 area, South Orange for example, has become 973; Westchester remains primarily 914. All calls within New York City require dialing the area code plus the seven-digit number.

CELL PHONES

Cell phone technology continues to change rapidly, and costs are accessible for most people. If you are considering a cell phone purchase, find out as much as possible before signing a contract. Better yet, try to find a service that does not require a long-term contract. And be sure to determine whether the cell phone you want to purchase is only operable if you subscribe to a particular service plan. The Better Business Bureau, www.bbb.org, has a page on its website dedicated to complaints against cell phone service providers—a few of the larger providers are notorious for over-billing and aggressive collection practices.

Several companies provide cellular service in the metropolitan area:

- **AT&T**, 800-IMAGINE, www.wireless.att.com
- **Sprint**, 866-866-7509, www.sprint.com
- **T-Mobile**, 877-353-3615, www.t-mobile.com
- **Verizon**, 800-256-4646, www.verizonwireless.com

INTERNET SERVICE PROVIDERS

Choices in Internet service providers (ISPs) in the metro area are numerous, varied, and change rapidly as technology advances. Many of the local cable providers now offer high-speed Internet service as part of a home technology bundle, which might also include phone service and/or cable television.

When picking your provider, be sure to call around, as plans and pricing vary. Some ISPs currently available in the metropolitan area are:

- **RCN**, 800-746-4726, www.rcn.com

- **TimeWarner Cable**, 212-358-0900, www.timewarnercable.com
- **Verizon**, 800-837-4966, www.verizon.com

All of the above offer some form of **broadband**, high-speed connection via cable, telephone, or satellite. Costs depend upon both the provider and level of speed you order, as well as whether you select one or more of the bundled services. Go to **www.dslreports.com** to evaluate local plans. If this service is important to you, when looking for a place to live, be sure to inquire about which service is available in prospective apartments you are viewing.

CITY WATER

Considering the quantity of commercially bottled water consumed by its residents, you might think that New York City water is either unpalatable or unsafe. In fact, city water, which flows at a rate of over a billion gallons a day from vast supply systems north of the city in Westchester, the Catskills, and the Delaware River watershed, is both safe and exceptionally tasty when compared to water in other cities. Except in the infrequent years of extreme drought, the supply is ample and unrationed. In most buildings, tenants are not charged for water but are encouraged to avoid water waste, especially in summer.

A slight rust-colored tint appears occasionally in water drawn from the Croton system (a small percentage of the total water supply), caused by a bloom of microorganisms, which are tasteless and harmless, if unappealing. Water in parts of Brooklyn appears milky white at first from suspended minerals, but this soon dissipates and is harmless. If the pipes have not been used for a while when you first move into your new apartment, let the water run for about ten minutes to clear out rust and the water will then be fine. Questions about water quality or about the water system should be addressed to the **NYC Department of Environmental Protection**, Bureau of Public and Intergovernmental Affairs, 59-17 Junction Boulevard, 13th floor, Flushing, NY 11373, www.nyc.gov/dep. Or contact the department's 24-hour Communications Center through the city's 311 information line, where you can also address concerns about air quality, noise, hazardous materials, sewers, or any number of city-related problems.

Most of the eastern and northern parts of New Jersey, closest to New York City, are served by **United Water New Jersey**, www.unitedwater.com/uwnj. Problems/concerns are handled by their customer service center, 69 DeVoe Place, Hackensack, NJ 07601, 800-575-4433.

For more on area water quality, go to the EPA's site, www.epa.gov, and read their guidelines on microbiological contaminants. Or call the **Safe Drinking Water Hotline**, 800-426-4791.

GARBAGE AND RECYCLING

Garbage service is provided by the city and is collected curbside in covered garbage cans or secured black plastic bags two to three times a week, depending on your location. Bulk trash, such as furniture and appliances, is picked up on the last day of regular garbage collection weekly. Refrigerators and other items containing CFCs, such as air conditioners, and larger appliances and electronics must be disposed of by special arrangement; you can make a request by calling 311 or requesting an appointment online at http://www.nyc.gov/html/dsny/html/collection/freon.shtml. Garbage disposal for those living in large apartment buildings will most likely entail locating the trash chute in your hall. Some of the rougher loft conversions may try and charge you for trash pick-up, but it is the landlord's duty to arrange and pay for this service if the building is residential (commercial spaces must also recycle, but it is not done through the NY governmental services). Check with your building super for any questions. To find out the pick-up days for your neighborhood call 311. (People in private homes in the boroughs, Westchester, and Long Island will need to supply their own trashcans and move them to the curb on specific pick-up days.)

Recycling is a part of life in New York City, and as with garbage collection, the service is provided by the city. Pick-up is weekly and is scheduled on one of your garbage collection days. Items to be recycled include paper: writing, copier, construction paper, glossy paper, envelopes, junk mail, postcards, smooth cardboard, wrapping paper, paperback books, and flattened boxes (no carbon paper, candy wrappers, takeout containers, napkins, paper towels, or hardcover books); glass; metal, including empty metal cans, aluminum foil trays, and general household items and appliances that are at least 50% metal; and number one and number two plastics (usually only bottles). FYI: returnable bottles and cans should be redeemed; in many neighborhoods they can be left neatly outside for the homeless to collect: often, it's their living. All recycled materials must be put in clear plastic bags. Paper products can also be put in special green-colored containers, while metal and plastics can go loose into special blue containers. Cardboard should be flattened and tied in a bundle.

For drivers with a New York driver's license and registration, the sanitation department operates self-help bulk sites (for large items) in four boroughs; call 311 for locations and hours. The Sanitation Department's "Digest of Codes" outlines regulations, penalties, and procedures for trash disposal. For more specifics, visit the department's website, www.nyc.gov/dsny. Fines for improper trash disposal range from $50 to over $250.

In New Jersey, garbage collection and recycling is provided municipally. The department to call for these services and the telephone number are listed here:

- **Edgewater**: Department of Public Works/Recycling, 201-943-1700
- **Fort Lee**: Department of Public Works, 201-592-3634

- **Hoboken:** Hoboken Environmental Services Department, 201-420-2049
- **Jersey City:** Waste Management, 201-435-1345
- **Weehawken:** Department of Public Works, 201-319-6070

CONSUMER COMPLAINTS—UTILITIES

If you have problems with a utility company (gas, electric, phones, water, steam, cable TV) you can contact the New York State Public Service Commission. By law, the commission is responsible for setting rates and ensuring that the public receives adequate service. You can file a complaint on the Internet at www3.dps. ny.gov or by calling one of several hotlines including:

- **New York Public Service Commission**'s helpline: 888-697-7728; regulates telephone, cable TV, and energy utilities
- **Gas or Electric** service shutoff hotline: 800-342-3355

In New Jersey, contact **PSE&G** at 800-436-7734. If you have any questions about your rights as a consumer, you can also call the **New Jersey Board of Public Utilities (BPU)**, which is responsible for regulating natural gas, water, telecommunications, and cable television, and for handling customer complaints: 601-341-9188, www.state.nj.us/bpu.

PRINT AND BROADCAST MEDIA

New York is one of the last great multi-newspaper towns in the U.S., with not only multiple mainstream dailies going toe-to-toe, but a veritable tidal wave of ethnic, specialty, and religious rags. What follows is only a partial listing.

MAJOR DAILIES

- *New York Post*, www.nypost.com; Rupert Murdoch's to-the-right entry into the Manhattan area has local news, opinion, gossip, sports, whose editors are in a daily battle for the most ingenious headline with their arch-rival, *The Daily News*.
- *New York Times*, www.nytimes.com; arguably the nation's premier source for national and world news, as well as the latest on sports, technology, health, and science. Sunday editions feature the respected *New York Times Magazine*.
- *Newsday,* www.newsday.com; Long Island's top-rated daily also covers Queens and NY.
- *New York Daily News*, www.nydailynews.com; which offers local New York news in the timeless Slash! Stab! Greed! Sex! Sex! Sex! tradition.
- *The Star-Ledger*, www.nj.com/starledger; New Jersey's largest daily paper.
- *The Wall Street Journal*, www.wsj.com; the bible of Wall Street, though this daily is hardly limited to financial news.

OTHER PUBLICATIONS

- *AMNY*, www.amny.com; this and its near twin (*Metro*, www.metro.us) are nearly identical free daily news digests distributed primarily at subway entrances in the mornings.
- *Brooklyn Daily Eagle*, www.brooklyneagle.com; once the most read newspaper in the country, this institution, founded in 1841, is now the only Brooklyn daily.
- *The Brooklyn Downtown Star*, www.brooklyndowntownstar.com; a weekly that focuses on downtown Brooklyn.
- *Brooklyn Rail*, www.brooklynrail.org; alternative monthly with arts focus and lots of essays and some reviews.
- *Brooklyn Spectator*, www.brooklynspectator.com; another Brooklyn weekly.
- *The Caribbean Voice*, caribvoice.org; a monthly that covers news and events of the Caribbean and Caribbean diaspora in NYC.
- *Carnarsie Courier*, www.canarsiecourier.com; an independent weekly in operation since 1921, covering the Brooklyn neighborhood of Canarsie.
- *Catholic New York*, www.cny.org; official newspaper of the Roman Catholic Archdiocese of New York and the largest Catholic paper in the U.S.
- *Columbia Spectator,* columbiaspectator.com; daily paper for Columbia University.
- *Community News Group* (CNG), www.cnglocal.com; the publisher of 11 community and topical newspapers around the city, including *Caribbean Life* and *Gay City News*.
- *Crain's New York Business*, www.crainsnewyork.com; daily financial and business news.
- *El Diario*, www.eldiariony.com; one of New York's Spanish language dailies; another is *Hoy*.
- *Greek News*, www.greeknewsonline.com; Greek-American weekly paper based in Astoria, Queens.
- *Greenpoint Gazette*, www.greenpointnews.com; a very local weekly paper for Greenpoint, Brooklyn.
- *India Tribune*, www.indiatribune.com; English language weekly paper for the local Indian community.
- *The Irish Echo*, www.irishecho.com; Irish-American newspaper.
- *The Jewish Daily Forward,* www.forward.com; paper that has focused on the Jewish community since 1897.
- *The Jewish Post of New York*, www.jewishpost.com; another Jewish paper.
- *The Jewish Week*, www.thejewishweek.com; printed in three regional editions: Manhattan, Westchester/The Bronx, and Long Island/Queens/Brooklyn/Staten Island.
- *The L Magazine*, www.thelmagazine.com; a pocket-sized freebie distributed every two weeks; covers all things relating or nearly relating to neighborhoods along the L subway line.
- *New York*, www.nymag.com; biweekly arts and culture glossy, with extensive restaurant and bar guides, geared toward the young, media-obsessed, semi-ironic, and middle- to upper-crust professional.

- *New York Amsterdam News*, www.amsterdamnews.com; weekly broadsheet with an extensive history focused on African-American news.
- *The New York Law Journal*, www.newyorklawjournal.com; a daily paper for NY's many, many lawyers.
- *The New York Observer*, www.observer.com; this weekly is terribly Manhattan, with an emphasis on socialite gossip, the arts, and media.
- *The New Yorker*, www.newyorker.com; New York's premier take on all things literary, cultural, artistic, and political; now that you live here you can finally make solid, pragmatic use of those sterlingly belletristic "Tables for Two" reviews.
- *Queens Courier*, www.queenscourier.com; everything you wanted to know about Queens; published weekly.
- *The Queens Tribune*, www.queenstribune.com; another Queens weekly.
- *Russian Bazaar*, www.russian-bazaar.com; weekly Russian language newspaper.
- *Staten Island Advance*, www.silive.com; the borough's only daily paper; over a century old.
- *TimeOut NY*, www.timeout.com/newyork; a comprehensive entertainment listings, with information about new bars, restaurants, and events; published weekly.
- *Tribeca Trib*, www.tribecatrib.com; a community newspaper covering Lower Manhattan, including Tribeca, Battery Park City, the Financial District, and the Seaport/Civic Center area.
- *The Village Voice*, www.villagevoice.com; long-time readers complain that this weekly is a shadow of its former self; the left-leaning free newspaper was once renowned for its investigative features focused on issues relevant to the city. That may be true, but it's still a good source for event and activity listings.
- *The Villager*, www.thevillager.com; small weekly focusing on the West and East Villages, Lower East Side, Soho, Union Square, Chinatown, and .

TELEVISION

LOCAL NETWORK CHANNELS

The major networks in New York City are: Channel 2–WCBS; Channel 4–WNBC; Channel 5–WNYW (FOX); Channel 7–WABC; Channel 11–WPIX, offers the CW during primetime evening hours (otherwise local programming). Two PBS channels are available: Channel 13–WNET (Public Broadcasting System) and Channel 21–WLIW (Long Island's public network channel). They broadcast similar PBS programming but at different times.

You'll find weekly programs for the broadcast channels as well as cable channels (including HBO, Showtime, and the like) printed in *TV Guide* and the Sunday *New York Times'* "Television" section. This supplement also carries a complete "Station Guide" detailing the ownership and/or focus of broadcast and cable stations. For a full list of stations, visit www.stationindex.com.

CABLE TELEVISION AND THE DISH

The introduction of digital television and the competition introduced by online streaming have changed both the provision and access of television in New York City. Add the fact that pre-war buildings have different wiring than newer luxury buildings, and it can be confusing to figure out which service you need. Your best bet is to speak to the super or manager of your building about the existing wiring and which cable television provider is best equipped to serve the building. Companies include:

- **TimeWarner Cable**, 212-674-9100, www.timewarnercable.com
- **RCN**, 800-RING-RCN, www.rcn.com
- **Optimum**, 718-617-3500, www.optimum.net
- **Verizon,** 800-837-4966, www.verizon.com

If you want to avoid the uncertainties of digital broadcast reception and the tyranny of cable companies, another option is **direct broadcast satellite (DBS)**, more commonly known as "the dish." DBS provides the clearest reception available and hundreds of channels, now including the local channels, though only if you are in a position suitable for mounting an 18- to 36-inch dish outside your home, a difficult proposition for most Manhattanites. Basically, you'll need to own your building so you can use the roof—or have a southwest-facing balcony on which to mount the thing—and there can be no taller building to block the signal from the southwest. Clearly, TV junkies in the outer boroughs and the suburbs, where buildings are lower and spread out, have the advantage here. Currently two DBS signal providers compete in the metropolitan area: **DirecTV**, 800-347-3288, www.directv.com, and **Dish Network**, 800-333-3474, www.dishnetwork.com. You buy the receiver and dish, pay a one-time installation fee, and a monthly programming fee.

Along with pay cable networks such as HBO, Showtime, and Cinemax, plus numerous basic cable offerings, New York City has several of its own channels, including NY1, www.ny1.com, which provides round-the-clock New York news, weather, and information for TimeWarner customers, and the YES Network, www.yesnetwork.com, owned and operated by the New York Yankees, among others. Public access also allows for several channels to be set aside for pay-as-you-go programming, most of which is less than mediocre and some of which is more than a bit risqué.

RADIO

RADIO STATIONS

Music lovers are best served by their FM dials; news and talk shows dominate the AM band. However, on either broadcast frequency, most stations specialize further still, emphasizing one specific format. Check below to find your station. If your reception is subpar—or you just want more variety—you can take advantage of free or subscription-based online or satellite radio, including Pandora, www. pandora.com, and SiriusXM, www.siriusxm.com.

AM Stations

- **AM news, sports, talk**: WCBS 880—"News Radio" and WINS 1010—two round-the-clock news stations, plus sports, weather, traffic reports, etc. WCBS also carries the Yankees games. WABC 770 and WOR 710 are talk radio stations with popular talk radio personalities (770 also plays Jets games); WLIB 1190 is religious and spiritual radio; WNYC 820 features cultural and consumer-oriented broadcasts, as well as National Public Radio's "All Things Considered."
- **AM Spanish news, talk, sports**: WADO 1280; also carries Mets, Yankees, and Jets games
- **AM Christian radio**: WMCA 570; WTHE 1520 for gospel
- AM easy listening music: WHLI 1100
- **AM sports**: WFAN 660 and ESPN sports radio 1050: both offer sports talk and live game coverage/commentary; 1050 is Spanish-language
- **AM children**: WQEW "Radio Disney" 1560, pop favorites for children

For a complete listing of area AM stations, visit www.nyradioguide.com.

FM Stations

- **FM Caribbean**: WVIP 93.5
- **FM news/talk public affairs and NPR**: WNYC 93.9
- **FM urban**: WQHT "Hot 97" 97.1; WWPR "Power 105.1" 105.1; WBLS 107.5; contemporary stations featuring hip-hop and R&B
- **FM adult contemporary**: WLTW "Lite FM" 106.7; WFAS 103.9
- **FM classical**: WQXR 105.9
- **FM current hits**: WPLJ (Power 95) 95.5; WQHT 97.1; WHTZ "Z-100" 100.3; WKTU 103.5
- **FM jazz**: WCWP 88.1; WBGO, "Jazz 88" 88.3
- **FM listener sponsored radio**: WBAI 99.5
- **FM oldies**: WCBS 101.1; hits from the 1960s and '70s; WKHL "Kool" 96.7
- **FM rock**: WAXQ 104.3
- **FM Spanish**: WQBU 92.7; WPAT "Amor 93.1" 93.1; WXNY 96.3; WSKQ "Mega" 97.9

In addition, nearly a dozen New York college radio stations between 88.1 and 90.9 on the FM dial offer a wide variety of musical styles and occasionally some interesting talk. For a full list of stations, visit www.nyradioguide.com.

OWNING A CAR IN NEW YORK

DRIVER'S LICENSES, AUTOMOBILE REGISTRATION (AND STATE IDs)

New residents with valid foreign or out-of-state licenses have 30 days to apply for a New York State driver's license and to register their cars and/or motorcycles.

These exchanges are now handled by the DMV's License Express office, 145 West 30th Street, open Monday–Friday, 8:30 a.m. to 4 p.m. Most other transactions related to licenses, registration, and the like can be completed here as well. Pick up a license application (which will have a convenient voter registration form attached), driver's manual and, if necessary, an automobile registration form at the District Office, or have them sent by calling 212-645-5550 (if you can get through), or simply download the form from the DMV website (see below). A valid out-of-state license exempts you from the road test, but you must pass the vision, road sign, and written tests, which means waiting on line at the DMV. You cannot drive in NYC with an out-of-town learner's permit.

If you are replacing an expired license, or acquiring a new one, you must make an appointment in advance to take the written test. You can stop by your borough's Preliminary Test Office of the Department of Motor Vehicles to schedule your test appointment or call the New York State Road Test Scheduling System at 518-402-2100—or sign up online at www.roadtest.dmv.ny.gov. The written tests, based on the driver's manual, are given between 9 a.m. and 3 p.m. The best place for information on rules and regulations for obtaining a driver's license, plus motorcycle licenses, address changes, and more is at the **DMV website**, www.dmv.ny.gov.

Tests are scored upon completion of your exam, and if you pass, you are issued a temporary license allowing you to drive immediately. Your official license, the one with the photograph, is mailed to you. On testing day, you must have the completed application form and your current license. New York State licenses are valid for eight years.

If your license has lapsed or this is your first, you'll need to pick up the materials and take the vision, road sign, and written tests noted above at the DMV, which also means waiting on line. You'll then be eligible for a learner's permit. With this in hand, after a five-hour course at a licensed driving school, it is possible to take the road test, the ultimate qualification for the New York Driver's License. Examiners can be finicky, but the most frustrating aspect of the road test is getting an appointment to take it. If you can arrange to take the test out of Manhattan, do so. If you make road test arrangements, pay your fee, and then have to cancel, make sure you provide 72-hours' notice or you will be charged a cancellation fee.

If you do not drive but wish to have a **state identification card**, visit any DMV office with at least two original identification documents, a combination of passport and Social Security card, for example, at least one of which must show date of birth and one with your signature. You can have your picture taken on site and receive a temporary ID. Yes, you'll wait in line. The permanent ID will arrive by mail in four to six weeks. For more details go to www.dmv.ny.gov.

To register your car or motorcycle you will need: a registration application or title (completely filled out), proof of ownership, proof of insurance, proof of vehicle inspection, sales tax clearance, and proof of your identity and birth. Read the back of the registration application to determine what "proofs" are acceptable.

The registration fee depends on vehicle weight. New York State requires **liability insurance** on all automobiles, upon the purchase of which, from a licensed insurance company, you will be provided with an FS-20 card, which is your proof of insurance. New York is a no-fault insurance state. Auto emission tests are part of the annual inspection procedure necessary for operating a registered vehicle.

You may find it easier to do your DMV business at one of these offices (all can be reached at 212-645-5550 or 718-966-6155), but be sure to call in advance to make sure that the office conducts the business you need to have done:

- 159 E 125th St, 3rd floor, 212-645-5550, Monday–Friday, 8:30 a.m. to 4
- 625 Atlantic Ave, 2nd floor, Brooklyn, Monday–Friday, 8:30 a.m. to 4 p.m.
- 2875 W 8th St, Brooklyn, Monday–Friday, 8:30 a.m. to 4 p.m., Thursday, 10 a.m. to 6 p.m.
- 696 E Fordham Rd, Bronx, Monday–Friday, 8:30 a.m. to 4 p.m., Thursday 10 a.m. to 6 p.m.; no original license, permit, or non-driver ID transactions
- 1350 Commerce Ave, Bronx, Monday–Friday, 8:30 a.m. to 4 p.m.; license or non-driver IDs only
- 168-46 91st Ave, 2nd floor, Jamaica, Queens, Monday–Friday, 8:30 a.m. to 4 p.m.
- 168-35 Rockaway Blvd, Jamaica, Queens, Monday–Friday, 8:30 a.m. to 4 p.m., Thursday, 10 a.m. to 6 p.m.
- 30-56 Whitestone Expressway, Flushing, Queens, Monday–Friday, 8:30 a.m. to 4 p.m., Thursday, 10 a.m. to 6 p.m.

Long lines are a Department of Motor Vehicles tradition. Best time to go is early in the week, but bring reading material along, *War & Peace* perhaps. Fridays are particularly busy. The last workday of any month can find the line spilling out onto the sidewalk and is to be avoided. Note: for a quickie (10-minute) renewal of your New York State driver's license or car registration, go to the DMV's License Express office. You can also submit your renewal online, though you will need a credit card to pay the fee and will be required to submit proof that your vision has been tested. To renew online, visit www.transact.dmv.ny.gov/PhotoDocRenewal.

For information about the **New Jersey DMV**, go to www.nj.gov/nj/trans.

PARKING

Signs such as "Don't even think of parking here" give you an idea of how difficult it is to park in parts of New York City—particularly Manhattan. You can park legally on city streets if you are prepared to spend several hours a week switching parking spots to conform to the city's alternate-side-of-the-street parking laws. In addition, you will need a crash course in reading the complex street signs that regulate parking on every block—often you'll find several signs regulating various sections of the same block. Call 311 to find out what regulations are in effect on any given day. Certain radio stations, including 1010WINS (1010 on the AM dial) and WNYC (93.9 on the FM dial) also remind listeners of the parking rules of the day during their news broadcasts.

In the boroughs, you'll find street parking in residential areas more easily, though neighborhoods close to Manhattan often become parking lots by day, when commuters leave their cars in less expensive garages or in the dwindling number of street spaces that don't require payment. Some owners of private homes rent daily parking in their driveways and garages to supplement their income; if you intend to take them up on a space, look for discreet "Parking for Rent" signs in outer-borough neighborhoods adjacent to Manhattan. Along main thoroughfares and in commercial shopping areas, such as Forest Hills in Queens, you may have to find garage space if you own a car. While many apartment buildings have garages, some have very long waiting lists, and most residences charge an additional monthly fee for parking (be sure to ask, before signing the lease, whether a parking space is included or whether it will incur an additional fee). In Manhattan monthly garage rates rival the price of monthly rent in other cities.

Note: city residents are exempt from 8% of the 18.375% parking tax. To apply for the exemption, go to www.nyc.gov/html/dof/html/parking/manhattan_parking.shtml, where you can apply or renew online. You must send the name and license number of the lot or garage you use and proof of residence, which can be a copy of your car registration and driver's license. The process must be repeated yearly, but the savings makes it worth the trouble.

If you use a car only occasionally, consider a private garage in a nearby community that is easily accessible by public transportation.

If you are frequenting Manhattan—other than midtown—for shopping or other purposes for a day or evening visit, you can usually find meters. Have plenty of quarters or your credit or debit card ready. Recently, stand-alone meters assigned to each parking space have been replaced by one or two automated machines on each block. You'll need to pay in quarters or with a bank or credit card and obtain a receipt, which is to be displayed on the dashboard of the driver's side of your car. The hours and costs of metered parking vary considerably from one neighborhood to another, so be sure to check signage in the area where you are parking. Nighttime parking can sometimes be easier in parts of the city where parking limits are not in effect between late night and early morning.

Many Manhattanites don't bother owning a car since lack of parking coupled with heavy traffic makes driving to and from the office stressful and inefficient, not to mention the added expense of inevitable parking violations. The cost of renting a car for the few times you really need one—such as taking a trip out of town—is cheaper than paying for parking, car insurance, taxes and fees, and maintenance. Using mass transit, taxis, or car services such as Uber are the preferred methods of getting around the city—especially on weekdays. See the **Transportation** chapter for information about car rentals, including **ZipCar**, an hourly car rental subscription service. For tips on auto services and repair, go to **Helpful Services**.

PARKING TICKETS AND TOWING

What's the price if you get caught?

To help you decide whether to take that parking chance or not, keep in mind that parking tickets issued below 96th Street in Manhattan range from $50 to $165, depending on the violation. (Note: the website for the New York City Department of Finance Parking Violations Operations, www.nyc.gov/html/dof, includes a wealth of parking information, including specifics about how to pay your ticket online, requesting a hearing, and information about towed vehicles.) You can challenge a parking ticket in person, online, or in writing, but the odds of your success are pretty slim, as the city has developed sophisticated ways to substantiate its own case against you.

Should you decide to take a chance and let your meter run over or double-park for a quick errand, you can be sure that a ticket will be waiting on your windshield. If you do get a ticket, you may pay by mail, online, or by phone.

But tickets are only a part of the penalty. The real deterrent to joining the ranks of New York's parking scofflaws is the threat of having your automobile towed. It costs $185 to retrieve your car from the pound, plus $10 a day (which jumps to $15 a day on the third day) for storage, plus a fixed $70 "execution" fee. You'll also have to pay any outstanding tickets before your car will be released. To retrieve your auto, you must first determine who towed it: the NYPD, the Sheriff's Office, or the City Marshal. You'll also need to know whether it was booted before it was towed to the pound. To find out who towed your car and whether it was booted, call 311 or visit the "Locate a Towed Vehicle" page on the city's Department of Finance website: www.nyc.gov/html/dof/html/parking/parking.shtml. You'll need to know your car's license plate number.

When you go to retrieve your car, you'll need to produce the car's registration, insurance card, and your driver's license, as well as a vehicle release form. Each borough has its own tow pound; consult the NYPD's tow pound website for locations, days, and hours: www.nyc.gov/html/nypd/html/towed_vehicles/tow_pounds.shtml. Note that if you haven't retrieved your car within 72 hours of it having been towed, it will likely be sold at auction.

If your car isn't in the pound (and you haven't misplaced it), your car has been stolen, and you should report it to the police. To find out if you have an accumulation of tickets (they sometimes blow off the windshield or are taken by other drivers who put them under their windshield wipers in order to fool cops), you can download your tickets online: www.nyc.gov/html/dof/html/parking/ticket_copies.shtml. You can search by violation number, if you have it, or by your license plate number. Residents outside of New York City should check with their municipality for information regarding traffic/parking citations. In New Jersey, you can pay parking citations online by going to www.judiciary.state.nj.us/atswep/njmcdirectmain. To contact the New Jersey Motor Vehicle Commission, call 609-292-6500.

KEEPING PETS

Can you bring your Portuguese water dog and your Burmese cat to New York? Will that pose a problem? Yes and maybe. The biggest hurdle to clear will be the first: finding an apartment that will accept pets (fish don't count). Many landlords and co-ops prohibit pets in their buildings, which means you may have to choose between the perfect apartment and the perfect pet. Even those landlords and co-ops that do allow pets often put owners through the kind of vetting (pun intended) that's usually reserved for diplomats or high government officials with special security clearance. Expect to produce veterinarian reports, shot records, and even references from people who can attest to your pet's sweet, non-destructive nature. You may even have to appear with your pet for an interview. And be prepared to pay a premium for having a pet. Those buildings that allow them often require a special pet deposit to protect the property against pet-related damage, and they may not allow every size or every breed. Be sure to inquire as you search for a pet-friendly home, and don't plan to sneak one in where they are prohibited. Dogs and cats being the most common city pets, we'll address their needs here. If yours is an exotic pet, say a miniature pig, you're on your own.

You will want to have a vet lined up before you need one. Start by calling the **Veterinary Medical Association of New York City**, 212-246-0057, www.vmanyc. org, for a list of accredited vets in your neighborhood. Visit the dog run, park, or vacant lot in your neighborhood frequented by dogs and their owners to glean information on local vets and the whole range of dog-owner concerns. Choosing a vet, like choosing a physician, is largely a subjective thing. Beyond the cleanliness and friendliness of the establishment, you and your pet will want to be comfortable with this vet. You may want to inquire to be sure your vet is available or covered after hours by an answering service. In case of a serious emergency after hours, the **Manhattan Veterinary Group**, a private animal hospital at 240 East 80th Street, 212-988-1000, www.vcahospitals.com/manhattan-veterinary-group, is open Monday–Friday, 8 a.m. to 7 p.m., and 9 a.m. to 5 p.m. on weekends; the **Animal Medical Center** at 510 East 62nd Street, 212-838-8100, www.amcny.org, is open 24 hours and is one of the premier pet facilities in the city.

Dogs must be licensed by the city's Department of Health. You can call 311 to request a license or download one online at www.nyc.gov/doglicense. The annual fee for licensing is $8.50 if your dog is spayed or neutered and $34 if it is not. The license tag must be worn on the dog's collar. Dogs must be leashed, except inside fenced dog runs; they may not enter playgrounds. Note: besides keeping your dog leashed, you must clean up after your dog. Failure to leash or clean up after your dog can result in a fine.

Dogs typically need to be walked at least three times a day. That's not a problem if you work at home or someone is at home during the day. If you are away for more than eight hours a day, you will probably need a **dog walker**, a person who has your keys and who will come in and take your dog out for 15 to

60 minutes. Expensive? Yes. To find a reliable walker check with other dog owners and your vet for recommendations. Some of the better pet-care establishments keep a list of walkers whose credentials they can vouch for. Some dog walkers will also pet-sit when you are away, either staying in your home to care for your pets and plants or visiting three times a day to feed, water, play with, and walk your pet. The price? Currently a minimum of $22 a day for cats, $25–$35 a day for dogs, more in some neighborhoods. There are kennels in the city, at least one without pens; those out of town, most of which will pick up and deliver your dog, tend to be roomier and less expensive. You may also want to look into doggie day care, an ever-growing specialty business, especially in Manhattan. Again, vets and other pet owners can be a great source of information and recommendations for these and other services.

Dog runs, fenced-in enclosures where dogs can play off-leash, are a New York City institution of sorts, not only a place for pets to socialize, but their owners too. Most, such as those in Riverside Park, are open to all non-aggressive dogs that are not in heat. A few are by membership only and may have a waiting list to get in. To find a dog run in your neighborhood, go to the city's parks website, www. nycgovparks.org/facilities/dogareas, which maintains a list of dog runs and off-leash areas; the list is searchable by borough or by ZIP code. The same site also has a pet owner's guide and a list of rules related to pets in parks.

Other useful websites for pet owners include www.animalalliancenyc.org and www.dogspin.com. If you're looking for pet-friendly places to travel outside the city, www.bringfido.com and www.petswelcome.com are two websites worth bookmarking.

If you're looking to **acquire a dog or cat**, the best place to start is one of the city's shelters or rescue programs. **Center for Animal Care and Control (CACC)**, www.nycacc.org, the largest animal adoption organization in the city, has centers in all five boroughs, and when you adopt, you are saving an animal from almost certain euthanasia. For about $50 to $150, you can adopt a dog or a cat, complete with vaccinations and spaying/neutering. In Manhattan the shelter is at 326 East 110th Street, 212-788-4000, open for adoptions daily, 12 p.m. to 7 p.m. Call for the location and hours of the other four shelters or visitwww.nycacc.org. The **ASPCA Shelter and Adoption Center**, 424 East 92nd Street, 212-876-7700, www.aspca. org, also offers animals for adoption. The **Bide-A-Wee Manhattan Shelter** at 410 East 38th Street, 866-262-8133, www.bideawee.org, does not destroy animals and offers dogs and cats for adoption at minimal cost.

Pet insurance is never a bad idea, especially in New York City, as are vet discount plans. One option for the latter is Pet Assure, which offers members 25% off all medical care and supplies for pets using participating veterinarians and up to 35% off the cost of pet foods, supplies, training, grooming, and boarding at participating establishments in the five boroughs, Manhattan especially. Call 888-789-7387, www.petassure.com. For straight medical coverage, try Veterinary Pet Insurance, 888-899-4VPI, www.petinsurance.com.

Should you lose your dog or find someone else's dog, you can use the city's eLocator system, which uses the dog's license information to reconnect a lost pet with its owner, www.nyc.gov/html/doh/html/environmental/dog-locator.shtml.

FINDING A PHYSICIAN

"What about how to find a doctor?" a plaintive reader inquires, adding, "It's been tough." Indeed. They're out there, more than 13,000 of them in Manhattan alone, but choosing a personal physician is more like choosing a mate than buying a car. You're looking for a doctor who has graduated from an excellent medical school, done residency in a good teaching hospital, is board-certified, has practiced long enough to know what he/she is doing but not so long as to be out of touch with the latest research and technology, and has just the right professional manner—concerned, straightforward, a listener with, perhaps, a good sense of humor. In short, you want a doctor you can rely on. If you put it off until you need one, you're apt to wind up sitting miserably in the nearest emergency room, followed by a big bill.

Most people who are insured will have their choices narrowed down for them somewhat, being forced to choose among a list of in-network, approved doctors. How to narrow that list still more?

Conventional wisdom says that one should have a doctor who is on staff or is an attending physician at one of the **teaching hospitals**. These physicians have been carefully screened and their credentials certified, the reasoning goes, and the teaching hospitals tend to offer a wider range of services and sophisticated procedures than do the smaller community hospitals. Bear in mind also, that as a patient in a teaching hospital, you may be poked and probed by students and residents, and some care may be provided by residents without additional supervision. Many of these hospitals also have student clinics which offer low-cost care, sometimes with financial aid, although this is on a case-by-case basis. In any case, these hospitals have referral services, which is one place to start your search. Referrals are based on medical specialty and location. The major academic hospitals in Manhattan, with their physician referral lines, are:

- **Mount Sinai Beth Israel**, First Ave at 16th St, 212-420-2000, www.bethisraelny. org
- **New York-Presbyterian Hospital**, 650 W 168th St, 212-305-7367, www.nyp.org
- **Mount Sinai Hospital**, Fifth Ave at 100th St, 800-MD-SINAI, www.mountsinai. org
- **New York Presbyterian Hospital-Weill Cornell Medical Center**, 525 E 68th St, 212-746-5454, www.nyp.org
- **NYU Langone Medical Center**, 550 First Ave, 212-263-7300, www.med.nyu. edu
- **Mount Sinai Roosevelt Hospital**, 1000 Tenth Ave, 212-523-4000, www. roosevelthospitalnyc.org

Some of these hospitals also have treatment centers elsewhere, and their doctors practice throughout the metropolitan area.

Another source of referrals is the county medical society, which in Manhattan (NY County Medical Society, 12 East 41st Street, NYC 10017, 212-684-4670, www. nycms.org) has some 6,000 members. The caller can specify the area of choice, hospital of choice, specialty, sex, and be given three names. Note: you can also check on the credentials, training, and board specialties of a physician.

Referral(s) in hand, call the specific doctor's office to ask about an introductory visit. Inquire about office hours and their procedure for an introductory interview, which may be by phone or in person, and what the charge will be. Is the office staff helpful? Before talking with the physician, have your questions written down: in which hospital does he/she practice, who covers for him/her when he/she is unavailable, can he/she be reached by phone after hours if need be, what are his/ her billing procedures, etc. You may also want to discuss such sensitive issues as his/her views on abortion and life support. If you are satisfied so far, you'll probably make an appointment for a physical exam and some tests to establish a baseline profile. Ask about that and what it will cost. If you are not satisfied, go elsewhere.

To assist in the choice of a physician, look into *New York Magazine's* annual "Best Doctors in New York" issue, in which you can gather names of physicians in various fields of medicine. The list is also available online, www.nymag.com/ bestdoctors.

Should you have a **serious complaint** that you cannot resolve with your physician, contact the **New York State Office of Professional Medical Conduct**, NY State Department of Health, 150 Broadway, Suite 355, Albany, NY 12204, 518-402-0836, www.health.ny.gov. In New Jersey, contact the **NJ State Board of Medical Examiners**, 140 East Front Street, Second Floor, Trenton, NJ 08608, 609-826-7100, www.state.nj.us/lps/ca/medical.htm.

VOTER REGISTRATION

Registering to vote is as simple as calling the New York State Board of Elections voter registration hotline, 800-FOR-VOTE, to request a voter application. You can also call the **New York City Board of Elections** at 212-487-5400, www.vote.nyc. ny.us, for an Application for Registration and Enrollment by mail. Complete this form and return it to the board. If you live in another borough, the Manhattan Board will pass the completed application along to the appropriate borough board: Bronx, 718-299-9017; Brooklyn, 718-797-8800; Manhattan, 212-886-2100; Queens, 718-730-6730; and Staten Island, 718-876-0079. Pre-stamped applications are also available in post offices, libraries, and some public agencies. If you enroll in a political party, the form must be received by the Board of Elections 25 days before the primary or general election. You can also register in person at Election Board headquarters, 32 Broadway, 7th floor.

For information on voter registration in New Jersey, visit the website of the state's Division of Elections: www.njelections.org.

LIBRARY CARDS

The New York Public Library, www.nypl.org, is one of the city's great, enduring treasures, with dozens and dozens of branches in neighborhoods across Manhattan, The Bronx, and Staten Island (Brooklyn and Queens have their own library systems). Among its branches are exceptional non-circulating research libraries, numerous special divisions for various disciplines (including the performing arts, science, and business), and famous reference collections. Neighborhood branch libraries are listed at the end of each neighborhood profile in the **Neighborhoods** section.

Library cards are free and entitle you to borrow or request circulating books from any branch in the system. To obtain a card, give your name, address, and proof of residence to the librarian at the return desk of the nearest branch library. Visit www.nypl.org for library hours, which vary widely from branch to branch (some are even open as late as 11 p.m.!).

A wonderful and underutilized resource is ASK NYPL, New York Public Library's telephone reference service, 917-275-6975. Library researchers try to answer all possible questions and, if they cannot, will refer you to the department most likely to have the required data. You can also renew books online by going to the www.nypl.org website.

In New Jersey, library information is available at the New Jersey Library Association's website, www.njla.org, or try one of the following contacts:

- **Edgewater Public Library**, 49 Hudson Ave, Edgewater, NJ 07020, 201-224-6144, www.edgewaterlibrary.org
- **Fort Lee Public Library**, 320 Main St, Fort Lee, NJ 07024, 201-592-3615, www.fortlee.bccls.org
- **Hoboken Public Library**, 500 Park Ave, Hoboken, NJ 07030, 201-420-2280, www.hoboken.bccls.org
- **Jersey City Public Library**, 472 Jersey Ave, Jersey City, NJ 07302, 201-547-4500, www.jclibrary.org
- **Weehawken Public Library**, 49 Hauxhurst Ave, Weehawken, NJ 07086, 201-863-7823, www.weehawken-nj.us/library.html

For more on New York's fabulous literary traditions and opportunities, see **Literary Life** in the **Cultural Life** chapter.

PASSPORTS

Whether you are applying for a passport for the first time or renewing, do not wait until just before your summer or Christmas vacation to do so. Apply early and relax. First, call New York **Passport Agency at 877-487-2778** to schedule an appointment. For detailed information and to download the proper mail-in forms, you can visit the **US Department of State Bureau of Consular Affairs'** link, www. travel.state.gov, or call them at the same number listed above. The automated line works 24 hours a day. Appointments, which are required, are scheduled for slots between 7:30 a.m.–3 p.m. Monday–Friday. General travel information and advisories are also available at the site.

If you are applying for a passport for the first time, you must (1) fill out the U.S. passport application form, #DS-11, which can be downloaded on this website: http://travel.state.gov/content/passports/english.html; (2) submit evidence of U.S. citizenship, which can include a birth certificate, naturalization certificate, or certificate of citizenship; (3) submit one form of primary identification, which can include a driver's license or current government or military ID; (4) bring photocopies of the identification documents; (5) bring payment for your passport; and (6) bring a passport photo. For specifications about size, format, and type of each document, visit the website listed above.

To **renew a passport**, download form **DS-82** from the website listed above and mail it as directed with one passport picture, your expired/expiring passport, and the relevant fee. Allow four to six weeks, more if you're applying in high summer season, or mention the date of your departure on the form; passports are processed on the basis of departure date. You can also pay a higher fee for expedited processing of your renewal request. A passport is good for ten years and can be renewed within two years after expiration.

Visit the New York City Passport Agency for passport processing only if you have an appointment s (see below). The government agencies and post offices listed on this site, referred to as "passport acceptance facilities," can also process your passport application: www.iafdb.travel.state.gov. Enter your ZIP code to find the passport acceptance facility that is closest to you.

Suppose you've got to go to Botswana on short notice, you don't even know what documents and shots you need, and you're too busy to get it together. What to do? For a fee (up to $200 for a same-day passport renewal) the knowledgeable staff at **Passport Plus**, 20 East 49th Street, 212-759-5540, www.passportplus.net, will handle it for you. Be aware, though, they're only open from 9:30 a.m.–5 p.m., Monday-Friday.

BUILDING STAFF

New Yorkers rely on the staff of their buildings in ways that are unique to the city—and they reward their staff in an equally unique manner.

Most multi-unit residences have a superintendent (the "super") who is responsible for the maintenance and day-to-day operation of the building. Some superintendents may be assisted by porters and hallmen. There are also doormen (and today, the occasional doorwoman) in many buildings, and in luxury buildings, perhaps a concierge who runs the building's wine cellar and will bring you up your bottle, not to mention in-house massage therapists.

Because many New Yorkers do not rely on their cars to accomplish their daily tasks, goods and services are delivered by businesses to the consumer's home even when they are not there, hence the importance of building staff. Other staff duties may include hailing cabs, supplying important building information, directing repair people, door holding and—in some buildings—even mail delivery. Most of all, your staff, particularly the doorman, is the first line of security in your building, making certain that anyone who seeks entrance truly belongs there.

In addition to the generally higher rents found in staffed buildings, there is an unspoken cost associated with the extra service. It is widely expected that a building's residents tip the staff at Christmastime for general services rendered throughout the year. (Anything beyond a general service, such as pet-walking or heavy lifting, is best attended to at the time the service is performed.) The tip is by no means mandatory, but individual service has been known to decline precipitously for tight-fisted residents. The custom varies widely from building to building, both in terms of cost and how the money is dispersed. It is a good idea to find out what is customary in your building and budget for the holiday season accordingly.

CITY SAFETY

The incidence of violent crime in New York City has declined significantly in the past two decades, and both city and federal law enforcement agencies responsible for monitoring crime statistics indicate that New York City is among the safest urban areas in the United States Despite this good news, it is still prudent to pay attention to your surroundings and be cautious, particularly for those new to an urban environment. Consider the following:

- Always remain alert to what is around you (in front and in back); if you don't pay attention to your surroundings, you make yourself a target for crime.
- Trust your instincts; they are usually right.
- Stay clear of deserted areas such as empty streets, uninhabited subway cars or platforms, and poorly lit automatic teller machines.
- If you must take the subway late at night, always get in the car that houses the brakeman (generally one of the middle cars). Typically, there is a black and white "zebra" sign marking the spot where the brakeman's car stops.
- Look for children playing outside or women walking on their own as signs that an area is safe.
- If you do find yourself on an ominous-looking block, avoid the sidewalk and walk directly in the street to be in view of traffic.
- If you feel you are being followed, walk into the nearest restaurant or store, or flag a cab.
- Conceal your valuables, and if you wear a ring, turn it around so only the band is showing. Cover watches and necklaces or put jewelry away when riding the subway.

- Avoid using smartphones or other electronic devices on the subway. Though it appears everyone else is doing so, theft of electronic devices is among the top crimes in the city.
- Hold your handbag close to you, wearing the strap across your chest, keeping the bag in front of you. Don't hang a purse on a restaurant chair or restroom hook. Men, don't put your wallet in your back pocket.
- Do not count your money in public or use big bills. Tuck your money in a safe place before leaving an ATM vestibule or bank lobby.
- If you're walking alone, or even as a pair, avoid crowds of teens (or any groups) congregated or hanging out on street corners. Cross the street and walk on the other side.
- Beware of operators working as a team: someone who tells you she just dropped her contact lens might well have a friend who is reaching in your handbag.
- Do not hold or open doors that are supposed to be locked in your apartment building for anyone you do not know.
- Remember: you do not owe a response to anyone who asks for one. This may seem callous, but it is better to err on the side of bad manners rather than bad judgment. Go with your instincts.

The New York City Police Department publishes free brochures on safety. These booklets include safety precautions addressed to men, women, children, and the elderly—even to runners. Brochure topics also include how to safeguard your apartment, car, and small business. See the final section of this book for emergency phone numbers. Residents outside of New York City should contact their local police station for similar pamphlets and safety initiatives.

Police officers, being human, can err, and unfortunately, sometimes these are errors of judgment. If you witness or experience inappropriate behavior or actions by an officer and wish to register a complaint, you may do so by contacting the Civilian Complaint Review Board at 100 Church Street. You may also submit a complaint online, at https://www.nyc.gov/html/ccrb/html/complaint/online.shtml. To speak directly with a CCRB representative, call 1-800-341-2272.

If your security desires can only be satisfied by high-tech gadgetry, you may want to pay a visit to one of the city's many spy shops, including the aptly-named Spy Shops at 138 East 34th Street, 212-SPY-SHOPS, www.spyshopsinc.com.

Finally, become involved in your neighborhood. All over town, people organize block associations to monitor crime and make stronger communities by helping out and working together. To find out if a block association exists in your neighborhood, or to set one up, call **Citizen's Committee for NYC** at 212-989-0909, www.citizensnyc.org.

Contrary to popular belief, when it comes to the good of the common cause, New Yorkers have shown a remarkable ability to go above and beyond. In numerous instances, including the citywide power outage in 2003, transit strikes, paralyzing snowstorms, the tragedy of September 11, 2001, and Hurricane Sandy in 2012, New Yorkers have pulled together and helped each other. You'll likely be surprised to see otherwise hurried and harried New Yorkers stop to offer directions or assistance to bewildered visitors in subways or street corners, and as a newcomer, you may benefit from neighbors who are far friendlier than dramatic movies and TV shows might lead you to believe.

I T SHOULD COME AS NO SURPRISE THAT THE INTERNATIONAL SERVICE CAP-
ital is as energetic in supplying the needs of New Yorkers as it is of those the
world over. Multitudinous talents and supremely innovative minds combine
to provide a mind-boggling array of services, for individuals as well as for industry.
Local magazines and newspapers seldom let an issue go by without feature articles about umbrella repair specialists, third-generation tapestry re-weavers, or
the pair of clever Upper East Side women available to organize your closets and
your life. We'll leave these summaries of the city's more *recherché* services to the
press and provide instead the names of a few representative firms and organizations that supply basics such as house cleaning, mail and shipping services, auto
and computer repair, as well as organizations to contact for consumer protection.
We also provide listings for organizations that address the concerns of women
contemplating pregnancy and childbirth, the lesbian and gay communities, the
needs of senior citizens, people with disabilities, and immigrant newcomers.

Note: the listing in this book is merely informational and is not an endorsement or recommendation by First Books. Addresses are in Manhattan unless
otherwise noted.

HOUSE CLEANING

Practically any service can be retained—for a price—in New York City, and house
cleaning is among the most common of them. Even if you associate house
cleaning with the upper crust, you might be surprised to learn that a whole crop of
affordable and professional cleaning companies have sprung up around the city
in recent years, with one of the most popular and affordable being Handybook,
www.handybook.com. Rates are typically set by the hour and include your choice
of specific cleaning services, which may range from light cleaning (dusting, vacu-
uming, and the like) to more involved jobs, such as refrigerator and oven cleaning

and other deep cleaning tasks). Below are some reputable companies that provide home cleaning services.

- **Flatiron Cleaning Co.**, 231 W 29 St, 212-876-1000, www.flatironcleaning. com; founded in 1893, it was the first cleaning agency in New York. For regular service, the same person will be sent when possible. One or two days' notice required. Help is bonded. Maids use your supplies. Provides online estimates.
- **Handybook**, 888-847-6036, www.handybook.com; perhaps the city's most affordable and professional cleaning service, with easy-to-book reservations (including last-minute services). Cleaners arrive with their own equipment and supplies. In addition to cleaning, clients can also book handyman services, including minor repairs, furniture assembly, and electronics installations. Discounts are provided for customers who sign up for multiple cleanings (either weekly, biweekly, or monthly).
- **Lend-a-Hand, Inc.**, 350 5th Ave, 59th floor, 212-614-9118, www.lendahandny.com; actors, musicians, and dancers moonlight as housecleaners through this company, which is also a one-stop-shop for party, clerical, and dog walking services.
- **Maid in New York**, 118 E 28th St, 212-777-6000, www.maidinnewyork.com; homes as well as industrial sites and business offices are serviced by some 100 employees. Times and schedules are arranged to suit the client: weekly, bi-weekly, or just once for a thorough spring cleaning. Provides online estimates. Fully insured and bonded.

MAIL AND SHIPPING SERVICES

The **General Post Office** has sat prominently at 421 Eighth Avenue between 31st and 33rd streets since 1913. It is open 24 hours a day, seven days a week, though agents are not available at all hours (stamps and other postal services can still be purchased via automated machines). Be advised that last collection is 5 p.m., Monday through Sunday). Addresses for neighborhood post offices are listed in the information provided following each neighborhood description; the telephone number and website are 1-800-ASK-USPS (1-800-275-8777) and www.usps.com.

If you want to rent a post office box in order to receive your mail, expect the cost to vary based on several factors, including location of the post office and size of the box. You will typically have the option to rent and renew your P.O. Box for either six months or a full year. Inquire at the window for specific rates and requirements. To snag a box at a high-occupancy station, line up early on the 15th of the month, when leases expire.

If you need more than a box, a mail service center, which will also forward mail and typically offer fax and copy service, may be your best bet. Such services have even been known to accept dry cleaning and flowers for their customers. The UPS Store is the most prolific chain in the city. Check its website, www.theupsstore.com, for a comprehensive list of locations and services. Less expensive are neighborhood businesses that take in mail and offer no services beyond renting boxes and notifying their occupants of package arrival.

Need to send a set of golf clubs to your brother in Kansas? Then you need a shipping service. National package delivery services include:

- **Craters & Freighters**, 333 Cedar Ave, Middlesex, NJ 08846, 877-744-7535, www.cratersandfreighters.com; for especially heavy or bulky items
- **DHL**, 800-527-7298, www.dhl.com
- **FedEx, and FedEx Ground**, 800-463-3339, www.fedex.com
- **United Parcel Service (UPS)**, 800-742-5877, www.ups.com
- **US Postal Service Express Mail**, 800-222-1811, www.usps.com

JUNK MAIL

Junk mail will surely follow you to your new locale. In order to curtail this kind of unwanted mail, visit the website of **Direct Marketing Association** at www.dmachoice.org, and complete the online form to register for the "name removal file." Some catalogue companies will need to be contacted directly with a purge request. You can also opt out of junk e-mail on the same website. The service will accept three non-business e-mail addresses at a time. This should reduce the amount of e-mail you receive from national e-mail lists; however, keep in mind that it will not eliminate junk mail completely. Another option is to call the "opt-out" line at 888-567-8688, and request that the main credit bureaus not release your name and address to interested marketing companies. Finally, you can **curb phone solicitations** by going to the government's do-not-call registry, www.donotcall.gov, and registering your phone number.

AUTOMOBILE SERVICES AND REPAIR

There are hundreds of auto repair shops throughout the city, and many of them are competent and honest. Which ones? Alas, there is no consumer rating system for auto repair shops. Talk to friends and colleagues for their recommendations before you have a problem; you may find a gem of a repairman. If so, try to establish a good rapport—they're often just as valuable as a good doctor. Recommendation in hand, before taking your car in, it's still a good idea to check with the Better Business Bureau to see if any complaints have been filed against a repair shop. Membership in AAA (American Automobile Association), $52–192, depending upon the level of membership, is probably the best investment you can make in your car in the city. The emergency road service alone, with free battery charge and free towing within a three-mile radius to an AAA-affiliated service station, is worth the membership fee. Their list of affiliated stations is a valuable starting point. Members also receive free maps, trip-planning services, trip interruption insurance, the service of AAA travel agents, travel discounts, and a host of products and services. For a list of membership levels and the benefits of each, visit www.ny.aaa.com. When all else fails, try the website for NPR's popular radio show "Car Talk," www.cartalk.com. The site has useful information on buying, selling, and owning cars, and a helpful "find a mechanic" section.

COMPUTER REPAIRS

Of course, you should always back up your files, but still: computer problems happen. If you need your computer repaired, the first thing you should do is call the manufacturer's tech support line to see if they can help, especially if you're still covered by a warranty or an optional protection plan you bought when you purchased the computer. If you can't get the troubleshooting help you need via phone, call a repair shop and describe the problem; a good shop may be able to talk you through a diagnosis and self-repair. Before taking the computer in, ask if the shop stocks spare parts for your system, how long repairs typically take, if there is a diagnostic fee, and if that fee will be applied toward any work they do to fix the computer. Be sure to get an estimate and confirm that they are not to do any work until it has been authorized by you. If the technician seems vague or intimidating, call someone else. As with auto repair shops, be sure to check with the Better Business Bureau to see if any complaints have been filed against a particular shop before you take your computer in for repairs.

New York City repair shops with solid reputations include:

- **Apple Store Genius Bar**, multiple locations, including inside Grand Central, 45 Grand Central Terminal, 212-284-1800, www.apple.com/retail/grandcentral; Macs only
- **New York Computer Help**, 53 E. 34th St, 212-259-0339, www.newyorkcomputerhelp.com; Macs, PCs, and smartphones
- **Tekserve**, 119 W 23rd St, 212-929-3645, www.tekserve.com; Macs only

CONSUMER PROTECTION—RIP-OFF RECOURSE

It goes without saying that the best defense against fraud and consumer victimization is to avoid it. Read all contracts (including the fine print), save your receipts and canceled checks, get the name of telephone sales and service people with whom you deal, and check a contractor's license number with the Department of Consumer Affairs for complaints. Still, getting stung can happen. A dry cleaner returns your blue suit, but now it's purple and he shrugs. A shop refuses to give you a refund as promised on the expensive gift that didn't suit your mother. Your landlord fails to return your security deposit when you move. After $733 in repairs to your automobile's engine, the car now vibrates wildly, and the mechanic claims innocence. Negotiations, documents in hand, fail. You're angry and embarrassed because you've been had. *There is something you can do*:

- File a complaint with the **New York State Division of Consumer Protection,** 518-474-8583, www.dos.ny.gov/consumerprotection, or the **New York State Consumer Frauds and Protection Bureau**, Office of the Attorney General, 800-771-7755, www.ag.ny.gov/bureau/consumer-frauds-bureau. Both have complaint forms you can complete and file online. Again, have all your documentation organized and in hand.
- Consult the **NYC Department of Consumer Affairs**, Complaints Department, http://www.nyc.gov/html/dca/html/resources/complaint.shtml, for information on filing a complaint.
- File suit for relief, up to $5,000, in **small claims court**. You do not need a lawyer, and precise steps for pursuing a case in small claims court are provided on the city's website at www.nyc.gov/html/dca/html/publications/publications_small_claims.shtml. You can also call 212-791-6000 for additional information. There are five small claims locations in the city, one in each borough. Be advised that winning in small claims court is much easier than ever collecting on a judgment.
- In New Jersey, file a complaint with the **New Jersey State Office of Consumer Protection**, 124 Halsey St, Newark, NJ 07102, 973-504-6200, www.njconsumeraffairs. gov.

Before doing any of the above, inform your adversary of your intentions, politely but firmly. You may force a settlement, thereby saving yourself the trouble of following through.

IMMIGRANT NEWCOMERS

Multinational New York City has been a doorway—and homestead—for immigrants since its very founding. It is probably easier here than anywhere else for transplanted citizens to find one another. According to the 2010 census, 36.9% of the city's populace is foreign-born. But New York is still very much an American city, and navigating its bureaucracies, legalities, and idiosyncrasies can be baffling. For advice and legal matters, your best first resource may be your embassy or consulate, many of which are listed below. For a full listing, check www.nyc. gov/html/ia/html/affairs/consular.shtml. To better understand the ins and outs of everything from American states to American business etiquette, consult the *Newcomer's Handbook for Moving to and Living in the USA* by Mike Livingston, published by **First Books**. Call 503-968-6777 or visit www.firstbooks.com.

CONSULATES

There are over 80 consulates in New York City. Here are a few:

- **Consulate General of Australia**, 150 E 42nd St, 34th floor, NYC 10017, 212-351-6500, www.newyork.consulate.gov.au/nycg/home.html

- **Consulate General of Brazil**, 225 E 41st St, NYC 10017, 917-777-7777, http:// novayork.itamaraty.gov.br/en-us/
- **Consulate General of Canada**, 1251 Ave of the Americas, NYC 10020, 212-596- 1628, www.can-am.gc.ca/new-york/menu.aspx
- **Consulate General of China**, 520 12th Ave, NYC 10036, 212-868-2078, www. nyconsulate.prchina.org
- **Consulate General of the Federal Republic of Germany**, 871 United Nations Plaza, NYC 10017, 212-610-9700, www.germany.info/newyork
- **Consulate General of France**, 934 Fifth Ave, NYC 10021, 212-606-3600, www. consulfrance-newyork.org
- **Consulate General of Great Britain**, 845 Third Ave, NYC 10022, 212-745-0200, www.gov.uk/government/world/organisations/ british-consulate-general-new-york
- **Consulate General of Italy**, 690 Park Ave, NYC 10065, 212-737-9100, www. consnewyork.esteri.it
- **Consulate General of Japan**, 299 Park Ave, 18th floor, NYC 10171, 212-371- 8222, www.ny.us.emb-japan.go.jp
- **Consulate General of Mexico**, 27 E 39th St, NYC 10016, 212-217-6400, http:// consulmex.sre.gob.mx/nuevayork/
- **Consulate General of Poland**, 233 Madison Ave, NYC 10016, 646-237-2100, www.nowyjork.msz.gov.pl/en
- **Consulate General of the Russian Federation**, 9 E 91st St, NYC 10128, 212- 348-0926, www.ruscon.org

IMMIGRATION AND NATURALIZATION SERVICE

US Citizenship and Immigration Services (CIS) for New York City is in lower Manhattan: USCIS New York City District Office, Jacob Javits Federal Building, 26 Federal Plaza, 3rd floor, NYC 10278, 800-375-5283, www.uscis.gov.

IMMIGRATION RESOURCES

- **Bureau of Immigration and Customs Enforcement**, www.ice.gov
- **Customs & Border Protection**, www.cbp.gov
- **Department of Homeland Security**, www.dhs.gov
- **General Government Questions**, 800-333-4636, www.usa.gov
- **International Center of Catholic Charities Community Services**, 80 Maiden Ln, 14th floor, NYC 10038, 646-794-3745, www.newintlcenter.org; English con- versation and American culture for immigrant newcomers
- **Social Security Administration**, 800-772-1213, www.ssa.gov
- **U.S. Department of Consular Affairs**, www.travel.state.gov
- **U.S. Department of State**, www.usvisas.state.gov, Visa Services

- **U.S. Immigration Online**, www.uscis.gov, Green Cards, Visas, Government Forms,

PUBLICATIONS

"America is too rich in contradictions for any definition of it to be possible." This quote from British economist John Gray opens the **Newcomer's Handbook for Moving to and Living in the USA** by Mike Livingston (First Books), and fittingly. A wealth of information in a compact volume, this handbook is an excellent reference for everything from currency to street signs to the public education system. It will help you sort through the nuances (and oddities) of American culture and behavior. Visit **www.firstbooks.com**.

MOVING PETS TO THE US

- **The Pet-Moving Handbook** (First Books) covers domestic and international moves, via car, airplane, ferry, etc. Primary focus is on cats and dogs.
- **Cosmopolitan Canine Carriers**, based in Connecticut, 800-243-9105, www.caninecarriers.com, has been shipping dogs and cats all over the world since 1972. Contact them with questions or concerns regarding air transportation arrangements, vaccinations, and quarantine times.

PREGNANCY, LABOR & DELIVERY, AND POSTPARTUM SERVICES

Stories about challenges related to certain aspects of child-rearing in the city (namely, getting your kid into a good, safe, and affordable school) are both legion and legendary, but no one really tells you what to expect *before* you ever get to that stage of family decision-making.

Specifically, no one ever tells you that your plans for pregnancy, labor and delivery, and postpartum services should really be laid out long before you actually ever *get* pregnant in New York City. As with schools, you have so many options that you'll seem spoiled for choice. However, so many women and their partners are seeking these services that there are often waiting lists or other factors that may delay your access to them. Midwives, in particular, tend to have long waiting lists, as many women seek alternatives to a traditional OB/GYN. Becoming aware of the alternatives as early as possible and making some preliminary decisions about your prenatal, labor and delivery, and postpartum care will make your pregnancy and the period beyond go much more smoothly.

New York's major hospitals, all listed in the neighborhood sections, have traditional labor and delivery units. Out-of-pocket costs for labor and delivery vary dramatically from one hospital to another, so if you have insurance, check to see what services are covered, at what institutions, and by which providers. From there, you can start to narrow down your choices. Another factor to consider is the C-section rates of each hospital, which vary as dramatically as the costs of giving birth.

If you are interested in natural birth, there are two birthing centers that are currently operating in the city. One is located in Mt. Sinai Roosevelt Hospital in Manhattan. You must be under the care of a midwife or OB/GYN who has privileges to practice and deliver in the birthing center; a list of those providers, as well as detailed information about the birthing center, is available here: www.nywomenshealth.com. This center is ideal because it is located on the same floor as the labor and delivery unit; if any complications should arise, you'll have immediate access to other specialized care.

The other birthing center is a private, free-standing clinic in Brooklyn, Brooklyn Birthing Center, www.brooklynbirthingcenter.com. You must be under the care of one of the midwives in the Brooklyn Midwifery Group, which is in the same building. Staff has admitting privileges at Maimonides Medical Center. If you live in The Bronx, it's worth looking into the Birthing Spa at Bronx Lebanon Hospital, www.bronxcare.org.

Home births, while controversial, have become wildly popular in the city. For more information, consult the website of Homebirth Midwives of New York, www.nyhomebirth.com.

As with traditional labor and delivery in a hospital setting, you'll want to check with your insurance provider to determine whether services provided by a birthing center or home birth specialist are covered.

The New York State Department of Health has produced a useful booklet that details many other factors to take into consideration when planning a pregnancy: www.health.ny.gov/publications/2935.pdf.

Both traditional hospitals and OB/GYNs, as well as midwives, provide follow-up postpartum care. When considering a provider and setting, be sure to ask about the extent of postpartum resources provided.

LESBIAN AND GAY CONCERNS

In a city with large and established lesbian and gay communities, there are many organizations, businesses, and publications that address their various needs and interests—too many to detail here. We mention one important umbrella organization and five other resources as starting points. All are in Manhattan.

- **The Lesbian, Gay, Bisexual & Transgender Center**, better known as "The Center," 208 W 13th St, 212-620-7310, www.gaycenter.org; is just that, and it offers numerous services seven days a week, 365 days a year in a renovated, 150-year-old former schoolhouse in Greenwich Village. Besides social, cultural, and recreational offerings and events galore, there are alcohol and substance abuse counseling; adoption and parenting support; a gender identity project; a variety of HIV/AIDS-related services, counseling and bereavement support; couples mediation; and public policy programs, among others. Center orientation provides newcomers to the city with "a map of New York's organized lesbian and gay community"; it offers a monthly open house known as the "Orientation Welcome Wagon" and a "Welcome Packet" for gay, lesbian, bisexual, and transgender tourists, which includes entertainment guides listing gay bars, clubs, and restaurants; fliers on cultural programs; and a monthly calendar of events. The center's website is updated regularly and hyperlinked with most New York City and national gay organizations; it also contains a daily calendar of events.

- **Callen-Lorde Community Health Center**, 356 W 18th St, 212-271-7200, www. callen-lorde.org, is the largest primary health care center in the country devoted to lesbians, bisexuals, gay men, and transgendered people. Uninsured patients pay on a sliding scale, according to their income.
- **Rainbow Roommates**, 75 West End Ave, 212-757-2865, www.rainbowroommates.com, is an apartment share referral service for the gay and lesbian community throughout the city and in New Jersey. Access to listings is by subscription; subscriptions range from one day to 90 days.
- **Services & Advocacy for Gay, Lesbian, Bisexual & Transgender Elders (SAGE)**, 305 7th Ave, 15th floor, 212-741-2247, www.sageusa.org, is a nonprofit community support agency that offers workshops, discussion groups, and day trips for gay seniors, many of them for free. With an annual membership, which starts at $35 for individuals, one receives a monthly events calendar and discounts on Broadway, Off-Broadway, and other performing arts events tickets.

RESOURCES AND SERVICES FOR PEOPLE WITH DISABILITIES

Living in New York City with a disability has never been easy, but after passage of the federal Americans with Disabilities Act (ADA) in 1990, the city began to address the needs of the disabled more seriously. Increasingly, street curbs and public buildings were modified to become wheelchair accessible. Following are some New York services, organizations, and resources that make life safer, easier, and more pleasant for people with disabilities. For a complete listing of services in New York City, call 311 or visit the website of the Mayor's Office for People with Disabilities, www.nyc.gov/html/mopd/html/home/home.shtml. (In New Jersey, call 888-285-3036 or go to the **New Jersey Department of Human Services**, Disabilities Services section www.state.nj.us/humanservices/clients/disability.)

GETTING AROUND

- **Buses**: All buses operated by the Metropolitan Transit Authority (MTA) are wheelchair-accessible. Some have lifts at the rear door, while others have lifts at the front door. If you have a qualifying disability or are 65 years of age or older, you are eligible for reduced fare travel on MTA buses and subways. To get the reduced fare card and for more information, go to http://web.mta.info/nyct/fare/rfapply.htm , where you can download an application form.

- **Subway:** Keep in mind that the New York City subway system is more than 100 years old and stations are in various states of accessibility. On the MTA website, you can access a complete list of the subway stations that are accessible to people in wheelchairs and with other assistive devices, http://web.mta.info/accessibility/stations.htm. Elevators and escalators are frequently out of service; before you head out, be sure to check the MTA website for the current status of service at the stations where you plan to transfer, http://advisory.mtanyct.info/EEoutage/. For additional questions, call the MTA customer service line at 511.
- **Access-a-Ride** is a city program that contracts with private carriers to provide rides for customers who are unable to use city bus or subway service for some or all of their trips. For more information, go to http://web.mta.info/nyct/para-tran/guide.htm.
- **Parking Permits for People with Disabilities (PPPD):** The city Department of Transportation issues two types of permits for citizens with disabilities: the New York State permit, which allows the driver to park in spaces marked by the International Symbol of Access, which in the city are all off-street in parking lots; and the NYC permit, which allows the driver to park on city streets in all "no parking" and "restricted parking" zones. For more information and to request an application for either or both permits write: Parking Permits for People with Disabilities (PPPD), NYC Department of Transportation, 28-11 Queens Plaza North, 8th floor, Long Island City, NY 11101-4008, or call 718-433-3100; TTY 212-504-4115. You can also visit the city's website for parking permits at www.nyc.gov/html/dot/html/motorist/pppdinfo.shtml. There, you can apply for or renew your permit.

COMMUNICATION

- **New York Relay Center**, TTY 800-662-1220; others 800-421-1220
- The **Verizon Center for Customers with Disabilities,** 800-974-6006 (voice and TTY), offers information, services, and a variety of adaptive communications equipment necessary or useful to people with various disabilities, including TTYs, videophones, amplified phones, and large print or Braille bills.

OTHER RESOURCES

- *Able*, a monthly newspaper "Positively For, By, and About the Disabled," with news, commentary, a calendar of events, and ads of interest to people with disabilities. Write P.O. Box 395, Old Bethpage, NY 11804, or call 516-939-2253. The online edition is available at www.ablenews.com.
- **Andrew Heiskell Braille and Talking Book Library**, 40 W 20th St, 212-206-5400, TTY 212-206-5458, www.nypl.org/locations/heiskell; wheelchair accessible,

offers books in Braille and recorded books, an extensive collection of large-print books, print and non-print materials on disabilities. Also here, a collection of community information services on resources for people with disabilities, as well as recreational, cultural, and service-oriented programming for and about people with disabilities.

- **Associated Blind**, 135 W 23rd St, 212-620-9109, manages more than apartments for the blind and wheelchair bound at this address, but there is a long waiting list and reviews of both the property and the management are not positive.
- **Center for Hearing and Communication**, 50 Broadway, 6th floor, 917-305-7700, www.chchearing.org; provides a range of services, including hearing rehabilitation. Call for their resource manual or get information on their programs and services from their website.
- **Con Edison Special Services** for the hearing and sight-impaired, as well as people with physical disabilities. Visit www.coned.com/customercentral/specialservices.asp for more information, as well as a listing of phone numbers that correspond to the variety of services available.
- *Exceptional Parent Magazine*, 800-372-7368, www.eparent.com, is a guide for parents of children and young adults with disabilities or health problems. Also publishes an annual resource guide available in bookstores or through the magazine.
- **Goodwill Industries International**, 4-21 27th Ave, Astoria, Queens, 718-728-5400, www.goodwillnynj.org, offers a host of job training and computer classes for people with physical and mental disabilities. The organization also hosts a day treatment program for adults with psychiatric disorders.
- **Healing Arts Initiative (HAI)**, 33-02 Skillman Ave, 1st floor, Long Island City, 212-284-4100, www.hainyc.org, provides access to the arts for New Yorkers with disabilities. Discount tickets for Broadway shows and a community performing arts series are among their services.
- **Institute for Career Development (ICD)**, 123 William St, 5th floor, 212-585-6009, TTY 212-585-6060, www.icdnyc.org, provides primary medical care, vocational evaluation, and job training and placement for learning and physically disabled.
- **Learning Disabilities Association Helpline**, 212-645-6730, www.ldanyc.org; operated by the Learning Disabilities Association of New York, 237 W 35th St, Suite 1101; provides information and referrals in English and Spanish from their database of resources for the learning disabled.
- **The Lighthouse, Inc.**, 111 E 59th St, 212-821-9200 or 800-829-0500, www.lighthouse.org, provides vision rehabilitation and other services to the visually impaired. Services include readers, mobility training, computer training, career services, a child development center, and adaptive skills classes.
- **Mayor's Office for People with Disabilities**, 311; www.nyc.gov/html/mopd/html/home/home.shtml, for information and referrals.

- **Metropolitan Museum of Art**, 1000 Fifth Ave, 212-535-7710, TTY 212-570-3828, www.metmuseum.org/learn/for-visitors-with-disabilities, is wheelchair accessible and has programs with sign language interpretation for the hearing impaired; guides by appointment only for the visually impaired; tours and programs for the developmentally disabled.
- **National Center for Learning Disabilities**, 381 Park Ave S, Suite 1401, 212-545-7510, www.ncld.org; provides information and referrals concerning learning disabilities in children and adults; website has links to related organizations and resources, publications, and relevant events. Areas of focus include dyslexia and adult literacy.
- **New York Public Library Branches** (see also Andrew Heiskell Library above). At present, 70 of the branches in the NYPL system are fully wheelchair accessible; many others are classified as partially accessible. The listing of branches found at www.nypl.org/locations includes indications about which are fully accessible. Many branches in the Brooklyn and Queens systems are accessible too; call your local branch to determine if it is fully accessible.
- **Resources for Children with Special Needs**, 116 E 16th St, 5th floor, 212-677-4650, www.resourcesnyc.org, bills itself as the city's "only independent nonprofit that works for families and children with all disabilities, across all boroughs, to understand, navigate, and access the services needed to ensure that all children have the opportunity to develop their full potential."
- **Rusk Institute of Rehabilitation Medicine**'s driver training program, www.rusk.med.nyu.edu/driver-rehabilitation-program, offers technicians to evaluate the particular needs of prospective drivers with physical handicaps, adapting each car with special devices, and train the driver to operate the adapted car.
- **TAP Accessibility Program, Theater Access Project of the Theatre Development Fund**, 520 8th Ave, Suite 801, 212-912-9770, TTY 212-719-4537, www.tdf.org/nyc/33/TDFAccessibilityPrograms, offers a wide range of services for an equally diverse range of people with special needs, including autism, hearing and vision loss, and limited mobility.
- **TechWorks Technology Resource Centers** operated by United Cerebral Palsy of New York City, can be visited in Manhattan and Brooklyn to view, learn about, and try a range of adaptive products and get information about others through a resource specialist and catalogues. Products range from adapted toys to augmentative communication devices, computers, home products, and accessibility modifications. Call 877-827-2666 for addresses, hours, and additional information.
- **Visions Services for the Blind and Visually Impaired**, 500 Greenwich St, 3rd floor, 212-625-1616, www.visionsvcb.org; offers free and low-cost rehabilitation and social services to the blind and multi- , including those who are non-English speaking. Self-help audio guides at cost teach life skills, and there are peer support groups and recreation year-round at Vacation Camp for the Blind in Rockland County, transportation provided.

RESOURCES AND SERVICES FOR SENIORS

The prime source of services and assistance for seniors here is the city's **Department for the Aging (DFTA)**, whose website, www.nyc.gov/html/dfta/html/home/home.shtml, is useful in discovering and accessing these services. Call 311 for information.

The Department for the Aging also operates several hundred senior centers throughout the boroughs, where meals are served, cultural trips originate, and outreach gives access to other services. The department offers guidance on government benefits and referral to community services; provides transportation for health care, social services, and necessities; arranges home care for the qualified; helps victims of elder abuse; offers job training for the employable unemployed; subsidizes part-time employment; offers computer training and customer service skills and placement in jobs in private industry; arranges legal assistance to those in need; and more.

Some useful resources:

• **Alzheimer's and Caregiver Resource Center of the New York City Department for the Aging**, 212-442-3086, offers counseling and referrals for families of seniors with Alzheimer's disease.
• **Elderly Pharmaceutical Insurance Coverage (EPIC) Program**, 800-332-3742, www.health.state.ny.us/health_care/epic, offers savings on the cost of drugs for qualified individuals.
• **Health insurance information and counseling**, www.nystateofhealth.ny.gov
• **Housing**, for the department's *Alternatives in Senior Housing: A Comprehensive Guide for New York City*, visit www.nyc.gov/html/dfta/html/benefits/housing. shtml, where you can download guides for each borough. The same link provides many resources about affordable housing, home sharing, emergency housing, and other housing resources specific to seniors.
• **Legal assistance**: Call 311 for legal resources specific to seniors. A list of services can also be accessed online at www.nyc.gov/html/dfta/html/services/legal.shtml.
• **Reduced fare for seniors**: people with disabilities and those 65 and older can purchase a reduced fare MetroCard. You can learn more about eligibility requirements and apply for a reduced fare card online at http://web.mta.info/metrocard/.
• **Senior Citizen Rent Increase Exemption (SCRIE)** is for those over 62 whose income falls below $50,000; this is a city subsidy. Call 311 for more information or visit www.nyc.gov/html/hpd/html/tenants/scrie.shtml.
• **State School Tax Relief (STAR)** offers reduced school property taxes for homeowners (condos and co-ops included) on limited incomes. Visit www.tax.ny.gov/pit/property/star/index.htm for more information.

Under state law **new rental housing** in the city is frequently classified **80/20**, which means that 20% of the apartments are reserved for people classified as low-income; the apartments are rented at below-market rates. Applicants are chosen by lottery, and the waiting list is long. Get on the list before you need the apartment. To find out if you are eligible and to get on a waiting list, visit the website of the **New York State Housing Finance Agency (HFA)** at www.nyshcr.org.

The city abounds in culture at a discount for seniors. Museums, movie theaters, and some theaters discount admission for seniors, and state parks and historic sites are free to seniors who present a photo ID that includes date of birth.

Exercise programs for seniors, free or low cost, are widely available. Exercise classes, stress management, and walking clubs are located in many senior centers. Call **Health Promotion Services (HPS)**, 212-442-0954, to find out more. The Parks and Recreation Department operates nearly 50 recreation centers in the city (membership, $25 annually for seniors, $150 for adults), some of which offer senior aerobics and other classes. The Parks Department also sponsors concerts in the parks and other activities. For all parks information, call the citywide information line 311 or visit www.nycparks.org. Finally, there are exercise programs for seniors at many YMCAs (see **Health Clubs and YMCAs** in the **Sports and Recreation** chapter).

Access to college courses on a "space available" basis is offered to seniors at a discount by most of the major universities and colleges in the city. To name some:

- **Brooklyn College**, Brooklyn Lifelong Learning Program, 718-951-5647, www.brooklyn.cuny.edu/web/academics/centers/irpe.php
- **City University of New York**, Quest Learning Community Program, 212-925-6625, www.questlifelong.org, offering free course auditing to those 60 and older in the four-year colleges, enrollment courses (for credit) in the community colleges.
- **College of Staten Island**, Adults Returning to the Classroom, 718-982-2470, www.csi.cuny.edu/admissions/arc.html
- **Columbia University**, Lifelong Learners, 212-854-0419, www.ce.columbia.edu/auditing/lifelong-learners-auditing-program
- **Fordham University**, College at Sixty, 212-636-6372, www.fordham.edu
- **New School**, Institute for Retired Professionals, 212-229-5682, www.newschool.edu/institute-for-retired-professionals
- **NYU School of Continuing and Professional Studies**, 212-998-7200, www.scps.nyu.edu
- **Pace University**, Senior Programs, 212-346-1244, www.pace.edu/continuing-professional-education/senior-programs
- **Queens College**, Senior Citizens Programs, 718-997-5600, www.qc.edu

A host of volunteer opportunities are available to seniors (see **Getting Involved** chapter) and some of the resources detailed above (**Resources and Services for People with Disabilities**) are valuable for seniors as well. A few other resources are worth noting:

- **Alzheimer's Association**, 1-800-272-3900, www.alz.org; useful for those who are diagnosed with the disease and for their families.
- **Con Edison**, 800-872-8846, in their "Concern" program for seniors age 62 and older, provides a newsletter and advice on bill payments, financial assistance, a Home Energy Assistance Program (HEAP), and turn-off protection for seniors who are blind or disabled.
- **New York Foundation for Senior Citizens**, www.nyfsc.org, 212-962-7559, offers a free home safety audit to homeowners (condos and co-ops included) 60 and older. They also have a home repair program, providing minor electrical, plumbing, masonry, and carpentry repairs.
- **SAGE, Services & Advocacy for Gay, Lesbian, Bisexual & Transgender Elders**, is a nonprofit community support agency described above under Lesbian and Gay Concerns, 212-741-2247, www.sageusa.org.

P LENTY OF PEOPLE FIND IT HARD TO BELIEVE, BUT RAISING CHILDREN IN New York City—while expensive and not without its idiosyncratic challenges—is actually remarkably rewarding. Though it can sometimes feel that you should have planned for prenatal care and your child's entire elementary education before you ever considered conceiving him/her (there are elements of childrearing here that are nothing less than a competitive sport), the resources and opportunities for children who are raised as New Yorkers are really and truly unparalleled. From the Broadway theatre devoted expressly to programming for young ones to a near-endless array of sporting and arts activities and spaces intended to give kids the same kind of rich experiences adults in the city enjoy, kids who grow up in this city are exposed to some exceptional experiences.

But what about that competitive sport aspect of parenting in New York City? Choosing a school or a childcare provider (and paying for it) are just a couple of the tasks of being a New York City parent that can come to seem like a full-time job, and even the most resourceful, savvy parents are likely to need a little bit of hand-holding to help them navigate the ins-and-outs of these challenges. This chapter attempts to make parenting like a New Yorker a little easier by describing the available options in childcare, nursery schools, primary, and high schools—public, private, and parochial—with information to help parents choose among them. We begin with babysitters and infant care and wind up with high schools, followed by a brief look at some of the opportunities for higher education in the city.

Please note: listing in this book is merely informational and is *not* an endorsement or a recommendation. Always be careful when entrusting your child with strangers. Addresses given are in Manhattan unless otherwise indicated.

CHILDCARE

Quality daycare, now typically called childcare, can be hard to find and is usually more expensive in New York than anywhere else in the country, thanks to the tremendous cost of real estate and the need for stringent standards governing the operation of daycare centers. According to the National Association of Childcare Resources (www.naccrra.org) in 2012, daycare and preschool costs in New York City averaged over $14,000 annually, among the country's most expensive relative to income. And that's *average*: costs can be considerably higher, depending upon the number of children you have and the setting in which they are receiving care.

High prices aside, there are many options, and not all are with such high price tags; some take into consideration your financial situation and childcare needs. Nonprofit agencies, which act as go-betweens for parents and daycare providers, are proliferating. We list some below under **Information Sources**. Your employer may have daycare information and some even offer on-premises facilities.

Also below, you'll find thumbnail descriptions of the kinds of preschool care (and education) available in New York City. Arranged chronologically by ages covered—from birth through six years—these categories are followed by the names of organizations that provide specific daycare recommendations.

New York State establishes the eligibility requirements for publicly funded daycare, be it family daycare in a private home or group care at a center. To be eligible, a family must meet established maximum income requirements. Almost all those entitled to assistance still pay something. For information about income eligibility for Head Start and Early Head Start programs, visit this website: https://otda.ny.gov/workingfamilies/headstart.asp.

The U.S. Department of Education provides a useful source of parenting information covering such topics as children's television viewing habits, sleep problems, childcare, and behavioral issues, with a library of articles and book abstracts and links to special interest organizations; visit www.ed.gov, or call 800-USA-LEARN. KinderStart's website, www.kinderstart.com, has a handy "childcare locator," which can help you find childcare in your neighborhood. For a daycare safety-hazard checklist and safety recalls, you can call the Consumer Product Safety Commission, 800-638-2772 or go to www.cpsc.gov. Available free in school lobbies, pediatricians' offices, and laundromats, a variety of monthly parent magazines, the most ubiquitous of which is *Big Apple Parent* (as well as *Queens Parent* and *Westchester Parent*), offer useful advice and information on everything from nutrition to single parenting, daycare, schools, and child health and recreation. *Big Apple's* website, www.nymetroparents.com, has links to current and past articles, an extensive monthly calendar of events for parents and children, and a bulletin board worth checking for babysitters, nannies, playgroups, Spanish classes for children … the list goes on.

AU PAIRS AND NANNIES

When it comes to sitters, New York's no different than the suburbs. Neighborhoods are filled with reliable teenagers looking for jobs. But it takes time to meet them. As with many personal services, the best sources for good babysitters or nannies are recommendations from friends, relatives, or colleagues. You can also stop by a crowded playground and talk to the many nannies that you'll find watching the neighborhood children. Naturally, before hiring anyone to watch your children, you should carefully screen applicants and check all references. In case networking fails, we've listed a number of alternatives. Some of the agencies also provide full-time, sleep-in, or day-only help.

Au pairs are young women (between 18 and 25), usually European, who provide a year of in-home childcare and light housekeeping in exchange for airfare, room and board, and a small stipend ($300–400 per week; since 2007, minimum salaries for au pairs have been tied to the federal minimum wage). Less expensive than nannies, they are also less experienced, may be less mature, and are gone in a year. The program is certainly valuable for the cultural exchange it offers the host family and the au pair. The U.S. Department of State is responsible for issuing J-1 visas to au pairs to authorize them to work in the United States; parents who are interested in the services of an au pair should review the Department of State's au pair page, where information about the au pair's and the parents' obligations are detailed: www.j1visa.state.gov/programs/au-pair. Either of the national agencies listed below will connect you with a local coordinator who will match up your family with a suitable au pair:

- **Au Pair in America**, 800-928-7247, www.aupairinamerica.com
- **InterExchange Au Pair USA**, 800-AU-PAIRS, www.interexchange.org

Good fortune is having a friend who passes on to you her excellent **nanny**, her children having outgrown the need, just when you need one. Failing that, there are want ads, the Internet, and nanny agencies to fall back on. On the Internet, www.4nannies.com carries classified nanny listings, allowing you to avoid agency fees, which can vary considerably and are often calculated based on a percentage (often 12–15%) of the nanny's annual salary. You simply pay the application fee. The site has links to firms that do background checks and some that provide nanny tax advice and/or service. According to nanny agencies, New York City area nannies make about $600–900 a week, though the total can be higher, depending upon the number of children under her care, the variety and extent of her responsibilities, whether she is live-in or live-out, and how many hours per week you retain her.

An agency, on the other hand, will have checked the nanny's background, perhaps by detective, her Social Security record, driving record, credit record, and as far as possible, any chance of criminal record. Note that there are no national criminal records available to investigators. But the agency will also have interviewed the nanny, in person or by phone, and will have checked her references. It has probably also obtained her medical records and can confirm whether she has First Aid and/or CPR training or other specialized skills. The agency can inform you about necessary nanny tax procedures and insurance and benefits required by law, and should provide a detailed contract. The **International Nanny Association** maintains a useful website, www.nanny.org, which provides information about nanny agencies and the nanny selection process. Another site, which is advertiser supported, www.nannynetwork.com, contains a database of nanny placement agencies and referral services, nanny insurance services, and background verification services as well as a library of articles.

However you find your nanny, be sure to check at least three of the prospective nanny's references, questioning them carefully, and repeatedly, if necessary. You will also want to interview the nanny in your home if possible in order to ensure a good fit.

NANNY AGENCIES

- **Fox Agency**, 19 E 65th St, 212-753-2686, ww.thefoxagency.com, providing baby nurses and nannies since 1936. Rates are hourly, daily, or weekly. Nannies are screened by the agency, which charges a fee for its services.
- **Lucky Lil Darlings**, formerly the New York Nanny Center, Inc., 212-265-3354, www.luckylildarlings.com, has both live-in and -out nannies, who are screened and background checked. The agency charges a placement fee equivalent to 16% of the nanny's annual salary.
- **Pavillion Agency, Inc.**, 15 E 40th St, Suite 400, 212-889-6609, www.pavilliona-gency.com, one of the larger companies, specializes in nannies (as well as butlers, chefs, domestics, and chauffeurs) who negotiate their rates depending on the needs of their clients. The agency fee is 15% of the annual salary. Pavillion includes a 30-day trial period, during which clients do not pay, and performs both background and motor vehicle checks (where appropriate).

BABYSITTERS

AGENCIES

Most babysitting is via word of mouth; short of that, try:

- **Baby Sitters' Guild**, 60 E 42nd St, 212-682-0227, www.babysittersguild.com; hourly fee for one child starts at $30 (with a four-hour minimum), with higher rates for more children. With enough advance notice, a sitter with a nursing background can be provided for children under one year. Bilingual or multilingual sitters are available with notice and for an additional fee. All fees include the agency's commission. Call between 9 a.m. and 9 p.m. seven days a week.

While requests made the same day can usually be filled, it is better to call a day prior. The guild was established in 1940.

- **Pinch Sitters**, www.nypinchsitters.com, 212-260-6005; babysitters, on short notice if necessary, starting at $22 per hour, with a four-hour minimum. After 10 p.m., a travel surcharge of $15 is applied, plus transportation at night, four-hour minimum. There is a transportation fee, depending on the hour. Sitters are available in all boroughs except Staten Island.

NONPROFIT

- **Parents League**, 115 E 82nd St, 212-737-7385, www.parentsleague.org; benefits included in the $185 annual membership fee include advisory services related to school selection and admissions; summer camp advice; support groups for parents of children with special needs; and workshops and publications on a variety of topics of interest to parents raising kids in the city.

SCHOOLS

- **Barnard Babysitting Agency**, Elliott Hall, 2nd floor, 49 Claremont Ave, 212-854-2035, www.barnardbabysitting.com; to preregister, fill out an online form or call in your name, address, phone number, and name of your pediatrician. Once you are in their file, call to confirm days and hours you'll need a sitter. Hours change regularly based on students' schedules. Rates start at around $10 per hour, but most parents pay at least $15 in this competitive market. There is also a $30 initial registration fee.

FAMILY DAYCARE

More and more parents who can afford the service are electing family care for their toddlers. Here in New York City the Health Department and the New York State Office of Children and Family Services establish regulations for providers who care for children in their own homes. These "providers" are often mothers of young children drawn to childcare as a means of remaining at home with their own youngsters. City regulations establish that "one caregiver may care for a maximum of six children younger than school age, or eight children when at least two of the eight children are school aged" in their dwelling at one time. Typically, parents who do not qualify for assistance pay between $40 and $50 per child for a six- to eight-hour day, approximately 25% less than the more traditional daycare centers. To obtain a list of licensed daycare facilities in New York City, visit https://a816-healthpsi.nyc.gov/ChildCare/ChildCareList.do, where you can search by borough. Another city site, www.nyc.gov/html/doh/html/living/childcare.shtml, is a clearinghouse of information about regulations and resources.

GROUP DAYCARE CENTERS

These city-licensed facilities, be they in the private or public sector, offer educational as well as care-taking programs for groups of children primarily, but not exclusively, between the ages of two and six years for an extended (beyond normal nursery school hours) or a full eight-hour day.

- **Publicly funded daycare centers** are usually found in, or contiguous to, neighborhoods with the greatest economic need. Even with an income above the maximum allowed by the state, parents proving "social" need—those working full-time qualify—can apply to publicly funded daycare centers, if they are prepared to pay the full cost for their child's care. Depending on the facility, full-time care now runs approximately $13,000 a year for an infant and $10,000 a year for a four-year-old (or about three times the national average).
- **Private centers** tend to be either nursery schools, which have added full-day care to the regular school curriculum, or centers established to supply childcare, which also offer education. Private daycare centers in New York City can exceed $30,000 a year, depending on facilities and educational components.

For a list of publicly funded daycare centers, contact the city's **Agency for Children's Services** through the city information line, 311, during business hours or online at www.nyc.gov/html/acs/html/child_care/child_care.shtml. You can also contact the **Department of Health, Bureau of Day Care**, also at 311. Ads for private centers and for the occasional playgroup will be found in parent magazines; the popular website www.mommypoppins.com also has an entire section devoted to preschools and childcare.

INFANT CARE

Formal programs for the two-month-old to two-year-old set are almost all publicly funded and appended to daycare centers. Call the New York City Health Department's Bureau of Day Care at 311, for the names of city-licensed facilities. Infants can also be placed in family daycare homes; costs are around $10,000 a year full-time.

PLAY GROUPS

Neighborhood parents often band together informally, usually in cooperative fashion, to care for a small group of preschoolers for a half-day or so, one, two, or three times a week. Do some networking, a little research, and use your best judgment about such existing groups, or start your own. You can often meet other parents interested in play groups at playgrounds or during sports or artistic activities in which your child might be enrolled.

INFORMATION SOURCES

- **Day Care Council of New York, Inc.**, 2082 Lexington Ave, Suite 204, 212-206-7818, www.dccnyinc.org, has over 60 years' experience as a nonprofit, providing free information, counseling, and referrals on all types of childcare, including babysitters, nannies, and daycare throughout the five boroughs.
- **The Parents League of New York**, 115 E 82nd St, 212-737-7385, www.parentsleague.org, provides parenting help, support, and special workshops and programs for a $185 annual membership fee.

OTHER LEADS

Check out some of the following resources for referrals in your particular neighborhood: **churches** and **temples**, large and small; old-fashioned, wall-mounted **bulletin boards**, most often found in larger supermarkets and around universities; **private schools**, ask the admissions director for the names of feeder schools, daycare centers, or playgroups; **pediatricians**; **hospitals**, talk with the administrative officer in charge of residents and interns; and last, but perhaps most accessible and knowledgeable of all, **playgrounds** and **neighborhood parents**.

SCHOOLS

NURSERY SCHOOLS

It is at this point, typically, that parental anxiety sets in. And it needn't. In Manhattan alone there are more than 175 privately run preschool programs, generally geared to three-, four-, and five-year-olds, often including toddlers' groups and sometimes all-day care as well. They vary widely in educational philosophy and style, and admission to none of them is essential to a child's later success at Harvard—although some cost almost as much. Talk with parents in the parks you frequent and with parents of children in neighborhood nursery schools. The search process typically begins just after Labor Day preceding application, and many schools will have open houses; this is also the time to request information from the schools you might wish to consider. And finally, in helping you decide what might be the best school for your child (and for you), the two sources below should be helpful:

- **The Independent Schools Admissions Association of Greater New York** (ISAAGNY, www.isaagny.org), has a searchable database of more than 120 private member schools, from preschool through high school. Nursery schools and toddler groups, as well as numerous elementary and secondary schools, along with preschool groups, are listed.

- **Parents League of New York, Inc.**, 115 E 82nd St, www.parentsleague.org, 212-737-7385; with 100+ member schools, mainly in Manhattan, the Parents League is an excellent source of private school information. One counseling session with a specialist from their School Advisory Service—for example, their expert on toddlers' groups and nursery schools—is well worth the league's annual $185 membership fee. A panoply of other child-related services comes with membership.

GRADE SCHOOLS

Here, decision-making can become more difficult because there are so many options. To begin with, there is the choice among public, private, and parochial schools. For some, it is a choice easily made; they know they want one or the other, or they can't afford private school. A word to the undecided: know that there are some excellent public schools in the city, just as there are some dreadful ones.

Those opting for a **private school** will find the resources above under **Nursery Schools** helpful. When trying to determine which school is right for your child—public or private—it is possible to do a lot of research on your own. For starters, you can go to each school's website, which will offer quite a bit of preliminary information. Ask parents whose children attend area schools. Contact schools directly and arrange a time to visit, and be sure to ask the administrators and staff about school philosophy, structure, and performance indicators. Read the school literature carefully. Examine the physical facility. Observe the relationships among children, staff, and administration. Consider the program, in theory and in practice. Finally, what is your gut reaction? Remember, you and your child may spend the next eight to twelve years here, and no decision is irrevocable. Just hard. In the case of private schools, school advisors are available, for a fee.

Catholic **parochial schools**, which cost considerably less than many of the city's private schools, have found favor in recent years with non-Catholics as well as Catholics as an attractive alternative to public schools. The Archdiocese of New York, www.adnyeducation.org, 646-794-2885, operates 218 schools in Manhattan, The Bronx, and Staten Island. The Roman Catholic Diocese of Brooklyn and Queens operates nearly 200 schools. Contact the Superintendent's office (718-965-7300, www.mybqcatholicschool.com/) for more information. There is no source of comparative evaluation of the parochial schools, which are independently run, so interested parents are left to make their own evaluation on a school-by-school basis.

Parents considering **public school** should begin by contacting the community school board in their district (see **Neighborhoods**) for a list of schools and to find out in which school zone they reside. Many school boards have brochures from which it is possible to get a sense both of the character of the district and its schools. When visiting schools, try to get a grasp of teacher-student interaction, school safety, PTA involvement, class size, and the overall feel of the school. Apparently, some Manhattan parents even hide out in the bathroom to eavesdrop on middle-schoolers' conversations and get the real scoop on goings-on at the school. You likely needn't go this far. But do ask questions.

It is often possible to send a child to a school outside of his/her zone, space permitting, and if the process is begun early enough. One reason to do this is if your workplace is in a different district; inquire with that district about the required variance procedure.

In recent years, several grade groupings have evolved among the city's schools, making choice more complicated. And within these groupings are schools with varying focus. The most common configurations below the high school level are:

- **Early childhood schools**, pre-kindergarten to second or third grade, popular for their focus on the needs of young children.
- **Elementary schools**, K–fifth or –sixth grades, are the most common configurations. Many districts are now shifting sixth grade to middle schools to avoid crowding.
- **Grammar schools**, K–8, are very rare but can serve as an alternative to middle school.
- **Middle schools or intermediate schools**, containing sixth through eighth grades or, sometimes, seventh and eighth. Some of these are theme schools, focusing on a particular subject area, such as the performing arts or technology; some require entry exams. These are the most common schools following K–fifth and have essentially replaced the junior high school. Middle school is often where crowding, social issues, and transportation issues (children taking buses and even subways to get to school) begin. It is, therefore, a time when some families head for the boroughs or the suburbs, or opt for private schooling for their kids. This is not to say there aren't good public middle schools. It just takes perseverance to find the right one.

For further guidance and encouragement in choosing public schools for your child, you can turn to one of the many websites devoted to rating and comparing the city's schools. Among these sites are www.insideschools.org and www.great-schools.org. The Chancellor's office keeps track of performance and accountability of all New York public schools, and you can get the latest information about these indicators on the website, http://schools.nyc.gov.

HIGH SCHOOLS

Decisions at this level, however fraught with anxiety, are made somewhat easier by the guidance procedures at your child's current school, as well as by the fact that your about-to-be-a-high-schooler will participate in the decision. Again, public or private? Information sources for the private schools are as noted above.

Admission to many of the public high schools is citywide, a trend that is increasing as theme schools proliferate at this level. Parents and students often find themselves in a mad scramble for entry into the "best school." Competition can be fierce, as the number of good high schools—particularly in Manhattan—is limited. Depending on the high school and the specific program, students may be selected by audition (for performing arts programs), by test scores, middle school grade averages, or a combination thereof. If not applying to a specific school, students are selected by lottery, or in some cases (generally in the boroughs outside of Manhattan), they attend the school nearest them. Typically, parents of Manhattan middle school students start scouting high schools much in the manner of college selections. Key concerns are safe transportation to and from the school, special programs, and how the school rates both academically and in terms of student safety.

The various categories of high school include the following major groupings:

- **Audition schools**, such as Fiorello LaGuardia High School of Music and Art and Performing Arts, and High School of Art and Design, to which the student must be recommended and must audition or present a portfolio for admission.
- **Competitive schools**, to which admission is by competitive exam; Bronx High School of Science, Brooklyn Technical High School, Hunter College High School, and Stuyvesant are the most well-known and desirable schools in this group.
- **District schools**, which range from abysmal to excellent.
- **Special interest schools** include the High School of Fashion Industries and the High School of Graphic Communication Arts, among others.

CHARTER SCHOOLS

Since 1999, charter schools have been among the choices that New York City parents and children have when considering what school best meets their needs. Charter schools are a popular alternative to public, private, and parochial schools; they embody some of the most attractive attributes of a public school (open to anyone; tuition-free) and private schools (free from the strictures that bind public school curricula, hiring practices, school vacation days, and more). While they tend to enjoy greater flexibility and freedom than other schools in the city, they are still obligated to uphold city, federal, and state standards.

Given their benefits, it's little wonder that admission to charters can be—and often is—just as competitive as it is to the city's top public and private schools. In 2014, a record number of students—nearly three times the number of students as available seats—applied for admission to one of the city's nearly 200 charter schools.

Unlike public schools, students do not necessarily need to live in the same district or zone where the charter school is located, though preference is given to residents of the school's neighborhood. Other characteristics may give students an admissions edge, including whether a sibling already attends the school. Students are usually admitted to a charter school by lottery, which is managed by the school, as is its application and admissions process.

Just as with public and private schools in the city, parents considered charter schools should make a list of schools that interest them and call the school to schedule a tour. There are a number of resources that provide information about charter school operations, the names of charters and their varying accreditation and performance standards, and more; these are below.

Resources include:

- **New York City Charter School Center,** www.nyccharterschools.org
- **New York City Department of Education**, Charter Schools Accountability and Support, http://schools.nyc.gov/community/planning/charters/default.htm

INFORMATION SOURCES

- **New York City Department of Education**, 52 Chambers St, 718-935-2000, http://schools.nyc.gov; contact them for a free "Public High School Directory."
- **The Division of Assessment and Accountability of the Board of Education**, 52 Chambers St, 311, http://schools.nyc.gov; publishes an annual report, commonly known as the "Progress Report," which describes each of the public schools statistically for the previous year. It's a source of information on enrollment, ethnic composition, reading scores, etc.
- **SchoolMatch**, 614-890-1573, www.schoolmatch.com; is a private organization that provides information about schools, public or private, that best suit your requirements as determined by a questionnaire.

COLLEGES AND UNIVERSITIES

New York City offers a wide variety of higher education opportunities, many of which are listed below. In addition to graduate degrees and an inviting array of evening courses, these schools also host lectures and workshops of interest, not to mention musical and theatrical performances. You can also visit some of these institutions on their websites via links at www.ny.com/academia/colleges.html.

MANHATTAN AND THE BRONX

- **Bank Street College of Education**, 610 W 112th St, 212-875-4400, www.bnkst. edu
- **Barnard College**, 3009 Broadway, 212-854-5262, www.barnard.edu
- **Baruch College of Continuing and Professional Studies**, 1 Bernard Baruch Way, 646-312-5000, www.baruch.cuny.edu
- **City College**, CUNY, 160 Convent Ave, 212-650-7000, www.ccny.cuny.edu
- **City University of New York**, 365 Fifth Ave, 212-817-7000, www.cuny.edu
- **Columbia University**, Broadway at 116th St, 212-854-1754, www.columbia.edu

- **Cooper Union**, 30 Cooper Square, 212-353-4120, www.cooper.edu
- **Fordham University**, Campuses in The Bronx, Manhattan, and Westchester, 800-FORDHAM or 212-636-6000, www.fordham.edu
- **Hebrew Union College–Jewish Institute of Religion**, One W 4th St, 212-674-5300, www.huc.edu
- **Hunter College**, 695 Park Ave at 68th St, 212-772-4000, www.hunter.cuny.edu
- **Jewish Theological Seminary**, 3080 Broadway, 212-678-8000, www.jtsa.edu
- **Manhattan College**, 4513 Manhattan College Pkway, Riverdale, 718-862-8000, www.manhattan.edu
- **Marymount Manhattan College**, 221 E 71st St, 212-517-0430, www.mmm.edu
- **New School University**, 72 Fifth Ave, 212-229-5600, www.newschool.edu
- **New York University**, 70 Washington Sq South, 212-998-1212, www.nyu.edu
- **Pace University**, 1 Pace Plaza and 535 Fifth, 866-772-3338, www.pace.edu
- **Parsons School of Design**, 66 Fifth Ave, 212-229-8900, www.parsons.edu
- **Pratt Institute**, Manhattan campus, 144 W 14th St, 718-636-3600, www.pratt.edu
- **Union Theological Seminary**, 3041 Broadway, 212-662-7100, www.utsnyc.edu
- **Yeshiva University**, 500 W 185th St, 212-960-5400, www.yu.edu

BROOKLYN

- **Brooklyn College**, 2900 Bedford Ave, 718-951-5000, www.brooklyn.cuny.edu
- **Pratt Institute**, Brooklyn campus, 200 Willoughby Ave, 718-636-3600, www.pratt.edu
- **St. Joseph's College**, 245 Clinton Ave, 718-940-5300, www.sjcny.edu

QUEENS

- **Queens College**, 65-30 Kissena Blvd, Flushing 718-997-5000, www.qc.cuny.edu
- **Queensborough Community College**, 222-05 56th Ave Bayside 718-631-6262, www.qcc.cuny.edu
- **St. John's University**, 8000 Utopia Pkwy, Jamaica, 718-990-2000, www.stjohns.edu

STATEN ISLAND

- **College of Staten Island**, CUNY, 2800 Victory Blvd, 718-982-2000, www.csi.cuny.edu
- **St. John's University**, 300 Howard Ave, 718-390-4500, www.stjohns.edu
- **Wagner College**, 1 Campus Rd, 718-390-3100, www.wagner.edu

BIG CITY LIVING ENCOURAGES IDIOSYNCRATIC LIFESTYLES. AND NEW Yorkers pursue their interests and goals singularly unencumbered by considerations as to "what the neighbors might think." Home decoration is a striking case in point. Anything (within the terms of the lease) goes, and when it comes to providing all the goods and services necessary for us to feather our wildly divergent, albeit mainly minuscule, nests, the city really comes through for its residents. Generally speaking, there are at least three approaches to shopping in Manhattan: (1) largish, fairly priced, standard sources; (2) signature shops and boutiques; and (3) discounters, warehouse-style superstores, and/or alternative resources such as wholesale districts and sample sales. There are also a number of thrift stores, such as Housing Works, which have a small but eclectic inventory of home goods and furniture.

Note from the shopping strategies department: unless you are literally sitting and sleeping on the floor of your new apartment, it pays to wait until winter for the annual, city-wide furniture and housewares sales to make major purchases. In both department stores and specialty shops, the savings in January and February are considerable, 20% to 50% off. And it's worth noting, especially if you anticipate making a major purchase, the **sales tax** in New York City (combined city and state sales tax) is 8.875%, but the tax bite in New Jersey is 7% and most clothing items are exempt. Depending on the "spree," the savings in New Jersey may more than pay for the toll to cross the Hudson.

While most stores are open on Sundays, except in Paramus, New Jersey, where blue laws are still in effect (though contested hotly by local and state politicians), store hours will vary, with many stores cutting hours during the summer and staying open late as the end-of-year holiday season approaches. Many run specials during Memorial Day, President's Day, Independence Day, etc.—check ads and call stores for hours and sales. In some cases you can get on their e-mail lists to find out about sales and other happenings. In the sections below, addresses are in Manhattan unless otherwise indicated.

FULL-SERVICE DEPARTMENT STORES

As designer sections fragment the more traditional uniform displays of merchandise, one-stop shopping at full-service department stores has lost some of its cohesiveness. Still, many shoppers prefer the one-stop-shop to making 15 stops in a 20-block neighborhood. Although more difficult than it once was, it's comforting to take a 15-item list—electronic organizer through silk sheets—and pass the afternoon under one roof. So we lead off with the royalty of New York's department store scene:

- **Bloomingdale's**, at 59th St and Lexington Ave, 212-705-2000, and 504 Broadway, 212-729-5900, and other locations, www.bloomingdales.com; for all the zap and glitter, Bloomie's has a sturdy core: you can leave your watch for repair, order Christmas cards, shop the best white sales in town—January and August—buy a TV, a mattress, and socks, as well as try out glittery shoes to a funky beat, or nosh the food of the moment at one of several chic cafés. The main floor offers a full array of make-up and makeovers, plus exquisite jewelry and other top-of-the line items. Once above the initial frenzy of the main floor, you'll find designer clothing and much more in calmer environs. Services include At Your Service personal shoppers, 212-705-3135, translators, a bridal registry, decorators, dining, and 24-hour telephone order service.
- **Century 21**, 22 Cortlandt St, 212-227-9092; 1972 Broadway, 212-518-2121; 472 86th St, Bay Ridge, Brooklyn, 718-748-3266, and other locations, www.c21stores.com; not the nationwide real estate broker but something unique to New York City—a full-service department store where nearly everything is discounted. There are many bargains here and the service is pleasant and no-nonsense. Beware: the Manhattan stores can be a zoo around Christmastime.
- **Kmart**, 770 Broadway, 212-673-1540, 250 W 34th St, 212-760-1188, www.kmart.com; essentially the antithesis of Bloomingdale's, the big "K" offers practical goods at reasonable prices. Fairly comprehensive, including even a houseplants department, as well as clothing, furniture, housewares, and appliances, not to mention Martha Stewart linens, paints, and furniture.
- **Lord and Taylor**, 424 Fifth Ave, 212-391-3344, www.lordandtaylor.com; wide selection and helpful sales staff. Lots of women's clothing, including formal wear and smart business suits.
- **Macy's**, Broadway at 34th St, 212-695-4400, www.macys.com; enormous! Complete! The crown jewel of New York City department stores. And, yes, it can be overwhelming! First-timers take advantage of the multilingual assistance and location maps at the first floor information booths. Others might opt for Macy's By Appointment, the personal shopping service, and the 24-hour telephone ordering service, 212-494-4181. Included are special events and a bridal registry. On the basement level you'll find the superb Cellar, a bazaar-like warren of individual food and housewares shops. Even if you're not setting out with a specific shopping goal, Macy's is a great place to browse and browse and browse ... .

- **Macy's**, 422 Fulton St, Brooklyn, 718-875-7200, www.macys.com; talk about full service! Lucky Brooklyn residents need travel no further than the Hoyt Street stop on the #2 or #3 train for practically any nicety or necessity. Macy's has both an optometrist and a podiatrist on duty and a fur storage and restyling service. From TVs, furniture, and electronics on the lower level to fabric on six, this rather reserved, no-nonsense institution also heeds the latest fashions with up-to-the-minute styles from leading designers on three.
- **Macy's**, 90-01 Queens Blvd, Elmhurst, 718-271-7200, www.macys.com; not as vast as Herald Square, but it provides full service and is convenient to the entire borough from a Queens Boulevard location. Macy's also has a furniture gallery nearby at 88-01 Queens Blvd, 718-760-7101, and another store in Flushing at 136-50 Roosevelt Ave, 718-358-9000.
- **Saks Fifth Avenue**, 611 Fifth Ave at Rockefeller Center, 212-753-4000, www.saksfifthavenue.com; carefully coifed customers, calm and self-assured, and elaborate bouquets that cascade nonchalantly into the glowing, wood-paneled aisles characterize Saks Fifth Avenue. So do the most refined escalators in New York. They float you silently past eight well-lit shopping floors against a backdrop of perfectly placed plants, mirrors, and pinky-beige marble. Luxurious Saks exudes well-being from every tasteful counter. Departments are stylish and help is generally available. Saks also harbors a useful set of shops along 49th and 50th Streets. Housewares, luggage, bathing suits, and sportswear, the bath and linen shop, and the art gallery all have private entrances. The Fifth Avenue Club, on the third floor, shelters five personal shopping services, among them the Executive Service for women executives.
- **Sears**, Cross County Pkwy and Route 87, Yonkers, 914-377-2100, www.sears.com; other Sears stores at 50 Mall Dr W in the Newport Mall, Jersey City, NJ, 201-420-5300; 2307 Beverley Rd, Brooklyn, 718-826-5800; 96-05 Queens Blvd, Rego Park, Queens, 718-830-5900; 5200 Kings Plaza, Brooklyn, 718-677-2100, call for hours. For those with wheels, this reliable old standby represents convenience and good value with plenty of selection. Parking is free, and in the New Jersey store just outside the Holland Tunnel, the sales tax bite is less painful.
- **T.J. Maxx**, 620 Ave of the Americas (Sixth Ave), 212-229-0875; 250 W 57th St, 212-245-6201; www.tjmaxx.com; again, not one of the grand old department store dames, but it's more than just off-price clothing. You'll find housewares and some small furniture items.
- **Target**, 517 E 117th St, 212-835-0860; 40-24 College Point Blvd, Flushing, 347-532-9942; 135-05 20th Ave, College Point, 718-661-4346; 139 Flatbush Ave, Brooklyn, 718-290-1109; 543 River Rd, Edgewater, NJ, 201-402-0252, www.target.com; this popular department store has furniture and hardware departments, in addition to clothes, appliances, and household products for the garden, kitchen, and living room.

The city is full of stores that specialize in any and every type of product you might want. Some of these stores provide savings and offer minimal customer service, while others will practically hold your hand through the purchase—of course, you'll spend a little more. Either way, you can find a vast selection of goods throughout the city, so don't settle—shop around and get what you want. Most stores also have websites, so you can go online to view and make purchases.

APPLIANCES, ELECTRONICS, CAMERAS

These three categories have been lumped together because many of the stores listed below cross merchandise lines.

- **B&H Photo Video**, 420 9th Ave, 212-444-6615, www.bhphotovideo.com; if photography buffs have a Mecca, this is it. People come from all over the city and all over the world to shop at B&H and marvel at its conveyor belt system of shuttling goods from one floor to another. The store is always hectic and service, while knowledgeable, is often curt. Note that the store, owned by Orthodox Jews, closes early on Fridays and is closed on Saturdays.
- **Macy's**; see Full-Service Department Stores, above.
- **Sears**; see Full-Service Department Stores, above.
- **Willoughby's Konica Imaging**, 298 Fifth Ave, 800-378-1898 or 212-564-1600, www.willoughbys.com; offers phone quotes. Complete rental and service departments complement an extensive stock of new and used photographic equipment. Willoughby's also has a computer department.

SPECIALTY SHOPS

- **Duggal Visual Solutions**, 29 W 23rd St, 212-786-5753, www.duggal.com; Professional photographers prefer Duggal for small and large-format printing, as well as for studio photography and special effects printing. The store specializes in a number of other services, as well, including fine art printing and vehicle wraps.
- **Innovative Audio**, 150 E 58th St, 212-634-4444, www.innovativeaudiovideo.com; perhaps a bit higher-end, but they offer a full range of quality equipment. They are noted for their helpful sales staff.
- **Lyric HiFi and Video**, 1221 Lexington Ave, 212-439-1900, www.lyricusa.com; "Only the finest stereo components." A good selection of speakers.
- **Sound by Singer**, 242 W 27th St, 212-924-8600, www.soundbysinger.com; full range of audio equipment, quiet listening rooms, and an extremely knowledgeable sales staff. Specializes in American brands.
- **Stereo Exchange**, 627 Broadway, 212-505-1111, www.stereoexchange.com; this established sound emporium specializes in home theater, audiophile stereo, and new components. Used high-end components, expertly repaired in-house and sold at 60% to 70% off what they might cost new, are a real draw.

DISCOUNT STORES

Appliances and electronics are sold all over the city at less than retail. A few of the many discounters in Manhattan:

- **Adorama**, 42 W 18th St, 800-223-2500; mail order: 212-741-0052, www. adorama.com, is a favorite of professional photographers and filmmakers. Carries a staggering array of cameras, accessories, video equipment, lighting, lenses, VCRs, and more. Call for their specialty catalog or drop by for one.
- **B&H Photo-Video-Pro Audio**, 420 Ninth Ave, 212-444-6670, www.bhphotovideo.com; whether you need an English-made Billingham photographer's vest, a point-and-shoot, or a Hasselblad, professional lighting and movie equipment, or camcorder, you'll find it in this sprawling audio-video bazaar with knowledgeable sales staff, a large professional clientele, and an encyclopedic catalog. Biggest price breaks are on professional equipment.
- **Bondy Export**, 40 Canal St, 212-925-7786; Offers photographic equipment, small as well as major appliances, audio equipment and supplies, TVs, and DVD players.
- **P.C. Richard & Son**, 120 E 14th St, 212-979-2600; 53 W 23rd St, 212-924-0200; 205 E 86th St, 212-289-1700;, 2372 Broadway, 212-579-5200, www.pcrichard.com; also at more than 60 other locations in Brooklyn, Queens, Westchester, Long Island, and New Jersey. Home appliances, digital cameras, DVDs, and video games.
- **Vendome Trading Corp.**, 55 W 45th St, 212-279-3333; offers phone quotes. A member of a cooperative buying group that has its own warehouse, Vendome sells air conditioners, washing machines, and other major, as well as small, appliances, computers, TVs, and stereos.

BEDS, BEDDING, AND BATH

Department stores can take care of all your bedding needs under one roof. Lay in supplies during January and August, traditional white sale months. Bloomingdale's becomes particularly generous at these times, stocking irregular Martex towels and name-brand sheets at great savings.

SPECIALTY SHOPS

- **Bed, Bath & Beyond**, 620 Sixth Ave, 212-255-3550; 410 E 61st St, 646-215-4702; 96-05 Queens Blvd, Rego Park, Queens, 718-459-0868; 459 Gateway Dr, Brooklyn, 718-235-2049; Edgewater Commons Mall at 489 River Rd, Edgewater, NJ, 201-840-8808, and other locations across the city and in Westchester, www. bedbathandbeyond.com; this popular and affordable chain store has almost everything for your household needs. Helpful service too. The Manhattan stores boast wide aisles, plenty of departments, easy checkout, and a special escalator for your shopping cart.

- **Dixie Foam**, 113 W 25th St, 212-645-8999, www.dixiefoam.com; in this factory/showroom, 4" and 5 1/2" thick foam mattresses are the forte. Choose standard sizes or have irregular sizes cut and covered to order.
- **Gracious Home**, 1220 Third Ave, 212-517-6300, 1992 Broadway, 212-231-7800, 45 W 25th St, 212-414-5710, www.gracioushome.com; imported linens, bathware, fabrics, stationery, and giftware. Free gift-wrapping and delivery in Manhattan, not to mention phone orders.
- **Laytner's Linen & Home**, 2276 Broadway, 212-724-0180, 237 E 86th St, 212-996-4439, www.laytners.com; outfit your bedroom and bath here, and then some. Besides a limited selection of handsome cotton drapes, you'll find bedding, feather beds, duvets, spreads, towels and bathroom and closet supplies, tablecloths, chenille throws and pillows, but none of it in overwhelming quantities. Scattered among these soft goods are items of Mission-style furniture, also for sale.
- **Sleepy's**, 962 Third Ave, 212-755-8210; huge chain offering beds, beds, beds of all kinds; frames and headboards; and mattresses as well. Call 800-SLEEPYS or go to www.sleepys.com for a location near you.

ALTERNATIVE SOURCES

Household linens on the **Lower East Side** are squashed into two blocks on Grand Street, between Allen and Forsyth. An uptown look has intruded on the cram-jammed bargain basement fustiness always considered *de rigueur* in the city's most raffish bazaar area. The uninitiated will find comparatively sleek **Harris Levy**, 98 Forsyth at Grand Street, 212-226-3102, www.harrislevy.com, a satisfying shopping opportunity with goods from Laura Ashley, Marimekko, Martex, Wamsutta, Cannon, and Stevens, in addition to the scores of other stores along Grand. All closed Saturday, open Sunday. Department store white-sale prices match those you're likely to find on the Lower East Side, but if you avoid the Sunday crush, you'll discover sales personnel often more knowledgeable and helpful than their uptown counterparts.

- **ABC Carpet & Home**, 881 and 888 Broadway, 212-473-3000; 1055 Bronx River Ave, Bronx (warehouse outlet), 718-842-8772; www.abchome.com; it's certainly not just carpets anymore. Imported and domestic designer linens, spreads, and towels, along with a fetching array of country furniture, folk art objects, decorative pieces, and scatter pillows. There's crystal, earthenware, Limoges, bone china, and flatware as well. The Manhattan location also has several delightful restaurants, including a Jean-Georges Vongerichten hotspot featuring seasonal menus.

CARPETS AND RUGS

For an overview, check the department stores, in particular Macy's for broadlooms and Bloomingdale's for imports.

- **ABC Carpet & Home**, 881 and 888 Broadway, 212-473-3000; just across from the main store is this carpet only emporium occupying four floors. Expensive but high quality.
- **Safavieh**, 902 Broadway, 212-477-1234, www.safavieh.com. They sell a variety of handmade Oriental rugs new and antique, silk and wool, and an assortment of Aubusson weaves. Watch for their sales. See their website for stores in Connecticut, Long Island, and New Jersey, some of which also sell antique reproduction furniture.

ALTERNATIVE SOURCES

Carpets and rugs also turn up at thrift shops, auctions, and flea markets. See **Furniture** for details.

COMPUTERS AND SOFTWARE

A number of the big computer stores have decamped, but personal computers can be bought in a variety of places, from comparatively cozy neighborhood centers to barn-like discount warehouses.

- **The Apple Store**, 767 Fifth Ave, 212-336-1440; 45 Grand Central Terminal, 212-284-1800; 103 Prince St, 212-226-3126; 1981 Broadway, 212-209-3400; 401 W 14th St, 212-444-3400; 2655 Richmond Ave, Staten Island, 718-568-2230; www.apple.com; all but the Staten Island location are mega-stores that are always overrun with customers trying out the newest models of Macs. The stores' "Genius Bars" are where you can go for technical support; most of these locations also host free workshops and classes for beginning and advanced computer user interests.
- **Staples**, 5-9 Union Square, 212-929-6323; and several other locations, www.staples.com. Everything for the (home) office, including computers, peripherals, and software.

FABRIC—DECORATING

Ringed around the **Decoration & Design Building**, 979 Third Ave, wholesale fabric showrooms marked "to the trade only" usually require shoppers to be accompanied by a decorator or to possess a decorator's card. No entrée? Try the department stores or the retail fabric importers or discount merchants listed below, all of whom stock dress goods as well as slipcover, curtain, and upholstery fabrics. For more information, call 212-759-5408 or go to www.ddbuilding.com.

DISCOUNT STORES

- **Beckenstein Fabrics + Interiors**, 32 W 20th St, 212-366-5142, www.beckensteinfabrics.com; for nearly 100 this bastion of discount fabric is somewhat upscale. With fabric on racks and some furniture as well, the selection in decorating fabric remains broad and prices still represent a savings over the uptown boutiques. If you need any furniture reupholstered, this is the place.
- **Martin Albert Interiors**, 257 W 39th St, 212-673-8000, www.martinalbert.com; formerly located on Grand St, this discounter still sells uptown fabric at downtown prices.
- **Zarin Fabrics**, 72 Allen St, 212-925-6112, www.zarinfabrics.com, holds down the fabric fort on what used to be the fabric bastion, the Lower East Side. Prices for the curtain, upholstery, and slipcover fabrics in stock are almost always a better bargain than materials you select from the sample books, but those too are discounted. You'll find stellar names printed on the selvages of velvets, embroideries, cottons, and tapestries: Brunschwig & Fils, Givenchy, Schumacher, and Stroheim & Roman among them.

FURNITURE

Antique furniture dealerships tend to cluster in the same neighborhoods. Rare pieces from the 17th, 18th, and 19th centuries are most likely to be found in elegant shops along Madison Avenue north of 67th Street. Increasingly, retail outlets for less prestigious pieces are infiltrating the wholesale "to the trade only" antique district located in the quadrant formed by University Place, Broadway, East 9th, and East 11th streets in the Village. Art deco dealers and those specializing in the Depression era, in retro furniture, and in the now-fashionable Fifties clump together in SoHo and NoHo. A handful of good sources can also be found in Greenwich Village.

Look for furniture sales post-Christmas. Those held by New York department stores at their warehouses in the boroughs and suburbs offer especially large savings for anyone with a car and enough stamina to brave the stampede.

- **Carlyle Custom Convertibles**, 122 W 18th St, 212-675-3212, www.carlylesofa.com; offers quality custom-made sofas in a variety of fairly conservative styles and fabrics. Allow four to six weeks for delivery.
- **Crate & Barrel**, 650 Madison Ave, 212-308-0011, and 611 Broadway, 212-780-0004, www.crateandbarrel.com; somewhat incongruously located at the base of a sleek office tower, this emporium of handsome, country-ish furniture, dish- and cookware, decorative items, and linens is theme-decorated in natural pine. The earth tones are muted, and the selection of reasonably priced glassware is extensive. It's affordable and stylish one-stop home furnishing.

- **Ethan Allen**, 1010 Third Ave, 212-888-2384, www.ethanallen.com; handsome, well-made traditional furniture for the whole house.
- **George Smith**, 47-09 30th St, Long Island City, 212-226-4747, www.george-smith.com; this is high-end, meticulously English-made furniture in the classic style, and requires space most city apartments don't have. Upholstered to order in your fabric or theirs, in cotton brocades, florals, checks, antique kilim, or leather, they'd all look splendid in a paneled home library. Custom orders take 10 to 12 weeks, or you can buy off the floor.
- **Ikea**, One Beard Street in Red Hook Brooklyn; 1000 Ikea Dr, Elizabeth, NJ; 100 Ikea Dr, Paramus, NJ; 1100 Broadway Mall, Hicksville, Long Island; 888-888-4532,www.ikea.com; worth the trip from the city for excellent deals. Selections range from inexpensive pine dressers to kitchen tables, beds, and living room furniture, all designed Swedish-style with clean lines and natural materials. Pick up sheets, glasses, wallpaper, lamps, and more—for less. At the Jersey and Red Hook stores, have a Swedish meatball lunch for less than $5 in the spacious, clean (if slightly antiseptic) cafeteria, also open for breakfast and dinner. Delivery is available and there are free buses on the weekend (and sometimes ferries to the Red Hook outlet).
- **Jennifer Convertibles**, 111 Third Ave, 212-260-0522; 902 Broadway, 212-677-6862; www.jenniferfurniture.com. No question, stores in this chain, which bills itself "America's largest sofa bed specialist," have the city's widest selection of relatively inexpensive convertible sofas, including Sealy and Simmons models.
- **Jensen-Lewis**, 89 Seventh Ave, 212-929-4880, 969 Third Ave, 212-434-0990, www.jensen-lewis.com; famous for deck chairs, satchels, backpacks, and other canvas products in lots of zippy colors. Puffy sofas and easy chairs, beds, and an expanding housewares department fill the showroom.
- **Pottery Barn**, 1965 Broadway at 67th St, 212-579-8477, 117 E 59th St, 917-369-0050, 100-104 7th Ave, 646-336-7160, www.potterybarn.com; where's the pottery? Mostly gone now. This former emporium of tableware has evolved into a design studio and catalogue operation focusing on home furnishings in a country-chic mode. Reasonably priced sofas and chairs often covered in tough cotton, rugs, dining and occasional furniture, drapes, and decorative items fill their catalogs and the stores. There's also a selection of inexpensive to moderately priced imported glassware, china, and table settings, augmented by quality cookware, sometimes below list price, and occasional gourmet items. Their periodic sales of specific merchandise are worth catching.
- **Restoration Hardware**, 935 Broadway, 212-260-9479, plus stores in Queens and New Jersey, www.restorationhardware.com; hardware? In fact, there are some drawer pulls, some bathroom hardware, and fireplace and cleaning supplies, but these spacious showrooms, part of a nationwide chain, are furniture and housewares emporia. You can buy sturdy garden furniture and the garden clogs and tin floral buckets to go with it, along with rugs, picture frames, and

the like, but the draw here is the Mission-style furniture with its clean lines and sturdy oak construction.

ALTERNATIVE SOURCES

- *Art & Antiques Magazine* can be helpful. Pick up their magazine at newsstands or check out their website, www.artandantiquesmag.com, for a list of New York City antique dealers.
- **Auction houses**: diverting, and occasionally rewarding, auctions are another way to obtain basic necessities, such as mattresses, as well as moth-eaten moose heads, which, in fact, make poor hat-racks. Check the auction pages at the back of the "Arts and Leisure" section of the Sunday *Times* for sale descriptions and viewing hours. The big three: **Christie's**, 20 Rockefeller Plaza, 212-636-2000, www.christies.com; **Phillips,** 450 Park Ave,t, 212-940-1200, www.phillips.com; and **Sotheby's**, 1334 York Ave, 212-606-7000, www.sothebys.com, hold specialty auctions of interest to collectors and connoisseurs (and voyeurs) once or twice a week in season. For erratic quality, more fun, and lower prices than the big three, try **Swann Galleries**, 104 E 25th St, 212-254-4710, www.swanngalleries.com, and Hutter Auction Galleries, 444 W 55th St, 6th floor, 212-247-4791, www.hutterauctions.com.
- **Flea markets**: this raffish country custom is almost extinct in New York City, but has been reinvented by hipsters peddling homemade, handmade craft goods, everything from artisanal ice cream to knitted scarves. Occasionally, you'll find some legitimate antiques and vintage home goods, mostly of the décor variety. Many of these flea markets operate seasonally, so check their websites for current dates and other information. Among the city's favorite fleas: Brooklyn Flea, www.brooklynflea.com; Chelsea Flea Market, www.hellskitchenfleamarket.com/home/?page_id=79; Hell's Kitchen Flea Market, www.hellskitchenflea-market.com; LIC Flea, www.licflea.com.
- **Housing Works Thrift Shops**; www.housingworks.org; more than a dozen shops spread across the city sell clothes, books, dishes, and other household goods, but furniture is the best buy here, where proceeds go to house and service homeless people with AIDS/HIV. Come early for the best buys. Higher-end goods are auctioned through the stores' online portal.
- **Nonprofit thrift stores**: Like Housing Works, a number of nonprofit organizations around the city have thrift stores that funnel profits back into providing services for people in need. Many of these line East 23rd Street in Manhattan and benefit everyone from cancer survivors to firefighters to arts organizations. If you're making a donation of goods, be sure to ask for a receipt for tax deduction purposes.
- **The street**: It's not for everyone, but believe it or not, New York City's streets can be one of the best places for incredible—and free—finds. Resourcefulness, a strong back, and willing cabbies are all that's required for street shopping—

well, that and a knowledge of the Department of Sanitation's collection days for whatever area you're combing. It's legal to put large items on the sidewalk after dark on the evening before any regular collection day. The Upper East Side tends to be fertile territory for found furniture, so if that's your game, Sunday, Tuesday, and Thursday evenings after 8 p.m. are the time to canvas. For other neighborhood collection days, consult the Department of Sanitation via the city service number, 311, and navigate the menus. Be careful, though. If an item has been sitting outside on the street for more than a few hours, it may not be something you want to bring into your home … or touch for that matter.

HARDWARE, PAINTS, AND WALLPAPER

On Saturdays, slow-moving lines make local hardware stores as good a way of meeting people as local bars later that night. But once you've made new friends along with those seemingly endless purchases, you may require more than the good old, all-purpose neighborhood reliable to fill decorating needs. Some specialty resources, then (the behemoth **Home Depot** is listed below under **Superstores**):

- **Gracious Home**, 1220 Third Ave, 212-517-6300; 1201 Third Ave, 212-517-6300; and 1992 Broadway, 212-231-7800, www.gracioushome.com; the sprawling hardware/houseware/home-furnishings center for the Upper East Side, and its slightly smaller Upper West Side version, are both well organized and staffed. From screws to decorative bathroom fixtures, paints, electrical fixtures, and power tools, to glassware and hard-to find vacuum cleaners.
- **Janovic Paint & Decorating Center**, 10 area locations including 2680 Broadway, 212-531-2300; 1491 Third Ave, 212-289-6300; 771 Ninth Ave, 212-245-3241; 215 Seventh Ave, 212-645-5454; 80 Fourth Ave, 212-477-6930; and 292 Third Ave 212-777-3030, www.janovic.com; the Bloomingdale's of the paint-and-wall-paper scene, Janovic's image is as glossy as its enamels and printed foil papers. For the latest colors and trends, as well as an overall view of what's available, Janovic can't be beat.
- **Simon's Hardware and Bath**, 421 Third Ave, 212-532-9220, www.simons-hardware.com; join the inevitable throng of contractors and decorators shopping Simon's first-rate stock of brass, bronze, pewter, plastic, wood, steel—whatever!—decorative hardware. They've expanded to include tile, bath fixtures, and lighting as well.

ALTERNATIVE SOURCES

Hardware and plastics—nuts and bolts made dingy by neighboring bright, bouncing baubles—overflow rows of cut-down cardboard boxes that alternate with the racks of surplus and flea market clothing lining Canal Street between West Broadway and Broadway. Most of this sidewalk hardware and pretty plastic bric-a-brac is useful only to the professional handyman or collage artist, but inside, generalists revel in complete selections of quality merchandise at exceptionally fair prices. Try any of the stores sitting side by gray dilapidated side on Canal, west of Broadway.

HOUSEWARES

Of course, any department store or furniture store will offer scads of traditional and funky housewares, particularly Crate & Barrel, Pottery Barn, and Ikea, as well as Target, Kmart, and the list goes on (see above). Those specializing in housewares include:

- **Design Within Reach**, 110 Greene St, 212-475-0001; 341 Columbus Ave, 212-799-5900; 957 Third Ave, 212-888-4539; 903 Broadway, 212-477-1155, www.dwr.com; contemporary design.
- **Jonathan Adler New York**, 53 Greene St, 877-287-1910; 37 Greenwich Ave, 212-488-2803; 304 Columbus Ave, 212-787-0017, and 1097 Madison Ave, 212-722-2410, www.jonathanadler.com; contemporary home furnishings.
- **Pier One Imports**, 1110 Third Ave, 646-358-1360, and 71 Fifth Ave, 212-206-1911, www.pier1.com; glassware, crystal, housewares, plenty of gift items, and even some furniture at reasonable prices.
- **Zabar's**, 2245 Broadway, 212-787-2000, www.zabars.com; housewares department on the mezzanine. Expansive Zabar's, mecca to millions for unequaled edibles, houses an equally esteemed and often bargain-priced selection of supplies for the home and kitchen in four rooms on the mezzanine. Try to avoid weekend forays there.

SPECIALTY SHOPS

- **Bowery Kitchen Supplies**, 88 10th Ave (inside Chelsea Market), 212-376-4982, www.bowerykitchens.com; the aisles can feel a little claustrophobic, but this small-ish kitchen supply store has everything you need to kit out your kitchen (and plenty of stuff you probably don't). A favorite among pro chefs.
- **Broadway Panhandler**, 65 E 8th St, 212-966-3434, www.broadwaypanhandler.com; discounted cookware (Calphalon, All-Clad, Le Creuset) and quality kitchen tools for the serious cook.
- **The Container Store**, 725 Lexington Ave, 212-366-4200; 629 Sixth Ave, 212-366-4200; 370 Route 17 North, Paramus, NJ, 201-265-9004; 145 Westchester Avenue, White Plains, NY, 914-946-4767, www.containerstore.com; organize your closets, your kitchen, your drawers, your desk, your life! This is the last word in containers: garment bags, shelving, shoe holders, drawer dividers, wicker boxes, closet accessories.

- **Fishs Eddy**, 889 Broadway, 212-420-9020, and 2555 Richmond Ave, Staten Island, 718-7494-7020, www.fishseddy.com; offers surplus restaurant china where you can buy just one piece. Plenty of New York themed wares here, too, and always something a little clever to make you laugh and to serve as a party conversation piece. Everything guaranteed chip- and crack-free.
- **Hammacher Schlemmer**, 147 E 57th St, 212-421-9000, www.hammacher.com; a department store of sorts for the eclectic, has plenty of off-beat luxury items, gadgets, electronic toys, and a premier collection of quality kitchen- and barware. They tend to carry the best of any given machine and it's worth visiting just to get an idea of what's quality.
- **S. Feldman Housewares, Inc.**, 1304 Madison Ave, 212-289-7367, www.sfeldmanhousewares.com; upscale cookware, including Calphalon, LeCreuset, and All-Clad, as well as the popular Miele vacuum cleaners. Watch for their sales.
- **Sur la Table**, 75 Spring St, 212-966-3375; 1320 Third Ave, 646-843-7984; 306 W 57th St, 212-573-8340, www.surlatable.com; From cookie cutters to coffee makers, Sur la Table stocks a range of reliable, name-brand cookware. Some locations also host cooking classes.
- **Tiffany and Co.**, 727 Fifth Ave, 212-755-8000, www.tiffany.com; stand up straight, speak softly, and be on your best behavior when entering the hallowed halls of the famous high end department store. The main-floor jewelry draws oohs and ahs from a multitude of tourists, but if you ask the elevator operator for "three, please," you'll find shimmering ivory walls and plates by Picasso nudging Royal Crown Derby place settings. The selection of fine china and glassware is exquisite. Tired of jelly glasses? Crystal's to your right. And if you're getting married, for many this is *the* place to register.
- **Williams-Sonoma**, 110 Seventh Ave, 212-633-2203; 121 E 59th St, 917-369-1131; 1175 Madison Ave, 212-289-6832; 10 Columbus Circle (inside Time Warner Center), 212- 581-1146, www.williams-sonoma.com; known through their appealing catalogue to serious cooks nationwide, this California-based firm specializes in quality cookware, handsome glassware, and mostly imported country-style tableware. The familiar pieces, and then some, are available here, along with gourmet food items and cookbooks. For lovers of color-coordinated kitchens, it's a treasure trove.

ALTERNATIVE SOURCES

- **Pearl River**, 477 Broadway, 212-431-4770, www.pearlriver.com; "Over 15,000 products, from the amazing practical to the chic and stylish to the curious and exotic"; that's how the owners of Pearl River describe their inventory, which includes nearly an entire floor (the basement) devoted to Chinese bowls, serving platters, chopsticks, and cookware, including bamboo steamer baskets and knives. The store also has small appliances and household goods such as curtains, shoji screens, and laundry baskets, as well as gifts, stationery, and clothing.

- **The Restaurant Supply District**: as the use of professional kitchenware in the home increases, the wholesale restaurant strip along the section of Bowery between West Houston and Broome streets has become a destination for retail shoppers. Pots, pans, butcher block, Robot Coupes, Garland ranges, bar ware and thick, nearly unbreakable dishes are available from most stores at less than uptown retail. Outlets include **Bari Restaurant Equipment Corp.**, 240 Bowery, 212-925-3845, www.bariequipment.com, for a grand assortment of pots, pans, strainers, stirrers and such must-haves as pizza ovens and gigantic wooden pizza peels; and **Chef Restaurant Supplies**, 298 Bowery, 212-254-6644, www.chefrestaurantsupplies.com, is "unbelievably cheap" and favored by uptown chefs. It's also well worth checking out the cookware available in Chinatown, which can be outrageously cheap.

LAMPS AND LIGHT FIXTURES

You can't beat the department stores for variety and choice; wait for the winter sales if you can. But if you want better prices or the newest imports, shop some of the sources below.

SPECIALTY SHOPS

- **Gracious Home** (see above listing under Beds, Bedding, and Bath)
- **Just Bulbs Ltd.**, 220 E 60th St, 212-888-5707, www.justbulbsnyc.com; an eclectic and funky mix of bulbs (and more bulbs!). Can make you a little "light" headed.
- **Oriental Lampshade Company**, 816 Lexington Ave, 212-832-8190; 223 W 79th St, 212-873-0812, www.orientallampshade.com; hand-made shades to order and less expensive ready-mades in a great variety of colors, shapes, and styles. Lamp repair, too.
- **Lee's Art Shop**, 220 W 57th St, 212-247-0110, www.leesartshop.com; yes, this is an art store, but there's also a large section devoted to lamps and light fixtures, many of them design-conscious.

ALTERNATIVE SOURCES

The **Lamp and Light Fixture District** concentrated on The Bowery between Broome and Canal streets abuts wholesale restaurant supply stores that begin at Broome and end a few blocks north at Houston. If you know what you want, don't be daunted by lurid window displays of fantasy fixtures. Push on past high kitsch, find a salesperson, and describe your product. Chances are, the fixture can be ordered or will be in stock at less than retail. But don't count on tender loving care. That's reserved for large wholesale buyers. Try **Just Shades**, 21 Spring Street,

212-966-2757, www.justshadesny.com, which covers the gamut from burlaps to fine pleated ivory silks in all sizes.

SUPERSTORES

Well established in the suburbs and rural areas across the country, big box stores such as Home Depot arrived in the outer boroughs in the late 1990s, and now even inhabit Manhattan. The cost of space and community resistance to their establishment poses the ultimate challenge to these warehouse-style behemoths. For those who have the stamina to roam their vast aisles and the storage space at home for, say, 32 rolls of toilet paper, they represent real savings, though some require yearly membership fees. Note: a car is a definite asset, if not a necessity, when shopping these outlets.

- **BJ's Wholesale Club**, more than 20 locations in the boroughs and New Jersey, including 137-05 20th Ave, College Point, Queens, 718-359-9703, and 610 Exterior St, Bronx, 718-292-5410, www.bjs.com; sells everything from tires to oven mitts to peanut butter—in gigantic family size. Bring some muscle to carry everything to and from the car (or van, or rental truck, or blimp). Members pay $50 annually for access.
- **Costco**, 32-50 Vernon Blvd, Long Island City, Queens, 718-267-3680; 61-35 Junction Blvd, Rego Park, Queens, 718-760-6470; 517 E 117th St, 212-896-5873; 2975 Richmond Ave, Staten Island, 718-982-9525; 976 Third Ave, Brooklyn, 718-965-7600; also several New Jersey locations; www.costco.com. Vast stores housing books, jewelry, computers, cameras, hardware, groceries, the list goes on. Membership is $55 per year.
- **Home Depot**, nearly 20 locations in metro NYC, New Jersey, and Westchester, including the original Manhattan store at 40 West 23rd St, 212-929-9571; www.homedepot.com. Home Depot offers clinics on how to build it, paper it, paint it, wire or plumb it, and plant it; and they stock everything you'll need to do it from nuts and bolts to toilets and hot tubs. Make a list before you go.

SAMPLE SALES

These are special sales of a designer's leftover inventory (from jewelry to furniture to upscale bathroom fixtures), and they offer considerable savings for the determined shopper. Sample sales are usually announced in *New York Magazine*; also keep an eye on New York-specific shopping websites, including www.ny.racked.com.

FOOD

New York eats, but in ways that take some getting used to. The city is host to some of the finest and some of the most expensive restaurants in the world, as well as hundreds of excellent eateries of every ethnic and national persuasion, large and small. For this you're on your own to explore the city's restaurant riches as far as your pocketbook permits, and with perhaps a *Zagat's Restaurant Guide* or the "Food" section of the *New York Times* in hand. You're also on your own to explore the possibilities of takeout, which is a ubiquitous part of the city's food life. It seems you're never more than a block away from a source of takeout; many New Yorkers depend on it. And the host of corner delis throughout the city providing late night sandwiches, coffee, milk, beer, and snack food, needs no chronicling. You have one in your immediate neighborhood. Chances are, you also have an open-air fruit and vegetable stand operated nearly round-the-clock and stocked with beautifully displayed fresh produce. These islands of color, almost invariably operated by Korean-Americans, brighten the city streets while also offering convenience and a sense of neighborhood. New York is sometimes referred to as "the city that never sleeps," perhaps because New Yorkers have too much fine food available 24 hours a day.

Sooner or later, though, you'll need that jar of spaghetti sauce, steak, box of rice, or shaker salt, not to mention some toilet paper. Supermarkets used to be scarce in many neighborhoods and lackluster in others, but happily, the supermarket scene has changed dramatically in recent years, particularly with the arrival of Whole Foods and Trader Joes and the expansion of NYC favorite, Fairway. Residents of outer boroughs are particularly lucky, benefiting from chains like Trade Fair and specialty groceries like EuroMarket in Astoria, which carry produce and dry goods from nearly every corner of the world. Depending on where you live, specialty shops may provide the best selection for fresh meats and produce, and summer finds many New Yorkers shopping for the freshest fruits and vegetables at sidewalk carts. If stocking up suits you, but you don't have access to a car, consider signing up with the online grocery delivery service **Fresh Direct** at www.freshdirect.com. More reasonably priced than you might imagine, this company delivers groceries right to your door (or your doorman).

Other local grocery chains include:

- **Associated Food Stores and Supermarkets**, www.afstores.com
- **D'agostino**, www.dagnyc.com
- **Food Emporium**, www.foodemporium.apsupermarket.com
- **Gristedes**, www.gristedes.com
- **Met Foodmarkets**, www.metfoods.com

You want some good French or Italian bread, a decent paté, fresh smoked salmon, and some frisée for Sunday brunch? Manhattan especially is well served by excellent bread bakers in just about every neighborhood, and by gourmet shops, which carry good breads and every other imaginable edible—at a price. Here are just a few:

- **Agata & Valentina**, 64 University Pl, 212-452-0690; 1505 First Ave, 212-452-0690, www.agatavalentina.com
- **Citarella**, 2135 Broadway; 1313 Third Ave; 424 Sixth Ave, 212-874-0383, www.citarella.com
- **Dean & Deluca**, 560 Broadway, 212-226-6800; 1150 Madison Ave, 212-717-0800, www.deandeluca.com
- **E.A.T. Gourmet Foods**, 1064 Madison Ave, 212-772-0022, www.elizabar.com
- **Eli's Vinegar Factory**, 431 E 91st St, 212-987-0885, www.elizabar.com
- **Fairway**, 2127 Broadway, 212-595-1888; 2328 12th Avenue, 212-234-3883; 240 E 86th St, 212-327-2008; 766 6th Ave, 646-676-4550; 550 2nd Ave, 646-720-9420; 255 Greenwich St, no phone; 480-500 Van Brunt St, Red Hook, Brooklyn, 718-254-0923, www.fairwaymarket.com
- **Garden of Eden Farmers Market**, 7 E 14th St, 212-255-4200; 162 W 23rd St, 212-675-6300; 2780 Broadway, 212-222-7300; 180 Montague St, Brooklyn, 718-222-1515, www.edengourmet.com
- **Gourmet Garage**, 117 Seventh Ave S, 212-699-5980; 489 Broome St, 212-941-5850; 301 E 64th St, 212-535-5880; 1245 Park Ave, 212-348-5850; and 155 W 66th St, 212-595-5850; www.gourmetgarage.com
- **Grace's Marketplace**, 1237 Third Ave at 71st St, 212-737-0600, www.graces-marketplacenyc.com
- **Todaro Bros**, 555 Second Ave, 212-532-0633, www.todarobros.com
- **Trader Joe's**, 142 E. 14th St, 212-529-4612; 675 6th Ave, 212-255-2106; 2073 Broadway, 212-799-0028; 130 Court St, Brooklyn, 718-246-8460; 90-30 Metropolitan Ave, Rego Park, Queens, 718-275-1791; 2385 Richmond Ave, Staten Island, 718-370-1085; numerous stores in New Jersey; www.traderjoes.com
- **Whole Foods Market**, 808 Columbus Ave, 212-222-6160; 250 Seventh Ave, 212-924-5969; 10 Columbus Circle, 212-823-9600; 4 Union Square South, 212-673-5388; 270 Greenwich St, 212-349-6555; 226 E 57th St, 646-497-1222;95 E Houston St, 212-420-1320; 214 Third St, Brooklyn, 718-907-3622; numerous stores in New Jersey; www.wholefoodsmarket.com.
- **Zabar's**, 2245 Broadway, 212-787-2000, www.zabars.com

Vegetarians and those in search of organic foods will find that farmers' markets and most of the major grocery store chains have dedicated organic sections, but there are also stores catering exclusively to this market. Some of the better-known health food stores are listed here:

- **Commodities Natural Market**, 165 First Ave, 212-260-2600, www.commoditiesnaturalmarket.com
- **Integral Yoga Natural Foods**, 229 W 13th St, 212-243-2642, www.integralyoganaturalfoods.
- **LifeThyme**, 410 Sixth Ave at 8th St, 212-420-9099, www.lifethymemarket.com

- **Park Slope Food Co-op**, 782 Union St, Brooklyn, NY 11215, 718-622-0560, www.foodcoop.com; provides fresh organic foods and household supplies to community members, who now number over 16,000. Each member pays a one-time $25 joining fee and then contributes a $100 investment to the co-op (returnable when the member leaves the co-op), and each member must do a minimal work share. The co-op buys food and sells it to members for much less than competing grocery stores.
- **Westerly Natural Market**, 911 Eighth Ave, 212-586-5262, www.westerlynaturalmarket.com

ETHNIC FOODS

The ongoing immigration history of New York is displayed in the sidewalk stalls and food markets of its ethnic neighborhoods. For every conceivable item of **Chinese** vegetable, ingredient, and condiment, not to mention fish, and **Korean**, **Japanese**, **Thai**, and **Malaysian** food items, all very reasonably priced, New Yorkers go to Chinatown on either side of Canal Street downtown, or to Flushing on either side of Main Street, or to Sunset Park in Brooklyn. For the ultimate in Japanese food shopping, Mitsuwa Marketplace on River Road in Edgewater, NJ, is the place to go. **Little Italy**, just north of Chinatown, isn't the only place to buy Italian food items; it just feels more authentic, despite the fact that many of the area's Italian restaurants and shops have disappeared in recent years. There are also pockets of Italian specialty stores in the Village, on Ninth Avenue in the Thirties, and along legendary Arthur Avenue in The Bronx. Pungent **Indian** spices scent the air along Lexington Avenue between 23rd and 28th Streets; a favorite shop (selling more than Indian spices and specializing in global dry goods) is Kalustyan's, 123 Lexington Ave, 212-685-3451, www.kalustyans.com. **Polish** and **Ukrainian** foods hold their ground among other ethnic outlets along First and Second Avenues between 14th and Houston Streets, but Greenpoint, Brooklyn, is the Polish food capital of the city. **Latino** food specialties are to be found throughout the city, especially in East Harlem along 116th Street, along Broadway in Washington Heights, and in Jackson Heights, Queens. No city outside Israel has more to offer in the way of **Jewish** foods than New York, in parts of The Bronx, Brooklyn, and Queens. In Manhattan, aficionados go to Broadway on the Upper West Side, East Houston Street near Orchard, and elsewhere in the Lower East Side especially for "the best" bagels, lox, pastrami, smoked whitefish, stuffed derma, etc. It's Brighton Beach, Brooklyn, no question about it, for **Russian** food (and some more Jewish, as well), and Astoria is still the epicenter of Greek culture and culinary life in New York City.

GREENMARKETS/FARMERS' MARKETS AND ARTISANAL MARKETS

One of the joys of New York food shopping is the range of options available. While New York has major grocery stores (among the best chains are Whole Foods,

Fairway, and Trader Joe's), it also has indoor artisanal markets, such as Chelsea Market and an ever-growing number of outdoor greenmarkets. Some of these run year-round, but spring, summer, and fall are the seasons for fresh, choice fare, much of it brought in by farmers from the Hudson River Valley area, just outside the city., GrowNYC, 212-788-7900, www.grownyc.org, manages the greenmarkets, where you can buy fruits, vegetables, meats, fish, dairy, bread and other baked goods, cheese, and flowers. Prices may be slightly higher for some items, but the quality and freshness are superior to anything else in the city. GrowNYC has made numerous efforts to make the market accessible to New Yorkers of all backgrounds and budgets; it accepts EBT payments (food stamps) and hosts workshops and events, such as free cooking demonstrations. Market hours are generally 8 a.m. to 6 p.m., but be advised: the later you arrive, the fewer vendors and goods you'll find.

- **Chelsea Market**, 75 9th Ave, 212-652-2110, www.chelseamarket.com; the best covered marketplace in NYC, with wine cellars, excellent cafés and restaurants, the best fish and produce providers, and even the Food Network upstairs! Other attractions include a gelateria, a bookstore, bakeries, and specialty purveyors of items such as nuts and tea. All done in the former Nabisco factory.
- **Essex Street Market**, 120 Essex St, 212-312-3603, www.essexstreetmarket. com; since 1940, this indoor market has been bringing low-cost produce, fish, cheese, and other products to the Lower East Side. It still has some of the least expensive fish and produce in the city, as well as a recent infusion of more upscale stands selling local cheeses and some nice little eateries.

ONLINE STORES OFFERING HOME DELIVERY

A growing number of businesses have foregone bricks-and-mortar storefronts and exist only online, offering convenience, variety, and speed—and, usually, competitive prices—to customers who want goods delivered straight to their homes. Here are some of the most popular ones providing service in and around the city:

- **Amazon**, www.amazon.com, is, perhaps, the original online shopping portal, selling everything from books to groceries.
- **Fresh Direct**, www.freshdirect.com, was the original grocery delivery service in New York City and still outdoes its competitors.
- **Google Shopping Express**, www.google.com/shopping/express, was launched recently and provides a similar range of products (i.e., practically everything) and services (i.e., same-day delivery in Manhattan) as Amazon. Keep in mind that delivery is not free.
- **Soap.com**, www.soap.com, started as a site where users could order household goods and toiletries; it still has a mind-boggling inventory of these items, but has launched nearly 10 additional satellite sites, each specializing in some other product domain: pet food (www.wag.com), groceries (www.vinemarket.

com), baby goods (www.diapers.com), and furniture and home appliances (www.casa.com). You can shop across all of the sites using a single account and deliveries can arrive as quickly as the next-day. A convenient "Easy Reorder" function keeps track of the items you order frequently so you can shop even more quickly. The sites also have a single app for smart phones for shopping and ordering on the go.

Keep in mind that many major bricks-and-mortar stores in the city also offer delivery services, among them **Barnes & Noble** (books); **Gracious Home** (household appliances); **Office Depot** and **Staples** (office supplies and furniture); and **Whole Foods** (groceries), to name only a few.

THE INCREDIBLE DIVERSITY AND DEPTH OF THE CITY'S CULTURAL, INTEL-
lectual, and artistic life is a magnet for many of the people who move
here. Nowhere else can such an enormous range of interests and avoca-
tions be accommodated on so many levels. While it is impossible to cover all the
opportunities New York offers, we can help the newcomer, young and old alike,
access this cultural variety by providing a compilation of ticket, subscription, and
membership information for leading opera companies, symphony orchestras,
dance companies, theatrical repertory groups, and museums. We've also included
cultural opportunities for children, as well as a section called **Literary Life** that
focuses on libraries and bookstores. Addresses provided are in Manhattan unless
otherwise noted. For more cultural life and opportunities, see the community
resources listed at the end of each neighborhood profile at the beginning of the
book. And while it's easy to forget that New York is a college town, don't forget
to check out the many offerings of colleges and universities around the city,
including Columbia, CUNY, and NYU (see **Higher Education** at the end of the
Childcare and Education chapter).

First, what is showing, where, and when? Two particularly useful sites for
tracking down event details are the *New York Times'*, www.nytimes.com, and the
extensive website of the Alliance for the Arts, **NYC-Arts** at www.nyc-arts.org. The
latter comprehensive compendium lists concert halls, galleries, museums, theaters, historical structures, monuments, and parks throughout the five boroughs,
with links to websites, information about hours and admission, timely articles, performance calendars, and a culture guide for children. Area publications offering
event information include:

- "**Weekend**," two sections in the *New York Times'* Friday edition, features
  reviews, articles, and tips on the endless arts and entertainment possibilities for
  Friday, Saturday, and Sunday.

- **"Arts and Leisure,"** the arts supplement in the *New York Times'* Sunday edition, offers reviews and critical articles on current trends and upcoming events in the arts, plus listings for the arts with thumbnail reviews.
- *The New Yorker*, www.newyorker.com; on stands each Wednesday, includes not just plays, opera, and museums in its comprehensive "Goings on About Town," but also poetry readings, sporting events, and nightlife. Most listings include abbreviated reviews. If you have a smart phone, the magazine also has a free "Goings on About Town" app, which is quite handy.
- *New York Magazine*, on stands each Monday, covers all manner of the arts, from newly opening visual arts exhibits to movies and everything in between. (www.nymag.com)
- *Time Out New York*, www.timeoutny.com; on stands each Wednesday, offers comprehensive listings and reviews in all aspects of entertainment and the arts, as well as gay and lesbian features, and listings of events for children.
- The *Village Voice*, www.villagevoice.com; free on the street each Wednesday, is filled with entertainment ads and carries a "Listings" column of weekly free events. Particularly good for alternative events.
- *Club Free Time* is a website maintaining listings of free cultural activities around the city. Search by date or genre.

For New York Theater listings you can also check out **TheaterMania** at www.theatermania.com or the **Theatre Development Fund** at www.tdf.org.

ELECTRONIC RESOURCES

A huge range of curated e-mail listings gives subscribers (almost always free) insight into events around New York. Many are just for a particular organization, some focus on a discipline or media, but they're excellent ways to find out about events, especially those that might not get listed elsewhere. You go to the list's website to sign up and then receive weekly emails of listings. Here are a few of the larger ones:

- **Flavorpill**, www.flavorpill.com; this curated weekly listing is emailed to sub-scribers with a listing of editors' picks of exciting performances/events, with an emphasis on alternative-type events. It's actually an international service, but with a NY franchise. Free.
- **Nonsense NYC**, www.nonsensenyc.com; this low-key and very personal enter-tainment listing bills itself as "a discriminating resource for independent art, weird events, strange happenings, unique parties, and senseless culture." Sign up on its website for weekly newsletters listing some of the city's odder, off-beat events. Free, but donation suggested.
- **Vulture**, www.vulture.com; this site and newsletter of *New York Magazine* is dedicated to all things pop culture. Amidst reviews and commentary about

popular TV shows and celebrities, you'll find coverage of other (slightly) higher-brow events and activities.

TICKETS

How can you buy tickets to New York's plays, concerts, ballets, operas, and special mega-events? Let us describe the ways.

BOX OFFICE

To get the best seats for the day you want, go to the venue's box office in person well in advance of the performance desired, cash or charge card in hand. Not only can you check the theater's seating diagram (usually posted near the ticket window), you won't pay a handling fee. When ordering by telephone or mail, you usually have no control over the exact row or seat issued, because orders are filled automatically on a "best available" basis. Box offices are usually open from 10 or 11 a.m. until the evening performance. Note: sometimes producers, directors, or actors release their personal tickets and these go back to the box office for sale at the last minute, making it possible for the persistent to see a hot show that has officially sold out.

TELEPHONE ORDERS

Most theaters list a special number to call for reservations. Billed to credit cards, tickets are mailed if time allows; otherwise pick them up at the theater's "Will-Call" window the day of the performance. **Telecharge.com**, 212-239-6200, www.telecharge.com, represents some 20 Schubert Theaters in New York City and adds a service fee and handling charge for the entire order; the total of those fees varies by venue. **Ticketmaster**, 800-745-3000, www.ticketmaster.com, may be better known as a vendor of concert tickets, but it handles theater productions as well. Note that it also collects a service and convenience fee, so the total cost of the ticket you're buying can add up quickly. While usually not at all convenient, the theater box office is much cheaper if you're buying more than one ticket to an event.

ONLINE ORDERS

Individual tickets and subscriptions to most major concert series, operas, dance programs, and the like can be ordered online from the host venue's website using a major credit card. Likewise, tickets to plays, sporting events, and popular entertainment generally can be ordered through www.telecharge.com or www.ticketmaster.com.

TICKETMASTER

Promoters determine how tickets to their events will be sold: at Ticketmaster outlets, by calling Ticketmaster, or both. First, call 800-745-3000 or go to www.ticketmaster.com to find out what performances they are offering and whether tickets can be ordered by phone and charged to a credit card (fees range, depending on the venue and type of ticket) or whether they must be picked up in person and paid for in cash at one of Ticketmaster's outlets in the U.S. or Canada.

BROKERS

Unless you have a friend with a personal broker or an "in" with a hotel concierge, don't expect to walk into a ticket agency and get front row center for the town's hottest musical the day of the performance. These seats are held for valued clients. However, for most people, events brokers, who usually handle only orchestra, mezzanine, and box seats, are still probably the easiest way to get into a show or sporting event in a hurry. Expect to pay 20% to 50% over the total price for their service. Note: deal only with licensed brokers in the city; out-of-town brokers operating with 800 numbers are not regulated, and you can get burned. American Tickets, www.american-tickets.com, and Continental Guest Services, www.continentalguestservices.com, operating out of major hotels, are large and well established. Scalping is illegal, so think twice before buying from the guy hawking tickets in the street. If you want to check seating charts, most venues have these available on their official websites.

ALTERNATIVE SOURCES

Tickets to sports events, tours, and other entertainment, as well as theater tickets, can be bought at the city's **Official NYC Information Center**, 810 Seventh Ave, 212-484-1222, www.nycgo.com, Monday–Friday, 8:30 a.m. to 6 p.m., and Saturday and Sunday, 9 a.m. to 5 p.m. There is a service charge for these tickets. Also available here is the CityPASS, a steeply discounted ticket to six major tourist attractions good for nine days, plus maps, brochures, and multilingual tourist counselors.

DISCOUNTS

- **TKTS** is one of the city's great bargains, and a rite of passage for the theater-bound. The Theatre Development Fund operates three outlets for half-price and 25%-off day-of-performance tickets to Broadway and Off-Broadway shows. Shows and availability change daily, and information about both is posted on large boards near ticket sales booths. A small fee—currently $4.50—is charged for each ticket; tickets can be paid for in cash or by credit card or traveler's check. Note: ticket selection is better and lines shorter early in the week.

- **TKTS Times Square**, W 47th St and Broadway, sells discount tickets for evening performances of Broadway, Off-Broadway, dance, and music events from 3 p.m. to 8 p.m., Monday and Wednesday–Saturday, and from 2 p.m. to 8 p.m. on Tuesday. Selling hours for matinee performances are 10 a.m. to 2 p.m. Wednesday and Saturday, and 11 a.m. to 3 p.m. on Sunday. They accept credit cards and cash. For more information go to the Theatre Development Fund website at www.tdf.org.

- **TKTS South Street Seaport**, on the corner of Front and John Streets (the rear of the building at 199 Water Street), sells same-day discount tickets for evening performances and next-day discount tickets for matinees. Also, tickets for matinees are available the day before, a service not provided at the midtown location. Hours are 11 a.m. to 6 p.m. Monday–Saturday; this booth is closed on Sunday. Cash and credit cards accepted.

- **TKTS Downtown Brooklyn Booth**, at 1 Metro Tech Center (corner of Jay and Myrtle), sells discount tickets to evening shows on the day of the performance, next-day discount tickets for matinees, and full price tickets for arts events in Brooklyn. Hours are 11 a.m. to 6 p.m. Tuesday–Saturday; the booth is closed Sunday and Monday. The booth is also closed from 3–3:30 p.m. for lunch each day. Cash and credit cards accepted.

- **Theatre Development Fund**, 520 8th Ave, Suite 801, Attention: TDF Membership, NYC 10018, 212-912-9770, www.tdf.org; offers tickets to a variety of plays, musicals, dance, and jazz performances at reduced prices, often for as much as 70% off the face value. Memberships are available to seniors (62 or older), students, teachers, performing arts professionals, union members, staff members of a nonprofit organization, and members of the clergy or armed forces. Download the application from the TDF website and mail it in. The annual membership fee is $30.

- **Audience Extras**, www.audienceextras.com, provides free tickets to plays in preview or in other special circumstances when the producer wants to "paper" the house, i.e., fill it with audience members to build buzz. For $115 you get a one-year membership card, renewable for $85, with a reserve fund against which a $3 service charge per ticket is charged, as well as access to their 24-hour hotline, which lists available shows. There is no limit on free shows.

- **Quicktix**: a small allotment of seats for each of the various performances at the New York Shakespeare Festival's Public Theater on Lafayette St (see **Theater** section) go on sale at 5:30 p.m. on the day of performance, for about half the price of regular tickets. You need to be a **Public Theater** member. Call 212-260-2400 after 1 p.m. for information. The Public Theater is online at www.publictheater.org.

- **Ask**: many theaters offer rush tickets, often at discounts, that are made available only hours before a performance. Typically, rush tickets are reserved for students or seniors, or are assigned through a lottery (usually two to three hours before a show). Limited-view seats are also discounted, and are more likely to be found at the box office than through a second- or third-party vendor. Contact the theater for specific details.

- **StubHub**, 1440 Broadway, 866-788-2482, www.stubhub.com; this service is the eBay of tickets—sporting, Broadway, what have you. It's scalping by another name, but here it is guaranteed, because the auctions are online and everyone selling has to register a credit card. Even better, they have an office at Broadway and 40th Street where you can pick up your tickets last minute.
- **Student tickets** at half price or less are often available to those holding bona fide student IDs as follows:
- **New York Philharmonic** at Avery Fisher Hall, Lincoln Center, has two arrangements. They sell $16 tickets for rehearsals about a month before the actual date. For shows with high availability, students and seniors can receive rush tickets for $13.50 (call 212-875-5656 on day of show, or go to Avery Fisher Hall box office; students may also phone to reserve tickets up to 10 days before the performance). For more information, go to www.nyphil.org/rush.
- **Carnegie Hall** sells $10 tickets, when available, on a first-come, first-served basis, to select events. You can call 212-247-7800 on the day of the concert starting at noon to see if tickets will be available. Day-of tickets are available at the box office from opening time until one hour before the performance. For more information, visit the venue's discount ticket page, www.carnegiehall. org/Tickets/Discount-Ticket-Programs.

High school students have access to the best deal of all on tickets to music, theater, museums, dance, and more through **High 5 Tickets to the Arts**. Students 13 to 18 years old can get $5 tickets to arts and cultural performances and two-for-$5 museum passes. Interested students will need to sign up for a free account on the High 5 website; tickets must be purchased online or at the High 5 office, 529 8th Avenue, Suite 321. A credit card is required. Call 212-750-0555 for information or visit www.highfivetix.org for a list of current performances on sale. The School Theater Ticket Program also offers discount vouchers for Broadway and Off-Broadway shows. Visit www.schooltix.com.

A few of the smaller to mid-size Manhattan theaters (generally Off-Broadway and Off-Off-Broadway), including Manhattan Theatre Club, www.manhattantheatreclub.com, will exchange admission for volunteer ushering, a boon to the theater devotee who is light of wallet. Call around for participating theaters.

SUBSCRIPTIONS

Common practice dictates that new subscriptions to any series—symphonic, operatic, dance, theatrical—must wait to be filled until the previous season's subscribers are given an opportunity to renew. Once the renewal deadline is past, new subscriptions are processed on a first-come, first-served basis. The initial announcement of each new season's schedule is sent to everyone on the mailing list anywhere from six weeks to six months before performances are scheduled to begin. To assure a position near the beginning of the line, call whatever institution interests you well in advance of its season and ask to be put on the mailing list. Upon receipt of the announcement schedule, choose your series and return the coupon and payment quickly. Often this can be done online at the appropriate website. Full-page ads in the *New York Times* Sunday "Arts and Leisure" section herald symphonic, operatic, and dance seasons five to six months before performances begin, but usually a week or two after the first public subscription mailers have been sent out.

Incidentally, certain nights are traditionally more popular than others. If good seats are more important than sitting next to the right people, find out which night or series has the best tickets available.

One great bargain:

- **People's Symphony Concert Series**, www.pscny.org; this series of a half-dozen classical performances each year has some of the world's greatest ensembles—but tickets can be as low as $7 if you buy a subscription. They have three different series every year.

GRAND OPERA

- **Metropolitan Opera**, Metropolitan Opera House, Lincoln Center, 212-362-6000, www.metopera.org; subscriptions range from $184 for an eight-opera series high up in the Family Circle to $3,115 for an eight-opera series in the Parterre. The Met charges $35 per subscription for handling. Renewal notices are mailed to current subscribers, and once these orders are processed in the spring, new subscriptions are filled. The Met's season is broken into three periods for the sale of individual seats: fall, winter, and spring. Subscribers are given first crack, then seats for single performances are offered to the public, first through a mailing, then via newspaper ads about a month and a half before each of the three seasons begins. Standing room goes on sale the Sunday before performance. You might also catch the Met during its free concert series in the parks during the summer. They visit each of the five boroughs. Check their website for a schedule as the summer approaches.
- **Opera Orchestra of New York**, at Carnegie Hall, 57th St and 7th Ave, 212-906-9137, www.operaorchestrany.org; under the musical direction of Eve Queler, performs three non-staged (that is, concert style) operas per season at Carnegie Hall. Performed by singers of the first rank, but not superstars; these are usually operas by major composers that are rarely staged.

CLASSICAL MUSIC

- **New York Philharmonic**, Avery Fisher Hall, 10 Lincoln Center, Plaza 212-875-5656, www.nyphil.org; numerous series are available for a September–June season. Easiest to obtain are subscriptions to the three-concert mini-series. Fall schedules are announced in late February/early March.
- **Carnegie Hall**, 57th St and Seventh Ave, 212-247-7800, www.carnegiehall.org; nearly 125 years old and still counting, Carnegie, featuring splendid acoustics, is still the concert hall preferred by many performers, and it continues to host programs by a variety of virtuosos and orchestras, plus popular superstars and even chamber music, with age-given grace. Call Carnegie Hall for subscriber information.

CHAMBER MUSIC

Several halls traditionally host the extraordinarily popular chamber music groups that perform here regularly, among them the hometown Juilliard String Quartet might give three or more New York concerts during any given year, each at a different location. Only the Chamber Music Society of Lincoln Center has a hall—Alice Tully Hall in Lincoln Center—that it can call home. Good seats go fast once the *Times* advertisements appear, so it's important to get on each group's mailing list. The following spaces are most likely to host chamber music performances. Call them or keep your eyes on the "Arts and Leisure" section of the Sunday *New York Times* in late spring and summer.

- **Merkin Concert Hall**, 129 W 67th St, box office, 212-501-3330, www.kaufmanmusiccenter.org
- **Alice Tully Hall**, Lincoln Center, 1941 Broadway, 212-721-6500, www.lc.incolncenter.org; concerts by the Chamber Music Society of Lincoln Center as well as other groups
- **Bargemusic**, Fulton Ferry Landing, under the Brooklyn Bridge (yes, it's actually on a barge), 718-624-4924, www.bargemusic.org
- **Metropolitan Museum of Art**, Grace Rainey Rogers Auditorium, 83rd St and Fifth Ave, 212-570-3949, www.metmuseum.org
- **92nd Street Y**, Kaufmann Concert Hall, 1395 Lexington Ave, 212-427-6000, www.92y.org

DANCE

It could be argued that New York is the dance capital of the world. Certainly, it is possible to see a performance of some form of dance—ballet, modern, jazz, ethnic, avant-garde—just about any night of the week somewhere in the city, from the most storied venues to those that are considered alternative. Among the latter are **Danspace Project** at St. Mark's Church, 131 East 10th Street, 866-811-4111, www.danspaceproject.org; **Performance Space 122**, 150 First Ave, 212-477-5829, www.ps122.org; **The Joyce Theater**, 175 8th Ave, 212-691-9740, www.joyce. org; and **The Riverside Theatre**, 91 Claremont Ave, inside the Riverside Church, 212-870-6784, www.theriversidetheatre.org. Below we've listed the established troupes and theaters to which one can subscribe. Get yourself on one mailing list and others are likely to find you.

- **American Ballet Theatre**, 890 Broadway, 3rd floor, 212-477-3030, www.abt. org; subscription series are offered for the ABT's spring season at the Metropolitan Opera House, April–June. The first announcement, mailed to friends in late December, is followed shortly by a new subscriber mailing, then a week or so later by the traditional January *New York Times* ad. Subscriptions for seats vary. Individual tickets at the box office and by phone go on sale in March.
- **New York City Ballet**, David H. Koch Theater, 20 Lincoln Center, 212-496-0600 for subscriptions or 212-870-5570 for performance information, www.nycballet. com; two seasons provide balletomanes the opportunity of feasting on dancing by Balanchine's company. Both the winter season, November–February, and the spring season, April–June, have 16 four-performance series, and good seats are easiest to come by for weekend matinees. First announcements go out nine weeks before the season begins. A tip for *Nutcracker* ballet fanciers: first orders for single, non-subscription performances of the *Nutcracker* are accepted in late October and tickets go fast for this seasonal family favorite. Call 212-870-5585 for prices and dates, and if certain seats for special performances are important, make your order several weeks before that time.
- **The Joyce Theater**, 175 Eighth Ave, 212-691-9740, www.joyce.org; celebrating dance of all kinds—ballet, modern, flamenco—The Joyce is an elegantly revamped former Art Deco movie house in Chelsea. Your reward for buying tickets to performances by four different dance groups during the fall or spring season is a membership that entitles you to 25% off on all tickets purchased subsequently. Your membership card also entitles you to priority seating and various discounts at more than 10 Chelsea restaurants located between 14th and 23rd Streets and Sixth and Tenth Avenues.
- **New York City Center**, 131 W 55th St, 212-581-1212, www.nycitycenter.org; dance companies once dominated the City Center's performance schedule; today they vie with a variety of musical comedy performances. The following **dance troupes** are among the major groups performing here regularly:
  » **Alvin Ailey American Dance Theater**, 405 W 55th St, 212-405-9000, www. alvinailey.org
  » **American Ballet Theatre**, 890 Broadway, 3rd floor, 212-477-3030, www.abt. org
  » **Dance Theatre of Harlem**, 466 W 152nd St, 212-690-2800, www.dancetheatreofharlem.com

» **Mark Morris Dance Group**, 3 Lafayette Ave, Brooklyn 718-624-8400, www. mmdg.org
» **Martha Graham**, 55 Bethune St, 212-299-9200, www.marthagraham.org
» **Paul Taylor Dance Company**, 551 Grand St, Broadway, 212-431-5562, www. ptdc.org

As with the chamber music ensembles, it is best to get on each company's mailing list. Call the company direct or City Center's Subscription Department. Prices vary for each series.

THEATER

Broadway, besides designating Manhattan's longest avenue, refers to the midtown theater district on and around "the Great White Way," home to the greatest theatrical productions in the nation, ranging from grand musicals and comedies to classic dramas. It's the big time and a magnet for theater-lovers everywhere. But a high percentage of the most critically acclaimed plays and musicals produced in any given year originate Off-Broadway, more often than not in theaters that offer subscriptions as a means of financing productions. Season tickets not only ensure exposure to new artists, playwrights, and directors, but in most cases, save money as well. A few of the most established groups are mentioned here, but please don't be limited by this list. Many more experimental but no less rewarding companies exist and should be explored.

- **Circle in the Square Theatre School**, 1633 Broadway, 212-307-0388, www. circlesquare.org; professional conservatory and acting and musical theater. Beginning in the 1950s in the Village, plays by Tennessee Williams and Eugene O'Neill premiered at Circle in the Square with such young actors as Jason Robards and George C. Scott. Uptown now, the theater continues to stage some of the best contemporary drama and comedy with first-rate actors and directors.
- **CSC Repertory Theater**, 136 E 13th St, 212-677-4210, www.classicstage.org; founded in 1967, CSC has been performing Ibsen, Strindberg, Brecht, and other mostly contemporary classics in this comfortably intimate theater since then. It's not a resident company, but three or four plays are performed in repertory throughout the season, with an occasional lecture bonus.
- **Joseph Papp Public Theater**, 425 Lafayette St, 212-539-8500, www.publictheater.org; Joseph Papp, who died in 1992, was perhaps the single most important figure in the post-WW II American theater. This venue, complete with the New York Shakespeare Festival's Public Theater and the cabaret Joe's Pub, offers events that are hailed for their diversity as well as their excellence. A membership package plan allows the public inexpensive access to productions and flexibility in choosing which of the season's productions one wishes to see. A small allotment of the seats for any performance at The Public are held for

same-day sale at a discount. The tickets, called Quicktix (see **Discounts** section), go on sale at 6 p.m. for about half the price of regular tickets.

- **Lincoln Center Theater**, 150 W 65th St, 212-239-6200, www.lct.org; members in this innovative theater program have access to a potpourri of presentations, from Shakespeare to Mamet, with an occasional first-rate musical thrown in, be it at Lincoln Center on Broadway or Off-Off-Broadway at the experimental La Mama. The $50 membership fee buys one year's access to Lincoln Center Theater plays already in progress around town and first crack at six new productions a year as they come up. Popular productions with outstanding casts have included *Our Town*, *Waiting for Godot*, and *Anything Goes*. For tickets, call Telecharge, 212-239-6200.
- **Manhattan Theatre Club**, 261 W 47th St and 131 W 55th St, 212-399-3030, www.manhattantheatreclub.com, has been producing critically acclaimed plays since its founding on the Upper East Side in 1970. After some years with one foot at City Center on West 55th Street, MTC has settled in there, at 299-seat Stage I and at 150-seat Stage II. Productions that prove to be especially successful typically move to larger Broadway or Off-Broadway venues. Single tickets can also be purchased through City Tix, 212-581-1212.
- **The Pearl Theatre Co.**, 555 W 42nd St, 212-523-9261, www.pearltheatre.org; a repertory theater company, it mounts regular productions of theater classics such as Ibsen, Chekhov, and Shakespeare for a loyal audience. Various subscription plans for three to five performances range from $105 to $150.
- **Roundabout Theatre Company**, 231 W 39th St, Suite 1200, 212-719-1300, www.roundabouttheatre.org; with a subscription base of some 20,000, this not-for-profit theater company is obviously doing something right. What that involves is presenting revivals such as Pinter's *Betrayal* and O'Neill's *Anna Christie*, along with musicals such as *Cabaret*, with star wattage.

ALL OF THE ABOVE

- **Brooklyn Academy of Music**, 30 Lafayette Ave, Brooklyn, 718-636-4100, www.bam.org; is a center for all the performing arts. Best known for its annual Next Wave Festival, BAM (as it is popularly known) is a prime showcase for cutting-edge dance, theater, music, and opera. From the intimate Lepercq Space to the magnificent Opera House and the rejuvenated Majestic Theater, BAM presents everything from small chamber performances to alternative new age music. With several series taking place year-round, it is best to call and get on the mailing list in order to have a shot at getting tickets. Subscriptions represent a real value here, and if you become a Friend of BAM, you'll get priority seating.
- **Queens Theatre in the Park**, Flushing Meadows-Corona Park, Flushing, 718-760-0064, www.queenstheatre.org; brings major dance companies, Off-Broadway plays, and children's theater to its two theaters located in the Philip Johnson—designed New York Pavilion of the 1964–65 World's Fair. From *Charlie and the*

Chocolate Factory to *Dames at Sea* to lazer vaudeville to the Latino Culture Festival, Queens Theatre offers a variety of performances for a wide range of tastes.

FILM

New York is a movie buff's paradise. Screening of new filmmakers' works is a constant at the **Whitney Museum of American Art**, 945 Madison Avenue, 212-570-3600, www.whitney.org, and at the **Guggenheim Museum**, 1071 Fifth Avenue 212-423-3500, www.guggenheim.org, as well as at most of those all-encompassing, art-encouraging alternative spaces sprinkled throughout New York. **New School University**, 66 West 12th Street, 212-229-5600, www.newschool.edu, and the Skirball Center for New Media, home of New York University's Cinema Studies program, 721 Broadway, 6th floor, 212-998-1600, www.cinema.tisch. nyu.edu, explore movies in depth through numerous seminars and courses and, almost every semester, sponsor a film series or two as well.

Some of Manhattan's remaining revival and art film showcases include: **Angelika Film Center and Café**, 18 W Houston St, 212-995-2570, www.angelikafilmcenter.com; **Anthology Film Archives**, 32 Second Ave, 212-505-5181, www.anthologyfilmarchives.org; **Cinema Village**, 22 E 12th St, 212-924-3363, www.cinemavillage.com; **Film Forum**, 209 W Houston, 212-727-8110, www.filmforum.org; **Landmark Sunshine Theater**, 143 E Houston, 212-260-7289, www.landmarktheatres.com; and the **Walter Reade Theater**, 165 W 65th St at Broadway, 212-875-5600, www.filmlinc.com. Weekly schedules for these theaters are found in the "Arts and Leisure" section of the Sunday *Times* and *New Yorker*.

Additional film societies and museums include:

- The **Film Society of Lincoln Center**, 140 W 65th St, 212-875-5600, www.filmlinc.com, presents the New York Film Festival each fall (late September through October) at the Walter Reade Theater (see above) as well as the New Directors/New Films series in conjunction with the Museum of Modern Art each spring. Established in 1963, the Film Festival presents some 20 films during its annual run. A $75 membership in the Film Society provides the following perks: the right to buy discounted tickets for all screenings, discounts on concessions and Film Society merchandise, and a free subscription to the society's magazine, *Film Comment*. Tickets can be purchased in advance online.
- The **Museum of the Moving Image**, 36-01 35th Ave, Astoria 718-784-0077, www.movingimage.us, is a continuous movie, animation, and video art retrospective with exhibits, speaker series, symposia, celebrity appearances, and film series throughout the year to quicken the pulse of the true movie maven. Membership, $75 for individual, $125 for family, gives you admission, reservation privileges for screenings, a subscription to the Quarterly Guide, a 15% discount at the museum shop, and reduced admission to special programs and celebrity appearances. You need not be a member to visit; day rates available.

- **Tribeca Film Institute**, 32 Ave of the Americas, 27th Floor, 212-274-8080, www. tribecafilminstitute.org, offers year-round cultural events, including comedy, film, music, and theater, as well as the annual Tribeca Film Festival. Established by Robert De Niro and Jane Rosenthal in an effort to make Lower Manhattan a "centerpiece for culture and the arts."

Of course, there are plenty of movie theaters around the city showing the latest in Hollywood's big-screen hits. Theaters range from the small screens and tight seating in the multiplex theaters to more spacious and comfortable movie houses. The IMAX Theater at 1998 Broadway with a four-story screen is worth checking out, especially with children. New Yorkers love to get out to the movies so expect to find lines for the hottest new flicks. Call the **Moviefone**, 777-FILM, or go to www.moviefone.com or www.fandango.com to find out what is playing in your neighborhood and when.

BROADCASTING

The Paley Center for Media, 25 W 52nd St, 212-621-6600, www.paleycenter. org, shouldn't be missed as a chance to revisit your childhood and to experience American culture in video and audiotape form. "The Shadow knows," Fred Allen on radio, *All in the Family*, *I Love Lucy*—it's all there. The museum offers 96 video monitors for individual viewing of any television program in their collection. Call for schedule listings of special screening events. Annual memberships vary, with special prices for students, which allow admission to the museum's theaters and screening and listening rooms. Membership also gives you a discount on museum seminars and magazines, as well as all gift shop items.

MUSEUM MEMBERSHIPS

The benefits to be reaped by joining any of the city's myriad nonprofit institutions are really quite amazing. There seem to be museums and societies for every possible interest, so if you're an aficionado of a particular discipline, seek out the institution that best reflects your avocation and join. You'll be inundated with free literature, offered perquisites of many kinds, and probably be invited to teas, cocktail parties, and even banquets if your contribution is big enough. For the generalist, membership in one or two of the city's established cultural citadels is a wonderful way of obtaining well-researched information on any number of subjects. As an indication of the kind of benefits memberships provide, we've noted below details for a few of New York's major institutions:

- **American Folk Art Museum**, 2 Lincoln Sq, 212-595-9533, www.folkartmuseum. org; a wide array of folk art from weathervanes to textiles is found depicting America's history from the 18th century to the present. Membership ranges from $70 annually for an individual to $90 for a family and includes free admission to the museum, discounts on gift shop purchases, a subscription to the museum's newsletter, access to the museum's library, and other perks.

- **American Museum of Natural History**, Central Park West at 79th St, 212-769-5100, www.amnh.org; an associate membership here entitles you to as many visits to the dinosaurs as you wish, to say nothing of the Rose Center for Earth and Space, a subscription to *Natural History* magazine, and a 10% discount in the store. A $140 family membership adds a monthly newsletter and calendar, 25% discount on Hayden Planetarium tickets, and invitations to previews of the exhibitions. You also receive a 10% discount on most educational programs at the museum and a hefty discount at the IMAX Theater, with its oversized retractable screen and a dizzying IMAX projector.
- The **Bronx Zoo** (its official name: **New York Zoological Society International Wildlife Conservation Park**), Fordham Rd and Bronx River Pkwy, The Bronx, 718-220-5100, www.bronxzoo.com, is the largest zoo in the five boroughs and, stretching over 265 acres, the largest urban zoo in the world. Membership includes admission to this zoo, as well as to the **Central Park Zoo**, Central Park, E 64th St and Fifth Ave, 212-439-6500; the **New York Aquarium**, Surf Ave and W 8th St, Coney Island, Brooklyn, 718-265-3474; the **Queens Wildlife Center**, 718-271-1500, and **Children's Farm**, 111th St at 54th Ave, Corona Park, Flushing, Queens. Bronx Zoo membership also includes four free parking passes and discounts at gift shops, certain zoo restaurants, and on educational classes. These organizations are all part of the Wildlife Conservation Society, online at www.wcs.org.
- **The Frick Collection**, 1 E 70th St, 212-288-0700, www.frick.org; membership in Friends of the Frick entitles you to unlimited admission to the collection, a subscription to the *Members' Magazine* with information on special exhibits, lectures, and concerts, and a 10% discount in the museum shop, as well as a discount on concerts and educational programs hosted by the museum.
- **Guggenheim Museum**, 1071 Fifth Ave, 212-423-3500, www.guggenheim.org; even the basic individual membership confers an architectural bonus, providing free admission to the justifiably famous Frank Lloyd Wright spiral uptown and the Peggy Guggenheim Collection in her palazzo on the Grand Canal in Venice. In addition, members get invitations to parties, private viewings, book signings, and discounts at Guggenheim stores and the Guggenheim café.
- The **Jewish Museum**, 1109 Fifth Ave, 212-423-3200, www.thejewishmuseum.org; Jewish culture is represented in 28,000 objects, including fine arts, Judaica, and through the broadcast media. The permanent collection, Culture & Continuity: The Jewish Journey, depicts 4,000 years of Jewish history, including ancient times in Egypt, the Holocaust, and the formation of the State of Israel to the present. Membership includes unlimited admission, invitations to special previews of new exhibitions, discounts in the museum store and Café Weissman, guest passes, invitations to the Family Hanukkah Party, and various other perks.
- **Metropolitan Museum of Art**, Fifth Ave at 82nd St, 212-879-5500, www.met-museum.org; the sumptuous *Bulletin* published quarterly by the Met, filled with

high-quality color photographs and illuminating texts of catalog caliber, comes free with the museum's $110 individual membership. Other bonuses include the quarterly *Members Calendar,* free admission to the museum and The Cloisters, invitations to previews and private viewings of two exhibitions a year, and copies of the Met's Christmas and spring catalogues illustrating the museum's publications and glamorous reproductions of everything from Chinese scarves to early American pewter pitchers, which, as a member, you can buy at a 10% discount. But probably the biggest bonus you'll receive is the program and exhibition information, which will impel you to get over to the Met more often than you might otherwise.

- The **Museum of Modern Art (MoMA)**, 11 W 53rd St, 212-708-9400, www.moma.org; MoMA offers an unparalleled collection of 20th century art in its six-story gallery building and eight-story Education and Research Center, with the top floors dedicated to the expanded library and archives; the lobby offers views of the sculpture garden. Entry-level memberships receive a 10% discount at the museum store and on catalog and online merchandise, as well as free admission to the galleries and daily film programs, and invitations to exhibition previews and special events. It also houses an exceptional restaurant, The Modern, and an excellent communal table café, as well as a more intimate café with a terrace. This is also an excellent museum for membership if you have children; the museum's MoMA Art Lab is an educational and creative play space where themes and objects with which to play change regularly.

- **The New Museum of Contemporary Art**, 235 Bowery, 212-219-1222, www.newmuseum.org; known for its distinctive architecture—it's a stack of offset, aluminum-shelled boxes—this museum showcases an über-modern collection of the latest of the latest and supposedly the greatest. Four floors, with a pretty comprehensive collection of the cutting edge in visual arts of all kinds.

- **South Street Seaport Museum**, 12 Fulton St, 212-748-8600, www.southstseaport.org, encompasses the Fulton Market with its intriguing stores and jolly restaurants, restored Schermerhorn Row's handsome brick houses, and the Museum Block with old shops and new walkways. Membership tends to be a youngish crowd, drawn as much by the ambiance and the idea of the museum as by the perks, which include free admission to the museums, galleries, and ships at the Seaport Gallery, invitations to gallery openings and educational programs, plus discounts in several stores at the seaport.

- **Whitney Museum of American Art**, 945 Madison Ave at 75th St, 212-570-3676, www.whitney.org; membership benefits its holder with museum admission for two, discounts on classes and lectures, discounts at the museum store, invitations to exhibition opening receptions, and a free museum publication, as well as a calendar of events. If American art or experimental film interests you particularly, it is worth belonging to the Whitney to have ready access to its excellent series of large and small exhibitions and also to the works presented by the museum's New American Filmmakers series in some 25 to 30 different programs every year.

CULTURE FOR KIDS

Perhaps the greatest asset in raising children in the city is the astonishing wealth of theater, film, museums, and programs designed for them. It goes without saying that all of the institutions and organizations above are accessible to and appropriate, sooner or later, for children: the New York City Ballet's exquisite *Nutcracker*, the popular armor collection at the Metropolitan Museum, so much of the Museum of Natural History including the famed dinosaurs, the Bronx Zoo, children's museums in Manhattan and Brooklyn, to name just a few. Many of them design exhibits and programs specifically for children. And there are institutions and groups that exist specifically for the younger population.

How to find it all? You'll pick up a lot about what's going on where from school bulletin boards, from other parents, and from the parent magazines distributed free in school lobbies and libraries. One of the most popular one-stop-shops for finding information about kid-friendly and kid-specific activities and events is the website www.mommypoppins.com, which is updated daily. You can also sign up for their newsletters (daily or weekly), which provide advance notice about upcoming events and include information about discounted tickets.

Other resources include:

- *Time Out New York Kids*, www.timeout.com/new-york-kids, publishes a print magazine, but up-to-date information is accessed more easily on its website.

THEATER FOR CHILDREN

Venues offering theater for children include the following:

- **Brooklyn Academy of Music**, 30 Lafayette Ave, Brooklyn, 718-636-4100, www.bam.org
- **Brooklyn Arts Exchange**, 421 Fifth Ave at 8th St in Park Slope, 718-832-0018, www.bax.org; also has classes for kids in theater, dance, and choreography
- **Henry Street Settlement, Abrons Art Center,** 466 Grand St, 212-598-0400, www.abronsartscenter.org
- **New Victory Theater**, 209 W 42nd St, 646-223-3010, www.newvictory.org; engaging programming ranges from the pleasingly silly to the avant-garde, but remains respectful of the audience's age and maturity. Some performances are for children as young as infants, and other programs are designed especially for children with autism.
- **The Shadow Box Theatre**, venues vary, check website for current shows and locations 212-724-0677, www.shadowboxtheatre.org
- **Swedish Cottage Marionette Theater**, Central Park, 212-988-9093, www.cityparksfoundation.org/arts/swedish-cottage-marionette-theatre/
- **Symphony Space**, 2537 Broadway, 212-864-5400, www.symphonyspace.org
- **Theatreworks USA**, 151 W 26th St, 212-647-1100, www.theatreworksusa.org

• **Thirteenth Street Repertory Company**, 50 W 13th St, 212-675-6677, www. 13thstreetrep.org

MUSEUMS AND LIBRARIES FOR CHILDREN

Many of the major museums and libraries host events and exhibitions specifically for children; others are dedicated entirely to kids.

• **American Museum of Natural History**, 79th St and Central Park West, 212-769-5100, www.amnh.org; a must, naturally
• **Brooklyn Children's Museum**, 145 Brooklyn Ave Crown Heights, 718-735-4400, www.brooklynkids.org; wonderfully hands-on and inventive
• **Brooklyn Museum of Art**, 200 Eastern Pkwy at Prospect Park, 718-638-5000, www.brooklynmuseum.org
• **Children's Museum of the Arts**, 103 Charlton St, 212-274-0986, www.cmany. org
• **Children's Museum of Manhattan**, 212 W 83rd St, 212-721-1223, www.cmom. org
• **Historic Richmondtown**, Staten Island Historical Society, 441 Clarke Ave, Richmondtown, Staten Island, 718-351-1611, www.historicrichmondtown.org
• **Intrepid Sea, Air and Space Museum**, Pier 86, W 46th St at 12th Ave, 212-245-0072, www.intrepidmuseum.org
• **Madame Tussaud's Wax Museum**, 234 W 42nd St, 212-512-9600, www.nycwax. com
• **Museum of the City of New York**, 1220 Fifth Ave, 212-534-1672, www.mcny.org
• **New York City Fire Museum**, 278 Spring St, 212-691-1303, www.nycfiremuseum.org
• **New York Hall of Science**, 47-01 111th St, Corona, Queens, 718-699-0005, www.nyscience.org
• **New York Public Library**, various branches, 212-340-0849, www.nypl.org
• **Queens Museum**, Flushing Meadows-Corona Park, 718-592-9700, www. queensmuseum.org; home to the most amazing miniature panorama of the city with some 800,000 buildings capturing almost every structure in the five boroughs—a must see to believe.
• **Queens Library**, various branches, 718-990-0700, www.queenslibrary.org
• **Staten Island Children's Museum at Snug Harbor Cultural Center**, 1000 Richmond Terrace, Livingston, Staten Island, 718-273-2060, www.sichildrensmuseum.org

FILM FOR CHILDREN

The **Museum of Modern Art** (see above) screens movies for children, some of them about art, some artful, 11 West 53rd Street, 212-408-6663. Children and their parents who attend the annual **New York International Children's Film Festival** at NYU's Cantor Film Center, 36 East 8th Street, 212-998-1212, choose the grand prize winners; www.gkids.com describes the films and gives show times.

MUSIC AND DANCE FOR CHILDREN

Many of the major venues for music and dance in the city present special programs for children. Among them:

- **Brooklyn Arts Exchange**, 421 Fifth Ave at 8th St in Park Slope, Brooklyn, 718-832-0018, www.bax.org
- **Carnegie Hall**, family concerts, 57th St and 7th Ave, 212-247-7800, www.carnegiehall.org
- **The Joyce Theater,** 175 Eighth Ave, 212-691-9740, www.joyce.org
- **Lincoln Center, Jazz for Young People**, venues vary; check http://academy.jazz.org/jfyp/ for current events and schedules
- **Little Orchestra Society**, 330 W 42 St, 212-971-9500, www.littleorchestra.org
- **Symphony Space**, 2537 Broadway St, 212-864-5400, www.symphonyspace.org
- **The Town Hall**, 123 W 43rd St, 212-840-2824, www.the-townhall-nyc.org

PARKS

The city's parks and botanical gardens are hopping with children's programs and activities year-round. To name just several:

- **Central Park** always has a variety of activities for children; venues include the Swedish Cottage Marionette Theater, Belvedere Castle, and the Charles A. Dana Discovery Center; visit www.centralparknyc.org for a calendar of activities. Registration may be required for some events. The Central Park Zoo and Children's Zoo are perennial favorites and more accessible than the Bronx Zoo, although much smaller.
- **New York Botanical Garden**, 2900 Southern Blvd, The Bronx, 718-817-8700, www.nybg.org, has a Children's Adventure Garden in addition to occasional programs for children and the wonderful Christmastime miniature train extravaganza. The garden also has an annual pumpkin carving event, typically with massive pumpkins.
- **Prospect Park Zoo**, 450 Flatbush Ave, Brooklyn, 718-399-7339, www.prospectparkzoo.com, features sheep, chickens, rabbits, and a friendly snake, as well as activities for children.

Not to be forgotten, of course, are the **Bronx Zoo**, the **New York Aquarium**, and the **Queens County Farm Museum**.

LITERARY LIFE

Given that New York is home to many of the largest publishing houses in the world, it's no surprise that New Yorkers love to read. From breakfast over the book section of the Sunday *New York Times* to lunch hours spent browsing the shelves at proud indie bookseller The Strand, New Yorkers enjoy their literature.

Just over 200 public libraries can be found in the five boroughs, and several private membership libraries still survive, some dating back to the 18th century. In addition, several of the city's museums have libraries and nearly all have well-stocked book sections in their gift shops.

PUBLIC SPECIALTY LIBRARIES

Along with the neighborhood branches (see the list of resources following the neighborhood profiles at the beginning of the book), New York City is home to several public premier research libraries pertaining to specific areas of interest:

- **The New York Public Library**, Stephen A. Schwarzman Building, Fifth Ave, between 40th and 42nd Streets, 917-275-6975, www.nypl.org/locations/schwarzman; beyond the spectacular floor-to-ceiling marble entranceway, you'll find an amazing collection of nearly 40 million items in the form of books, periodicals, newspapers, manuscripts, microfilm, maps, paintings, ephemera, and CDs. All are tucked away within this magnificent structure guarded by two larger-than-life stone lions flanking the grand Fifth Avenue entrance. Built over a ten-year period from 1901 through 1911, at a cost of nine million dollars, this world-famous library is home to the first five folios of Shakespeare's plays, ancient Torah scrolls, a Gutenberg Bible, and many other historic literary items. Free tours meet at the front entrance between 11 a.m. and 2 p.m. Monday–Saturdays. Note: this is not a lending library.
- **New York Public Library for the Performing Arts**, Dorothy and Lewis B. Cullman Center, 40 Lincoln Center Plaza, 917-275-6975, www.nypl.org/locations/lpa; located in Lincoln Center, this library features an extensive collection items related to the arts: posters, correspondence, sheet music, scripts, press clippings, periodicals, books, and recordings. Patrons include many performers, playwrights, choreographers, and musicians.
- **Science, Industry and Business Library**, 188 Madison Ave, 917-275-6975, www.nypl.org/locations/sibl; opened in 1996 at the price of $100 million dollars, this state-of-the-art facility is devoted to science, technology, economics, and business; features over 60,000 volumes of reference materials, 50,000 circulating titles, and over 100,000 periodicals.
- **Schomburg Center for Research in Black Culture**, 515 Malcolm X Blvd, 917-275-6975, www.nypl.org/locations/schomburg; featuring a vast array of resources collected by Arturo Schomburg, the library is part of the larger exhibit

space, which displays African-American culture. The Jean Blackwell Hutson General Research and Reference Division includes rare books and writings available in text and electronic formats.

MEMBERSHIP LIBRARIES

Before there were public libraries, there were private membership libraries, three of which survive in New York, a clubby step back in time and a haven for the book lover.

- **The Center for Fiction (formerly known as The Mercantile Library)**, 17 E 47th St, 212-755-6710, www.centerforfiction.org; formed in 1820 and houses only fiction. It is noted for its lively panel discussions. Individual membership is $120. Check their calendar for upcoming events.
- **The General Society Library**, 20 W 44th St, 212-840-1840, www.generalsociety. org; founded in 1820, it seems little changed over the last century. More than 150,000 volumes can be found on its old wooden shelves, including a special collection of the works of Gilbert & Sullivan. Membership starts at $50 per year.
- **The New York Society Library**, 53 E 79th St, 212-288-6900, www.nysoclib.org; the oldest library in the city, founded in 1754. Offers members the opportunity to search extensive holdings and even borrow some of the titles. Membership costs $275 per year or $225 for six months per household.

BOOKSTORES

Bibliophiles are amply served in New York City, although rising real estate costs and the widespread adoption of e-readers have definitely impacted the number and variety of bookstores among which to choose. Still, amidst the Barnes & Noble stores scattered around the city, you'll find independent booksellers whose knowledgeable staff have cultivated a base of loyal customers. Many of these shops specialize in a particular type of book, and most host readings and other events, including children's story time and even language lessons. Here are a few favorites:

- **Argosy Book Store**, 116 E 59th St, 212-753-4455, www.argosybooks.com; rare books, antique maps, photos, and documents.
- **Bauman Rare Books**, 535 Madison Ave, 212-751-0011, www.baumanrarebooks. com; first editions and rare books, many of which are kept in cabinets under lock and key. Don't let that intimidate you; staff is friendly and happy to show you any book that piques your interest.
- **Bank Street Bookstore**, 610 W 112th St, 212-678-1654, www.bankstreetbooks. com; offers books for and about children.
- **Book Culture**, 536 W 112th St, 212-865-1588, www.bookculture.com; university press and scholarly books and journals.

- **Books of Wonder**, 18 W 18th St, 212-989-3270, www.booksofwonder.com; offers a lovely selection of children's books, readings, and events.
- **Bonnie Slotnick's Cookbooks**, 163 W. 10th St, 212-989-8962, www.bonnieslotnickcookbooks.com; inarguably the city's most interesting and charming bookshop, especially if you love cookbooks. Slotnick specializes in them; many of the titles are vintage or first edition.
- **Complete Traveler Bookstore**, 199 Madison Ave (at 35th), 212-685-9007; in a world where so many travelers plan their trips using TripAdvisor, it's amazing this bookstore has managed to survive. But its titles are less guidebook oriented and more vintage; the shop has a lovely selection of rare and first edition copies of everything from WPA guides to coffee table photo books.
- **Housing Works Used Book Café**, 126 Crosby St, 212-334-3324, www.housingworks.org/bookstore; sip espresso, browse books, or take in a reading; proceeds go to provide services to people with HIV/AIDS.
- **Idlewild Books**, 12 W 19th St, 212-414-8888, www.idlewildbooks.com; popular bookstore for those interested in travel; sells current guidebooks as well as fiction, memoir, and any genre related to place. The store also hosts language classes and readings, and recently opened a second location in Brooklyn.
- **Kinokuniya**, 1073 6th Ave, 212-869-1700, www.kinokuniya.com/us/; unknown even to many book lovers, this three-story store is a treasure, especially (though not solely) for those who are looking for books in Chinese and Japanese. It also has an ample children's and gift section (including fine goods such as ceramics, silks, wallets, and home accessories) and a café overlooking Bryant Park.
- **Kitchen Arts & Letters**, 1435 Lexington Ave, 212-876-5550, www.kitchenartsandletters.com; new and hard-to-find books on food and wine, as well as an extensive selection of food-focused magazines.
- **La Casa Azul**, 143 E. 103 St, 212-426-2626, www.lacasaazulbookstore.com; New York City's only Spanish-language bookstore (though it has titles in English too), La Casa Azul opened in 2012 after a successful crowdfunding campaign raised $40,000 via Kickstarter. The shop has a full calendar of events and is engaged in a number of social projects, including book drives for at-risk children.
- **McNally Jackson**, 51 Prince St, 212-274-1160, www.mcnallyjackson.com; a favorite of the hip, contemporary lit set. Has a café, a lovely children's section, magazines that are hard to find elsewhere in the city, and a smart calendar of events and readings.
- **Posman Books**, 9 Grand Central Terminal (stores also in Chelsea Market and Rockefeller Center), 212-983-1111, www.posmanbooks.com; offers an eclectic selection of books and frequent author readings; has a robust section of New York City and state-themed titles.
- **Shakespeare & Co.**, 716 Broadway, 212-529-1330; 939 Lexington Ave, 212-570-0201; also one Brooklyn location at 150 Campus Rd, 718-434-5326; www.shakeandco.com; many students shop here for textbooks, but the shops also have a full selection of current and recent titles from many genres.

- **Strand Bookstore Inc.**, 828 Broadway, 212-473-1452, www.strandbooks.com; the world's largest used bookstore, they say ("18 miles of books"), and mind-boggling. New, used, and rare books; shelves full of specialty genres and titles.

Also, keep in mind that most museums have excellent book and gift shops, as does the Schwarzman branch of The New York Public Library.

N NEW YORK YOU CAN ROOT, ROOT, ROOT FOR THE HOME TEAM, CANTER along Central Park's cinder track, join a pickup basketball game, swim laps after work, or sit spellbound at the US Open Tennis Championships. The city hosts events for every season and activities for every appetite. To help you sort out the teams you wish to follow and the activities you wish to pursue, details about the area's major teams are listed below, followed by a section devoted to **Participant Sports**. For specifics about ticket sales see also **Tickets** in the **Cultural Life** chapter. Locations are in Manhattan unless otherwise specified.

PROFESSIONAL SPORTS

BASEBALL

The season begins at the end of March and lasts until early October (or longer, as is often the case for the Yankees). Tickets range from $15 for bleacher seats to $300 for field level seats that are generally long sold out. There are also special $9 ticket nights: see the team schedule available at the box office or at www.yankees.mlb.com. Mets tickets range from $17 to more than $400, depending on the location of the seats and which team they are playing. You can purchase tickets for Mets or Yankees games through Ticketmaster, 212-307-7171 or www.ticketmaster.com; charge tickets to a credit card and have them sent, or pick them up at one of 20 locations in Manhattan. Note: as with theater tickets, there is a service charge tacked on to the price of each ticket purchased through Ticketmaster, which can be costly. To save some money, you can purchase tickets at the stadium box office. Tickets can also be purchased through each team's website. Schedules for upcoming Mets or Yankees games are always easy to find in the newspapers or at www.mlb.com, the official site of Major League Baseball.

- **New York Mets** (National League), Citi Field, 126th St and Roosevelt Ave, Flushing, NY 11368; 718-507-METS for information; box office: 718-507-8499, www.newyork.mets.mlb.com; along with season tickets, the Mets have innumerable subscription plans, and buying single-game tickets in advance is generally not difficult, as they typically only sell out a few times a year. There are plenty of fun promotional days for kids, with giveaway items. You can drive to Citi Field on the Grand Central Parkway and park for a fee in the stadium lot or take the #7 train, which takes about 50 minutes from midtown and brings you right to the stadium.
- **New York Yankees** (American League), Yankee Stadium, 161st St and River Ave, Bronx, NY 10451, 718-293-6000, www.newyork.yankees.mlb.com; the Yankees have several ticket subscription plans ranging from season tickets to several games. Games against top teams will sell out, but generally, tickets for weeknight games—and certainly weekday games—are usually available on game day. The new Yankee Stadium (or the house that Ruth built) replaces the classic ballpark from the 1920s and is a great place to watch a ballgame. Monument Park just over the centerfield fence pays tribute to classic Yankee teams and is a fun place to explore prior to the game. There are also pre-game and "classic" tours offered of the stadium, starting at $20. You can drive to Yankee Stadium, which is just off the Major Deegan Expressway, and park in one of several lots (for a fee) or take the #4 train from Manhattan—it's about 25 minutes from midtown and an easy trip, as the subway stops right behind the bleachers.

BASKETBALL

The NBA basketball season begins when baseball leaves off, around late October, and continues through mid-April or into May or even June if the teams are in the playoffs. Knicks' home games are played in Madison Square Garden; the Nets play at the Meadowlands. Single seats for the Nets and the Knicks range between $25 and $1,500. Call Ticketmaster, 212-307-7171, to order tickets, or visit a Ticketmaster outlet to pick up your tickets.

- **New York Knickerbockers** "Knicks" (NBA), Madison Square Garden, 33rd Street between Seventh and Eighth Avenues, NYC 10001, 212-465-5867, www.nba.com/knicks; season plans cost several thousand dollars, but there are some limited plans available. Individual tickets go on sale in early September and can be purchased at Ticketmaster outlets, 212-307-7171, as well as at the Garden Box Office. Seats are not easy to get, so plan to purchase well in advance. To get to Madison Square Garden it's best to take the subway—1, 2, 3, 9, A, C, E trains—or the Long Island Railroad, which stops at Penn Station under the Garden. If you drive, your best bet is parking after 7 p.m. on side streets (24th through 29th Streets), otherwise you'll end up in costly lots waiting for up to an hour to get your car after the game.

- **Brooklyn Nets** (NBA) play in the Barclays Center in Brooklyn, which is easily accessible by subway; call 718-NETS-TIX or go to www.nba.com/nets for ticket information. Ticket plans range from season tickets for the 41-game home season, plus exhibition games, to short plans of six to ten games. You can always purchase single game tickets in advance and usually on game night. Parking is limited to expensive fee-based lots; take the subway instead.
- **New York Liberty** (WNBA), Madison Square Garden, 33rd Street between Seventh and Eighth Avenues, NYC 10001, 212-465-6073, www.wnba.com/liberty, is professional women's basketball at its best. Tickets can be purchased at the Madison Square Garden Box Office or at Ticketmaster outlets, 212-307-7171. Tickets are easy to get. The season runs from May through August.

FOOTBALL

The popularity of Jets and Giants games during the pro football season, September–December, is clearly demonstrated by ticket scarcity.

- **Giants** (NFL), MetLife Stadium, Meadowlands Sports Complex, East Rutherford, NJ 07073, 201-935-8222, www.giants.com; regular season tickets are sold out years in advance. Your best bet: become chums with a season ticket holder or buy through a ticket broker.
- **New York Jets** (NFL) also play at MetLife Stadium in the Meadowlands Sports Complex. Call 201-935-8222 for ticket information, www.newyorkjets.com. Renewals for season tickets to the eight home-game season games are filled by May 15. New subscriptions are then issued from the fairly long waiting list on a first-come, first-served basis in early June. Good luck.

HOCKEY

The New York Rangers and Islanders, and New Jersey Devils play NHL hockey starting at the end of September and going into the spring.

- **New York Rangers** (NHL), Madison Square Garden, 33rd Street between Seventh and Eighth Avenues, NYC 10001. Call Ticketmaster to order tickets by phone, 212-307-7171. Whether the Rangers are playing well or not, tickets are very hard to come by as most season ticket holders keep their seats for years. Be on line at the box office when tickets go on sale for the season or sign up in advance for a mini-plan if any are still available. Get ticket information at the team website, www.rangers.nhl.com. For information on Madison Square Garden see above.
- **New York Islanders** (NHL), Nassau Coliseum in Uniondale, Long Island, NY 11553, 516-501-6700, www.islanders.nhl.com; tickets also available through Ticketmaster. Islander tickets are easier to get than Ranger tickets. In fact, if

you want to see a Rangers game, this is one way to do it—just don't let on that you're a Rangers fan while at the Coliseum—or for that matter, if you're an Islander fan, be quiet at the Garden.

• **New Jersey Devils** (NHL), Prudential Center, Newark, NJ, 973-757-6200, www. devils.nhl.com; they've won three Stanley Cups since 1995, making them the area's most successful hockey team and making tickets harder to get.

RACING: HARNESS AND THOROUGHBRED

All the local tracks are easily reached by public transportation. For those who enjoy betting but do not feel the need to be at the racetrack, the city features numerous off-track betting locations. More information can be found at the New York Racing Association's website, www.nyra.com. Off-track-betting offices are listed here: www.offtrackbettingnewyork.com. Call the numbers listed below for directions.

• **Aqueduct**, Jamaica, Queens, 718-641-4700, www.nyra.com; the track is open from October until May for thoroughbred races starting at 12:30 p.m. daily, except Mondays and Tuesdays.
• **Belmont Park**, Elmont, Long Island, 516-488-6000, www.nyra.com; thorough-bred races May–July and September–October.
• **Saratoga**, Saratoga Springs, NY, 518-584-6200, www.nyra.com; home of the Travers Stake, America's oldest thoroughbred race; season runs from the end of July through early October; post time 1:00 p.m.
• **Meadowlands Racetrack**, Meadowlands Sports Complex, East Rutherford, NJ, 201-THE-BIG-M, www.thebigm.com; open at 6 p.m. nightly Tuesday–Saturday; December–August harness racing; thoroughbreds run October–November.
• **Monmouth Park**, Oceanport, NJ, 732-222-5100, www.monmouthpark.com; thoroughbred races daily Wednesday–Sunday at 12:55 p.m., late May–September.
• **Yonkers Raceway**, Yonkers, NY, 914-968-4200, www.yonkersraceway.com; the post time is 7:40 p.m.; daily schedule varies as the track is sometimes used for festivals and other events, so call in advance.

SOCCER

• **New York City Football Club** (MLS), Yankee Stadium, 161st St and River Ave, Bronx, NY, www.nycfc.com; the first New York City-based MLS team, New York City FC begins competing in 2015. Plans for their own stadium are in progress.
• **New York Red Bulls** (MLS), 600 Cape May St, Harrison, NJ, www.newyorkred-bulls.com; founded in 1996 and one of the ten charter clubs of the MLS, the team was previously known as the MetroStars, but became the Red Bulls in 2006.

TENNIS

The biggest tournament held in the New York area is the US Open.

- **United States Open Tennis Championships**, United States Tennis Center, Flushing Meadows Park, Queens, NY 11365; for ticket information call 866-OPEN-TIX or visit www.usopen.org. The nation's premier tennis tournament, the US Open, consists of nearly two weeks of afternoon and evening matches held in late August and early September. The finals take place the weekend after Labor Day. Individual tickets for the finals and semifinals are sold as soon as the first mailing goes out in late March or early April. Tickets for matches earlier in the tournament aren't as hard to come by and are sold at Ticketmaster outlets, as well as the Tennis Center. If you drive, there is parking in lots for a fee. If the Mets are also playing that day, the area gets more congested, as Citi Field (formerly Shea Stadium) is practically across the street. You can also take the #7 train from Manhattan.

PARTICIPANT SPORTS

Swimming pools, tennis, squash and racquetball courts, bowling alleys, and billiard parlors, as well as roller and ice skating rinks dot the island for your sporting pleasure, and practically any outdoor recreation you want can be found in New York City, and especially in Central Park. It's not just a super place to ride bikes or listen to classical performances on summer evenings; you can also schedule football and softball games, play tennis, or row a boat around the Lake. Flanked by Central Park West and Fifth Avenue to the east, the park covers some 750 acres between 59th and 110th Streets and is Manhattan's prime outdoor recreation area. So, before listing information about sports citywide, as well as multipurpose facilities such as health clubs and YMCAs, we've detailed opportunities to be found in the park, sport by sport. To learn more about the park itself, see the chapter on **Greenspace and Beaches**. For information about city parks you can call the **NYC Department of Parks & Recreation** at 212-360-3456 or visit their website at www.nycgovparks.org.

CENTRAL PARK

The park's **Visitor Information Center** is located at the Dairy, 65th Street between the zoo and the carousel. It is open daily from 10 a.m. until 5 p.m. The Arsenal, 830 Fifth Avenue at East 64th Street in front of the zoo, is the park's administrative hub. It also plays host to occasional art exhibits, often related to park history. For event and park information, call the **Central Park Conservancy**, which runs the park under contract from the city, 212-310-6600, or go to www.centralparknyc.org.

- **Ball: Baseball, Softball, Football, Rugby,** and **Soccer** fields are located in the North Meadow, at the Great Lawn, and Heckscher Playground. Visit www.nyc-govparks.org to apply for permits.
- **Bicycling** is popular when the park drives (but not the sunken cross-town transverses) are closed to motorized traffic on weekends from 7 p.m. Friday until 6 a.m. Monday (all day on holidays), and from 10 a.m. to 3 p.m. and 7 p.m. to 10 p.m. weekdays, from April through October. For rentals, see **Bicycling** below for names of bicycle shops near the park.
- **Boating:** the Loeb Boathouse, near East 74th Street, 212-517-2233, rents rowboats for outings on the Lake, from 10 a.m. until between 4 p.m. and 6 p.m. You can also glide beneath Bow Bridge in a black Venetian gondola, complete with a gondolier. Armchair sailors can enjoy the comfort and cuisine of meals at Boathouse Café, which is open daily from 8 a.m. until 8 p.m. Evening dining and weekend brunch are offered at The Loeb Restaurant from April through November.
- **Ice Skating:** the park boasts two beautiful main rinks: Wollman Memorial on the East Side near 62nd Street, 212-439-6900, and Lasker Memorial at Lenox Avenue at 110th Street, 917-492-3856. Both are open November–March. Of the two, Lasker is less crowded. At both rinks, mornings and weekdays offer the best ice time: i.e., fewer skaters.
- **Paddleball and Handball:** you can use the ten courts located near the North Meadow at West 97th Street and Transverse Road on a first-come, first-served basis.
- **Roller/In-Line Skating:** in-line skaters and old-fashioned roller skaters can be found strutting their stuff throughout the park, but the road west of the Sheep Meadow near 69th Street is designated specifically for blading and skating. Skates can be rented for use at Wollman Memorial, 212-439-6900, April–November. Call for hours and admission.
- **Running:** joggers traditionally work out on the 1.58-mile cinder track girdling the Reservoir between East 85th and 96th Streets, but running isn't limited to that patch. The **New York Road Runners**, 9 East 89th Street, 212-860-4455, www.nyrrc.org, sponsors races and clinics during the season. (See **A New York City Year** at the end of the book for specifics on New York Road Runners' New Year's Eve midnight run.)
- **Sledding:** the park has hills for all levels of experience. For children or timid sledders, a perfect spot is Pilgrim Hill by the 72nd Street and Fifth Avenue entrance closest to the pilgrim statue. For more of a challenge, try Cedar Hill close to the Belvedere Castle at the 77th Street entrance off Central Park West.
- **Tennis:** twenty-six clay and four all-weather courts, open from 7 a.m. to dusk, are located on the west side of the park near 95th Street. In season, play necessitates a seasonal tennis permit, which costs $200. Permits can be purchased online at www.nycgovparks.org/permits/tennis-permits. You can also purchase single play tennis tickets at $15 for one hour of court time, which are also available online. Courts can be reserved online too, at www.nycgovparks.org/tennisreservation.

BEYOND CENTRAL PARK

The New York City **Department of Parks and Recreation (DPR)** directs and maintains baseball fields, basketball courts, and more throughout the city. The best resource is their website at www.nycgovparks.org. On the website, you can find up-to-date listings of every facility, as well as apply for permits directly.

BASEBALL

Most of Manhattan's more than two dozen diamonds (seven of which are located in Central Park) are under the direction of the DPR. Call 212-408-0226 or visit www.nycgovparks.org. Fields can be difficult to get onto in the spring due to corporate softball leagues.

BASKETBALL

The DPR, www.nycgovparks.org, maintains more than 1,000 courts throughout the city in gyms (see **Swimming** below) as well as in city parks, large and small. Some of the health clubs and YMCAs have basketball courts, and the **Chelsea Piers Sports and Entertainment** complex, www.chelseapiers.com, includes two courts with electronic scoreboards used in league basketball, which is open to players of all skill levels for a fee.

BICYCLING

One of the most significant—and exciting—changes that has taken place in New York over the past decade has been the surge in the number of city dwellers braving Manhattan's crazy, traffic-clogged streets from the vantage point of a bike saddle. In fact, city officials say that the number of New Yorkers riding bikes has more than doubled in the past 10 years. Though there have always been cyclists who take the two wheel commute to work, the massive expansion of bike lanes across the city and the spring 2013 launch of the bike-share program, Citi Bike, www.citibikenyc.com, prompted thousands of New Yorkers to diversify their modes of transportation. Suddenly, it was no longer necessary to find space in one's already overcrowded apartment to store a bike; with Citi Bike, riders just paid an annual membership fee ($95, plus tax as of this writing) and began checking out bikes at stations all across the city. The program has proven so popular as to be problematic: bike stations haven't yet made it to key outer borough neighborhoods, like Long Island City and Astoria, and demand often exceeds supply. Hopefully, these growing pains will be resolved as the program matures.

For now, you can buy your own bike, join Citi Bike, or rent a set of wheels from one of the many bike shops around the city. For rules on biking in the city (avoid fines for riding on sidewalks, riding against traffic, and running red lights), information about bike safety, and to download bike maps, visit the city's Department of Transportation website, www.nyc.gov/html/dot/html/bicyclists/ bicyclists.shtml. Additional maps and recommended routes can be found at www. nycbikemaps.com. If you're so passionate about cycling that you want to join a local bike club, here are a few popular ones:

- **Bike New York**, 475 Riverside Dr, 13th floor, 212-870-2080, www.bikenewyork. org; organizes bicycling events, rides, and courses, including the annual Five Boro Bike Tour.
- **Century Road Club Association**, P.O. Box 348, NYC 10113, www.crca.net; is a racing club, which provides free coaching clinics for beginners and sponsors friendly competitions for people of all ages. You must become a member to enjoy these services, however. Fees range from $25 for students to $70 for "racing members," depending upon the time of year they join.
- **Fast and Fabulous Cycling Club**, www.fastnfab.org; is a cycling club for people who identify as LGBT. They organize training, morning rides in city parks, and road trips.
- **New York Cycle Club**, www.nycc.org; sponsors rides in and around the city, offers training, and its members receive discounts from a handful of bike shops in the city.

If you don't own a bike, you may well want to rent one on a beautiful spring day. At least half of Manhattan's bike dealers rent bikes. Rates average $8 to $10 an hour and about $30 a day. You'll have to leave money, or a driver's license or major credit card, behind as a deposit, although you might hesitate to do that with some of the street operators who operate at Columbus Circle. A handful of the many bike rental outfits include:

- **Bicycles Plus**, 1400 Third Ave, 212-794-2929, 1690 Second Ave at 87th St, 212-722-2201
- **Central Park Bicycle Tours and Rentals**, 5 W 63rd St at the YMCA, 212-541-8759, offers bike rentals ($20 for an hour, $65 for all day), and bike tours of Central Park

BILLIARDS

The popularity of pool halls waxes and wanes in New York, but a few have managed to hang on despite rising rents and other pastimes competing for New Yorkers' attention.

- **Amsterdam Billiard Club**, 110 E 11th St, 212-995-0333, www.amsterdambilliards.com; an old stalwart with a clubby atmosphere—think oak wood and maroon-colored décor. It boasts over 25 tables and a full-service bar as well as lunch and dinner. Also on-site are ping-pong tables, dart boards, foosball tables, and pinball machines.

- **Eastside Billiards & Bar**, 163 E 86th St, 212-831-7665, www.eastsidebilliards. com; features 17 tables (16 Brunswick Gold Crown IIIs and one coin-operated table), as well as skee-ball, foosball, and ping pong. If you fancy becoming a regular, consider joining their co-ed pool league.
- **Ocean's 8 at Brownstone Billiards**, 308 Flatbush Ave, Brooklyn, 718-857-5555; with 30 tables, six ping-pong tables, and two bowling alleys, as well as a fully-stocked bar, Brownstone has positioned itself as a complete entertainment center.
- **Slate Billiards**, 54 W 21st St, 212-989-0096, www.slate-ny.com; a two-floor, all-in-one restaurant/lounge/ping-pong room/pool parlor, complete with 25 pool tables. Yet you might still have to wait for a table, Friday nights especially. Best times are mornings and Sunday daytime. The size makes this venue particularly popular for parties.

BIRD WATCHING

People who have never been to New York like to poke fun—Bird watching? In New York City?—but avid birders and other naturalists know that the Big Apple actually has incredible biodiversity, including birds, and there's plenty to see here. And, no, it's not just limited to pigeons. Central Park is one of the city's popular places to go birding; join one of the groups or walks below for other prime birding spots and experiences:

- **American Museum of Natural History**, 212-769-5700 (discovery tours), www. amnh.org; the **Brooklyn Botanic Garden**, 718-623-7200, www.bbg.org; and the **New York Botanical Garden (Bronx Park)**, 718-817-8700, www.nybg. org, are all prime birdwatching areas. **Rare Bird Alert**, 212-979-3070, provides recorded information on interesting sightings in the New York City area.
- **Brooklyn Bird Club**, www.brooklynbirdclub.org, founded in 1909, hosts lectures, monthly meetings, and weekly field trips, open to both non-members and members (membership $20) alike. Their website includes detailed maps and descriptions of some excellent bird locations in Brooklyn and Queens, directions, some history, and lists of the species one is likely to find at each site.
- **New York City Audubon Society**, 212-691-7483, www.nycaudubon.org, hosts birding events in Central and Prospect Parks, local and overnight trips, classes, lectures, and volunteer opportunities. Birders with a special interest in photography may be interested in joining their photography club. Annual membership ranges from $25–$100.
- **Urban Park Rangers** sponsor a variety of bird walks, such as the fall hawk watch, in all five boroughs, as well as courses in animal tracking and survival. For times and meeting places, call 212-628-2345 for more information, or visit www.nycgovparks.org/programs/rangers.

BOWLING

Check online for the alley nearest you. Here are a couple:

- **Bowlmor Chelsea Piers**, Pier 60, West Side Hwy at 23rd St, 212-835-2695, www.bowlmor.com/chelsea-piers; 40 lanes, open seven days. There's a bar and restaurant on site, a pro shop, and arcade with video games to keep the kids occupied. Thursday, Friday, and Saturday nights they offer "extreme bowling" (glow-in-the-dark bowling). League bowling and lessons are also available. Call for lane availability and/or to reserve. Be forewarned: bowling here ain't cheap.
- **Frames Bowling Lounge**, 550 9th Ave, 212-268-6909, www.framesnyc.com; Frames has 28 lanes, but it's also a dance club and pool hall. Reservations are recommended.
- **Strike 10 Lanes**, 6161 Strickland Ave, Brooklyn, 718-763-6800; the city's biggest bowling alley.

BOXING

- **Church Street Boxing Gym**, 25 Park Place, 212-571-1333, www.csboxinggym.com; bills itself as "New York's last authentic boxing gym" (translate: Manhattan's). It's not a health club or fitness center; it's about boxing. The 8,000-square-foot gym has two full-size rings and co-ed membership classes in boxing, kickboxing, Thai boxing, and mixed martial arts. Membership is by the month, but you can also purchase a day pass. It's probably also the best place in the city to watch boxing; enthusiastic crowds pack the occasional Friday night fights.
- **Gleason's Gym**, 77 Front St, Brooklyn, 718-797-2872, www.gleasonsgym.net; going strong since 1937, it boasts seven world champions among its past or present membership, Riddick Bowe included. Women also work out in this old-style boxing gym. Get lean and mean working up a sweat on the equipment or work with one of more than 60 trainers for an hourly fee. A variety of membership levels also available. Closed Sunday.

CHESS

Though it's not a "sport," enthusiasts pursue chess with the intensity of an athletic competition. New York City, with its huge immigrant community, has a large and active chess community. If you're looking for information about where to play or compete, try the following leads (or head to Washington Square Park and Union Square Park, where "pick-up" games of speed chess are ongoing at the chess tables):

- **Chess Forum**, 219 Thompson St, 212-475-2369, www.chessforum.com

- **US Chess Federation**, 3PO Box 3967, Crossville, TN 38557, 931-787-1234; their website, www.uschess.org, contains a great list of places to play, as well as tournaments and other chess-related events around the country.

FENCING

- **Blade Fencing**, 115 W 30th St, 800-828-5661, www.blade-fencing.fencingnewyork.com; arms and dresses the duelist for competition with a full range of foils, épées, and sabers.
- **New Amsterdam Fencing Academy**, 2726 Broadway, 2nd floor, 212-662-3362, www.nyfencing.com; there are private and group classes for children through adults, beginner through Olympian, Monday through Saturday.

FOOTBALL

Most playing fields fall under the **Department of Parks and Recreation**; call 212-408-0226 for information and permits. More than 50 parks and recreation properties have football fields, some of which are suitable also for soccer, across the five boroughs. A complete list of them can be found at www.nycgovparks.org/facilities/football.

GAMES AND GAMING

From RPGs to LANs, whether you seek to buy board games or conquer animated nations, you can get your gaming fix at the location below:

- **Kings Games**, 1685 E 15th Street, Brooklyn, 718-336-1955, www.kingsgames.com; full-service Internet café, along with all the latest gaming consoles and old-school board games and trading card games.

GOLF

Manhattan boasts no 18-hole golf courses, but you'll find several city-owned public courses in the outer boroughs. A full list of city courses can be found on the Parks and Recreation website, www.nycgovparks.org/facilities/golf. You'll need a resident permit to play; these can be obtained at any course and currently cost $6 for adults and $2 for seniors and students. Greens fees are also listed on the same website. There are also plenty of nice public clubs on Long Island and in Westchester. Higher fees are the norm at suburban courses and you'll need to reserve tee times well in advance. Perhaps the nicest courses closest to NYC are those at Bethpage State Park at 99 Quaker Meeting House Road in Farmingdale, Long Island, 516-249-0700. The park has five 18-hole courses, several of which are award-winning greens that have attracted top tournaments, top players, and high ratings in the golf world. More information about the courses at Bethpage can be found on this website, www.nysparks.com/golf-courses/11/details.aspx.

New York City **public courses** include:

- **Clearview Golf Course**, 202-12 Willets Point Blvd, Queens, 718-229-2570, www.clearviewparkgc.com
- **Douglaston Golf Club**, 63-20 Marathon Pkwy, Queens, 718-224-6566, www.golfnyc.com/douglaston_home
- **Dyker Beach Golf Course**, 86th St and 7th Ave, Brooklyn, 718-836-9722, www.dykerbeachgc.com
- **Forest Park Golf Course**, 101 Forest Park Dr, Queens, 718-296-0999, www.golfnyc.com/forestpark_home
- **Kissena Park Golf Course**, 165-14 Booth Memorial Ave, Queens, 718-939-4594, www.golfnyc.com/kissena_home
- **LaTourette Golf Course**, 1001 Richmond Hill Rd, Staten Island, 718-351-1889; www.latourettegc.com
- **Golf Course**, 2880 Flatbush Ave, Brooklyn, 718-252-4625, www.golfmarinepark.com
- **Mosholu Golf Course**, 3545 Jerome Ave, The Bronx, 718-655-9164; www.mosholugolfcourse.com; also features a driving range
- **Pelham/Split Rock Golf Course**, 870 Shore Rd, The Bronx, near City Island, 718-885-1258, www.pelhamsplitrock.com; New York City's only 36-hole golf facility
- **Silver Lake Golf Course**, 915 Victory Blvd, near Forest Ave, Staten Island, 718-447-5686. www.silverlakegolf.com
- **South Shore Golf Course**, 200 Huguenot Ave, Staten Island, 718-984-0101, www.southshoregc.com
- **Van Cortlandt Park Golf Course**, Van Cortlandt Park at Bailey Ave, The Bronx, 718-543-4595, www.golfnyc.com/vancortlandt_home; a marvelous course dating back to 1895; it has seen everyone from Babe Ruth to the Three Stooges to presidents and diplomats tee off

Among the city's other **driving ranges** are:

- **The Golf Club at Chelsea Piers**, Hudson River at 17th St, 212-336-6400, www.chelseapiers.com/gc; this golf club, with its white-shingled clubhouse entrance, pro shop, putting green, and golf academy, has as its *pièce de résistance* 52 heated, weather-protected driving stalls with Japanese-designed, computerized automatic ball returns and tee-ups in four tiers fronting a 200-yard, net-enclosed, artificial turf fairway, with four target greens, overlooking the Hudson River... No you can't aim at passing boats. Pay according to the number of balls used.
- **Randall's Island Golf Center**, Randall's Island, 212-427-5689, www.randallsislandgolfcenter.com; as part of an island in the East River, nestled

between East Harlem, the South Bronx, and Astoria, Queens, Randall's Island is not the easiest place to get to, but there are shuttles from Manhattan to pick you up and drop you off.

Miniature golf courses can also be found in the outer boroughs.

HANDBALL

A city sport in which two or four players hit a rubber ball with their hands against a cement wall, volleying furiously for points, handball is played on outdoor courts all over the city. And at many sites it is also a spectator sport. Among the many handball courts in the city, two stand out as shrines:

- **"The Cage"** at W Fourth St and Sixth Ave, the Village; the action on the adjacent basketball court is equally spectacular.
- **Surf Avenue** at W Fifth St, Coney Island, on whose courts the Nationals are played. Attracts a colorful crowd of betting spectators.

To learn more about one of the world's oldest games go to www.ushandball.org.

HORSEBACK RIDING

Horseback riding in Central Park vanished as of 2007 with the closing of Claremont Riding Academy. But there are lots of options outside Manhattan.

- **Bronx Equestrian Center**, 9 Shore Rd, Bronx, 718-885-0551, www.bronxequestriancenter.com; open daily 9 a.m. until dusk, but call ahead for a guided trail ride, Western only, through the woods by the Split Rock Golf Course and Pelham Bay. Lessons, English or Western, are offered individually or as a group. Reachable by car from the New England Thruway. Alternatively, take the #6 train to the last stop and walk east, or take the City Island bus, number 29, which stops across the street from the stable.
- **Jamaica Bay Riding Academy**, 7000 Shore Pkwy, Brooklyn, 718-531-8949, www.horsebackride.com; located on some 300 acres of prime real estate, they offer a riding shop, lessons, wooded trails, and can accommodate birthday parties. No appointment needed for a guided trail ride along Jamaica Bay beach, open year-round. Bring your own helmet.
- **Kensington Stable**s, 51 Caton Place, Brooklyn, 917-940-9189, www.kensingtonstables.com; operates guided trail rides, English or Western, in lovely Prospect Park. Private and group lessons offered. Call ahead. Take the F train to Fort Hamilton Parkway.
- **Lynne's Riding School**, 88-03 70th Rd, Forest Hills, 718-261-7679, www.lynnesridingschool.com; you can take public transportation—the F train and then the

Q23 bus—to Queens, where Lynne's offers riders a choice between Eastern or Western tack. Private lessons are available, as are pony rides and boarding.

- **Riverdale Equestrian Centre**, W 254th St and Broadway, inside Van Cortlandt Park, 718-548-4848, www.riverdaleriding.com; four riding rings and an indoor Olympic-sized arena. Rabbits, raccoons, and other wildlife are a bonus on the guided trail rides in this large city park. Pony rides are available for children and pony parties can be arranged. All rides by appointment. To get there by public transportation take the #1 train to 242nd St (last stop) and the #9 bus (262nd St); ask to get off at the stables. Or take the Liberty Line Bx-M3 bus, which goes up Madison Avenue, stopping every 10 blocks, and drops you at the stable door; 20 minutes from the Upper East Side.

ICE SKATING

In addition to the Wollman and Lasker rinks in Central Park (see above), and Conservatory Water (also known as Sailboat Pond) at 73rd Street when it freezes, New York City boasts many fine places to skate.

- **Ice Skating at Bryant Park**, www.wintervillage.org; each winter, Bryant Park, located right behind New York Public Library's Schwarzman branch, turns into a winter wonderland as the green that hosts movies during summer is converted to a large ice skating rink. Ringed by holiday shops and food concessioners, it has become as popular as the iconic Rockefeller Center rink. Skating is free, but you'll have to pay for skate, helmet, and locker rentals if you need them.
- **Riverbank State Park**, 679 Riverside Dr, 212-694-3600, www.nysparks.com/parks/93/details.aspx; skate outdoors just above the Hudson River in this beautiful 28-acre park. Skate rentals available. Roller-skating here during the summer.
- **Rockefeller Center Rink**, 50th St off Fifth Ave, 212-332-7654, www.rockefellercenter.com; open daily and evenings in season. Skate rentals available. One of the country's most famous skating rinks sits adjacent to a lovely café and, in December, below the massive Rockefeller Center Christmas tree. Plenty of onlookers, so brush up on your skating skills. October–April.
- **Sky Rink at Chelsea Piers**, Pier 61 at Hudson River and 22nd St, 212-336-6100, www.chelseapiers.com/sr; with two indoor rinks in use some 20 hours a day, this facility offers public skating, figure skating, and hockey instruction for adults and children, league hockey, a skating club, and ice theater. Rentals and a skate shop are on site, as well as audience seating for 1,600, including two skyboxes for special events, and a snack bar. You can even hold a birthday party here. Year-round.
- **World Ice Arena**, 111th St, Corona, Queens, in Flushing Meadows Park, 718-760-9001, www.worldice.com; you can walk to this large, indoor rink from the Citi Field stadium–111th Street subway stop on the #7 train. Skate rentals and weekend lessons available. Year-round.

RACQUETBALL

Devotees of this popular sport can burn calories at two of the Ys we mention below—the West Side YMCA at 5 West 63rd Street and the 92nd Street Y at Lexington Avenue—as well as:

- **New York Health and Racquet Club**, 20 E 50th St, 212-593-1500; 110 W 56th St, 212-541-7200; 39 Whitehall St, 212-269-9800; www.hrcbest.com; though NYHRC has several other locations, these three are the only ones with racquetball facilities at present.

ROLLER/IN-LINE SKATING/SKATEBOARDING

For exhilarating outdoor fun, try **Central Park** for blade action. Every once in a while, especially during mid-summer, you'll find old-school roller skaters gathered here too, showing off their smooth moves. Other in-line skating hot-spots: **Battery Park City**, Brooklyn's **Prospect Park**, and especially the greenway along the Hudson River, which runs almost the entire length of Manhattan's west side.

- **Blades Board and Skate**, 156 W 72nd St, 212-787-3911; 659 Broadway, 212-477-7350; www.blades.com; with the help of the friendly staffers at any of these locations, you too can join the fun. Rollerblades, the best-known brand, can be rented for the day with wrist guards and kneepads included. You can also buy skates, equipment, and gear.
- **Chelsea Piers Skate Park and Roller Rinks**, 23rd St and Hudson River, 212-336-6200, www.chelseapiers.com; besides general skating in two outdoor, regulation-sized in-line and roller rinks, there are classes at various levels: from basic technique to hip-hop to aggressive, as well as league hockey games for adults and youths. Also, two half-pipes with 11- and 6-foot walls respectively. Or you can just watch.
- **Pier 62 Skatepark**, Pier 62, Hudson River. www.hudsonriverpark.org/explore-the-park/activities/pier-62-skatepark; free and open to skateboarders and rollerbladers, this 15,000 square foot, California style skatepark on the Hudson River's greenway is open from 8 a.m. until dusk every day.
- **Tribeca Skatepark**, N Moore St and Hudson River, www.hudsonriverpark.org/explore-the-park/activities/tribeca-skatepark; about half the size of the Pier 62 Skatepark, this site, also in the Hudson River Park, is popular with bladers and boarders.

RUGBY

- **Gaelic Park**, 718-548-9568, in The Bronx, is the center of rugby play in New York City. The park is located at Broadway and West 240th Street. To join in on the action, check the website of the NYPD Rugby Club, www.nypdrugby.com.

- **The New York Rugby Club**, www.newyorkrugby.com, supports rugby for men, women, boys, girls, and masters. It is billed as the oldest rugby club in the USA, having been originally formed in 1929.

RUNNING

- **Front Runners**, NY, www.frny.org, is the hyperactive local branch of Front Runners International, which organizes running, walking, cycling, and triathlon events for lesbians, gay men, and supportive non-gays. Their weekly "fun runs" take place in Central Park and Prospect Park in Brooklyn. Participants gather after the runs for a snack or a meal. The organization also offers coaching and training, events for cyclists and walkers, and competitions for runners and triathletes. Visit their website for a schedule of runs.
- **Hash House Harriers**, 212-427-4692, www.hashnyc.com, is a group of not-totally-serious joggers who meet at various locations throughout the city and in Westchester to follow a flour-marked trail looping four to five miles and winding up at a bar for post-run analysis fueled by food and copious quantities of beer. Runners are called "hashers" and the trails are set by "hares." You need only running shoes and about $15 in "hash cash" to join in. Some call it "the drinking club with a running problem." Hashing originated in 1938 in Kuala Lumpur and is now international, so you can hash away from home. Global information is on the web at www.gotothehash.net.
- The **New York Road Runners** claims to be "the world's largest running club," serving more than 300,000 people each year through its numerous events. The organization maintains an "International Running Center" at 9 East 89th Street, 212-860-4455, www.nyrr.org. The Road Runners Club sponsors the New York Marathon and more than 150 other races a year.

SAILING AND KAYAKING

If you want to bound over Long Island Sound, City Island in The Bronx is an accessible starting point. Take the #2 (Seventh Avenue) or #6 (Lexington Avenue) train to Pelham Parkway and transfer to The Bronx #12 City Island bus. This and some other watery options are listed here:

- **Manhattan Sailing School**, Battery Park City, 212-786-0400, www.sailmanhattan.com; sail out of classy North Cove in front of the World Financial Center. Beginners can take a 20-hour basic sailing course and continue on to basic coastal cruising, also 20 hours, in J-24 sailboats. Private lessons available.
- **New York City Community Sailing Association**, Lincoln Harbor Marina, 1500 Harbor Blvd, Weehawken, NJ, 646-360-0048, www.sailny.org; operating with nine 22- to 24-foot keel sloops, five of which are Solings, out of Lincoln Harbor Marina in Weehawken, NJ. This nonprofit organization was founded in

1996 with the idea that sailing ought to be easy and affordable. You must be a member to participate in recreational sailing and races. Call or check their website for more information.

- **New York City Downtown Boathouse**, 646-613-0375, 646-613-0740 (daily status line), www.downtownboathouse.org; an all-volunteer organization dedicated to providing free access to the Hudson River via kayak Boathouse locations in Tribeca, Chelsea, Uptown, and Governors Island. Contact them about sailing or kayaking lessons.
- **New York Sailing Center**, 10 Centre St (at Stuyvesant Yacht Club), City Island, The Bronx, 718-885-0335, www.startsailing.com; a sailing school and club. Courses include basic keelboat, basic and intermediate coastal cruising, and coastal navigation.
- **The New York Sailing School**, 22 Pelham Rd, New Rochelle, Westchester, 914-235-6052, www.nyss.com; offers sailing courses, programs, boat rental, and more.
- **Offshore Sailing School**, Pier 25, Tribeca, 888-454-7015, www.offshore-sailing.com; take the Learn to Sail course from this national sailing school, which offers a variety of options for signing up, including couple or pair lessons.

SCUBA

While no one's suggesting dives to the murky depths of the Hudson, you can take certification courses in local pools in preparation for a plunge into the Caribbean's turquoise waters.

- **Gotham Divers,** 125 E 4th St, 212-780-0879, www.gothamdivers.com; courses range from those for beginners to advanced certification and wreck diving.
- **PanAqua Diving**, 460 W 43rd St, 212-736-3483, www.panaquadiving.com; in addition to selling and repairing equipment, they organize group and individual diving travel and run certification courses evenings and weekends. Courses, held at the 92nd Street Y and Manhattan Plaza, range from a one-weekend intensive to five weeks of evenings. The open water dive required for certification is extra.

SKIING

You won't schuss downhill in New York City, but cross-country skiers take to the gentle slopes of Central Park and, in the boroughs, Van Cortlandt Park, Split Rock Golf Course in Pelham Bay Park in The Bronx, Prospect Park in Brooklyn, and Flushing Meadows Park in Queens. No official trail grooming, so break your own, or follow trails carved out by fellow skiers.

Downhill skiers take to the slopes two hours north of the city in the Catskills or at Bear Mountain, 909-866-5766, www.bearmountain.com, in northern Westchester. Lake Placid, www.lakeplacid.com, home of the 1980 Winter Olympics, is also a skiing destination. Mountain Creek, 973-827-2000, www.mountaincreek. com; bills itself as the closest ski resort to New York City, just 47 miles away. Check local sporting goods stores for day or weekend ski rental packages.

SOCCER

The **Cosmopolitan Soccer League**, 201-943-3390, www.cslny.com, represents amateur and semi-pro clubs from New York, New Jersey, and Connecticut. You don't have to join a club to play on a team, but club facilities are limited to members. Coaches are available for training; all age groups are welcome.

Year-round league play is available at **Chelsea Piers**, 23rd Street at the Hudson River, 212-336-6500, www.chelseapiers.com/fh/adult/leagues-soccer. Teams accommodating men and women at various skill levels play one night a week on an Astroturf indoor field. A season consists of 8 or 12 games consisting of two 25-minute halves and league playoffs.

Some city parks also have soccer fields. For permit information in New York, contact the NYC Department of Parks and Recreation, 311, www.nycgovparks.org/facilities/soccer.

SQUASH

When you consider that a tennis court takes up about ten times as much space as a squash court, it is easy to understand the great attraction squash holds for sports club operators, as well as for a population determined to exercise, but at the lowest cost possible. See **Health Clubs** and **Ys** for other locations with courts.

- **New York Health and Racquet Club**, www.nyhrc.com; multiple locations
- **New York Sports Clubs**, www.nysc.com; multiple locations

SURFING

It may not be Oahu, but New York City surfers need not abandon their beloved boards; a stretch of Rockaway Beach in Queens has been designated the city's sole "Surf Only" beach. Surfing at other city beaches may get you a summons, so unless you want to make the long haul to southern Jersey's Ocean City, Rockaway is your best (and cheapest) bet. Surfing is also permitted at a number of beaches on Long Island.

- **Rockaway Beach**, near Beach 90th St, Rockaway, Queens, 718-318-4000; take the A train to Rockaway and transfer to the S train. Check www.northeast-surfing.com for a listing of conditions.

SWIMMING—POOLS

The Department of Parks and Recreation, www.nycgovparks.org, maintains a number of indoor and outdoor pools throughout the city; the former are open year-round, while the latter are typically open late June until September 1. Hours at all outdoor pools are 11 a.m. until 7 p.m., with mandatory closure from 3 p.m. to 4 p.m. for cleaning. All of the city's pools are free of charge. Rules about what you can and can't bring are quite stringent, so check with department's website for up-to-date information about what's currently permitted: www.nycgovparks.org/facilities/outdoor-pools. Some pools are accessible for people with disabilities; a list of these can be found on the website. Shower before and after using city pools.

Here are a few to get you started:

- **Asser Levy Pool**, 392 Asser Levy Pl, 212-447-2020; built in 1906 as a public bath modeled on the Roman baths, this granite gem with a marble lobby and 20-foot ceilings reopened in 1990 after extensive renovations.
- **Hansborough Recreational Center**, 35 W 134th St, 212-234-9603, in Harlem has an indoor pool and gym with dance and aerobic classes.
- **Metropolitan Recreation Center**, 261 Bedford Ave, Greenpoint, Brooklyn, 718-599-5707; probably the most beautiful of the pools operated by the city. Light pours through a copper-framed skylight into the somewhat Andalusian pool area, which is handicap-accessible. Best to avoid early evenings and Saturdays. Mornings from 7 to 9:30 are quiet.
- **Tony Dapolito Recreation Center**, 1 Clarkson St, 212-242-5228, offers a 50' by 100' outdoor pool.

Health clubs and Ys with pools are described at the end of this chapter. Dedicated swimmers might wish also to check out other swimming locations such as:

- **Coles Sports and Recreation Center**, 181 Mercer St s, 212-998-2020, www.gonyuathletics.com; New York University's sports facility, with racquetball and squash courts, a weight room, and a 25-meter pool with six lanes beneath frosted glass windows, is available to residents from 14th to Canal Streets, Fourth to Eleventh Avenues, and students, faculty, and staff affiliated with NYU.
- **Manhattan Plaza Health Club**, 482 W 43rd St at Tenth Ave, 212-563-7001, www.mphc.com; the handsome, verdant, glass-enclosed 40' by 75' pool with four lap lanes is the main lure here, but there is also a gym and sauna. Of course, you'll need an annual membership and to get one, or to just get pricing information, you must first schedule an appointment for a personal visit with one of the club's consultants.
- **Metropolitan Masters**, www.metroswim.org; call or visit their website for a list of places where club members can swim in and around New York City. Options include several YMCAs, Chelsea Piers, and the New York Athletic Club.

- **Riverbank State Park**, 679 Riverside Dr at 145th St, 212-694-3600; this glorious facility atop a waste treatment plant over the Hudson River is a treasure for Uptowners who pay a couple of dollars to go for a swim in its indoor Olympic-sized pool (50 meters)—no membership or consultation needed. There are a host of water classes and activities between sessions, and there is an outdoor pool open in the summer. Call for hours.

TENNIS

The Department of Parks Permit Office in each borough issues tennis permits for city courts. Manhattan permit particulars are detailed above under Central Park—Tennis. Of the city's 535 public courts, more than 100 are located in Manhattan at nine sites. The largest single concentration, 30 courts, is in Central Park off 96th Street. Seven of the other locations are north of 96th Street, and the eighth is at East River Park at Broome Street on the Lower East Side. In Manhattan, the phone is 212-360-8131. Permits for all boroughs can also be secured online at www.nyc-govparks.org/permits/tennis-permits.

Five private clubs with four or more courts in Manhattan, Roosevelt Island, and across the East River in Queens are listed below.

- **Manhattan Plaza Racquet Club**, 450 W 43rd St, 212-594-0554, www.manhattanplazatennis.com; membership, hourly, and seasonal rates
- **Midtown Tennis Club**, 341 Eighth Ave, 212-989-8572, www.midtowntennis.com; hourly and seasonal rates
- **Roosevelt Island Racquet Club**, 281 Main St, Roosevelt Island, 212-935-0250, www.rirctennis.com; clay courts indoors, league play, a seniors' club, babysitting, membership, hourly rates
- **West Side Tennis Club**, 1 Tennis Place, Forest Hills, Queens, 718-268-2300, www.foresthillstennis.com, has 38 outdoor courts, including grass, clay, Deco-Turf, and Har-Tru courts under a bubble in cold weather. A membership club on the former site of the US Open and home to some 800 members, West Side hosts a variety of tennis programs and tournaments and includes on the premises a fitness room, platform tennis, basketball, and an outdoor pool complex. The club also draws surprisingly big-name acts to play concerts during the summer; in 2013 they hosted the extraordinarily popular group, Mumford & Sons. Membership dues vary depending on age and family status. Lessons with a pro are available at extra charge.

Of course, if you really want to play where the pros play, you can rent a court at the **Billie Jean King National Tennis Center**, which is open to the public almost all year (closed for Thanksgiving, Christmas, and for two weeks in late August/early September for a little tournament called the US Open). Located in Flushing Meadows Park, Queens—across from Citi Field stadium (take the #7 train). For rates and information call 718-760-6200 or visit the USTA website at www.usta.com. Junior and adult training programs plus junior summer camps are also available.

TRAPEZE

Yes, indeed, you too can planche and whip, execute twisting layouts, or pull off a double pirouette return. Of course, it will take time, practice and instruction, and there is no better place than Trapeze School New York. Established in 2001, TSNY has seen explosive growth, especially after exposure from *Sex in the City* and the *Today Show*. The school has three locations, including an outdoor set-up on the Hudson, and instructors cater to all levels, with special focus on beginners. Classes range from $50 to $70, with discounts for purchasing blocks of five or more classes. Visit www.newyork.trapezeschool.com for more information, or call 212-242-8769. Truly, this town has everything.

YOGA

Not a sport really, but available at nearly any health and fitness club. It's the un-sport in sports. Listed below are just some of the many sites other than health clubs where yoga, in one form or another, is taught and practiced.

- **Dharma Yoga Center**, 26 W 23rd St, 212-889-8160, www.dharmayogacenter. com, offers classical yoga, meditation, breathing classes, and posture classes for different levels.
- **Integral Yoga Institute**, 227 W 13th St, 212-929-0585, www.integralyogaof-newyork.org, offers open classes in Hatha I, beginners, intermediate, and advanced Hatha, prenatal and postpartum classes, Hatha in Spanish and for persons with HIV. They operate an adjacent health food store and a vitamin store.
- **Sivananda Yoga Vedanta Center**, 243 W 24th St, 212-255-4560, www.sivanan-dany.org, offers multi-level yoga for all ages, as well as courses and one-day workshops on meditation, philosophy, and vegetarian cooking. They also offer yoga retreats at their ranch in the Catskills.

HEALTH CLUBS, YMCAS, AND YWCAS

HEALTH CLUBS

Beyond offering personal trainers and customized fitness regimens, most health clubs offer various classes, ranging from kick-boxing and spinning to yoga and fencing. Facilities go from bare-bones weight rooms to ubiquitous all-purpose spas where you set your own pace using the most appealing facilities. These often include a pool (varying from postage stamp to Olympic in size), exercise

equipment (aerobic and weight), steam-rooms, whirlpools, and saunas. To indicate the amenities offered, a few of the dozens of health facilities located in the
city are described here.

Get a tour, and if possible a free pass or two, before signing on the dotted
line—you may decide that the reality of exercising to skull-pounding music is not
so healthful after all. When you're told that the club you're visiting is having a "sale,"
take it with several grains of salt; with few fixed prices, words like "special" and "discount" are next to meaningless in the fitness business. The person on the treadmill
next to you may have paid double or half what you paid. Ask at your place of
work if they offer an employer-sponsored program. Finally, don't let yourself be
pressured into signing up for a long-term commitment—unless you're *really* sure
you want that multi-year membership. One excellent way to get a feel for what's
available is the New York Fitness Passbook, which gives you passes to more than
165 private gyms and clubs in the area. The cost is $85, and there are also yoga and
other fitness passbooks available from the same company, The American Health
and Fitness Alliance, 212-808-0765, www.health-fitness.org.

- **Asphalt Green**, 555 E90th St, 212-369-8890, www.asphaltgreen.org; two
  gyms, indoor and outdoor running tracks, state-of-the-art cardiovascular and
  weight-training equipment at this community-oriented, not-for-profit 5.5-acre
  sports and fitness complex. But the centerpiece is its AquaCenter, a spectacular
  50-meter Olympic-standard pool. Membership is on a monthly, semi-annual, or
  annual basis. Non-members can purchase a day pass for full access to the facility.
- **Bally Total Fitness Clubs**, www.ballyfitness.com; this nationwide club has a
  number of New York area locations; consult the website for the one nearest
  you. Aqua fitness, step training, athletic training, dance fitness, conditioning,
  mind-body training, circuit training, yoga, spinning, and plenty of other classes
  are offered in the membership plans. Personal training is also available. Be sure
  to tour the club you will use most, as the clientele and facility vary greatly from
  place to place.
- **Crunch Fitness**, www.crunch.com, has nearly a dozen locations in New York
  City; check the website for the one nearest you. Crunch packs 'em in with catchy
  ads and fairly outlandish exercise classes, including pole dancing, which appeal
  to a mostly young crowd. Call it entertainment fitness. Amenities vary at the
  different clubs but include personal training, boxing, rock climbing walls, steam
  rooms, pools, saunas, and even tanning. Membership.
- **Dolphin Fitness Clubs**, Manhattan at 94 E Fourth St, 212-387-9500, www.dol-
  phinfitnessclubs.com; there are nine clubs total in The Bronx, Brooklyn, Queens,
  and Staten Island. Provides all the basics, including muscle toning and aerobic
  classes, Nautilus equipment, personal trainers, weight training, cardiovascular
  equipment, and pools, and racquetball courts at some locations. Membership.
- **Equinox Fitness Club**, www.equinox.com, has nearly 30 locations in and
  around New York City; check the website for the one that's most convenient

to you. Certified personal trainers and some 200 classes, from high- and low-impact aerobics to Aerobox, pre- and postnatal exercise to yoga and meditation. Besides up-to-date equipment, the club boasts boxing circuit training, one-on-one boxing (for women, too), and cardio/theater television with cardiovascular workout equipment. In addition, you'll find childcare, a juice bar, shopping and more at these health emporiums. A nutritionist supervises personal weight-loss programs. At the Amsterdam Avenue location, a physiology lab offers comprehensive metabolic testing for a fee to non-members as well as members. No boxing uptown. Membership.

- **Lucille Roberts**, 800-USA-LUCILLE, www.lucilleroberts.com; billing itself as "The Women's Gym," Lucille Roberts operates more than 20 gyms in the boroughs, and more in New Jersey, Long Island, and Westchester. Forget the sauna and the personal trainers, and bring your own towel. Classes are the draw, including one called "butt and gut." In some neighborhoods, there are classes in Spanish. The cost of membership, comparatively low, varies by location, as do hours. Individual gyms have occasional sales promotions, when it's cheaper to join; they're worth checking out.

- **New York Health & Racquet Club**, 212-797-1500, www.hrcbest.com, has nine locations in Manhattan (plus a yacht club on 23rd Street if you want to take a sea cruise). Rates go down considerably in the summer (watch for ads offering discounts, and ask about corporate discounts). Membership includes admission to any of its locations. Most locations have pools, saunas, and racquetball courts.

- **New York Sports Clubs**, over 50 locations around the city, www.nysc.com; check the website for the one closest to you. Eagle and Nautilus circuits, Lifecycles, StairMasters, Gravitron, and other equipment are available in all clubs. Most have one-on-one training, pools, squash courts, whirlpools, and saunas. Membership includes entrance to all clubs and access to tennis courts in Brooklyn (additional court fee). Fees vary by location. This is one of the few clubs that does not require payment for a full year upfront, but will bill you monthly.

- **Reebok Sports Club/NY**, 160 Columbus Avenue, 212-362-6800, www.reeboksportsclubny.com, is an upscale, landscaped urban country club. This state-of-the-art 140,000-square foot facility on six floors features a 45-foot climbing wall; a rooftop in-line skating and running track; full basketball and volleyball courts; swimming pool with underwater sound; sauna; a virtual reality sports simulator for skiing, wind-surfing, and golf; a bar; health food café; and a bistro. They even have a dry cleaning service.

- **Sports Center at Chelsea Piers**, 23rd St and Hudson River, 212-336-6000, www.chelseapiers.com; this 150,000-square-foot pier houses a four-lane, ¼-mile running track; competition track; three basketball courts; a 100-foot climbing wall and a bouldering wall; a six-lane, 25-yard swimming pool; two outdoor sun decks; cardiovascular, circuit, and strength training equipment; a boxing ring; aerobic studios; and an infield for volleyball, sand volleyball, and touch football. Also, training, sports medicine, spa facilities, and a physiology lab are available.

Members have the use of all the other Pier facilities at a 10% discount. Membership or day passes. Popular for kids' parties.

YMCAs AND YWCAs

- **92nd Street Y**, 1395 Lexington Ave, 212-415-5700, www.92y.org; annual athletic membership entitles you to participate in many programs, including indoor jogging, weight training, volleyball, and handball, as well as fitness programs and use of the 25-yard lap pool.
- **Brooklyn YWCA**, 30 Third Ave between State St and Atlantic Ave, Brooklyn, 718-875-1190; for a reasonably priced athletic membership plus a Y membership, both men and women can work out on the Universal machines, punching bags, the large basketball court, jogging track, and in the 20' by 60' swimming pool, and relax in the sauna.
- **Harlem YMCA**, 180-181 W 135th St by Lenox Ave, 212-912-2100, www.ymcanyc. org/harlem; offers two pools (for adults and children), Nautilus and weights, a track, basketball courts, table tennis, aerobics, yoga and karate classes, and personal trainers. Athletic membership (for men and women), plus joiner's fee.
- **McBurney YMCA**, 225 W 14th St, 212-912-2300, www.ymcanyc.org/mcburney; this Y has a carefully developed children's after-school program, as well as adult gymnastics, adult lap and recreational swimming, full-court basketball, indoor jogging track, fencing, handball, volleyball, and a weight lifting room. Annual adult membership plus joiner's fee for the first year. Excellent facilities.
- **Vanderbilt YMCA**, 224 E 47th St, 212-912-2500, www.ymcanyc.org/vanderbilt; has an after-school program (with escorts from certain neighborhood schools), plus yoga, handball, and paddleball, along with swimming, basketball, volleyball, indoor jogging, Nautilus, and aerobics. Regular membership plus joiner's fee includes use of the gym, 20' by 60' swimming pool, a 40' by 75' lap pool, and other sports facilities. Annual dues for the Businessman's Club and the men's Athletic Club are higher.
- **West Side YMCA**, 5 W 63rd St, 212-912-2600, www.ymcanyc.org/westside; justifiably proud of its Sports Fitness Department, which keeps both men and women members in the very best of shape. The seven-story building houses two pools, a wrestling room, indoor running track, handball, squash, and racquetball courts, universal exercise machines, and numerous other facilities. Annual adult membership plus initiation fee.

NESTLED AMONG THE CONCRETE, STEEL, AND GLASS OF NEW YORK'S riotous urban landscape are pockets of greenery and nature so lush and rich that even the most hard-nosed New Yorkers cannot help but forget their customary brusqueness and the madcap rush of the city itself. Though the buildings and blocks may be densely packed, it is the parks that New Yorkers truly share with one other. From the smallest community garden on a vacant lot in a dense neighborhood, where neighbors lovingly tend an iris bed and riotous morning glories, to green bands streaked with runners, bladers, and cyclists along watery borders, to Manhattan's great lush centerpiece, Central Park, and its sister, Prospect Park, in Brooklyn, New Yorkers use and cherish their parks. Beyond these groomed and cultivated parks familiar to most, there are about 9,000 acres of urban wilderness in the domain of the city's parks department, where the nature lover can wander wooded paths, meadows, and marshlands alone and silent among swans, egrets, herons, turtles, muskrats, and rabbits. For the price of a subway ride, one can spend the day in a national park, Gateway National Recreation Area, a birders' paradise, parts of which are within the city. And the city's beaches, seaside parks of a sort, guarantee sandy access to the Atlantic Ocean and Long Island Sound.

There are more than 1,700 parks and playgrounds throughout the 29,000 acres maintained by the Department of Parks and Recreation in the five boroughs. These range from vest-pocket neighborhood playgrounds to the 2,700-acre Pelham Bay Park in The Bronx. Suffice it to say, we can't describe or even list them all. Rather, this chapter focuses on the major parks in each borough, with brief descriptive mention of some others and, finally, a look at the city's beaches. For further information about parks in general or a particular park call 311 within New York City, 212-NEW YORK outside the city, or go online to www.nycgovparks.org.

Open from dawn to 1 a.m., all city parks are free and accessible by public transportation. Statistically speaking, the parks are very safe. That said, it is good to remember these are urban parks; common sense tells you it's not a good idea to stroll or jog through a wooded park area alone, day or night—there are plenty of trails in wide-open spaces. Unless you're watching one of the special concerts in the park, or visiting some other crowded park event, avoid the parks after dark. Dogs must be on leashes, and you are expected to clean up after your dog. It's the law.

PARKS

MANHATTAN

In 1858 Frederick Law Olmsted and Calvert Vaux won a design competition for the construction of the first public park to be built in America. It was to occupy swampy land inhabited by poor squatters, bone-boiling mills, and swill mills, an area described in one report as "a pestilential spot where miasmic odors taint every breath of air." The inhabitants were removed, buildings torn down, swamps drained, tons of earth moved, and Manhattan schist blasted away. Following plans for a picturesque landscape of glades alternating with copses, water, and outcroppings, and threaded with drives, footpaths, and bridle paths, over a period of 20 years the park emerged from wasteland. What Olmsted and Vaux had named Greensward became **Central Park**, 840 acres of man-made romantic landscape stretching rectangularly from 59th Street north to 110th Street, and from Fifth Avenue west to Central Park West (Eighth Avenue): the green jewel in the middle of Manhattan.

Today the park is managed, under contract with the city, by the **Central Park Conservancy**, www.centralparknyc.org, a nonprofit organization responsible for extensive restoration of the park. The most heavily visited area is the southern portion of the park, especially the area around the ever-popular **Central Park Zoo**, www.centralparkzoo.com, which includes the revamped Children's Zoo. The northern portion beyond the Reservoir, with its heavily used jogging track, contains the wildest terrain, including the Ravine area with its waterfall and the 1814 Blockhouse, as well as the only formal garden in the park, the elegant **Conservatory Garden** at 105th Street and Fifth Avenue. The **Charles A. Dana Discovery Center**, 212-860-1370, in the northeast corner of the park, features ecologically oriented exhibits and programs for all ages on a regular basis, and has fishing poles for use at the adjacent Harlem Meer. The Conservancy offers free seasonal events throughout the park, including birdwatching walks and ecological activities. Pick up the Conservancy's excellent Central Park Map and Guide at the Dairy Visitor Information and Gift Shop, just north of Wollman Rink near the 65th Street Transverse, open Monday–Sunday, 10 a.m.–5 p.m.

New Yorkers use Central Park for sports, from croquet to horseback riding to league softball (see the chapter on **Sports and Recreation**); for cultural events, such as Shakespeare in the Park and outdoor performances by the Metropolitan Opera and the New York Philharmonic; for children's recreation in its numerous playgrounds; for storytelling sessions, kite-flying, and carousel riding, and organized nature activities; for sunbathing on its rocky outcroppings or in bucolic Sheep Meadow; for birdwatching in the Ramble, especially during the annual spring warbler migration; for boating in the Lake or floating beneath Bow Bridge in a Venetian gondola; for sailing toy boats in the Lake; for weddings; and even for films, many of which have been shot in or around the massive park—the musical *Hair*, for example was primarily shot in Central Park. And it's used for daydreaming or reading a good book. In fact, sometimes just knowing it is there is enough.

Central Park is open from a half-hour before dawn to 1 a.m. As in the other large city parks, it is best visited in daylight or at night in the well-lighted areas along the edges and with companions. Check www.centralparknyc.org for an invigorating virtual visit and plenty of information. This excellent website offers a colorful virtual tour, park history, sporting events, a listing of park events, and links to other park-related sites.

Having completed Central Park, Olmsted and Vaux focused their attention on the banks of the Hudson River and designed most of what is now **Riverside Park**, www.nycgovparks.org/parks/riversidepark. This elongated ribbon of green, stretching along the river from 72nd Street to 152nd Street and bisected length-wise by the Henry Hudson Parkway, is particularly beautiful in the spring when daffodils dot the grassy banks and swarms of flowering trees create a haze of pink and white. Riverside Drive winds among great trees along the upper terrace, and the mighty Hudson, nearly a mile wide here, sweeps along past cyclists and joggers on the riverfront promenade. Sailboats and a few houseboats at the 79th Street boat basin bob at anchor, and in good weather, reasonably priced sailing lessons are to be had here (see **Sports and Recreation**). Tennis, handball, soccer, and volleyball are played here, and a facility for bladers and boarders, with ramps and half-pipes at 108th Street, draws youthful enthusiasts. Soaring Riverside Church and Grant's Tomb add to the appeal of Riverside Park. For more information, call the park administrator's office at 212-408-0264 or visit www.nycgovparks. org/parks/riversidepark. Farther along at 145th Street and Riverside Drive, an iron gate gives access to **Riverbank State Park**, 212-694-3600, www.nysparks.com/ parks/93/details.aspx, built atop a waste treatment plant, where ice skating, swimming, and other athletic activities can be pursued at way-below-health-club rates.

Fort Tryon Park, www.nycgovparks.org/parks/forttryonpark, in Washington Heights stands atop a ridge of Manhattan schist at the island's highest natural point. The site of one of the earliest Revolutionary War battles (we lost), this land was purchased in 1917 by John D. Rockefeller, Jr. He hired Frederick Law Olmsted, Jr., to design a park here, reserving four acres at the northern end of the 67 acres for a museum of medieval art, The Cloisters—a fortuitous pairing, those juniors. Taking advantage of the sweeping Hudson view at this 250-foot elevation, Olmsted designed a series of terraces with stone parapets and retaining walls, the whole threaded with eight miles of paths. The centerpiece of the park is the three-acre Heather Garden, with heaths, brooms, and thousands of bulbs, which bloom from January through autumn. Farther along the Promenade are leafy Linden

Terrace and The Cloisters, with its three medieval gardens. Bring a picnic lunch. For more information call Fort Tryon Park, 212-795-1388, or The Cloisters, 212-923-3700 (www.metmuseum.org for a schedule of exhibitions).

Just north of Fort Tryon Park at the very top of Manhattan, little-known **Inwood Hill Park** contains the last remaining natural woodland in Manhattan, not to mention arresting views of the Hudson River and the Jersey Palisades beyond. Interesting geology on the wooded ridge, which is crisscrossed with paved and graveled paths, includes glacial potholes and cliffs with a hodge-podge of blocky gray rocks, the Indian Rock Shelters, which once sheltered Algonquin Indians. From these rocky cliffs, paths descend to playing fields, grassy parkland, and marshland along swift Spuyten Duyvil Creek, across which the Henry Hudson Bridge soars to The Bronx. There is an excellent **Urban Ecology Center** here staffed by Urban Park Rangers. They lead occasional walks and canoe trips into the Hudson. For information call 212-304-2365.

South of Central Park, greenspace is measured out in much smaller portions. **Bryant Park** behind the Beaux Arts main branch of the New York Public Library at 42nd Street, between Fifth and Sixth Avenues, for example, is too small to encourage sports much more strenuous than chess, though it does host a few ping-pong tables in the summer months and is ringed with other passive recreational leisures, including a small reading area for both adults and children. It is now greenspace with a rather European feel, and those who work in the neighborhood are grateful for it. During the summer months it hosts concerts and festivals (www.bryantpark.org).

Union Square Park, www.nycgovparks.org/parks/unionsquarepark, is a 3½-acre rectangle south of the Flatiron District. Serving as a gateway into downtown Manhattan, the park is heavily trafficked and open 24 hours. There are dog runs and an al fresco restaurant at the north end, but the limited greenspaces within are made available only occasionally. The square has a long history as a meeting place for rallies, protests, and artisans, and in the winter hosts a labyrinthine holiday market, a complex of merchants housed in candy cane-striped kiosks. One of the city's best greenmarkets is found here (see **Greenmarkets** in the **Shopping for the Home** section), and the park is surrounded by shops, restaurants, theatres, and schools, www.unionsquarenyc.org. Not a place to picnic, but the people-watching is fantastic.

Farther downtown at the foot of Fifth Avenue, **Washington Square Park** provides greenspace for Greenwich Village and SoHo, where people-watching and attending the annual art show are the sports of choice. Nearly surrounded by New York University, which threatens to engulf it entirely, Washington Square Park has managed to retain a sense of its history, which has included being a potter's field, the site of the hangman's tree, a military parade ground, and an elegant park for the wealthy. Its Village location and the presence of college students keep it youthful and colorful.

To the east, **Tompkins Square Park,** truly a people's park with an English provenance and great old trees that have always made it a shady haven in the summer for a working-class population, is the front yard for the East Village. Gentrification has brought more young professionals and families to the area, and the park is often crowded. There are several dog runs there, including a "Small Dog Area" exclusively for dogs under 23 pounds. Way downtown you'll find a series of small parks connected by a sinuous, elegant **Esplanade** spacious enough to accommodate joggers, cyclists, bladers, walkers, and baby strollers moving at their own pace within sight of the Statue of Liberty and Ellis Island. Students from nearby Stuyvesant High School toss Frisbees in the offshore breeze, and children romp and climb in a fanciful playground. The landscape at the south end was designed to resemble the original shoreline.

Just to the south, at the very foot of the island, is **Battery Park,** once part of New York Harbor, with Castle Clinton surrounded by water rather than grass. This inviting, grassy stretch looks out on the harbor, the statue, and Staten Island, and invites a hop onto the free Staten Island Ferry. This is just the downtown end of the Manhattan Waterfront Greenway, a 32-mile stretch of car free pedestrian/biker paradise that almost encircles the entire island (the 10 blocks around the Queensborough Bridge remains un-green, as of yet). It is taboo to all motorized traffic, but anything else is a go. Combined with the crosstown bike lanes it's an excellent way for two-wheel commuters to avoid traffic.

Saving the smallest for last, don't forget the Green Thumb Community Gardens, throughout the Lower East Side area, www.greenthumbnyc.org; one of the city's man inspiring urban movements, the Green Thumb program began as a way for the crime-wracked Lower East Side community to take control of hundreds of trash-filled vacant lots in the 1970s. These lots—saved in part by a donation from singer Bette Midler (who was also responsible for the rescue and rehabilitation of Fort Tryon Park)—have been turned into hundreds of teeny community-run gardens that provide much needed relief from NYC congestion. Some are astonishing paradises of plants and flowers and sculpture, while some have stayed closer to their roots as vacant lots, but they're one of the most beloved movements in this part of town. The best ones are well worth a visit (check for what hours they're open to the public, usually weekend afternoons).

GOVERNOR'S ISLAND

Governor's Island, www.govisland.com, accessible by ferries from Lower Manhattan and Brooklyn Bridge Park's Pier 6 (check for current schedule), as well as from various ports on the East River Ferry almost lost to commercial development, this military base (closed in 1996) was instead sold to the people of New York for one dollar in 2003. It now is one of the more popular summer greenspace destinations, with a number of 18th-century forts and hundreds of acres of forest and waterfront with lovely views of the Statue of Liberty. Bring your own bicycle, or rent one, and explore this car-free island. It's become an immensely popular day trip for Manhattanites. In 2014, the park opened seven days a week. Check current schedules and event information at www.govisland.com

BROOKLYN

Who but Calvert Vaux and Frederick Law Olmsted could have designed **Prospect Park**, www.prospectpark.org, sister to Central Park and younger by just a few years? In fact, its designers considered it their masterpiece. Free of Manhattan's grid, it is irregularly shaped in a somewhat elongated ovoid, smaller at 526 acres, and unlike Central Park, it is undisturbed by crisscrossing traffic. Prospect Park was designed for strolling along a network of paths: on vast Long Meadow, the park's magnificent centerpiece, around Prospect Lake and the Lullwater, through The Ravine and the Midwood Forest, and by The Pools. Sounds English? It is. Olmsted and Vaux incorporated the natural terrain into their design, including water, magnificent old trees and geological features such as glacial kettle ponds, one of which became the charming Vale of Cashmere. To these features they added rustic bridges, a waterfall, and lakes, the final effect of which is vistas, surprising nooks and glades, and hilltop prospects. There's even a Quaker cemetery, among whose residents is the actor Montgomery Clift, and an elegant, Palladian-style boathouse. This is not to say that strolling is the sole Prospect Park activity. Birding is excellent in the park; jogging, tennis, softball, kite flying, and soccer flourish here; and on summer weekends the Bandshell at 9th Street and Prospect Park West features music, from calypso to jazz, klezmer, and Latin grooves. For more information and for upcoming events in the park visit www.prospectpark.org. The park is bounded by Ocean Avenue, Flatbush Avenue, Prospect Park SW, Prospect Park West, and Parkside Avenue.

Across Flatbush Avenue from Prospect Park, and behind the Brooklyn Central Library and the Brooklyn Museum, the **Brooklyn Botanic Garden**, 990 Washington Ave, 718-623-7200, www.bbg.org, has extended an open invitation to Brooklynites and visitors since 1912. Within its compact 52 acres it contains an extraordinary variety of greenery and flora, beautifully landscaped so as never to seem crowded. The Cherry Esplanade, said to be the finest in America, draws crowds in May when the cherry trees are in exquisite bloom. Don't miss it, but come early and on a weekday if possible. There's a rock garden, water-lily ponds, and a lilac collection, offering intoxicating blooms each spring. An herb garden is arranged as an Elizabethan knot, and the stunning Japanese garden is a perennial favorite. Year-round, the gently undulating terrain invites wandering, beginning in February, when the witch hazel blooms and the snowdrops begin to come up. Call it mid-winter botanical balm. Before you bliss out, don't miss the original Palm House. You may decide to get married there, as many have.

Green-Wood Cemetery, with its main entrance on Fifth Avenue at 25th Street, is at once a cemetery and one of the most beautiful, not to mention unusual, parks in the city. This is an active cemetery, so you will not play soccer here, and jogging its winding, hilly drives would be a challenge. What you can do, if not on a cemetery-related mission, is walk, bird watch, identify exotic trees, of which there are many, and look for the graves of the once-famous, including Lola Montez, Boss Tweed, Peter Cooper, and Samuel F. B. Morse, to name but a few. Opened in 1840, before Prospect Park was conceived, on 478 acres of glacial terminal moraine, and overlooking New York Harbor from the highest point in Brooklyn, it was promoted by its developers as an idyllic spot for strolling among the hills, ponds, superb vistas, and plantings. It was, de facto, the city's first park. The extraordinary mausoleums, obelisks, temples, pyramids, and rustic grave markers make it something of a museum of Victoriana and a draw for occasional guided tours. The main gate building, designed by Richard Upjohn, is a Gothic Revival extravaganza, housing the office where you pick up a pass, brochure, and a map of the cemetery. The office is open Monday–Friday, 9 a.m.–5 p.m., 718-768-7300, www.green-wood.com. If you wish to roam the cemetery on the weekend, you should pick up a pass in advance.

Stepping out of the car at the **Marine Park**, www.nycgovparks.org/parks/marinepark, parking lot on Avenue U, just west of Flatbush Avenue, you'll find yourself in a landscape of salt marsh and meadow somewhat reminiscent of Holland. This 798-acre park, most of it saltwater wetlands surrounding Marine Park Creek, north of Sheepshead Bay, contains playing fields, tennis courts, a running track, and a golf course, in addition to a watery urban wilderness. From the parking lot you can hike the Gerritsen Creek Nature Trail for about a mile, through grasses, sedges, and reeds with glimpses, perhaps, of diamond-back terrapin, horseshoe crabs, cottontails, marsh hens, myrtle warblers, cormorants, and peregrine falcons. It's hard to believe you're in New York City. For more information, call the Brooklyn Borough Office of the Department of Parks and Recreation at 718-965-8900. There's also the **Salt Marsh Nature Center** at 33rd Street and Avenue U, 718-421-2021, www.saltmarshalliance.org.

Even more unbelievable, and not known to many New Yorkers, is the presence of a 26,000-acre national park, **Gateway National Recreation Area**, www.nps.gov/gate, which encompasses most of Jamaica Bay in Brooklyn and Queens, and part of the Rockaways in Queens, a long stretch of the southern shore of Staten Island, and parts of the Jersey shore. Besides **Jacob Riis Park**, an ocean beach with a boardwalk (see **Beaches**, below), the best known point of interest in the area is the **Jamaica Bay Wildlife Refuge**, 718-318-4340, a prime birding preserve with salt water marshes, upland fields, and woods, where land and shore birds stop during migration. After obtaining a permit at the visitor center on Crossbay Boulevard in Broad Channel, Queens, visitors can explore diverse habitats by hiking an extensive trail system. Insect repellent in summer is strongly advised. Rangers give interpretive talks and lead nature walks; evening walks, workshops, and other programs are offered on a seasonal basis. Fishing can also be done for the cost of a permit. **Floyd Bennett Field**, 718-338-3799, the city's first municipal airfield, is now the site of the Historic Aircraft Restoration Project. Kayaking and urban camping can also be done here. Across Flatbush Avenue from the Field, **Dead Horse Bay** is a popular fishing area with a nature trail. **Canarsie Pier** just off the Beltway in Brooklyn is the site of summer concerts, excellent fishing, a children's playground, and a restaurant. Fishing is also popular, along with bird watching, at **Breezy Point Tip** on the Rockaway Peninsula and at **Fort Tilden**, 718-318-4300, www.nyharborparks.org, a 317-acre former Army base, where visitors can also hike and explore a military past, participate in organized athletics, or attend special events. On the south shore of Staten Island, **Great Kills Park**, 718-980-6130, offers ocean beaches, nature trails, a model airplane field, and fishing areas. Ranger walks at **Miller Field**, 718-351-6970, a former Army Air Corps defense station, and at **Fort Wadsworth**, 718-354-4500, dating from the 18th century, appeal to military buffs and children.

Admission to all portions of Gateway, except Sandy Point, NJ, is free. For the latest information on concerts, special programs, and ranger-led activities, visit Gateway on the web at www.nps.gov/gate. Or contact the National Park Service, Gateway National Recreation Area, Floyd Bennett Field, Building 69, Brooklyn, 718-338-3799, for a seasonal program guide, which includes transportation directions to all parts of the area.

QUEENS

At long last **Flushing Meadows-Corona Park**, 718-760-6565, www.nycgovparks. org/parks/fmcp, is coming into its own, becoming the grand park originally envisioned when the 1939 World's Fair was held there, and again at the time of the 1964 World's Fair. Built on what was once a garbage heap on Northern Boulevard, between Grand Central Parkway and the Van Wyck Expressway, both fairs were to pay for park construction, but neither made money, and the great park limped along with World Fair leftovers and a neighboring baseball stadium, Shea (now Citi Field). The Unisphere, the signature attraction of the 1,255-acre park, and its grassy surrounds have been renovated, and extensive landscaping and plantings have beautified the central portion of the park, which also hosts the **New York Hall of Science**, www.nysci.org, and its Science Playground, and the **Queens Museum**, www.queensmuseum.org, which emerged gorgeous and grand from extensive renovations in late 2013. Elsewhere in the park are the **Queens Theatre**, www.queenstheatre.org, the **Queens Zoo**, www.queenszoo.com, the **US Tennis Association's Arthur Ashe Stadium and National Tennis Center**, www. usta.com, the **World Ice Arena** with skating rink, www.worldice.com, an 18-hole pitch-and-putt golf course, www.golfnyc.com/flushing_pitchputt_home, running trails, and two large lakes lying to the south of the Long Island Expressway, one, Meadow Lake, with a boathouse.

Alley Pond Park, www.nycgovparks.org/parks/alleypondpark, sprawls and meanders south from Little Neck Bay to Union Turnpike. Despite being sliced by numerous parkways, it encompasses forests, meadows, salt marshes, and wet-lands, making it an ideal environment for a network of nature trails from which one can observe muskrats, bullfrogs, salamanders, and hawks. Up on the northern end near Alley Creek, an environmental center offers a variety of educational classes and workshops: 718-229-4000, www.alleypond.com.

Along Woodhaven Boulevard en route to the Rockaways, the beach, and JFK International Airport, you'll find **Forest Park**, 718-235-4100, www.nycgovparks. org/parks/forestpark. It offers a public golf course, playing fields, and a magnifi-cent 150-year-old oak forest honeycombed with picturesque nature trails. Summer concerts and other events take place at the band-shell. Call for information.

In the heart of Flushing, within cheering distance of Citi Field and the National Tennis Center, **Kissena Corridor Park**, www.nycgovparks.org/parks/Q300, con-tains the **Queens Botanical Garden**, www.queensbotanical.org, and connects with greater Kissena Park, a gracious greenspace surrounding a lake and mean-dering stream. There's also a bicycle track and a public golf course: 718-886-3800, www.queensbotanical.org

To the east, adjacent to Cross Island Parkway and Hempstead Turnpike, **Belmont Park**, www.nyra.com/belmont, is famous for its exceedingly beautiful racetrack, where thoroughbreds compete annually for the Belmont Cup. But you don't have to be a horse-lover to enjoy the park.

Nearing Long Island, in the eastern part of Queens, is **Cunningham Park**, www.nycgovparks.org/parks/cunninghampark. This small but busy park on Union Turnpike in Fresh Meadows has several tennis courts, baseball fields, and even bocce courts, as well as plenty of picnic locations.

And finally, Queens is home to much of **Gateway National Recreation Area**, www.nps.gov/gate/index.htm, bordering Brooklyn and described above.

THE BRONX

Up in the northeast corner of The Bronx, sprawling alongside and into Long Island Sound, is the city's largest park, 2,700 acres of it. **Pelham Bay Park**, 718-430-1890, www.nycgovparks.org/parks/pelhambaypark, has it all: a city beach, a golf course, miniature golf and a driving range, a stable, tennis courts, baseball diamonds, picnic grounds, and a historic mansion-museum, not to mention a range of hab-itats—the most diverse of any of the city parks. Just offshore and connected to the park by a bridge, City Island dangles like a fish on a line. The largest portion of the park lies on the north side of the Hutchinson River and Eastchester Bay, with Split Rock Golf Course and Pelham Bay Golf Course (see **Sports and Recre-ation**) scenically occupying the northernmost part. Also on Shore Road are **Bronx Equestrian Center** (again, see **Sports and Recreation**) and extensive bridle trails. Nearby is the **Thomas Pell Wildlife Refuge and Sanctuary**, home to a variety of owls, wild turkeys, and deer. Just to the north and east, off Shore Road, is the Bartow-Pell Mansion and Museum; dating from 1675 and with alterations done in the 19th century, it is the single manor house remaining of 28 country estates that once comprised the park area. It is well worth a visit. **Orchard Beach** (see **Beaches** below) cuts a great sandy arc on Long Island Sound. At its far end is **Orchard Beach Nature Center**, where you can pick up literature and a guide booklet to the **Kazimiroff Nature Trail**, which winds through the adjoining Hunter Island Sanctuary, perhaps the most beautiful section of the park. Mature woodlands give way to salt marsh, where a profusion of water birds can be spotted year-round, plus migrating hawks and ospreys in the fall. The great rounded boulders off-shore in the sound are glacial erratics, and the gray bedrock visible here is the southernmost extension of the ancient bedrock that forms most of the New England coast.

Directly to the west, abutting Riverdale and Yonkers, is **Van Cortlandt Park**, 718-430-1890, www.nycgovparks.org/parks/VanCortlandtPark, which also contains playing fields, two golf courses, a riding stable and trails, and a historic mansion-museum. Heavily used for recreation and once the site of an extensive Native American village, the Parade Ground is also home to weekend cricket competitions by largely West Indian teams. Nearby, you can visit the **Van Cortlandt Mansion and Museum**, 718-543-3344, www.nycgovparks.org/parks/VanCortlandtPark/highlights/6371, the oldest house in The Bronx (1748) and a lovely example of vernacular Georgian architecture. To the north, where the Henry Hudson Parkway crosses Broadway and slices through the park, the **Riverdale Equestrian Centre**, www.riverdaleriding.com, rents horses for trail rides and offers lessons (see **Sports and Recreation**). The **Van Cortlandt Golf Course**, www.golfnyc.com/vancortlandt_home, the oldest municipal course in the country, surrounds much of long, narrow Van Cortlandt Lake, while the **Mosholu Golf Course**, www.mosholugolfcourse.com, lies in the southeast corner of the park (see **Sports and Recreation** for both). Birders and nature lovers seek out two popular trails: the forested **Cass Gallagher Nature Trail** with its dramatic rock outcroppings in the northwest portion of the park, and the **John Kieran Nature Trail** in the southern portion. The latter, which skirts freshwater wetlands and the Tibbetts Brook area, is esteemed by birdwatchers; it follows a former rail corridor, where deer, wild turkeys, and coyotes are seen occasionally, and swings down along the lake, where egrets and great blue herons are to be found.

Bronx Park in the center of the north Bronx is comprised entirely of the **New York Botanical Garden** and the **International Wildlife Conservation Park** (Bronx Zoo), neither of which, properly speaking, is a park. Separated by Fordham Road and each bisected by the scenic Bronx River, they bear mentioning here because of their natural beauty, their accessibility, and their popularity. The **Botanical Garden**, 718-817-8700, www.nybg.org, on the north, is at once an internationally recognized botanical research facility and an extraordinary Victorian conservatory, with gardens and educational programs on 250 acres of geologically interesting virgin forest and a variety of landscaped gardens, all accessible by pathways and tram. Two cafés and picnic areas make it possible to spend the day here. Leave the dogs home and please don't pick the daisies. The **Bronx Zoo**, 718-220-5100, www.

bronxzoo.com, on similar wooded terrain with rock outcroppings and wonderfully varied flora, would be a great place to spend the day even without the animals. But it is, of course, a world-class zoo, where you can wander out of the northeast woods into a rain forest, a savanna, or a Himalayan mountain enclave. Avoid holiday weekends, and during warm weather, parking is easier on weekdays.

Another greenspace that bears mention, though it is not a park at all, is **Woodlawn Cemetery**, 718-920-0500, www.thewoodlawncemetery.org, just east of Van Cortlandt Park, between The Bronx River and Jerome Avenue. Less spectacular in terrain than Green-Wood in Brooklyn, Woodlawn is nevertheless a splendid array of mausoleums, memorials, and tombstones in a richly planted, peaceful setting. Stop by the office at the Webster Avenue entrance at 233rd Street for a map and brochure. You can drive or walk around the terminal mansions of Jay Gould, the Woolworths, Herman Melville, and Fiorello ("The Little Flower") LaGuardia, whose modest tombstone bears a simply carved little flower. The cemetery is open daily, 9 a.m.–4:30 p.m.

STATEN ISLAND

Well into the middle of the 20th century, most of Staten Island remained something of a sleepy backwater of woods, meadows, and farms. Unbridled suburban sprawl threatened to sweep that away until community action resulted in the preservation of significant chunks of remaining natural lands in the center of the island, now designated the **Staten Island Greenbelt,** www.sigreenbelt.org. Twelve individual parks strung together by narrow corridors form the 2,800-acre greenbelt, encompassing five distinct vegetative zones and an astonishing variety of terrain. The Wisconsin glacier stopped here some 10,000 years ago, which accounts for the rocky ridges and kettle ponds. Six trails, four of them woodland trails that permit bikes and motorized vehicles, traverse the area. The 12.3-mile **Blue Trail** runs roughly east-west, and the 7.6-mile **White Trail** runs roughly north-south—the two cross at Bucks Hollow in Latourette Park. And don't forget the bizarre Ship Graveyard on the northern end of the island where dozens of wrecks pop out of the waves—hardly a natural site, but it makes for fantastic afternoon kayaking. Ask locals for directions. For complete information about the features and strenuousness level of each trail, visit www.sigreenbelt.org/2010/05/15/hiking-trails.

One of the parks in the Greenbelt, **High Rock Park** on Todt Hill, 718-667-2165, www.nycgovparks.org/parks/highrockpark, happens to be the highest coastal point in the East south of Acadia National Park in Maine. Trails crisscross the 90-acre park, which was once a Girl Scout campground, winding in and out of woods, along the **Richmond Country Club**, www.richmondcountycc.org, golf course and freshwater wetlands, and down steep slopes to glacial kettle holes. It's a birdwatcher's paradise, with woodcock, indigo buntings, northern orioles, and other birds that generally shun urban areas. From the highest point on a clear day one can see the Atlantic Ocean.

Clay Pit Ponds State Park Preserve, 718-967-1976, www.nysparks.com/parks/166/details.aspx, near the southwest shore of the island, is the only state park preserve in the city, and its 265 acres perpetuate a remnant of Staten Island's rural past, through its bogs, meadows, ponds, sand barrens, woodlands, and swamps. Some 160 acres are designated state freshwater wetlands and unique natural areas, and as such, are closed to visitors. But the remainder has much to offer. Two interesting walking trails, with bridges and boardwalks through the wet areas, are easily hiked, even for children, who will marvel at the amphibians to be glimpsed along the way: black racer snakes, box turtles, frogs, lizards, and red-backed salamanders. One trail goes through part of one of the designated natural areas. A former pasture is now a meadow full of wildflowers and butterflies. An observation platform overlooks Abraham's Pond, a former clay pit abandoned in the 1920s. Look for muskrats, red-winged blackbirds, and painted turtles here. The park is free, open daily from dawn to dusk; the headquarters and restrooms are open weekdays, 9 a.m.–5 p.m. No pets allowed.

And, of course, there's **Miller Field** and **Great Kills Park**, Staten Island's share of Gateway National Recreation Area described above under **Brooklyn**; call 718-351-6970.

BEACHES

The air seems to bake in the concrete corridors of the city. The pungent aroma of the subway becomes nearly asphyxiating. You find yourself ducking into stores just to cool down. Then, on the train, you notice something odd: an assortment of men, women, and children in beach wear, carrying coolers and beach bags and towels. Summer-mad residents? Self-deluded European tourists? No: beach-savvy New Yorkers. There are city-run saltwater beaches in every borough but Manhattan, all one fare away—except for Jones Beach and Robert Moses State Park on Long Island, which are not city beaches but are included here because they are wonderful and many prefer them to the more crowded city beaches. If you venture to any of the beaches by car on those really hot summer weekends, prepare for a significant amount of beach traffic and make sure your a/c is working. City beaches are free, though costs for private parking lots may vary, unless you get lucky and find street parking.

City strands traditionally open on Memorial Day and close the day after Labor Day. Managed by city, state, or national park departments, all the beaches mentioned below are staffed by lifeguards. For information on beaches open to the general public, as opposed to residents with permits in Nassau and Suffolk counties, call the Long Island Convention & Visitors Bureau, 877-386-6654, or visit www.discoverlongisland.com for specific beach and park information. We begin with the northernmost beach, in The Bronx, and wind up on Long Island:

- **Orchard Beach**, 718-885-2275, www.nycgovparks.org/parks/pelhambaypark/ facilities/beaches, on a long, sandy crescent on Long Island Sound in The Bronx with all of Pelham Bay Park at its back, is exceptionally popular, so much so you'll need to get there early on weekends if you're driving. Parking can be difficult.
- **Coney Island**, 718-372-5159, www.coneyislandusa.com; Coney Island Avenue and West 8th Street, is more than just a beach; it's a state of mind and an icon. The vast sandy beach and the long boardwalk reaching from near the tip of the "island" to the Esplanade at Manhattan Beach is a scene for sure on summer weekends. You've seen the pictures, now try the beach. While you're there, don't miss the excellent New York Aquarium, the legendary Cyclone roller coaster, and Luna Park, a small but packed-with-fun amusement park. You might also catch a Cyclones game (the Mets class "A" minor league baseball team) at MCU Park. If nothing else, you should certainly stop by the original Nathan's for one of their world famous hot dogs.
- **Brighton Beach**, 718-946-1350, at Brighton Court and Brighton Second Street, in the heart of heavily Russian Little Odessa, makes for exotic people watching along the long, broad boardwalk. Stock up on Russian gourmet specialties and incredibly cheap produce at the stands along Brighton Beach Avenue before taking the subway home. For more about the beach and the area you can go to www.brightonbeach.com.
- **Manhattan Beach**, www.nycgovparks.org/parks/manhattanbeachpark, just east of Brighton Beach off Oriental Boulevard in Brooklyn, is a 40-acre public park and beach area with parking, a sandy beach, ball field, and concession stand, a favorite with families. Best reached by car. After a day in the water you can eat at one of Sheepshead Bay's popular restaurants and perhaps catch an outdoor concert at nearby Kingsborough Community College.
- **Jacob Riis Park**, 718-318-4300, www.nps.gov/gate/index.htm, in the Gateway National Recreation Area on the Rockaway Peninsula in Queens, has a 13,000-car parking lot, a mile of wide, sandy beach with a boardwalk, and handsome, WPA-era buildings. It is perhaps the preeminent city beach. Besides swimming and tanning, there's handball, paddle tennis, and shuffleboard. I Lifeguards come on duty here in mid-June.
- **Great Kills Park**, 718-987-6790, www.nycgovparks.org/parks/greatkillspark, in the Gateway National Recreation Area on Staten Island's south shore, boasts miles of trails for jogging and walking, a model airplane field, athletic fields, a fishing area and marina, as well as the guarded beach.
- **Beach State Park**, Long Island, 516-785-1600, www.nysparks.com/parks/10/ details.aspx, is six and a half miles long and beautiful, well worth the drive, the bus ride from the Port Authority Bus Terminal, or the train from Penn Station to Freeport, where there's a shuttle bus to the beach. Field six, the most popular, attracts a peaceful mix of seniors, families, and couples gay and straight, but on summer weekends, the parking lot fills up early. Field five is sheltered from waves, good for kids. West End two allows fishing and surfing and is the most

peaceful. Weekend traffic on the Long Island Expressway is daunting, to say the least. Easily accessible from all five boroughs, Jones is the most popular public beach. Also here, a pitch-putt golf course, a pool, and a much-loved summer concert series at the outdoor Jones Beach Theater featuring familiar name acts.

- **Robert Moses State Park**, Babylon, Long Island, 631-669-0470, www.nysparks. com/parks/7/details.aspx; just beyond Jones Beach, over two bridges on the Robert Moses Causeway, you'll find five more miles of beach; less well-known than Jones, but along the same Atlantic Ocean. There's a per-car fee and you can enjoy the beach or visit the picnic area until the sun goes down. You'll also find a pitch-putt golf course, playgrounds, a day-use boat basin, and more ... just 48 miles from Manhattan, or about 90 minutes when you factor in traffic.
- **Rockaway Beach**, Beach 9th Street to 149th Street, Rockaway, Queens, 718-318-4000, www.nycgovparks.org/parks/rockawaybeach; on the south shore of Long Island, though technically within city limits, Rockaway is an extremely long beach, with numerous handball courts and high, heaving waves. The weekend scene is dominated by families that live on the outer rim of Queens and hipsters attracted to the new wave of businesses that have opened here. Five hundred yards near Beach 90th Street are devoted to surfers alone, the only chunk of city beach so designated.

For information or travel directions to any of these beaches, call your preferred beach directly or the Transit Authority, 718-330-1234, for directions.

NEW YORK SEEMS LIKE THE LEAST GREEN CITY IN THE WORLD—THE average New Yorker creates four pounds of waste daily, more per capita than any other city in the world and totaling 24 million pounds of trash every day of the week. You see it everywhere, in the four-foot high piles of garbage bags on the pavement, the overflowing city garbage containers, and the rancid, smelly waters of the Gowanus Canal. But looks deceive. Thanks to its density and mass transit system, New York is also one of the most energy-efficient places in the world per capita per square foot. And now that green has become the new black, fashion-conscious Manhattanites have taken to zero-footprint living with a vengeance (if often more in image than fact). Here are some resources:

GREENING YOUR HOME

A green home or apartment is well-insulated and energy-efficient, incorporates nontoxic and sustainably produced materials, and/or has sustainable features like solar-assisted hot-water heating. Unfortunately, green materials and features tend to cost more upfront (sometimes significantly more) than non-green. Sometimes, depending on the feature, the savings gained over the lifespan of the efficiency product will recoup the premium paid in the beginning; other times, a clearer conscience is the primary reward. However, the cost gap between the idealistic and practical is rapidly closing as green technology continues to advance. Whether social consciousness or financial savvy motivates a homeowner, there are many features one can add to an existing home to make it greener.

GREEN REMODELING

Unless you own your apartment or building, traditional remodeling is not really an option in NYC. However, there has been of late a huge increase in greener building design, ranging from high-end, high-tech, entirely green-designed, and LEED-certified apartment complexes, to programs to put a lawn on everyone's roof. The New York City Department of Design and Construction, www.nyc.gov/ddc, has placed a priority on identifying and implementing cost-effective ways to promote greater environmental responsibility in building design, and its "High Performance Building Guidelines" (www.nyc.gov/html/ddc/downloads/pdf/guidelines. pdf) is one of the key works on minimizing a building's effect on the environment. Another leader in this area is the Green Building Council, which offers a national Leadership in Energy and Environmental Design (LEED) rating system. Under NYC's 2006 Green City Buildings Act, any nonresidential project costing $2 million or more must meet LEED standards. Ask your realtor if your prospective new home meets these standards.

For smaller remodeling projects, there's a whole host of tools and services. The city's **Department of Design and Construction** (www.nyc.gov/html/ddc) has a variety of publications for green remodeling on its website. The **Community Environmental Center**, 43-10 11th Street, Long Island City, 718-784-1444, www.cecenter.org, is a nonprofit group that helps smaller home-owners meet LEED standards and go as green as possible. Going green doesn't just mean micro-windmills. Some 70 million tons of building materials are thrown onto the streets of New York every day and using scavenged/recycled materials has a huge impact on the environment. **Build It Green!, with warehouses in Queens and Brooklyn,** 718-777-0132, www.bignyc.org, has 75 tons of salvaged building materials, making this nonprofit the area's leader in in low cost eco-friendly salvage. There's also Demolition Depot, 216 E 125th St, 212-860-1138, www.demolitiondepot.com, specializing in reclaimed vintage pieces, such as doors, fixtures, and the like.

Low-emission paints are now available in every serious hardware and paint store, but for more interesting possibilities, try **Green Depot**, www.greendepot. com, which has locations in Manhattan and Brooklyn. Green Depot offers a large range of eco-products, ranging from home mold-testing kits to low-flow shower heads. GrowNYC, 51 Chambers St, Room 228, 212-788-7900, www.grownyc.org, is a hands-on nonprofit dedicated to greening the city and promoting waste prevention and recycling. If you're thinking of making your building go solar, one recommended consultant is **Bright Power**, 11 Hanover Square, 21st floor, 212-803-5868, www.brightpower.biz.

ENERGY EFFICIENCY

Even if you're not able to build a 90-story green skyscraper or fund a million-dollar remodeling job, there are a number of small steps you can take to make your apartment more energy efficient without giving your landlord an excuse to evict you. The city's main website, www.nyc.gov, has a host of suggestions that are well worth looking at. Be sure to use energy-efficient appliances with the **Energy Star** label on them. Their website, www.energystar.gov, offers a store-locator engine for finding Energy Star–rated products. For smaller projects, contact **Green-HomeNYC**, www.greenhomenyc.org, a nonprofit NYC organization that helps apartment dwellers and smaller buildings become environmentally friendly. **Con Edison**, the main electricity supplier of New York, has a number of tips on its website, www.coned.com. It also lists rebates and incentives to assist with energy-saving improvements for your home.

The following are typical recommendations for boosting your home's energy efficiency:

- **Insulate and weatherize your home.** Poorly insulated walls, ceilings, and floors allow heated or cooled air to escape from your house, needlessly raising your energy use (and energy bill). In apartments, poorly sealed doors and windows can allow in huge amounts of cold air during the winter, so seal or caulk leaks around doors, windows, pipes, and vents. Replace leaky old windows with insulated windows.

- Many older apartments have central steam heaters controlled by the landlord, but this invariably means you need supplemental heat. **Be sure to investigate an energy-efficient mode of heating**—the differences can be up to 50%, in both energy use and energy bills. The same is true for air-conditioning units. For summer, utility companies suggest setting the thermostat for 78 or higher, and in the winter setting it to 68 or cooler.

- **Upgrade inefficient appliances**. Replacing old, inefficient washing machines, dishwashers, water heaters, and refrigerators with more efficient models can have a major effect on your energy consumption (and, in the case of washing machines and dishwashers, on your water consumption too). Forgo using the appliance entirely, if possible: let washed dishes and clothes air dry instead of using the dishwasher or clothes dryer.

- **Install efficient lighting**. Compact fluorescent light bulbs use 75% less energy and last up to ten times longer than standard incandescent bulbs. They also generate less heat. For an assurance of quality, choose ENERGY STAR® bulbs. (CFL bulbs do contain mercury and require special handling if they break. The state requires you to dispose of these bulbs at hazardous waste collection centers.)

- **Turn off appliances when not in use.** Many home electronics such as the TV, DVD player, computer printer, and microwave are actually in standby mode and continue to draw a small amount of power even when "off." Plug these appliances into a power strip and turn off the power strip when not in use to completely cut off the drain. Recharging devices continues to use energy even when not in use, so unplug them or attach them to a power strip and turn it off.

- **Go solar;** sure, it's pretty hard in a place like New York, but if you're determined there are small-scale solar rechargers for everything from fans to cell phones.

Going green is not cheap (although it can pay for itself in the long run). But New York State has a variety of green-building tax credits, as well as ones for using alternative energy that can be applied to various business and personal income taxes. The Green Building Tax Credit provides for tax credits to owners and tenants of eligible buildings and tenant spaces which meet certain "green" standards— talk to your accountant for more details. Federal tax credits are also available; visit the federal government's **Energy Star** website (www.energystar.gov) or the **Tax Incentives Assistance Project** (www.energytaxincentives.org) to review home-owner incentives.

RENEWABLE ENERGY

Consider buying green power from your utility. **Con Ed,** 800-752-6633, gives consumers the option of buying only wind or hydro produced energy for their home, thus increasing demand and lowering costs. Visit www.conedsolutions.com for more details. A number of alternative energy suppliers are now approved by the state to provide renewable energy. You can see which providers service your neighborhood by visiting New York State Public Service Commission's website at www.newyorkpowertochoose.com. Enter your ZIP code for a list of suppliers and a comparison chart of their services and prices.

Exhaustive water conservation advice, like washing full loads of laundry and taking shorter showers, can be found at www.dec.ny.gov, as well as at www.nyc.gov. Tax rebates are offered for installing high-efficiency clothes washers, showers, and ultra-low-flush toilets (or convert your own by putting a full liter bottle of water in the tank). The **Department of Environmental Protection** offers free water-conservation seminars on a regular basis, and will even send out inspectors to your home to check for water efficiency (you'll also get free faucet aerators and low-flow shower heads). You can call **311** to set up an appointment.

LANDSCAPING

The idea of landscaping in NYC might seem ridiculous, but a growing number of people with roof access are turning their roofs into cooling and heat conserving gardens. The state of New York recently even passed a tax credit for people who install a roof garden covering at least 50 percent of available rooftop space. One place to contact is **Sustainable South Bronx** at www.ssbx.org. Larger new buildings are now required to have a minimal amount of green covering on their roofs.

RECYCLING

It wasn't always the case, but New York now likes to brag that it has the "largest, most ambitious recycling program in the nation." True? It's hard to say for sure, but it is a fact that New Yorkers are required to recycle metal, plastic, paper, cardboard, glass, and certain electronics and household appliances. You can get a free chart detailing precisely what to recycle and how to prepare it for pick-up by calling 311 and asking for it. You can get even more detailed information and printouts, as well as a schedule for pickups of unusual materials, by going to the website of the **NYC Department of Sanitation** at www.nyc.gov/html/dsny.

In addition to the recyclables picked up by the Department of Sanitation, a host of other items is collected and recycled by private and public organizations and partnerships. Clothing, textiles, and certain electronics not collected by the city are recycled by GrowNYC, www.grownyc.org. The organization, which operates one of its main sites at the Union Square Greenmarket, also accepts certain food scraps for composting: www.grownyc.org/compost.

ENVIRONMENTALLY FRIENDLY PRODUCTS AND SERVICES

The best way to encourage the proliferation of environmentally friendly products and services is to support them. For businesses concerned about the bottom line, customer demand is the most compelling motivation to change. Here are a few resources for finding green products and services.

- *Greenopia, New York City: The Definitive Guide to More Than 1,300 Eco-Friendly Businesses and Resources* describes sustainable products and services from New York-based businesses; visit www.greenopia.com, which is far more up-to-date than the book, which was last updated in 2008.
- **Consumer Reports** maintains a website that assesses the environmental soundness of various products; the site also includes a report card for various environmental claims and labels, and assesses whether each claim is meaningful and/or verified. Visit www.greenerchoices.org.

FOOD

New York has traditionally had some of the worst, most environmentally unfriendly produce in the country. On the positive side, it was also the most expensive. Actually, it still *is* the most expensive, but the quality has increased enormously, and thanks to GreenMarkets and the locavore movement, as well as the arrival of the Whole Foods chain, it is becoming increasingly environmentally friendly.

For those concerned with eating locally, the hugely popular GreenMarket movement has been a blessing. Not only are products in these roving markets all produced locally, their quality is usually infinitely superior to anything available in stores. GrowNYC, 51 Chambers St, Room 228, 212-788-7900, www.grownyc.org, is the hands-on nonprofit dedicated to running what is now the largest farmers' market program in the country. Visit their site www.grownyc.org for market locations and times, but the one at Union Square is not to be missed, if only for the people watching.

Most grocery stores in New York have an organic produce section. In addition to seeking out organic labels, certifications such as **Salmon Safe** (www.salmon-safe.org) will assure that the source farm or vineyard uses watershed-friendly practices; the **Marine Stewardship Council** (www.msc.org) certifies seafood as being from sustainable fisheries; and the **Food Alliance** (www. foodalliance.org) certifies farms and ranches for sustainable and humane practices. Make sure the product actually says Certified Organic; the word "natural" means almost nothing.

Finally, because livestock production is resource intensive and can result in their mistreatment, the earth conscious and animal compassionate suggest reducing the amount of meat in your diet.

GREEN MONEY

Some banks, including large national banks, are making efforts to become greener in their operations and lending practices. **Bank of America** and **Citi** have promised to invest millions of dollars to go green. But the simplest way for consumers to conserve paper and fuel is to do their banking online.

For those looking to invest their money in a socially conscious manner, start your research with **GreenMoneyJournal** (www.greenmoneyjournal.com) or **The Progressive Investor** (www.sustainablebusiness.com). And don't forget **Working Assets** (www.workingassets.com), which donates a percentage of money you spend with their credit cards and landline and mobile service to worthy and environmentally friendly causes.

GREENER TRANSPORTATION

This is the one area that New York excels at. With millions of people riding the MTA every day, the car pollution problems of Los Angeles or Houston are virtually non-existent. It does, however, have its own particular form of pollution—noise. Decibel levels in the limbic netherland of the MTA can reach the level of an airplane taking off. This kind of constant noise has been associated with hypertension, exhaustion, and hearing problems. Some people wear earplugs to alleviate the noise. Others simply listen to their iPods at full blast, although the health benefit of this approach is in doubt.

If you can't bear spending over an hour ever day in the netherworld of the New York subway system, there's biking. New York is small enough to be covered on two wheels, and the city has made enormous strides to making this a viable alternative for commuters, with new bike lanes popping up on a number of major avenues. Go to www.nycbikemaps.com to see if biking makes sense for your commute. If you don't have your own bike, consider purchasing an annual membership in the city's bike share program, Citi Bike, www.citibikenyc.com.

If you have to drive, consider owning a more fuel-efficient vehicle. The most popular and efficient mass-production cars are gas-electric hybrids like the Toyota

Prius or the Honda Civic hybrid. A hybrid car consumes less fuel, and you may be entitled to federal tax credits if you buy one, as well as a New York state tax credit, plus a partial refund of your sales tax.

No matter what car you own, routine maintenance ensures that the engine runs as efficiently as possible. The nation's only environmentally friendly auto club, **Better World Club** (866-238-1137, www.betterworldclub.com), can provide roadside assistance and travel advice. They offer the full menu of auto-club services, along with discounts on hybrid rentals, bicycle roadside assistance, and an electronic newsletter.

GREEN RESOURCES

The following are just a fraction of the available resources on sustainability and environmental protection:

- **Build It Green! NYC** describes itself as the city's "only non-profit retail outlet for salvaged and surplus building materials." It has centers in Brooklyn and Queens. www.bignyc.org.
- **Carbon offsetting** relies on the theory that you can neutralize the carbon dioxide you generate by funding anti-CO_2 measures. Carbon offsets fund projects that store carbon or reduce carbon emissions from other sources, such as tree-planting projects, energy-efficiency projects, and alternative-energy investments. You can calculate how much CO_2 you're producing and buy carbon offset credits from sources like Terra Pass (877-210-9581, www.terrapass.com) or My Climate (www.myclimate.org).
- **City of New York's Department of Environmental Protection**, 311, www.nyc.gov/dep, offers information and seminars for local sustainability resources and environmental affairs.
- **New York State Department of Environmental Conservation**, 625 Broadway, Albany, New York 12233-0001, or Hunter's Point Plaza 47-40, 21st Street, Long Island City, NY 11101-5407, 718-482-4900, www.dec.ny.gov, oversees a wide range of environmental topics that affect New York residents.
- **United States Department of Energy's Energy Efficiency and Renewable Energy** website, www.energy.gov, informs consumers about renewable energy.

D ESPITE THE CITY'S RAPID PACE AND ANONYMITY, OR PERHAPS because of it, New Yorkers by the thousands volunteer their services to hundreds of worthy causes. Motivations are as varied as the tasks. So are the rewards.

A mind-boggling array of public, private, and nonprofit organizations will gladly put to use whatever talents or interests you have. Experience is not necessarily required; most institutions provide training. What kinds of jobs are available where? The single best way to connect with the right group is the **www.nycservice.org** website. It has up-to-date listings of all of New York's infinite groups and their current needs; you can search by interest, location, or both.

Below are the names of agencies that refer volunteers to other organizations or who are seeking help themselves. Addresses are in Manhattan unless otherwise noted.

AREA CAUSES

THE HUNGRY AND THE HOMELESS

Scores of volunteers concern themselves with shelter for the city's homeless. Jobs include monitoring and organizing the shelters; providing legal help; ministering to psychiatric, medical, and social needs; raising money; staffing phones; and caring for children in shelters. Many people solicit, organize, cook, and serve food to people in need at sites throughout the city. Still others deliver meals to the homeless and the homebound.

CHILDREN

If involvement with children is especially appealing, you can tutor in and out of schools, be a big brother or sister, teach music and sports in shelters or at local community centers, run activities in the parks, entertain children in hospitals, and accompany kids on weekend outings. Schools, libraries, community associations, hospitals, and other facilities providing activities and guidance for children are all worth exploring.

HOSPITALS

The need for volunteers in both city-run and private hospitals is manifold: from interpreters to laboratory personnel to admitting and nursing aides, many volunteers are required. Assistants in crisis medical areas—emergency rooms, intensive care units, and the like—are wanted if you have the skills, as are volunteers to work with victims of sexual abuse. If you just want to be helpful, you might assist in food delivery or work in the gift shop. Most city hospitals are large and busy, and many are in need of help.

THE DISABLED AND THE ELDERLY

You can read to the blind, help teach the deaf, work to prevent birth defects, and help the disabled, among others. You can also make regular visits to homebound elderly, bring hot meals to their homes, and teach everything from nutrition to arts and crafts in senior centers and nursing homes.

EXTREME CARE SITUATIONS

Helping with suicide prevention, Alzheimer's and AIDS patients, rape victims, and abused children is a special category demanding a high level of commitment—not to mention emotional reserves and, in many cases, special skills.

THE CULTURE SCENE

Museums all over the city are in need of volunteers to lead tours or lend a hand in any number of ways. Libraries, theater groups, and ballet companies have plenty of tasks that need to be done. Fund raising efforts also require many volunteers to stuff envelopes and/or make phone calls. The Public Broadcasting Service (PBS) is a good example. Its large volunteer staff raises money for its stations through extensive on-air fundraising campaigns that include collecting pledges.

THE COMMUNITY

Work in your neighborhood. Block associations and community gardens are run strictly by volunteers. You can help out at the local school, nursing home, or animal shelter.

WHERE YOU CAN HELP

SPECIFIC-NEED ORGANIZATIONS

Organizations in New York City that address a major disease, disability, or social problem are legion. For example, there's Memorial Sloan-Kettering Cancer Center, The Coalition for the Homeless, New York Association for the Blind (Lighthouse International), Literacy New York, the Gay Men's Health Crisis, Women in Need, and City Harvest, which collects and distributes food to the hungry.

INSTITUTIONS

New York's health, education, and—some would say—its very civilization rest upon the city's institutions. Hospitals, museums, libraries, schools, animal shelters, and opera and ballet companies are mostly under-funded and rely on an army of volunteers to survive.

THE RELIGIOUS CONNECTION

Individual houses of worship (in particular, those serving the homeless and the needy), and church federations such as Federation of Protestant Welfare Agencies, Catholic Charities, Lutheran Social Services, and United Jewish Appeal Federation, use volunteers for a variety of activities.

THE COMMUNITY

Block associations and neighborhood-wide organizations, such as Greenwich House in the Village and Yorkville's Civic Council, can use your talents. Citywide, there is a need for volunteers in schools, parks, and shelters, as well as in consumer affairs. The Natural Resources Defense Council, located in New York, www.nrdc.org, is a national organization dedicated to improving city centers and deterring urban sprawl.

MULTI-SERVICE ORGANIZATIONS

Don't forget such well-known groups as the Salvation Army, American Red Cross, March of Dimes, United Way, and Visiting Nurse Service (you don't have to be a nurse).

THE CORPORATE CONNECTION

Corporations encourage employee volunteerism through company-supported projects such as literacy programs, pro-bono work, and management aid to nonprofit groups. Check with the company personnel or public relations department to see if your firm is involved in any specific philanthropic projects.

REFERRAL SERVICES

If you don't know which way to turn, try one of several umbrella organizations that match volunteers with relevant organizations. At these referral services, staff members will help you determine the tasks you would be interested in doing, where, and when. Your interviewer will make specific suggestions and appointments at the places that sound appealing. Interview at several sites if you wish, and return to the referral agency until you find something you want to undertake.

- **Catholic Charities of New York**, 1011 First Ave, 11th Floor, 888-744-7900, www.catholiccharitiesny.org; affiliated with more than 100 different agencies, ranging from shelters to food kitchens. Some opportunities, such as recording books for people who have visual disabilities, can be done on your own time, from the comfort of your home. An interview may be requested.
- **Federation of Protestant Welfare Agencies**, 281 Park Ave S, 212-777-4800, www.fpwa.org; this ecumenical group, with connections to hundreds of agencies in the metropolitan area, finds jobs for volunteers of any religious background.
- **The Mayor's Volunteer Center 311**, www.nycservice.org; the center's mission: "to bridge individuals, corporations, government agencies, and non-profit organizations in order to connect people with meaningful volunteer opportunities that significantly improve the quality of life in New York City." As mentioned earlier, this enormous clearinghouse can place just about anyone in a useful position, especially in the human services, educational, and cultural areas.
- **New York Cares**, 65 Broadway, 19th floor, 212-228-5000, www.newyorkcares.org; a favorite volunteer organization among busy young professionals who are discouraged by the time commitments required by other organizations. New York Cares lets its thousands of volunteers choose from a monthly calendar of events set up with the more than 50 not-for-profit organizations they serve. Projects include reading with homeless children, serving brunch at soup kitchens, cleaning public parks, and visiting elderly homebound. Call to attend one of the weekly orientation meetings.
- **The United Jewish Appeal-Federation of Jewish Philanthropies**, 130 E 59th St, 212-980-1000, www.ujafedny.org; the Jewish Information Referral Service helps match volunteers with one of many projects, including revitalizing old neighborhoods and synagogues, as well as working with children, immigrants, the elderly, and the homeless.
- **The Volunteer Referral Center**, 161 Madison Ave, 212-889-4805, www.volunteer-referral.org; interviews by appointment. The center places adult and student volunteers at some 250 not-for-profit agencies throughout the city.

OTHER CONNECTIONS

- **Check bulletin boards** at your office, church, neighborhood grocery store, laundromat, and school.
- **Walk into local** churches, temples, community organizations, and/or libraries.
- **Big Brothers/Big Sisters of New York City**, www.bigsnyc.org
- **Hearts & Minds**, www.heartsandminds.org/linksnyc, for volunteering or donations
- **VolunteerMatch.org** offers a searchable database of volunteer options

What follows is a far-from-exhaustive listing of some of the main community, national, and international groups, broken down by category.

HUMAN RIGHTS

- **American Civil Liberties Union**, ACLU, 125 Broad St, 19th Floor, 212-607-3300, www.aclu.org/affiliate/new-york; specializes in constitutional, legal, and human rights
- **Brennan Center for Justice**, 161 Ave of the Americas, 12th floor, 646-292-8310, www.brennancenter.org; nonprofit focused on constitutional issues and human rights
- **The Legal Aid Society of New York**, 199 Water St, 212-577-3300, www.legal-aid.org; helps underrepresented defendants and does research to reform the legal system
- **The Osborne Association**, 809 Westchester Ave, 718-707-2600, www.osborneny.org; specializes in reforming the criminal system and aiding defendants

SUBSTANCE ABUSE

- **Alcoholics Anonymous of New York**, 307 Seventh Ave, Room 201, 212-647-1680, www.nyintergroup.org; the Manhattan central organization for Alcoholics Anonymous
- **Alcoholism Council of New York, Inc.**, 2 Washington St, 7th Floor, 212-252-7001, www.alcoholism.org
- **Cocaine Anonymous of NY**, 212-COCAINE, www.canewyork.org
- **El Regreso, Inc.**, 189-191 South 2nd St, 718-384-6400; specializes in substance abuse services, providing bilingual (English-Spanish) service for Hispanic populations
- **Narcotics Anonymous, Inc.**, 154 Christopher St, Suite 1A, 212-929-6262, www.newyorkna.org
- **Phoenix House**, 888-286-5027, www.phoenixhouse.org; national organization with NY centers specializing in drug abuse, especially among youth

MENTORING

- **Big Brothers and Sisters of New York**, 223 E 30th St, 212-686-2042, www. bigsnyc.org; local headquarters of this national organization
- **Catholic Big Sisters and Big Brothers**, 137 E 2nd St, 212-475-3291, www.cbsbb. org; Catholic-run group that has been working with children for over a century
- **iMentor NYC**, 30 Broad St, 9th Floor, 212-461-4330, www.imentor.org; specializes in arranging mentoring in schools
- **Mentoring USA**, 5 Hanover Square, 17th floor, 212-400-7000, www.helpusa.org; a national organization that will connect anyone with a mentoring opportunity

SENIORS

- **Jewish Association Serving the Aging (JASA)**, multiple locations across the boroughs, 212-273-5272, www.jasa.org; an organization that provides multiple services with a focus on the Jewish community
- **New York Foundation for Senior Citizens**, 11 Park Pl, 212-962-7559, www. nyfsc.org
- **SAGE**, 305 7th Ave, 15th Floor, 212-741-2247, www.sageusa.org; specializes in senior services for the gay, lesbian, and transgendered communities

CULTURE AND THE ARTS

- **Astor Place Theater**, 434 Lafayette St, 212-254-4370, www.blueman.com
- **Cherry Lane Theatre**, 38 Commerce St, 212-989-2020, www.cherrylanetheatre. com
- **The Joyce Theater**, 175 Eighth Ave, 212-691-9740, www.joyce.org
- **Lucille Lortel Theatre**, 121 Christopher St, 212-924-2817; www.lortel.org
- **Manhattan Theatre Club**, 261 W 47th St and 131 W 55th St, 212-239-6200, www.mtc-nyc.org
- **New York Philharmonic**, Avery Fisher Hall, 10 Lincoln Center Plaza, 212-875-5900, www.nyphil.org
- **New York Theatre Workshop (NYTW)**, 79 E 4th St., 212-780-9037, www.nytw.org
- **Roundabout Theatre Company**, American Airlines Theatre, 227 W 42nd St; 212-719-9393, www.roundabouttheatre.org
- **Second Stage Theatre**, 305 W 43rd St and 2162 Broadway; 212-787-8302; www.secondstagetheatre.com
- **Signature Theatre Company**, 480 W 42nd St., 212-244-7529; www.signaturetheatre.org

GAY ISSUES

- **Gay Men's Health Crisis**, 446 W 33rd St, 212-367-1000, www.gmhc.org; one of New York's oldest health organizations, servicing the gay, lesbian, bisexual, and transgender communities
- **Harlem United**, 306 Lenox Ave, 212-803-2850, www.harlemunited.org; provides a range of supportive services, from case management to medical and housing, to people living with HIV/AIDS
- **Housing Works**, various locations, 347-473-7400, www.housingworks.org; a full-service social service agency for people living with HIV/AIDS
- **International Gay & Lesbian Human Rights Commission**, 80 Maiden Ln, 212-430-6054, www.iglhrc.org; focuses on international and national human rights issues pertaining to the gay community
- **SAGE**, 305 7th Ave, 15th Floor, 212-741-2247, www.sageusa.org; specializes in senior services for the gay, lesbian, and transgendered communities

ANIMAL RIGHTS

- **ASPCA**, American Society for the Prevention of Cruelty to Animals, 212-876-7700, www.aspca.org

LITERACY

- **Community Impact at Columbia University**, 2980 Broadway, 105 Earl Hall, 212-854-1492, www.columbia.edu/cu/ci; serves the communities near Columbia University
- **Little Sisters of the Assumption Family Health Service**, 333 E 115th St, 646-672-5200, www.littlesistersfamily.org; working in East Harlem, this group offers a number of services, specializing in children and education

HOUSING AND THE HOMELESS

Scores of volunteers concern themselves with shelter for the city's homeless. Jobs include monitoring and organizing shelters; providing legal help; ministering to psychiatric, medical, and social needs; raising money; and organizing, cooking, and serving food at sites throughout the city. Still others deliver meals to the homeless and the homebound, or spend one night a month bedded down in a homeless shelter to make sure it runs smoothly. Many soup kitchens tend to be overwhelmed with well-meaning volunteers during the winter holidays, when they can use help year-round. So consider pitching in "off season." The list of shelters following the general organizations are actively seeking volunteers.

- **Bowery Mission**, 227 Bowery, 212-674-3456, www.bowery.org

- **Broadway Housing Communities**, 583 Riverside Dr., 212-568-2030, www. broadwayhousing.org; specializes in finding affordable housing for the homeless, including their own temporary apartment complex
- **Food Bank for New York City**, 39 Broadway, 212-566-7855, www.foodbanknyc. org; a key central resource for a variety of homeless organizations focused on food access and distribution
- **Grand Central Neighborhood Social Services Corporation (GCNSSC)**, 120 E 32nd St, 212-883-0680, www.grandcentralneighborhood.org
- **Holy Apostles Soup Kitchen**, 296 9th Ave, 212-924-0167, www.holyapostlessoupkitchen.org
- **Homes for the Homeless**, 50 Cooper Square, 212-529-5252, www.hfhnyc.org
- **New York City Department of Homeless Services**, 311, www.nyc.gov/dhs; umbrella group for official and unofficial homeless service groups
- **New York City Rescue Mission**, 90 Lafayette St, 212-226-6214, www.nycrescue. org
- **Part of the Solution**, 2759 Webster Ave, The Bronx, 718-220-4892, www. potsbronx.org
- **Sanctuary for Families**, 212-349-6009, www.sanctuaryforfamilies.org
- **Trinity Church's Services and Food for the Homeless**, Inc., 602 E 9th St, 212-228-5254, www.safhnyc.org
- **St. Paul's House**, 335 W 51st St, 212-265-5433, www.saintpaulshouse.org

WOMEN AND CHILDREN

- **A Caring Hand**, The Billy Esposito Foundation, 212-229-2273, www. acaringhand.org; helps people, especially children, deal with grief
- **Center Against Domestic Violence**, 25 Chapel St, Suite 904, Brooklyn, 718-439-1000, www.cadvny.org; counseling and placement for survivors of domestic abuse
- **Child Development Support Corporation**, 352-358 Classon Ave, Brooklyn, 718-398-2050, www.cdscnyc.org; specializes in a variety of services for children
- **Grace Institute**, 1233 Second Ave, 212-832-7605, www.graceinstitute.org; national organization whose mission is to empower uneducated women
- **Neighbors Together Corporation**, 2094 Fulton St, Brooklyn, 718-498-7256, www.neighborstogether.org; soup kitchen that provides social services

NEW YORK CITY TEEMS WITH PEOPLE, WITH FAITHS, AND WITH PLACES in which those people may practice those faiths and in many cases devote themselves to one of the many social problems listed above. Whether you seek the orthodox, the scholarly, the ecumenical, the activist, or an approach to faith beyond your previous experience, you can find a community here. There are an estimated 2,300 churches (not counting storefront Pentecostals) and some 650 synagogues in New York City. Finding a suitable church or synagogue may be as simple as following the suggestion of an acquaintance. Or it may be as intensely personal and complex as choosing a spouse. The houses of worship listed below alphabetically were chosen specifically for their possible appeal to newcomers. (Addresses are in Manhattan unless otherwise noted.)

BAHÁ'Í

- **New York City Bahá'í Center**, 53 E 11th St, 212-674-8998, www.bahainyc.org; conducts devotions and discussion Sunday at 11 a.m.

BUDDHIST

- **New York Buddhist Church**, 331-332 Riverside Dr, 212-678-0305, www.newyorkbuddhistchurch.org; a stunning bronze statue of Shinran Shonin in front of this landmarked building marks the presence of this Shin Buddhist Temple. Regular Dharma service in English at 11:30 a.m. Sunday is occasionally preceded by a service in Japanese. In addition, there are regularly scheduled Dharma study classes for adults and for children, meditation sessions, and other classes offered in various subjects.
- **Soka Gakkai International—USA**, 7 E 15th St, 212-727-7715, www.sgi-usa.org; with lectures, discussions, and group chants for some 5,000 area members

who practice the Buddhism of Nichiren Daishonin. It's a warm and accepting community in a harmonious Romanesque Revival building.

CHRISTIAN

BAPTIST

- **Calvary Baptist Church**, 123 W 57th St, 212-975-0170, www.cbcnyc.org, across from Carnegie Hall, is probably the largest Baptist Church in Manhattan. You might begin a typical Sunday at the 9:30 a.m. contemporary praise and worship service, followed by a Young Professionals' topical Bible study and fellowship at 11 a.m., and then coffee. Traditional worship service is at 11 a.m. Young Adult Ministries offers occasional weekend retreats, and there are outreach programs to the prison population, the poor, and children in need.

EPISCOPAL

- **Cathedral of St. John the Divine**, 1047 Amsterdam Ave at 112th St, 212-316-7540, www.stjohndivine.org, dwarfs its surroundings even as it awaits the (hopeful) completion of its stone towers. One of the largest cathedrals in the world—at once Byzantine, Romanesque, and Gothic—it is truly awesome, especially inside, where spectacular stained glass windows light the vast dark vaults and music echoes ethereally. It is also a bustling and exciting community church, a leader in the movement to feed and house the poor. And the performing arts flourish here almost around the clock. Don't miss the blessing of the animals on the first Sunday of October in honor of St. Francis.
- **Church of the Ascension**, Fifth Ave at 10th St, 212-254-8620, www.ascensionnyc.org; its communicants find this church especially pleasing aesthetically. A LaFarge altar fresco and a St. Gaudens altar relief enliven the quietly tasteful interior, and liturgical music of the highest quality in special evening concerts is a welcome treat.
- **Church of the Heavenly Rest**, 2 E 90th St at Fifth Ave, 212-289-3400, www.heavenlyrest.org, sits confidently but unostentatiously—in stripped contemporary Gothic in pale gray stone—facing Central Park. It's an upscale neighborhood family church, where the congregants stay for coffee after the morning service while the children play decorously about the door.
- **Grace Church**, 802 Broadway, 212-254-2000, www.gracechurchnyc.org, despite its rather patrician, lacy English Gothic elegance, is relatively low church. Worship is traditional, however, with wonderful music, especially on holy days. The congregation runs to young families and a variety of students and artists. Pastoral counseling is available, as well as adult classes on a variety of topics. Also: outreach groups to college students and people with HIV/AIDS, programs for

children and families, and the popular Bach at Noon program, an open service for prayer and meditation.

- **St. Bartholomew's**, 325 Park Ave, 212-378-0200, www.stbarts.org; this landmarked Romanesque-Byzantine church houses a friendly, welcoming community numbering about 1,000 worshipers each Sunday. Lay participation in all aspects of church life is encouraged. Sundays feature a stimulating Rector's Forum and Sunday School, in addition to several services, and Bible studies are offered during the week. Several adult social clubs offer a variety of social, athletic, and theatrical activities. Communicants and non-members alike volunteer at the homeless shelter and the feeding program operated by the church.
- **St. James'**, 865 Madison Ave, 212-774-4200, www.stjames.org; distinctly Upper East Side, this trim brownstone is a warm, neighborhood family church that is also decidedly activist in the community and beyond: feeding, mentoring, supporting, and sometimes even demonstrating. Despite its rather liberal bent, St. James' is moderately high church. Its education programs for adults and children are worthy of note.
- **Trinity Church**, 74 Trinity Place, 212-602-0800, www.trinitywallstreet.org; this Neo-Gothic church dominated New York's skyline when it was finished in 1846. Now a bit more tucked away, it offers a peaceful respite to bustling lower Manhattan. Daily services, community outreach, and fellowship are all part of Trinity's ministry. This was one of the key bases for relief work during the 2001 WTC attack.

GREEK ORTHODOX CHURCHES

- **Cathedral of the Holy Trinity**, 337 E 4th St, St, 212-288-3215, www.thecathedral. nyc.org; tucked away among the modern buildings on the Upper East Side of Manhattan, this church has stood since the 1890s when it was originally built as a Protestant church. Today the church includes a full parochial school program, nursery through eighth grade, as well as afternoon language classes and Sunday school classes. Cultural and human services programs can also be found.
- **St. Demetrios Cathedral**, 30-11 30th Dr, Astoria, Queens, 718-728-1718, www. saintdemetriosastoria.com/cathedral; Serving New York's large Greek Orthodox community, St. Demetrios was built in 1927 and features the architectural stylings of the Byzantine cathedrals of Athens. Adult Greek language courses and Sunday school classes are offered.
- **St. Irene Chrysovalantou**, 36-07 23rd Ave, Astoria, Queens, 718-626-6225, www.stirene.org; newer, and slightly larger than nearby St. Demetrios', St. Irene's is a large converted Protestant church with a grand and elaborate interior design. A full complement of elementary and junior high school programs is offered, plus many youth and teen activities. A daycare center is also available weekdays from 9 a.m. to 5 p.m.

INTERDENOMINATIONAL

- **Chelsea Community Church**, 346 W 20th St, 212-886-5463, www. chelseachurch.org, is a nondenominational Christian church welcoming "persons of all faiths and of uncertain faith" at its lay-led Sunday services at noon in historic St. Peter's Church.
- **Judson Memorial**, 55 Washington Square S, 212-477-0351, www.judson.org; worldly young adults and seminarians are attracted to this ornate Romanesque church designed by Stanford White and its fairly traditional Protestant liturgy with progressive elements, including a monthly Agape Meal. There is a consumer health library and support for people with HIV/AIDS.
- **Riverside**, 490 Riverside Dr, 212-870-6700, www.theriversidechurchny.org; this towering Gothic gift of John D. Rockefeller, Jr., dominates the heights overlooking the Hudson River. Inspired by Chartres, it boasts spectacular stained glass and beautifully carved stone in the large but simple nave and chancel, and about the entrance. The congregation is widely known for activism and political debate; there are also plentiful opportunities for involvement in musical, intellectual, and social, not to mention spiritual, activities.

LATTER-DAY SAINTS/MORMON

- **The Church of Jesus Christ of Latter-Day Saints**; in Manhattan, the Mormon temple is located at 125 Columbus Avenue at 65th St (across from Lincoln Center), 917-441-8220, www.lds.org; several different congregations (called "wards" and "branches") conduct worship services every Sunday in three-hour blocks, beginning at 9 a.m. These include English-speaking "family" wards, an English-speaking ward for single adults, Spanish-speaking wards, and a deaf branch. Also, each congregation offers social and musical activities during the week.

LUTHERAN

- **Holy Trinity**, Central Park at 3 W 65th St, 212-877-6815, www.holytrinitynyc. org; offers challenging preaching at traditional, rigorously Lutheran services. But it is music, at the regular services and at the Sunday vespers, featuring Bach cantatas with professional musicians for which Holy Trinity is widely known (go to www.bachvespersnyc.org for more information). The sturdy Gothic Revival church is the setting for frequent evening concerts as well.
- **St. Peter's**, 619 Lexington Ave, 212-935-2200, www.saintpeters.org; sleek and angular like a modern stone tent, St. Peter's is nestled beneath the towering Citicorp Center. A large Louise Nevelson sculpture punctuates the stark, light interior, scene of a sung Mass with traditional liturgy in the morning and Jazz Vespers with jazz as the sermon Sunday afternoons. Classical and jazz concerts, often free, theater, and provocative adult-forum lectures attract an ecumenical following.

METHODIST

- **Christ Church**, 524 Park Ave, 212-838-3036, www.christchurchnyc.org, is sedately Byzantine outside, dazzlingly so inside, every inch covered with mosaics in blazing blues, greens, and gold. It's a wonderful setting for the religious music-dramas occasionally performed here. The congregation, though relatively small, supports a weekly soup kitchen and excellent pastoral counseling.
- **John Street Church**, 44 John St, 212-269-0014, www.johnstreetchurch.org; to step into this landmarked little Italianate brownstone church (1841) among the towering monoliths of the financial district is to step out of place and time into a peaceful haven of creamy modest proportions and brass sconces. It's the oldest Methodist society in the U.S., and few know about it. Inquire about the occasional Wednesday noon hymn-sings.
- **Park Avenue United Methodist Church**, 106 E 86th St, 212-427-5421, www.parkavemethodist.org; a mixed and growing congregation, mostly young families and singles, is attracted by the moderately liberal approach and active social scene at this smallish, restfully intimate, Moorish-looking church. Adult Bible study precedes and a coffee hour follows the traditional Sunday service with volunteer choir.
- **Church of St. Paul and St. Andrew**, 263 W 86th St, 212-362-3179, www.stpaulandstandrew.org; with a large children's program, extensive outreach, and a devotion to the arts, this Romanesque church, more than a century old, is home to many: the sanctuary is shared with B'nai Jeshurun, a Conservative Jewish Congregation, and The Sacred Center of New York; the New York Arabic Orchestra's home is here; and the West End Theatre on the second floor houses five professional companies. Various ministries reach out to serve community needs.

PRESBYTERIAN

- **Brick Church**, 62 E 92nd St, 212-289-4400, www.brickchurch.org; staid neo-Georgian with a rather ornate interior, is distinctly Park Ave. But the welcome is friendly, including a popular coffee hour after the Sunday service. The church's day school is prestigious.
- **Fifth Avenue**, 7 W 55th St, 212-247-0490, www.fapc.org; the city's largest Presbyterian Church has a warm, woody interior behind its otherwise undistinguished brownstone facade. A variety of social fellowship groups attract large numbers to the traditional services. Activities of these groups may include Sunday night church suppers, after-church brunch, movies, and ski retreats, as well as dinner meetings with outside speakers at the Women's Roundtable (for businesswomen) and the Men's Fellowship. Also here, a Center for Christian Studies. Fees are minimal and non-members are welcome.
- **Madison Avenue Presbyterian Church**, 921 Madison Ave, 212-288-8920, www.mapc.com, has a cozy, Scottish feel, with its Gothic-timbered white walls,

carved pews, and galleries. The music program is strong, including a volunteer choir and frequent Sunday afternoon concerts. You'll also find an adult education program and young adult fellowship group that meets for Bible study, discussion, and socializing.

- **Redeemer Presbyterian**, church office at 1359 Broadway, 4th floor, 212-808-4460, www.redeemer.com; this congregation has three locations: one downtown at The Salvation Army at 120 W 14th St; one on the East Side at the Hunter College Auditorium at 695 Park Ave; and one on the West Side at 150 W 83rd St. The scripture-based emphasis is on preaching, which is intellectually engaging, and there is an array of spiritual, social, and outreach activities.

ROMAN CATHOLIC CHURCHES

Most Catholics attend Mass near their home or office. But there are a few churches that, for one reason or another, attract worshipers from beyond the parish confines. One of these may suit you. Contact the Archdiocese of New York, 212-371-1000, or the Archdiocese of Brooklyn (also handles Queens), 718-399-5900, for your local parish. Or go to www.ny-archdiocese.org.

- **Cathedral-Basilica of St. James**, 250 Cathedral Pl (at Jay St near Tillary St), Brooklyn Heights, 718-852-4002, www.brooklyncathedral.net, was built in 1822 and restored in recent years to a Georgian brick elegance befitting its prominence. St. James is Brooklyn's cathedral, a bishop's church, but it is also a non-territorial parish, and is especially popular among young professionals in the area, for whom the daily business communion at 12:10 is a special convenience. Mass here is traditional and the music quite wonderful.
- **Church of the Epiphany**, 239 E 21st St, 212-475-1966, www.epiphanychurchnyc. org; is at once striking and modest, an unusually successful modern structure of rounded verticals in brown brick. It's a family church, with a traditional Mass at noon and a popular family mass to guitar accompaniment at 10 a.m. There is also a Sunday evening mass. But there's a difference, for one thing, altar girls. Nuns are involved in work traditionally done by priests, and women's issues are addressed. The church is popular with young professionals in the community, and there is a social action group.
- **Church of St. Agnes**, 143 E 43rd St, 212-682-5722, www.stagneschurchnyc. org, is convenient to Grand Central Terminal and offers multiple daily masses, including a Latin Mass, Sundays at 11 a.m. There is also a small gift and book shop on site.
- **Church of St. Thomas More**, 65 E 89th St, 212-876-7718, www.thomasmore-church.org; stone Victorian Gothic, was built as an Episcopal Church and still feels a bit like one, with its intimately peaceful, fragrant interior beneath a timbered ceiling. Ever so decorous. You can linger for coffee after 10 o'clock Mass.

- **St. Francis Xavier**, 46 W 16th St, 212-627-2100, www.sfxavier.org; this hulking, gray stone Jesuit presence dominates the block between Fifth and Sixth Avenues. The style here is rather less formal than you might expect, perhaps because the congregation covers such a broad social spectrum: Hispanics, knowledgeable Catholic activists, and young professionals. Actively involved in the community, the church shelters the homeless and serves 800 meals a week. It's equally busy on the spiritual front, with lay spirituality group retreats, healing Masses, and discussion groups for a fiercely devoted following.
- **St. Ignatius Loyola**, 980 Park Ave, 212-288-3588, www.stignatiusloyola.org; this solidly limestone Italian Baroque structure is definitely high church and upscale: incense, ornate vestments, and a fine professional choir at the traditionally sung morning High Mass. But the rigorous Jesuit approach is apparent in a strongly social and economic outlook from the pulpit. At 11 a.m. you can attend a folk Mass in the undercroft (Wallace Hall) and linger over coffee. The church is also known for its series of formal musical programs featuring the fine choir and organist as well as visiting musicians. Contemporary music Sundays at 7:30 p.m.
- **St. John the Baptist**, 210 W 31st St, 212-564-9070, www.padrepioshrine.com; as a distinct sideline to its normal parish activities, is host to the Catholic charismatic movement in Manhattan. There are seminars, prayer meetings, and a monthly charismatic Mass.
- **St. Joseph's**, 371 Ave of the Americas at Washington Place, 212-741-1274, www.washingtonsquarecatholic.org; in the heart of Greenwich Village, appeals to a variety of Catholics in the neighborhood and even outside the city. At once a bustling family church and an aesthetic experience, with professional musicians performing at traditional Masses and at evening concerts; distinctly high church. The lovely stone and stucco Greek Revival structure, resplendent inside with creamy plaster, crystal chandeliers and wide, carved balconies, is the oldest Catholic Church in the city (1833), and the first to open a shelter for homeless men.
- **St. Patrick's Cathedral**, 460 Madison Ave, 212-753-2261, saintpatrickscathedral.org; this looming Gothic-style cathedral is the seat of the Archbishop of New York.

UNITARIAN

- **All Souls**, 1157 Lexington Ave at 80th St, 212-535-5530, www.allsoulsnyc.org; New England simple and elegant, from 1891, this Federal-style brick church looks Unitarian. As might be expected here, the busy church calendar tends toward activism on a variety of fronts including running a soup kitchen and tutoring children. A fairly intellectual approach to adult education features book groups, films, and lectures. Music is stressed. Social activities are many and varied, including a Career Networking Group.

ETHICAL SOCIETIES

Ethical societies offer a meeting place and fellowship to members and visitors. Their "focus is on core ethical values that people have in common." Acknowledging that humans are both individualistic and social in nature, the society explores what it means to understand the inner workings of self and how to relate to each other in a respectful/ethical/moralistic way. For more information go to www.aeu.org.

- **Brooklyn Society for Ethical Culture**, 53 Prospect Park W, Brooklyn, 718-768-2972, www.bsec.org
- **New York Society for Ethical Culture**, 2 West 64th St, 212-874-5210, www.nysec.org
- **Riverdale-Yonkers Society for Ethical Culture**, 4450 Fieldston Rd, The Bronx, 718-548-4445, www.rysec.org

HINDU

- **Ramakrishna Vivekananda Center**, 17 E 94th St, 212-534-9445, www.ramakrishna.org, is a Vedanta Hindu Temple of universal worship with a Sunday lecture service at 11 a.m. Tuesday evenings at 8 are devoted to the reading and discussion of the gospel of Sri Ramakrishna, and there's a Bhagavad Gita class each Friday at 8 p.m.
- **Vedanta Society**, 34 W 71st St, 212-877-9197, wwww.vedantany.org, is affiliated with the Ramakrishna Math and Mission in India. The shrine room is open for meditation daily from 9 a.m. to 6 p.m. There is a lecture Sunday at 11 a.m. and classes Tuesday and Friday evenings.

ISLAM

MOSQUES

- **The Mosque of New York**, in the Islamic Cultural Center, 1711 Third Ave, 212-722-5234, www.icc-ny.us; this imposing structure, the gift of a group of Islamic countries, houses the largest of more than 100 mosques in the city. The design is modern, with numerous references to traditional elements of Muslim architecture. The effect is at once peaceful and spiritual. In addition to the weekly congregational prayer service, the mosque is open for daily prayer at the five prescribed times. There are classes for children and adults, which cover a range of Islamic topics. There are Saturday classes for women only.
- **Muslim Center of New York**, 137-58 Geranium Ave, Flushing, 718-460-3000, www.muslimcenter.org, serves the large Muslim community in Queens and Long Island. In a modest neighborhood, an octagonal minaret rises from the polished rose quartz structure. Congregational prayers Friday at 1:15 p.m. are followed by Koranic studies. There are Sunday school and weekday afternoon religious school for children. Call for hours.

JEWISH

REFORM SYNAGOGUES

- **Brooklyn Heights Synagogue**, 131 Remsen St, Brooklyn, 718-522-2070, www. bhsbrooklyn.org; services here are characterized by a greater use of Hebrew and more congregational singing than is generally found in reform syna- gogues. The warmth and friendliness of this relatively small congregation and their purposeful inclusiveness makes this a particularly appealing synagogue for newcomers. Congregants come from all the boroughs; numbers swell so suf- ficiently on the high holy days that these services are held in a church nearby.
- **Central Synagogue**, 652 Lexington Ave, 212-838-5122, www.centralsynagogue. org, is the oldest Jewish house of worship (1872) in continuous use in New York. The Moorish brownstone structure with its interior richly stenciled in red, blue, and gold suffered extensive damage from a fire in 1998. Restoration is now complete and the traditionally oriented synagogue tends to the manifold inter- ests, worldly as well as spiritual, of its 2,300-family congregation in groups and classes ranging from Hebrew and Yiddish to Bible to bridge, teens' and singles' groups. Hebrew school.
- **Temple Emanu-El**, 1 E 65th St, 212-744-1400, www.emanuelnyc.org, is perhaps a little less traditional, nevertheless classical Reform in approach, and it is the largest reform temple in the US. The landmarked limestone Moorish-Roman- esque temple facing Central Park seats 2,500 beneath a high, colorfully painted wood ceiling and stunning stained glass windows. The temple has a large staff to run its many facilities, classes, and community outreach programs, as well as a large religious school. Services are broadcast every Friday evening at 5:30 over WQXR (96.3 FM).

CONSERVATIVE SYNAGOGUES

- **Ansche Chesed**, 251 W 100th St, 212-865-0600, www.anschechesed.org, houses four separate congregations, each with a different approach to Conser- vative Judaism, in one medium-sized, squat, brick building. Alternatives within a framework of Jewish tradition are stressed at this much-talked-about West Side synagogue, which offers an adult beginners' service, courses on a wide range of Jewish topics, and social action projects.
- **B'nai Jeshurun**, 257 W 88th St, 212-787-7600, www.bj.org; emphasis is on study, with a variety of adult courses and lectures, as well as a Hebrew school for children. The diverse congregation thinks of itself as a community, with a strong commitment to social action, Tikkun Olam, in the wider Jewish and non- Jewish community beyond. Plan to come early for services, which tend to fill up fast; non-members will want to call about high holy days.

- **Brotherhood**, 28 Gramercy Park S, 212-674-5750, www.brotherhoodsynagogue. org, occupies a landmarked (1859) Friends' Meeting House, starkly beautiful in Italianate brownstone and overlooking lovely Gramercy Park. About its courtyards are housed a shelter for the homeless, a religious school, adult education, and an educational program for the developmentally disabled.
- **Kane Street Synagogue**, 236 Kane St, Cobble Hill, Brooklyn 718-875-1550, www.kanestreet.org; has grown considerably in recent years, partly, perhaps, because of the emphasis on egalitarianism in its observances. Vibrant and involved, with challenging study groups, it is regularly packed with congregants, mainly young, from Cobble Hill and nearby Brooklyn Heights.
- **Park Avenue Synagogue**, 50 E 87th St, 212-369-2600, www.pasyn.org, is the city's largest conservative temple and an East Side Moorish landmark in carved golden stone. The rich interior boasts fine stained glass, sculpture, and paintings, and the traditional services are distinctly formal, with organ and choir. There are programs for children and a food pantry for the neighborhood's hungry.
- **Shaare Zedek**, 212 W 93rd St, 212-874-7005, www.sznyc.org; this congregation, founded nearly 200 years ago on the Lower East Side and housed now in a gray stone Greek Revival temple on the Upper West Side, experienced a revival in the mid-1990s with an infusion of college students and young professionals. Friday evening services, usually downstairs in the social halls, can be especially busy. Special events fill out the social calendar.
- **Town and Village Synagogue**, 334 E 14th St, 212-677-8090, www.tandv.org, stresses sexual egalitarianism in its informally innovative, traditional services and attracts an involved family congregation, largely from the adjacent community, including Stuyvesant Town and Peter Cooper Village. Adult education and a young married group are both popular. The Sol Goldman YW-YMHA of the Educational Alliance next door, with whom it shares a Hebrew school, offers members the advantages of a social center with a pool, gym, and classes.
- **United Synagogue of Hoboken**, 115 Park Ave, Hoboken, NJ, 201-659-4000, www.hobokensynagogue.org; Friday evening and Sabbath services are in the converted Victorian brownstone Hudson Street temple, the last of many serving the predominantly German Jewish community here. The small but growing egalitarian congregation is youngish and welcoming. Extensive adult education courses include Hebrew reading and Jewish history, a Hebrew discussion group, a book club, Jewish women's and men's discussion groups, karate, and adult bar and bat mitzvah instruction. There is also a Hebrew School for children.

ORTHODOX SYNAGOGUES

- **The 16th Street Synagogue** holds its weekday services at Congregation Etz Chaim at 11 East 11th Street and its Shabbat/Yom Tov services at The Sixth Street Community Synagogue at 325 East 6th Street, www.sixteenthstreetsynagogue. org; modern Orthodoxy, observing all the Orthodox forms, including separate seating of the sexes, but emphasizing programs serving the entire family. This includes communal singing and participation, youth and singles programs, outreach, adult education, and attention to community needs.

- **Kehilath Jeshurun**, 125 E 85th St, 212-774-5600, www.ckj.org; though old and rich and housed in classical Romanesque gray stone, this is probably the most progressive of the Orthodox congregations. Its size makes possible a host of activities for singles, couples, and children, recreational facilities, and an educational program. Emphasis is placed on outreach to beginners and singles, with classes, special services, and Friday night dinners for them.
- **Lincoln Square**, 180 Amsterdam Ave, 212-874-6100, www.lss.org, sometimes referred to as "the hip synagogue," might be described physically as synagogue-modern, thanks to its popularity among young professionals who pack its Saturday services.
- **Shearith Israel**, 2 W 70th St, 212-873-0300, www.shearithisrael.org; known as the Spanish and Portuguese synagogue, is the oldest Jewish congregation in the U.S., dating from 1654, when a group of Sephardic Jews arrived from Brazil. In the formal sanctuary scholarly rabbis conduct formal services, which offer the best opportunity to observe Sephardic tradition and music. Excellent adult education explores Sephardic and Ashkenazi culture and tradition, with visiting scholars leading seminars. There are special educational and social events for young adults.
- **Tribeca Synagogue** (also known as Synagogue for the Arts and formerly known as Civic Center), 49 White St, west of Broadway, 212-966-7141, occupies a small, award-winning, modern structure scrunched among cast iron manufacturing lofts and loading docks. Its flame-shaped interior houses a membership of about 100 families with about 1,000 supporters, including elderly members of long standing, as well as artists and young professionals from surrounding Tribeca, Independence Plaza, and Battery Park. There are both Hebrew and adult education classes, as well as parenting sessions conducted by Educational Alliance West.

OTHER

- **Congregation Beit Simchat Torah**, 57 Bethune St, 212-929-9498, www.cbst.org; purported to be the largest gay and lesbian Jewish congregation in the world, it was founded in 1973. The rabbi is Reconstructionist, the community liberal, and the services traditional, with egalitarian minyans rotating among traditional, liberal, tot shabbat, junior congregation, family minyan, and Hebrew egalitarian; Saturdays at 10 a.m. Friday evening services are so heavily attended the congregation moves to the Church of the Holy Apostles at 296 9th Ave.
- **Society for the Advancement of Judaism**, 15 West 86th St, 212-724-7000, www.thesaj.org; known as the SAJ, this is the original Reconstructionist synagogue. Reconstructionism, which attempts to reconcile traditional Conservatism with modern life, views Judaism as evolving rather than divinely inspired. The Torah

is observed, and services are largely traditional, but egalitarian. The approach here is distinctly intellectual, not social.

• **West End Synagogue**, 190 Amsterdam Ave, 212-579-0777, www. westendsynagogue.org, is a popular Reconstructionist congregation flourishing with a slightly more emotional, interpersonal emphasis and monthly Shabbat dinners as well as concerts, debates, and social action programs. Also a Hebrew school.

GETTING AROUND

BY SUBWAY

People are the lifeblood of New York City, and the subway is the circulatory system in which they travel. It is also the great equalizer: all manner of people, from the wealthy broker to the night-time porter, from the lowly tourist to the mayor himself vie for the same seats, inhale the same pungent odors, and curse the same just-missed train. It is the quickest way around town, and—despite regular fare hikes—still one of the cheapest. Its 660-plus miles of track and the trains that run on them are managed by the Metropolitan Transit Authority (MTA), which in conjunction with the NYPD, has managed to substantially decrease crime. One should of course remain aware of one's surroundings and use common sense.

As intimidating as the system is at first, it will be a short matter of time before you wonder why you had fretted. There are numerous resources that will help you better understand the subway system, including maps that are posted in every car and station (free maps are also available at station booths), and the MTA web page, www.mta.info, but your most ubiquitous resource for help will be your fellow citizens. Don't be shy about asking for help; everyone, even veteran New Yorkers, sometimes needs a little guidance when on unfamiliar lines.

Transfers, express trains, partial-service lines … and that's before getting into weekend construction and late-night redirections. How does one navigate this tangled web? Start with color. You will notice that the trains are grouped by color and then separated by letter or number. The 4, 5, and 6 trains are all green and run along Lexington Avenue in Manhattan. On the Upper East Side, you will see that while the 6 stops at 59th, 68th, 77th, and 86th streets, the 4 and the 5 stop only at 59th and 86th streets. This indicates that the 4 and the 5 are express trains, skipping local stops for a faster ride. You'll quickly become aware of which stations serve as express stops. Stations shared by local and express trains typically have easy transfers between them.

Transfers are also available at stations that serve more than one train line, and sometimes are available between separate stations. The 14th Street/Union Square stop serves the Lexington lines as well as the Broadway lines (the yellow N, R, and Q), as well as the crosstown L, which is gray. Moving between separate lines often means moving from one platform to another, and there are plenty of signs to direct you. Transfers between stations typically involve long walks in the city's underbelly, marked on the maps by a thin black line. The 42nd Street/Times Square stop is connected to the 42nd Street/Port Authority stop in this manner, connecting the Eighth Avenue lines (blue A, C, and E) to the multiple lines that run through Times Square. Such treks can be a drag, especially in the humidity of summer, but they can be a blessing on a rainy day!

A little more confusing are the partial-service lines. The orange trains on Sixth Avenue—B, D, F, and V—all run together at certain points and separate at others (this is true of most lines), but the B is different: it runs only on weekdays, and even then only from 6:30 a.m. until 9:00 p.m. For someone who lives near Central Park West and depends on this line, this means that in the B train's off-hours, another train will serve (in this case, the C train). This too is only a small example of what happens to the system at large at nights and on weekends, when service changes are most likely to take place. Express trains may run local, trains may be diverted, and lines might even be replaced with shuttle buses in the event of construction. Keep an eye out for signs posted in your station, check the MTA web page, or call 718-330-1234 for service changes. If you plan to ride an unfamiliar line, consult the Subway Service Guide at the base of the MTA map. The schedule for each line is broken down by day of the week and hour of the day.

Start with one line, and build from there. If you are closest to the 1 train (red, Seventh Avenue), start there, and gradually work your way into the 2 and the 3. Eventually you will find yourself exploring other lines that connect, and inevitably, you will make a mistake and end up in unfamiliar territory. Fear not: this is a rite of passage. Don't get discouraged, either; there will come a day when the unexpected will occur (sudden diversion, poorly marked service change, train stuck in a station or tunnel) and you can vent all your frustration at the vast, faceless machine that is the MTA.

If you are entirely vexed and want to take action or simply seek additional information, contact the Straphangers Campaign, a transit advocacy group that has been campaigning for riders' rights since 1979, 212-349-6460, www.straphangers.org.

New York's infamous subway tokens are long gone and in its place is the MetroCard. The card, available at vending machines (accepting credit and debit cards) in subway stations, is to be used on all subway lines and on all city buses (though coins may still be used on buses). There are several fare options for the card. The pay-per-ride card works like a debit card; when the card is empty you deposit more money. A single ride is $2.50 ($6 for express buses). To use, swipe the card through the turnstile slot, and one fare is subtracted. A more economical option is the unlimited usage pass, which is sold in weekly or monthly increments. The seven-day pass is $30, and a 30-day MetroCard is $112—good if you ride the subway frequently. Weekly and monthly passes purchased with a credit or debit card are insured against loss by the MTA, and if you want your money back, you can theoretically just mail it in and get a refund on the remaining value. You can also buy a single-ride ticket, which is slightly higher in cost at $2.75. And hang onto your card! The city recently introduced a $1 "new card" fee for each new MetroCard purchased. If you want to save yourself some money, hang onto your original card and refill it each time your fare or time runs out.

Seniors and people with disabilities are eligible for half-fare cards, while turnstile jumpers get a 100% discount, minus the occasional fine. Reduced fare information is available on the MTA website: www.mta.info. Children under 44 inches in height travel free (although they have to sit on their guardian's lap on express buses). School children are issued free passes if they attend a public or private school that is a specified distance from their home. Two-zone transfers mean riders with the MetroCard can move from subway to a bus (and vice versa) without paying another fare, although this is only applicable in certain areas. For general MetroCard information, call 212-METRO-CARD.

Subway trains operate 24 hours a day, but service slows appreciably after 11 p.m. At night, wait for trains near the subway booth or the turnstiles where transit cops seem to hang out. Be alert on subways or platforms and never leave personal items unattended. If you've come to New York to start a career in crime, you should know that the chip in your MetroCard actually keeps a record of where it was used—the police have solved several crimes using this bit of info.

BY PATH

The PATH (for Port Authority Trans-Hudson) tubes provide clean and efficient service connecting Manhattan with Hoboken, Jersey City, and Newark for $2.50 around the clock. Unlimited 30-day cards are $80. Trains leaving 33rd Street at Avenue of the Americas (Sixth Avenue) go to Hoboken or Jersey City, with stops along the way at 23rd, 14th, 9th, and Christopher Streets. Trains leaving World Trade Center terminate in Newark, stopping along the way at Exchange Place, Grove Street, Journal Square, and Harrison. Schedules are available in most stations, or call 800-234-7284 or visit www.panynj.gov/path.

BY BUS

Independent bus lines found mainly in boroughs other than Manhattan co-exist with those run by the MTA. Call 718-330-1234 for Transit Authority information as well as telephone numbers for the independents. You can also get up-to-date transit information on the MTA website: www.mta.info. Maps are sometimes available on the bus, but are usually easier to find in the few remaining information booths in subway stations. If you have difficulty finding a map, check the MTA's website. Buses cost $2.50 (express buses are $6). Transfers to other buses are free. Use the MetroCard or exact change. Note that in 2008 the MTA introduced a service known as "Select Bus" and has been expanding the number of routes and buses significantly in the past few years. The purpose of the service is, at least theoretically, to make boarding more efficient; passengers pay their fare at a kiosk at the bus stop (rather than on-board) and can enter any door on the bus (the select buses are usually articulated buses, double the length of regular buses). In lieu of paying fare with your MetroCard on the bus, the kiosk will give you a receipt when you pay your fare; this receipt must be presented to the driver or an MTA employee aboard the bus if it is requested. While some wise guys (and gals) try to use the Select Bus Service to avoid paying fare, it's not advisable; plain-clothes officers and MTA employees conduct regular spot checks and you can be fined if you fail to produce proof that you paid for your ride. Note that Select Bus Service is not available on every route, and that Select Bus Service buses do not stop at every bus stop on a given route. For more information, visit the SBS website: www. web.mta.info/nyct/sbs.

Call 212-564-8484 (Port Authority) for bus routes and schedules, or pick up a map at the Port Authority Bus Terminal at Eighth Avenue and 41st Street in Manhattan.

BY FERRY

There was, before the advent of the auto, a time when some 125 passenger-boats plied 50 different routes across the Hudson and East rivers. With the closing of the Hoboken Ferry in 1967, only the Staten Island Ferry remained, both a commuter necessity for Staten Islanders and an excursion delight for Manhattanites and tourists alike.

The water commute is once again a reality thanks to a handful of privately operated routes connecting Manhattan with New Jersey, Brooklyn, and Queens. And the Hoboken Ferry is back, faster than ever, docking at a floating terminal with a canvas marquee in Battery Park City. These ferries cruise at 35 miles per hour, twice as fast as the Staten Island Ferry. In increasing numbers, commuters are choosing this alternative to traffic gridlock, exorbitant parking fees, and expressway dementia, especially during the oppressive heat of summer. As more passengers take to the water, service increases.

- **Staten Island Ferry**, free, and certainly one of New York's best deals in transportation (and entertainment). Taking 25 minutes, the ferry leaves the South Ferry Terminal at Whitehall in Lower Manhattan for St. George, Staten Island, every 20 to 30 minutes daily, less frequently at night. Car service is available. Call 311 for information or go to www.siferry.com.
- **NY Water Taxi**, 212-742-1969, www.nywatertaxi.com; Boarding points include: Pier 79 on W 39th St; Pier 45 at Christopher St; Battery Park Slip 6; Pier 11 Slip

A; Pier 1 Brooklyn Bridge Park; World Financial Center Ferry Terminal; Pier 84 on W 44th St; and Ikea and Fairway in Brooklyn. The yellow and black boats offer commuter service, as well as leisure rides, and tickets can be bought online, by phone, or at the departure dock. Visit the website for information about fares and schedules.

- New Jersey passenger ferries are dominated by **NY Waterway**, 800-53-FERRY, www.nywaterway.com, which operates the Hoboken Ferry and service to Pier 11, the World Financial Center dock, and Pier 39 in Manahttan from Edgewater, Liberty Harbor, Port Liberté, Lincoln Harbor, Paulus Hook, Port Imperial/Wee-hawken, and Belford. Sightseeing cruises (known as the "booze cruise") and theater packages are also offered. You can purchase monthly passes on the NY Waterway website. Parking in New Jersey costs extra; parking passes are available at the website as well.
- NY Waterway also operates the **East River Ferry**, which runs along the East River, making stops at various docks in Manhattan, Brooklyn, and Queens, as well as Governor's Island (this last destination is seasonal). Bikes are allowed on the ferries, but a $1 surcharge will be added to the rider's fare. For information about schedules and fares, visit the East River Ferry website, www.eastriverferry.com.
- **Seastreak**, 800-BOAT-RIDE, www.seastreak.com, operates commuter ferries from Highlands and Atlantic Highlands, NJ, to Pier 11 at the foot of Wall Street, and to 35th Street on the East River. Hours are weekdays between 6 a.m. and 9:30 p.m. Fares are around $26 one way and $45 for round trip, depending on the hour. Call or visit the website for schedules.

BY BIKE

An increase in bike lanes, the introduction of the Citi Bike bicycle sharing program, and an aggressive public health campaign have all played a part on contributing to the increase in the number of people who are using cycling as their primary form of transportation in the city. The benefits of the bicycle are obvious: speed and economy. The downside? Vulnerability in city traffic. In addition to alert, defensive riding, there are also a number of **city laws** governing bicyclists that contribute to their safety:

- Bicycles are allowed on all city streets, but not on highways unless signs permit.
- Always ride with traffic and never on sidewalks.
- Traffic rules apply to bicycles as well as to cars. Riders must use hand signals.
- Bicycles must use bike lanes where they are provided.
- Bicycles must be equipped with a bell or horn, brakes, a headlight, and tail light.
- Accidents resulting in injury must be reported to the police.
- A rider may not wear more than one earphone to an audio player.
- Common sense mandates the wearing of a bicycle helmet.

Bicycles are permitted on subways at all times, but a few gates limit entry/ exit. MetroNorth and the Long Island Railroad require a one-time purchase of a permit to carry a bike on a train; the permit is $5 and is good for an entire lifetime. Bikes are not permitted on MetroNorth and LIRR during rush hour. You can purchase a permit aboard the train or check the bike section of the MTA website for more information about the permit and other bike rules, www.web.mta.info/bike. New Jersey Transit requires no permit on its trains, but bicycles are not allowed during rush hours or on certain holidays. The same rules apply on the PATH tubes. Check the Bike & Ride section of the NJ Transit website for complete information about bike rules, www.njtransit.com.

By the end of 2013, the city had developed 366.4 miles of bike lanes across the boroughs, and more miles are added every month. To find out where they are, download the NYC Bike Map at www.nyc.gov/html/dot/html/bicyclists/bikemaps. shtml or call 311 or visit a bike shop to pick up a free copy.

Transportation Alternatives, 127 W. 26th Street, Suite 1002, 212-629-8080, is a member-supported nonprofit citizens' group for the promotion of biking and public transportation. Their encyclopedic website, www.transalt.org, provides up-to-date news of interest to bikers links to biking organizations in the metropolitan area, lists shops offering discounts to members, and provides information on bike tours. There's also **Critical Mass**, www.times-up.org, which attempts to raise consciousness about the virtues of biking by holding riding rallies. They tend to take over an entire street and are not very popular with the police.

For more concerning biking in the city, see **Bicycling** in the **Sports and Recreation** chapter.

BY CAR

For the most part, New Yorkers don't get around Manhattan by car, except when they're in a cab. Why? Because on-street parking is so limited and off-street parking so expensive. So who are all those cars causing the periodic gridlock? Cabs, car services, delivery vehicles, and day commuters. Those living in Manhattan may own a car or rent a car occasionally. Many residents of outer boroughs own a car, and may drive into Manhattan for work, adding to major rush-hour delays. We'll continue with a few things you need to know about driving in and out of the city. (See also **Parking** and **Parking Tickets and Towing** in the **Getting Settled** chapter and **Auto Services and Repair** in **Helpful Services**.) For those who don't want to deal with the fuss of owning a car, but still want to have one readily available, you can join **ZipCar** (www.zipcar.com, 866-4ZIPCAR), an hourly car rental subscription service.

New York drivers are aggressive, cabbies especially. Get used to it. But New York pedestrians rarely follow the rules either: they cross against the light and mid-block when they feel like it; watch out for them. Also, keep your eye out for bike messengers and recreational and commuter cyclists, who defy all traffic rules as they weave in and out of traffic. Be especially vigilant when exiting a car; many a cyclist has been injured—and some severely—by car doors being opened.

Gridlock is a way of life here, at least on weekdays. "Don't block the box," means don't enter the intersection unless you are sure you can cross it before the light changes. Failure to heed this command causes gridlock and can cost you points on your license. If you can, avoid entering or leaving the city during rush hour traffic (roughly 7 a.m. to 10 a.m. and 4 p.m. to 7 p.m.). Friday and Sunday evenings are especially bad. In New York, street signs are everywhere, so pay attention for bus lanes and turning-only lanes. Unlike much of the country, right turns are NOT permitted on a red light in New York City, unless indicated by a rare sign.

Nonetheless, because of the logical street grid covering most of the island and because traffic is so slow, driving in Manhattan is easier than you might think. The north-south avenues for the most part are one-way, generally in an alternating pattern: hence, First Avenue runs uptown, and Second Avenue runs downtown. Park Avenue is two-way, as are portions of Third Avenue. The east-west streets are, for the most part, one-way, with the even-numbered streets running east (remember, even-east), and odd-numbered streets running west; the exceptions are typically major cross-town streets: Canal, Houston, 14th, 23rd, 34th, 42nd, and 57th streets, for example, which are two-way. Left turns are rarely permitted during the day, so watch signs closely. For driving in the other boroughs, you'll need a map, at least initially. AAA members can get them free; other New Yorkers can buy street maps at newspaper or magazine shops. A good selection of maps is also available at www.firstbooks.com.

Manhattan is bracketed by two major north-south arteries, the West Side Highway/Henry Hudson Parkway (Route 9A) along the Hudson River on the west side, and Harlem River/FDR Drive along the East River on the east side. At the southernmost tip of the island the Brooklyn Battery Tunnel (now also known as the Hugh L. Carey Tunnel) (toll) runs under the harbor to Brooklyn, where it connects to the Brooklyn-Queens Expressway (BQE), Route 278, which arcs around the Brooklyn shoreline and into Queens on either end. The BQE also connects with the Verrazano-Narrows Bridge (toll) to the Staten Island Expressway across the Goethals Bridge to New Jersey.

On FDR Drive, three bridges cross the East River to Brooklyn: south to north, the Brooklyn Bridge, the Manhattan Bridge, and the Williamsburg Bridge. At 34th Street, the Queens Midtown Tunnel (toll) shoots under the river to Queens and the Long Island Expressway running east to Long Island. The Queensboro Bridge (also called the 59th Street Bridge and, more recently, the Ed Koch Bridge—the city has been on a renaming spree) crosses from 59th Street into Long Island City for free, and the Robert F. Kennedy Bridge (formerly the Triborough Bridge) (toll) at 125th Street crosses into Queens and The Bronx (watch the signs carefully). The Willis Avenue Bridge also takes you across the East River from the FDR to The Bronx (no toll) and connects with the Major Deegan Expressway, a north/south highway that passes Yankee Stadium.

From the West Side Highway the Holland Tunnel (toll) at Canal Street goes under the Hudson to Jersey City, and the Lincoln Tunnel (toll) at 38th Street crosses to Weehawken, both connecting to the Jersey Turnpike (I-95) and Routes 78 and 22 west into New Jersey and the Garden State Parkway. Farther north, the George Washington Bridge (toll) sweeps across the Hudson River on two levels to connect with the Palisades Parkway, which runs north along the west bank of the Hudson, the New Jersey Turnpike and I-80, which heads west straight across New Jersey. The Cross Bronx Expressway, which runs onto the bridge, also runs (crawls is sometimes more like it) east, connecting with I-95 north into Connecticut, I-87 north into Yonkers and Upstate New York, and The Bronx River Parkway north. From the northernmost tip of Manhattan the Henry Hudson Bridge (toll) soars into Riverdale north on the Henry Hudson Parkway to Route 87 and other routes north into Westchester and on to New England.

Tolls on the bridges and tunnels range from $7 to $13, but drivers with an E-Z Pass can save money. The pass also saves time, as it doesn't require counting money and more lanes are open for pass holders. To get the E-Z Pass, which also works on the New York State Thruway and in neighboring states, go to www.e-zpassny.com and apply online, or call 800-333-TOLL for an application. The pass works like a debit card, subtracting the toll from your balance with each use; you can pay to keep the pass filled by check or money order, but if you pay by credit card the pass is automatically filled as necessary. Your monthly statement will tally your toll spending.

SERVICES AND RENTALS

TAXI AND CAR SERVICES

All car services in New York City, unlicensed as well as licensed, come under the jurisdiction of the Taxi and Limousine Commission (TLC). Call the commission via 311 with questions, complaints, or for lost and found, or go to www.nyc.gov/taxi.

Licensed cabs in New York City tend to be reliable and safe and are among the most recognizable taxis in the country, if not the world. In recent years, the city's fleet of cabs has diversified; no longer are bright yellow taxis limited to the Crown Victoria sedan; there are also small SUVs, hybrid vehicles, and even vans outfitted with lifts for people with disabilities. Read on to learn more about how to distinguish the different types of taxi and car service options in the city.

- **Yellow cabs**, or "medallion" cabs—so named for the medallion affixed to the hood—are, along with apple green borough taxis (described below) the only taxis authorized to pick up passengers on the street. A licensed cab (the kind you should get into) will have a photo license of the driver displayed on the Plexiglas partition behind the driver's seat, as well as the number of the taxi's medallion (it's never a bad idea to make a note of that number; it can come in handy if you have a complaint or if you happen to leave an item behind in the cab). There are more than 13,600 of these, each charging $2.50 upon entry and 50¢ for each additional "unit." A unit refers to every 1/5th of a mile when the taxi is moving and each 60-second increment of waiting time. A 50¢ surcharge is collected between 8 p.m. and 6 a.m. and a $1.00 surcharge is applied during afternoon rush hour, currently defined as 4 p.m.–8 p.m. There is no legal surcharge for luggage. Tips in the 15% to 20% range are expected. If you are crossing a toll bridge or tunnel you are responsible for paying the tolls. All taxis are now equipped with machines to process debit and credit card payments; if you'd like a receipt, be sure to ask for one. If you are headed to an outer borough, avoid telling the driver your destination until you get in the car; cabbies are legally required to take you as a fare regardless of your destination, even if they hate going to the boroughs. They are not permitted to ask you your destination before you get in the cab, though many do. If you're having a run of refusals, threatening to report them to the TLC (which you can do by phoning 311) can work wonders.

- **Boro taxis**, a bright green taxi that differs from yellow cabs only in color, were introduced to the city in 2013 with the goal of improving street-hail taxi access in the outer boroughs. Boro taxis can drop riders off anywhere in the city, but drivers are bound by restrictions about where they can pick fares up. Permitted pick-up zones include: areas north of West 110th Street and East 96th Street in Manhattan and anywhere in the outer boroughs. Like yellow cabs, fares are calculated by meter and the rate structure is the same as that in yellow cabs. Passengers can pay via debit or credit card if they wish.

- **Black cars** (aka: livery cabs), the trade term for high-quality, radio-dispatched fleet sedans, aren't licensed to stop for street hails. Corporations and private charges account for most of the "black car" business. In theory, these meterless "voucher cabs" (which charge by zone or by mileage registered on the odometer) will respond to telephone requests from "charge-accountless" individuals. If a driver sees you hailing a cab and offers to pick you up, he's doing so illegally and you are taking a risk.

- **Car services** are licensed to work only from a telephone base and can't legally pick up passengers on the street. The vehicles, of which there are some 36,000 licensed, range from the less-than-lovely to the pristine-upscale, but they are never yellow. Each vehicle, as proof of licensing, must display the decal of the Taxi and Limousine Commission on the passenger side of the front windshield. Especially useful to residents of the outer boroughs, where they are more common, these for-hire vehicles charge flat rates per trip, sometimes less than the cost of a metered cab. Agree upon the fare before getting into the car. This is the way to go when you need to get home from the boroughs at night—share with a couple of people if possible.

The car lurching to your side looks a wreck, and there's no decal? Then it's probably an unlicensed "gypsy cab," in which you'll ride at your own risk without recourse in case of bad service. Avoid them.

Ride-shares and taxi alternatives are growing increasingly popular in the city, and the best-known and most frequently used of these services is Uber, www.uber.com. Using an app on your smart phone, you order a car and driver, who picks you up at your current location based on GPS data beamed to a dispatcher. In other words, you don't even need to know your address to order a car. The car information, driver's name, and estimated arrival time will all be displayed on your phone, and payment is handled solely through the app via credit card you have stored on file. If you're riding with friends and want to split the fare, just choose the "Split Fare" option within the app. Taxi drivers have, of course, been resistant to services like Uber, which tend to have sexier vehicles and an air of exclusivity (despite their accessibility), but New Yorkers love Uber, and this and similar services, including Lyft, www.lyft.com, seem like they're here to stay.

LIMOUSINE SERVICE

For those occasions when you wish to ride in style or have a car and driver at your beck and call, consider hiring a limousine. Many car services also operate limousines; rates are usually on a per hour basis, although some firms set flat rates for trips to airports or for dinner-and-theater evenings. A variety of stretch vehicles are available, including 40-foot-long stretch Hummers, such as those operated by **Amex Limousine Service**, 718-946-2323, www.amexlimo.com. These block-long beauties carry up to 30 people, and some models even have an open-air Jacuzzi; the garden-variety limos offer stereos, color TV, and a stocked bar with ice for five or six. One day's notice is usually required, though cars (but not necessarily your first choice) are sometimes available on short notice. Most firms accept major credit cards, but check when you call. Add 15% to 20% gratuity for the driver. Several companies deal primarily with corporate accounts.

- **All-State Private Car and Limousine, Inc.**, 335 Bond St, Brooklyn, 212-333-3333, www.allstatelimo.com; All-State also offers good rates for black car service to LaGuardia, JFK, and Newark airports. Rates vary depending on the neighborhood you are traveling to/from; expect a 20% gratuity charge to be added to your bill. There are also various surcharges applied depending on the time of day and whether your route includes any tolls. Call for more information.
- **Carey International**, 800-336-4646, www.carey.com; call for rates.
- **Dav-El Livery**, 800-922-0343, www.davel.com; all trips are charged a two-hour minimum. Call for rates.
- **Fugazy International Corp.**, 1270 6th Ave, 212-661-4155, www.fugazy.com/transportation; call for rates. Sedans and stretch limos available.

- **London Towncars**, 40-14 23rd St, Long Island City, 800-221-4009; call for rates; sedans and limousines available.
- **Tel Aviv Car and Limousine Service**, 43-23 35th St, Long Island City, 800-222-9888, www.telavivlimo.com; *New York Magazine* called Tel Aviv "the best ride in town."

CAR RENTALS

If you need to rent a car, you'll have plenty of options for doing so; nearly every major national chain has at least one branch in New York City, and often, dozens. Prices vary widely from firm to firm, and special rates (for a weekend or even mid-week) are common; call around or check online for cost comparisons. Keep in mind that companies located just outside the city may offer rates low enough to more than make up for the hassle of getting there. Keep in mind that prices can also vary widely within the same company, so if the branch location isn't a significant issue for you, it can be worth your time and money to price check rental rates for one of the airport branches versus one of the in-city branches. Ask about any fees that may not be obvious; at the airport, for example, an additional airport concession fee is typically tacked on to your total bill. Finally, even if you only need a car for a day or two, check the day rate against the weekly rate; sometimes, the weekly rate ends up being cheaper—significantly so, at times—than the daily rate.

Be sure to ask if there is a charge for leaving the car at another location, if that is your plan. Some other helpful hints: Manhattan car rental companies run out of availability quickly, especially on holiday weekends. Do not wait until the last minute to try to reserve a car. Check with your employer as well, who may have a corporate account that can get you a reduced rate. When you book your reservation, ask for a confirmation number, which will help get the rate you were quoted when you reserved the car. It's also a good idea to arrive early to pick up your car. Also, if you plan to use a debit card, be sure to ask if the company from which you're renting accepts them and, if it does, the amount of deposit it requires for use of a bank card instead of a credit card.

If you expect to rent somewhat regularly, you may want to consider joining the rental company's customer loyalty program, which is free. Points accumulate with each rental, earning you free rental days and/or frequent flyer points and other incentives. Hertz's loyalty program, Gold Rewards, also offers members expedited rentals; if you make your reservation online or by phone and Hertz already has your credit card and license information on file, your car will be ready for you to drive straight out of the garage or lot once you arrive.

Here are some of the largest car rental companies. All have several Manhattan locations and most have locations at the three major area airports.

- **Avis**, 800-633-3469, www.avis.com.
- **Budget**, 800-218-7992, www.budget.com
- **Dollar**, 800-800-4000, www.dollar.com

- **Hertz**, 800-654-3131, www.hertz.com
- **National**, 877-222-9058, www.nationalcar.com
- **Thrifty**, 800-334-1705, www.thrifty.com

BUS AND TRAIN

COMMUTER AND NATIONAL RAIL SERVICE

Pennsylvania Station, between 31st and 33rd Streets and Seventh and Eighth Avenues, with the Long Island Railroad Station adjacent, between 33rd and 34th Streets, and Grand Central Terminal at 42nd Street, between Vanderbilt and Lexington Avenues at Park, are the railroad hubs in New York City. Grand Central has been restored to its former glory, its gray stone walls cleaned and the spectacular azure vaulted ceiling with gilded constellations uncovered. It is truly a destination worthy of its calling. The once dim and dirty passageways now house a spiffy shopping arcade (which, among other shops, features New York City's largest Apple Store), an expansive food court, fine restaurants (including the New York institution, The Oyster Bar), newsstands, and more. In winter, a holiday market selling artisanal goods is set up in its Vanderbilt Hall; during other seasons, the same hall is the site of cultural performances, exhibits, and other special promotional and marketing events that are open to the public. And don't miss the Grand Central Market; while most of its goods are terribly overpriced, it's worth strolling all the way to the eastern end of the market and gazing up at the stunning chandelier hanging above your head. Finally, the MTA has its transit museum annex here; it's a particularly popular (and crowded) spot in the winter, during an annual toy train exhibit.

Compared to Grand Central and its grandeur, Penn Station feels like a dive. Though it too has some shops and restaurants, the transit hub isn't a place where you'll want to slow down and stay a while. Its capital improvements remain a work seemingly ever in progress, and plans to restore it to its former greatness seem eternally stalled.

- **Amtrak** trains, 800-872-7245 for information and reservations, or go to www.amtrak.com, leave Penn Station for the Northeast Corridor—between Washington and Boston—and for destinations throughout most of the country and to Canada. Amtrak's high-speed Acela Express service is a sleek bullet train shooting along the Northeast Corridor between Boston and New York and on to Washington, D.C. at speeds peaking at 150 mph, cutting travel time by a third. Both Acela Express and the less expensive, and slower, Acela Regional come in two classes, first and business. Metroliner service between New York and Washington is also available. Look for "rail sale" announcements online.
- **Metro-North** trains, www.mta.info/mnr, leave from Grand Central and include the Hudson Line to Poughkeepsie, NY; the Harlem Line to Brewster, NY; and the

New Haven Line to New Haven, CT. Find up-to-date Metro-North information on the MTA website.

- The **New Jersey Transit Information Center**, 973-275-5555, is the place to call for Penn Station-New Jersey train schedules. Also, check www.njtransit.com.
- **Long Island Railroad** (LIRR) trains, 511, www.mta.info/lirr, leave from the LIRR station, which is inside Penn Station. You'll find up-to-date LIRR information on the MTA website.
- **Staten Island Railway,** 511, www.mta.info/sir, runs between St. George and Tottenville stations 24/7. At the St. George Station, riders can make connections with the Staten Island Ferry.

COMMUTER AND NATIONAL BUS SERVICE

- **The Port Authority Bus Terminal**, between 40th and 42nd Streets and Eighth and Ninth Avenues, www.panynj.gov/bus-terminals/port-authority-bus-terminal.html, is the center for almost all inter-city bus traffic. The exceptions are inter-borough expresses, which have designated pickup points at certain Manhattan intersections, and buses, mostly from New Jersey, that arrive and leave from the George Washington Bridge Bus Station at the George Washington Bridge in upper Manhattan. For lines that serve the George Washington Bridge Bus Station, visit this website, www.panynj.gov/bus-terminals/gwbbs-carriers-routes.html.
- **Greyhound Bus Lines**, 800-231-2222, www.greyhound.com, has its principal ticket offices in the Port Authority Terminal, and its buses arrive and depart from the Lower Level of the North Wing with entrances on both 41st and 42nd Streets.
- **Peter Pan Bus Lines**, 800-343-9999, www.peterpanbus.com; uses Adirondack Trailways as its local ticket agent in the Port Authority Terminal. Its buses also arrive at and depart from the Lower Level of the North Wing.

AIR TRAVEL

AIRPORTS

The Port Authority of New York and New Jersey manages John F. Kennedy, LaGuardia, and Newark Liberty airports, and strives mightily to upgrade airport transportation and services and to disseminate information to the public about the facilities. To this end, they distribute particularly helpful materials and staff several telephone information numbers.

The airport section of the Port Authority website, www.panynj.gov/airports, provides information on each of the three major New York City airports.

AIRPORT TRANSPORTATION

The cheapest route (and one of the slowest) to JFK is the subway. Take the A train (make sure it's to Far Rockaway, and exit at Howard Beach) or the E, J, or Z train to Sutphin Boulevard for just $2.50; once at either of these stations, you'll connect with AirTrain for all stops at JFK. You'll need to pay an additional $5 fare for the AirTrain. Allow an hour and a half or more for the ride.

You can, of course, drive to the airport and park there for up to 30 days at Kennedy International, LaGuardia, or Newark (costly at $250+). Short-term parking is available at all airports. Day rates vary from $18 to nearly $80, depending on the airport and the proximity to the terminal. Rate charts are available at www.panynj. gov/airports. Also, keep in mind that on Fridays and during holidays the lots fill up quickly. Business travelers fill short-term lots on Wednesdays. Arrive at the lot before 3 p.m. most days to be sure of a parking spot, and don't expect to find a space at LaGuardia on Sunday night.

For up-to-date information on transportation to any of the three airports go online to the Port Authority's website, www.panynj.gov, or call the individual airport, below.

If you are traveling with a companion, or can find someone to share with, it is probably worth taking a taxi to and from any of the major airports. Get taxis only at taxi stands and do not follow someone who claims to be a driver to his "parked" cab somewhere in an airport lot. More on airport transportation under each airport listing below.

JOHN F. KENNEDY INTERNATIONAL AIRPORT (JFK)

JFK is New York City's main international airport, a multi-terminal giant. Its AirTrain light rail system links the terminals, as well as the Long Island Railroad, city subway system, and buses at Jamaica Station and at Howard Beach. Travelers can now zip from Midtown to JFK in 45 minutes. For more information about AirTrain, call 877-535-2478 or go to www.panynj.com. Security at JFK is tight, so give yourself additional time and be patient. It should go without saying, but do not leave your bags unattended. Call 718-244-4444 for **airport information**, 718-244-4225 for lost and found, and 718-244-4168 for **parking**; online, go to www.panynj.gov/airports/jfk.html.

- **Taxis to Manhattan** cost a flat fee of $52, plus tolls and tip. If there is a second person going beyond the first stop in Manhattan, the meter is started after the first stop and this passenger pays the metered rate. From destinations in the other four boroughs, taxis will typically run from $28–$40 (Queens) to $67–$79 for Staten Island. Allow 45–90 minutes from Manhattan, depending on time of day, with rush hour being the longest commute. Remember, when leaving JFK get taxis only at taxi stands.

- **Go Airlink NYC,** 718-875-8200, www.goairlinknyc.com; buses leave from Penn Station, Port Authority, Bryant Park, and Grand Central Terminal every 30 minutes. The trip from Downtown takes about 40 minutes, more during rush hours, and costs between $12 and $15, depending on the stop. Discounts may be available if you purchase online.
- **SuperShuttle (Blue Van),** 800-BLUE-VAN, www.supershuttle.com; operates 24/7, shuttling passengers from all destinations in Manhattan to each of the three major airports. Call ahead and make reservations, which are required. You will be notified at the time of your reservation if delays of more than 15 minutes are expected. When arriving at JFK, you can go to the ground transport desk located by the baggage claim area to reserve pick up. You can expect about a 15-minute wait. Fares start at $20 and depend upon your destination.
- **Bus or subway**: if you're looking to save money but not time, you can take the A train to Far Rockaway, exiting at Howard Beach, or the E, J, or Z train to Sutphin Boulevard. From either of these stations, connect with AirTrain for all stops at JFK. Note that there's an additional $5 fare for the AirTrain, and you'll need to allow an hour and a half or more for the ride.

LAGUARDIA AIRPORT

Call 718-533-3400 for airport information; 718-533-3988 for lost and found; and 718-533-3850 for parking. Online, you can visit www.panynj.gov.

- **Taxis** to and from Midtown cost about $25–$37, plus tolls and tip. If you can find a friendly fellow Manhattan (or wherever you are going) bound traveler, you can split the fare.
- **Go Airlink NYC,** 718-875-8200, www.goairlinknyc.com; buses leave from Penn Station, Port Authority, Bryant Park, and Grand Central Terminal every 30 minutes. The trip from downtown takes about 40 minutes, more during rush hours, and costs between $12 and $15, depending on the stop. Discounts may be available if you purchase online.
- **SuperShuttle (Blue Van),** call 800-BLUE-VAN, www.supershuttle.com. This shuttle service operates 24/7, taking passengers from all destinations in Manhattan to each of the three major airports. You will be notified at the time of your reservation if van delays of more than 15 minutes are expected. Fares start around $16.
- **Public subway and bus**: for door-to-door directions via subway and bus (note that there are no subway stops at LaGuardia), visit www.mta.info and enter your information into the Custom Trip Planner. Total cost: $2.50 one way using a MetroCard (or coins—exact change, only—on the bus). If you're leaving from the Upper West Side and have 45–60 minutes to spare, take the M60 bus from Broadway and 116th Street, or anywhere along Broadway north to 125th Street to Second Avenue before midnight. It goes to LaGuardia for one fare. An MTA

Select Service bus was recently introduced on the M60 line, which is a speedier option for the same fare.

NEWARK LIBERTY INTERNATIONAL AIRPORT

Call 973-961-6000 for airport information; 908-787-0667 for lost and found; and 888-397-4636, then press 22, to receive parking information. Online, visit www. panynj.gov/airports/newark-liberty.html.

The Port Authority, which runs all three New York City area airports, supervises efficient, inexpensive transportation to and from Newark.

- **Taxis,** the trip from midtown to Newark Airport costs $50–$70, plus tolls. In addition, taxis can add a $15 surcharge. Returning to Manhattan, New Jersey cabs are limited to fixed fares determined by location. "Share and save" rates for groups of up to four passengers cut costs by almost half and are available between 8 a.m. and midnight. Check with the dispatcher at the terminal's hack stand.
- **Newark Airport Express by Coach USA,** 877-8-NEWARK, www.coachusa.com/ olympia/ss.newarkairport.asp service between Newark Airport and three Manhattan locations (Port Authority, Bryant Park, and Grand Central Terminal) for $16 (one way) or $28 (round trip). Comfy ride. Other drop-off points available. Contact Coach USA for more specifics.
- **SuperShuttle** (Blue Van), call 212-258-3826 on day of departure; from out of town or to reserve before day of departure, call 800-BLUEVAN, www.supershuttle.com. Operates 24 hours a day, shuttling passengers from home, office, or hotel to the three major airports. Call and make reservations, which are required. When arriving at Newark Airport, you can go to the ground transport desk in the baggage claim area and order a Blue Van pick up. There will typically be about a 15-minute wait until the van picks you up. The fare is $21.
- **Rail: NJ Transit,** 973-275-5555, www.njtransit.com; PATH, 800-234-PATH, www. panynj.gov/path; Amtrak 800-USA-RAIL, www.amtrak.com: trains operate from Penn Station in Manhattan to and from Newark Penn Station between 5 a.m. and 2 a.m. AirTrain is the light rail system that whisks you between the train station and airport terminals: 888-397-4636, www.panynj.com.

SATELLITE AIRPORTS

Three airports outside the city offer an attractive alternative to the JFK-LaGuardia-Newark axis: uncrowded access roads, easy parking, and fewer delays all around for domestic flights.

- **MacArthur Airport,** 100 Arrival Ave in Ronkonkoma, Long Island, 631-467-3210, www.macarthurairport.com; served by several major airlines, including

Allegiant, Penair, Southwest, and US Airways Express. Access is easiest via the LIRR. Ride to Ronkonkoma (about 90 minutes) and catch a shuttle to the airport.

- **Stewart Airport**, 1180 Windsor, New Winston, New York, 845-838-8200, www.panynj.gov/airports/stewart.html; a former Air Force base 60 miles north of the city in Newburgh, NY, at the juncture of I-87 and I-84, opened for commercial service in 1990. Airlines include: Allegiant, Delta Connection, JetBlue, and US Airways Express.

- **Westchester County White Plains Airport**, 240 Airport Rd, White Plains, 914-995-4860, http://airport.westchestergov.com; served by American Airlines, Cape Air, Delta, JetBlue, United, and US Airways. The airport has ample parking in a three-story lot. Lacking a car, take the Harlem Line out of Grand Central to White Plains, and the Bee Line #12.

AIRLINE FLIGHT STATUS AND COMPLAINTS

FLIGHT STATUS INFORMATION

Information about flight status, including delays, can be checked online on your airline's website, or at www.fly.faa.gov. Similarly, the site www.flightarrivals.com offers real-time arrival, departure, and delay details for commercial flights, as does www.flightaware.com.

CONSUMER COMPLAINTS—AIRLINES

To register a complaint against an airline, the Department of Transportation is the place to call or write: 202-366-2220, Aviation Consumer Protection Division, 1200 New Jersey Ave SE, Washington, D.C. 20590. You can also file a complaint online: www.dot.gov/airconsumer/file-consumer-complaint.

WHEN YOU FIND YOURSELF FLYING DOWN THE SIDEWALK—SHOULDER bag or briefcase in tow, feet sore, elbows jostling, grinding teeth ready to chew up the slowpokes in front of you—take heed: that pounding in your head is not a war drum, it's a warning. It is time to get out of the city. Like all great things, New York City is better appreciated when experienced with some moderation. It is infectious, but it is also exhausting, especially in the dog days of August. You'll be glad you left once you're gone, and you'll be glad you're back when you return.

By virtue of its location, its size, and the multitude of transit systems that pass through New York City, entire volumes could be devoted to getting out of town, and every magazine runs lists of seasonal getaway trips, ranging from bucolic swimming spots to places you can eat foie gras naked—of course, if it was in last week's *New York Magazine*, you'll end up squeezing in with the rest of the city, so you might want to peruse *last* summer's recommendations instead. And don't forget all-day escapes like Governor's Island or Fire Island! Here, we point you in the direction of some good resources, with a few trips suggested as well. The tri-state area is rich with destinations for a day trip, and the Northeast provides ample opportunity to get away for a weekend. Friends and co-workers will doubtless have a number of favorite spots (and suggestions on how to get there). And don't be afraid to venture out on your own. How fun, how 1950s, to simply board a train and ride until something grabs your fancy?

MODES OF TRANSPORTATION

TRAINS

- **Metro-North**, the MTA's regional rail service, offers numerous "One-Day Get-aways" to upstate towns, Connecticut casinos, biking regions, hiking trails, rafting purveyors, and more; "Manhattan Getaways" are package deals for travel to some of New York State's incredible destinations. Visit http://web.mta.info/mnr/html/outbound.htm for a listing of getaways.

- **Long Island Railroad**, the key for the car-less to Long Island, provides year-round service to destinations deemed best for the season: beaches and fishing villages in the summer, for example, and orchards and wineries in the fall; LIRR also has packages for the hobby photographer, the gambler, and the oenophile. Visit www.mta.info/lirr, or call 718-217-LIRR.
- **Amtrak**: perhaps you'd like to visit Boston or Philly or D.C. for a day, or maybe you're eyeing a long weekend in Montreal. Amtrak can get you there, and though it is more expensive than many other options, the ride is comfortable and the booking fees for short notice travel beat flying almost every time. See www.amtrakvacations.com for packages and deals, or call 800-268-7252.

BUSES

Fleets of **discount fare buses** have descended upon Manhattan, promising cheap, comfortable, and tech-connected (in the form of on-board Wi-Fi) rides to and from New York City and other major urban centers in the northeastern U.S. Among the two most popular providers are **BoltBus** (www.boltbus.com) and **MegaBus** (www.us.megabus.com).

- **Greyhound Bus** offers short and long-haul trips across North America. Check www.greyhound.com or call 800-231-2222.
- **Peter Pan Bus Lines** operates buses between New York City and other cities and towns in the northeastern U.S. Visit www.peterpanbus.com or call 800-343-9999 for route and fare information.
- **New York Trailways**, www.trailways.com, 800-858-8555, operates several fleets, each specializing in a distinct region in or around New York State, including Adirondack Trailways. Call for routes and fares.

Note: The "Chinatown buses" that became so popular for their budget tickets and quick transfers between NYC and other major northeastern cities are, as of this writing, beleaguered entities, and passengers should book fares with caution. Federal regulators shut down the popular Fung Wah bus in 2012 after numerous safety violations, and though Lucky Star (www.luckystarbus.com) has resumed service after a similarly forced hiatus, the future of these buses is somewhat tenuous.

CAR RENTAL

If you'd like to escape and set your own pace, or have a destination in mind that isn't served by train or bus, you may wish to rent a car. For a short trip on short notice, ZipCar (866-4ZIP-CAR, www.zipcar.com) is your best option, but note that you must have a membership. There are three levels of membership from which you can select, based on the frequency you expect to need or want a car. In addition to a monthly membership fee, which varies from $6 to $50, you'll pay hourly or daily rental fees. Gas and insurance are included in your rate, but keep an eye on your mileage: after 180 miles, you'll pay an additional mileage fee.

Apart from ZipCar, the city has numerous staffed and self-serve branches of all the major national rental car chains, including Avis, Budget, Enterprise, Hertz, and National, to name a few. Note that base rates for rentals picked up at airport locations may be cheaper; however, airport concession fees may offset the savings, so check the rate quote thoroughly. Also, be sure to compare daily rates versus weekly rates; sometimes, it is actually cheaper to rent for an entire week or longer rather than one or two days.

STATE RESOURCES

The tri-state area is not shy about self-promotion, and with good cause. There is plenty to see and do, and the variety of options are dazzling. Below is information pertaining to these three beautiful states.

- **New York**: www.iloveny.com is the state's enthusiastic and thorough official tourism website, rife with plans, packages, destinations, and deals—from "Culinary Adventures" to "Girlfriend Getaways." Additional info at 800-CALL-NYS.
- **New Jersey**: www.visitnj.org is the state's official travel and tourism website, with content organized by topical interests, including culture, history, and outdoors. The information is reliable and the Calendar of Events is excellent. Call 1-800-VISITNJ for more.
- **Connecticut**: www.ctvisit.com is extremely user-friendly and is loaded with practical travel planning information, including a comprehensive sampler of activities and trip ideas presented in the section called "52 getaways." New events are posted for each approaching weekend. Also call 888-CT-VISIT.

WEB RESOURCES

Online you will find a cavalcade of tourism sites, promotions, charters, and more. Here are some of the best.

- **About.com's Easy Escapes from New York City**, www.gonyc.about.com/od/daytrips, has a rotating list of activities, ranging from the decadent (drinking, gambling) to the special interest (Renaissance fairs, tours of the military academy).
- **Fun New Jersey**, www.funnewjersey.com, delivers on the promise of its name, with loads of listings about attractions and activities around the state, ranging from adult-specific to family-friendly.
- **North Jersey Day Trips for Kids**, www.fmfcorp.com/familyspot/trips.html, contains a comprehensive listing of events and destinations in North Jersey, with a focus on the family.

- **Mommy Poppins**, www.mommypoppins.com; *the* one-stop-shop of New York City "mommy blogs," updated daily with event calendars, reviews, and insider tips on discounted and exclusive activities.

S UMMER ACCOMMODATIONS IN UNIVERSITY DORMS, YMCAs, CHURCH-RUN women's residences, hotels, and B&Bs are among your options if you need temporary shelter en route to a permanent living situation or for out-of-town guests looking for affordable, short-term lodging. Descriptions of these varied lodgings are offered, together with a selection of hotels categorized by price and location. Addresses are in Manhattan unless otherwise noted.

A few generalizations regarding hotel rooms: rates are often negotiable and vary depending on time of the year; weekends and the summer months offer the best opportunity for lodging bargains; holidays and the fall months are usually the priciest times to stay in the city. To avoid sticker shock at checkout, note that New York hotel rooms are subject to a tax of 5.875%.

SUMMER ONLY

Several local colleges and universities designate a portion of their residential accommodations for interns who are in New York only for the summer. Eligibility and application requirements, fees, and rules vary widely. Below are several options, though this is not an exhaustive list.

- **International House New York** (near Columbia University), 500 Riverside Dr at 123rd St, 212-316-8400, www.ihouse-nyc.org; you don't have to matriculate at Columbia to be eligible for one of the dorm rooms and suites available to students, interns, and other scholarly visitors from mid-May to mid-August. Stays are monthly and accommodations also give you access to onsite facilities, such as the fitness center, computer lab, and dining room. Throughout the year, the International House also has 11 guest rooms it rents out; rates run from $140-205/night.
- **New York University Dormitories**, c/o New York University, Office of Summer Housing, 14A Washington Place, 212-998-4621, www.nyu.edu/summer/housing;

NYU dorms are open to interns and students affiliated with NYU during the summer months. Accommodations range from traditional dorm rooms to apartment-style halls; for the former, enrollment in the campus meal plan is obligatory. Rental rates also vary, starting around $181/week and running as high as $394/week. A $500 reservation payment is required at the time of application; deadlines are as early as March, so this option requires planning ahead.

See also **Sublets and Sharing** in the **Finding a Place to Live** chapter.

TRANSIENT YMCAs

Six YMCAs across the city—three in Manhattan, two in Brooklyn, and one in Queens—offer accommodations for both men and women; all rent rooms on a day-to-day basis only. To obtain reservations at the YMCAs listed below, contact each Y individually. Rates vary ($119 for a single and $129 for a double at the Vanderbilt in Manhattan, or $48/$68 for a small/large single in Greenpoint, Brooklyn). In all cases, the room rates include use of all athletic facilities on the premises (see YMCAs in Sports and Recreation). Note that you will be sharing a bathroom with your hallmates.

- **Harlem YMCA**, 180 W 135th St, 212-912-2100
- **West Side YMCA**, 5 W 63rd St, 212-912-2600
- **Vanderbilt YMCA**, 224 E 47th St, 212-912-2504
- **Greenpoint YMCA**, 99 Meserole Ave, Brooklyn, 718-389-3700
- **North Brooklyn YMCA**, 570 Jamaica Ave, Brooklyn, 718-277-1600
- **Flushing YMCA**, 138-46 Northern Blvd, Flushing, Queens, 718-961-6880

TEMPORARY RESIDENCES

Daily transients are not accepted by any of the residences noted below, which, with the exception of the 92nd Street Y Residence, are for women only. Weekly or monthly rates are the norm; some include two meals a day in the price. Full occupancy is the rule at most of these places, as is the requirement for a personal interview, and you should therefore make arrangements for a room well in advance of arrival. Some of the residences may also require an application fee and/or deposit; this may or may not be refundable upon your departure, so be sure to ask about policies. Some have special house rules, such as curfews, so inquire about these before booking.

- **92nd Street Y Residence**, 1395 Lexington Ave, 212-415-5650, www.92y.org/residence; co-ed, for men and women ages 18 and older, with 350 beds, minimum stay one month (by application only); rates for single rooms start at $1,850 shared double rooms are also available for around $1,450 a person, depending on size. Must be working full time at a job or internship, or going to school. Apply several months in advance. Occupants receive reduced or free admission to the Y's renowned concerts and lectures, as well as the on-site fitness center and pool. Wi-Fi is also free. Kitchens and laundry on the premises as well.

- **Brandon Residence for Women**, 340 W 85th St between Riverside Dr and West End Ave, 212-496-6901; 120 single rooms, shared baths, a handsome lobby, and 24-hour security. Applicants who will be working or students must apply in advance, with approval pending an interview. Rates range from $1,023 to $1,218 a month, breakfast and dinner included.

- **Markle Evangeline Residence** (Salvation Army), 123 W 13th St, 212-242-2400; private room and bath, includes two meals a day, 24/7 security, Wi-Fi, and an excellent location in the heart of the Village Operated by The Salvation Army. Single, double, and quad rooms are available and rates range from $1,210 to $1,820/month. You can apply in advance online at http://gny.salvationarmy. org/MarkleResidence/residence-application.

- **St. Mary's Residence** (Daughters of the Divine Charity), 225 E 72nd St, 212-249-6850, www.stmarysresidence.blogspot.com; with three-month commitment, $231/week for private rooms with shared baths and facilities. Otherwise, $263 a week with two-week minimum stay. Women between the ages of 18 and 40 only, and residents must be interns, students, or beginning professionals.

- **Webster Apartments**, 419 W 34th St between Ninth and Tenth Aves, 212-967-9000, www.websterapartments.org; call well in advance to reserve for a minimum of four weeks at this attractive establishment, which features gardens and a library. An interview is required of applicants in the area; out-of-towners write directly for an application. Weekly rates are determined based on a sliding scale, and they start at $315 per week and go up to $405 per week. That's not a bad deal, considering that included is a private room, housekeeping five days a week, and two meals a day. Prospective residents must provide proof that they have a full-time job and earn an annual salary of $20,000–$60,000; otherwise, they must provide proof that they are fulfilling requirements of a college internship at least four days per week. Many residents here stay for months at a time (the maximum stay is five years), so if you're moving to the city and your place isn't quite ready, or if you're looking for the right place, this is a good option for women.

BED AND BREAKFASTS

In Manhattan? Yes! Many a resourceful New Yorker has let out that extra room and thrown a continental breakfast into the bargain. It's even possible to have the whole apartment, in a charming brownstone or a high-tech high-rise, to yourself, which is to say un-hosted. In any case, it will be cheaper than comparable digs in a hotel, but the visitor may give up something in privacy, service, or convenience. However, don't look for hand-lettered shingles advertising availability, because owners require anonymity and an agency acts as intermediary.

This cottage industry is unregulated (and, increasingly, under attack by the city, which wants to tax it), though reputable agencies inspect the properties they represent and attempt to monitor the quality of service and accommodations on an ongoing basis through visitor critique cards. Shop around by phone; be as specific as you can be about preferred location, likes and dislikes, allergies, and other restrictions. There is usually a minimum stay, but there may be exceptions off-season. For the best choice, book well in advance (reasonable B&Bs have gotten as scarce as affordable hotel rooms) and expect to pay at least a 25% deposit (some charge 50%), which may or may not be refundable, so be sure to ask. The commission is included in the fee. A sales tax, which varies, is charged above the room price. Many accept credit cards. Many people also rent out their entire apartments on a weekly/monthly basis to supplement their incomes. Check www.craigslist.com and www.airbnb.com for listings, but buyer beware.

- **1871 House**, 130 E 62nd St, 212-756-8823, www.1871house.com; want to stay in a historic brownstone on the fashionable Upper East Side, just two blocks from Bloomingdale's? Now you can. High ceilings, oriental rugs, cozy sitting areas, fireplaces, and plenty of antiques (no, this isn't the place for the kids). Seven spacious apartments, including two suites, with plenty of first-class amenities. Check availability and rates on the website.
- **Abode**, 520 E 76th St, Suite 3E, NYC 10021, 212-472-2000, www.abodenyc.com, represents about 50 un-hosted apartments, all in Manhattan, some long-term locations. They request business references from guests. Four-night minimum, rates vary. Most rooms non-smoking.
- **City Lights Bed and Breakfast and Short Term Apartment Rental**, 212-737-7049, www.citylightsnewyork.com, lists several hundred rooms and apartments, hosted and un-hosted, all in Manhattan. Rates vary depending on the accommodation; three-night minimum.
- **Manhattan Lodgings, Inc.**, 212-677-7616, www.manhattanlodgings.com, offers a wide range of furnished, short-stay apartments in Manhattan. Five-night minimum, six-month maximum; rates range from around $175 per night to $9,000 per month.

EXTENDED-STAY HOTELS

If your initial visit to New York City involves an extended stay as you search for work or an apartment, and you've chosen against a temporary sublet, you can mitigate the high costs of a hotel by choosing a chain that specializes in extended-stays, offering amenities, services, and prices for a visitor who will be around for more than a few days. The official visitors' site of New York City, www.nycgo.com, maintains a list of some extended-stay hotels, or you can consult our list below:

- **Affinia Hospitality**, 866-233-4642, www.affinia.com; options for weekly or monthly packages at the Affinity-managed The Fifty in Midtown, where you'll have access to a 24/7 fitness center, free Wi-Fi, and a range of special and promotional amenities and credits for services such as grocery delivery and laundry.

Be sure to ask if your unit includes a kitchenette if you want to be able to cook for yourself.

- **AKA**, 646-744-3434, www.stayaka.com, promotes its five locations (Central Park, Times Square, Sutton Place, United Nations, and Wall Street) as the ideal pied-a-terre, and it's not hard to see why, what with ideal positions in posh or central neighborhoods, apartments with full kitchens, and full-service staff on hand 24 hours a day.

- **The Marmara Manhattan**, 301 E 94th St, 212-427-3100, manhattan.marmaranyc.com, has 108 apartments that were formerly condominiums. Amenities include an exercise room and a daily buffet breakfast (charged as extra). Studios, one-, two-, and three-bedroom units available.

- **The Phillips Club**, 155 W 66th St, 212-835-8800, www.phillipsclub.com; at the high end and designed for the corporate traveler, contemporary apartments in a sleek 32-floor building just north of Lincoln Center, a few short blocks from Central Park. From overnight stays to extended stays to owning a piece of Manhattan real estate, you can enjoy luxurious surroundings at this corporate minded hotel. From $8,000 to $22,000 a month. Fully equipped kitchens.

HOTELS

There are over 90,000 hotel rooms in New York City. Prices and occupancy rates fluctuate seasonally depending on location. The friendly, and sometimes frenetic, first-class commercial establishments along Central Park West and Lexington and Park avenues in the East 40s and 50s are impossibly full on weekdays in the fall, winter, and spring, but both occupancy and prices languish during the dog days of summer. Typically, the in-season rates in New York City begin in the fall and extend through the holiday season. The most affordable deals can be had during the summer months when many New Yorkers head for the Hamptons and other beach locales. Additionally, there is significantly less business travel to the city during the summer and hotels are looking to fill their rooms, so many will offer amenities as part of a package. Keep in mind, however, that if you're traveling in winter, you may want to hold out for the city's newish "Hotel Week" promotion, when rooms that often exceed $300 may be had for as little as $100.

Weekend rates are almost always lower than prices charged during the week. However, glossy "weekend packages" with champagne, flowers, and free brunches for two don't represent the best value. Ask about the no-frills prices available Friday, Saturday, and sometimes Sunday nights. Weekend rates are, in effect, contingency plans to fill the house as corporate weeknight visitors depart. If full occupancy looms, off they go.

One place to look for deals is at the website of the **New York Convention and Visitors Bureau**, www.nycgo.com/hotels. Go there, or drop in at their Visitors Information Center (810 Seventh Avenue at 53rd Street, 212-484-1200), for an extensive listing of discounted hotel rooms. This useful site includes pictures, hotel descriptions, and ratings listed by date of availability, number of nights, number of beds, and online booking.

Hotel discounters buy blocks of rooms from hotels at volume discounts and pass savings, some as high as 60%, on to consumers. Visit their website or call for specifics. Generally, cancellations must be made 24 to 72 hours in advance; be sure to check their cancellation policies in advance Keep in mind, unless you know the city, you should inquire about the location of the hotel. A discounted room in a less desirable neighborhood may not be worth the savings. **Reservation services** include:

- **Central Reservation Services**, 800-894-0680, www.crshotels.com; especially good at getting mid- to low-priced rooms in New York and in about a dozen other cities.
- **Quikbook Hotels**, 800-789-9887, or 212-779-7666 from outside the U.S., www.quikbook.com; will connect you with a reservation agent who can reserve rooms at dozens of moderate to deluxe hotels all over Manhattan and Brooklyn (and nearly 50 other cities).

Additionally, you can check with the following:

- **Expedia.com**, 800-397-3342, www.expedia.com
- **Hotels.com**, 800-246-8357, www.hotels.com
- **Hotwire.com**, 866-468-9473, www.hotwire.com
- **Orbitz,** www.orbitz.com
- **Priceline.com**, www.priceline.com
- **Travelocity,** 855-201-7800, www.travelocity.com

Other websites send users weekly alerts about special regional "flash deals," or short-term sales. The most popular among these include:

- **Groupon**, www.groupon.com/getaways
- **Jetsetter**, www.jetsetter.com

A growing number of hotel apps for smartphones are being used by hotels to sell last minute rooms that haven't been booked to tech-savvy customers in search of a deal. Free apps you can download to your smartphone include Hotel Tonight (www.hoteltonight.com). Most of the hotel discounters noted above (i.e., Expedia and the like) also have their own smartphone apps, which are free to download. Some can be programmed to send you "push" notifications about last-minute deals.

Finally, if you're the type of person who prefers home-style accommodations to hotel rooms, www.craigslist.com and www.airbnb.com are among the many websites where you can find a room or an entire apartment for a short-term stay. At press time, city officials continued their legal battle against these sites, contending that apartment owners should pay taxes for these sublet-style arrangements; however, many owners and travelers continue to circumvent the conflict.

INEXPENSIVE HOTELS

Doubles for less than $300 a night, not including tax, may not seem cheap, but that's the range that more or less separates New York's bargain hotel category from the rest of the flock. Options on the lower cusp of $200 (and under) can also be found.

- **Best Western Seaport Inn**, 33 Peck Slip, 212-766-6600, www.seaportinn.com; pleasingly restored 19th century building one block from the waterfront at the very lower tip of Manhattan. Rooms are a bargain, especially if you get one of the upper floor rooms with great views of the Brooklyn Bridge.
- **Chelsea Savoy Hotel**, 204 W 23rd St, 212-929-9353, www.chelseasavoynyc.com; convenient and safe location in Chelsea, small (90 rooms), and reasonable prices.
- **Clarion Hotel Park Avenue**, 429 Park Ave South, 212-532-4860, www.clarionhotelny.com; you're unlikely to find an affordable hotel that's more convenient to the Empire State Building and Midtown shopping.
- **Excelsior**, 45 W 81st St, 212-362-9200, www.excelsiorhotelny.com; a landmark building in a great location, facing the American Museum of Natural History and Central Park. Rates vary by season and range from very reasonably priced standard rooms to suites. Health club and concierge.
- **Gershwin Hotel**, 7 E 27th St, 212-545-8000, www.gershwinhotel.com; east side hotel, within walking distance of Madison Square Park and the popular Italian food emporium, Eataly.
- **Hampton Inn**, 108 W 24th St, 212-414-1000, www.hamptoninn.com; located in Chelsea, it prides itself on offering stylish contemporary rooms at reasonable rates.
- **Herald Square**, 19 W 31st St, 800-727-1888, 212-279-4017, www.heraldsquarehotel.com; with a handsome Beaux-Arts facade, it's a favorite with European travelers looking for a good value. Good location, especially if you want to shop at Macy's.
- **Holiday Inn SoHo**, 138 Lafayette St, 212-966-8898, www.hidowntown-nyc.com; near Chinatown and Little Italy.
- **Hotel Wolcott**, 4 W 31st St, 212-268-2900, www.wolcott.com; near the Empire State Building and about 10 blocks from the theater district.
- **Hudson**, 356 W 58th St, 212-554-6000, www.hudsonhotel.com; opened in 2000 with 1,000 small rooms behind a bland brick facade. Inside, however, hotelier Ian Schrager and designer Philippe Starck fashioned a fascinating interior, which includes a public library with a pool table, a lobby-as-town-square, and a witty garden. On-site restaurant gets raves and the hotel is just a half-block from the Time Warner Center, with a Whole Foods and various retailers and restaurants. Also an excellent base for visitors who want to attend events at Lincoln Center.
- **Off SoHo Suites**, 11 Rivington St, off the Bowery 800-633-7646, www.offsoho.com; walking distance to SoHo, Chinatown, Alphabet City, and Nolita. Accom-

modations are clean and comfortable, and a bargain, especially for a family or a group of four. There are 38 suites, an on-site café, and 24-hour parking (fee).

- **Paramount**, 235 W 46th St, 212-764-5500, www.nycparamount.com; the designer of the avant-garde Royalton, Philippe Starck, turned his charms on a lower-priced venue. This whimsical effort aimed at the young and hip includes an on-site restaurant, nightclub, and coffee shop, as well as a 24/7 fitness room. Ask about special weekend rates.
- **Pod Hotels**, 230 E 51st St, 212-355-0300, and 145 E 39th St, 212-865-5700, www. thepodhotel.com; minimally hip and enormously popular little crash pads with style and an appealing price point at just over $200 a bed.
- **Row NYC**, 700 8th Ave, 888-352-3650, www.rownyc.com; formerly Milford Plaza, this hotel reopened in 2014 as an ultra-affordable Times Square option, with bright, clean rooms.
- **Washington Square Hotel**, 103 Waverly Place, 212-777-9515, www.wshotel. com; some rooms with views of the historic Washington Square Park.
- **Yotel**, 570 10th Ave, 646-449-7700, www.yotelnewyork.com; an antidote to "boring, overpriced hotels," Yotel is probably the most affordable, tech-forward hotel within easy walking distance to Times Square.

LONG ISLAND CITY HOTELS

Hotel deals can still be found in some parts of Manhattan during certain parts of the year, but a growing number of visitors are discovering that the Queens neighborhood of Long Island City, just five minutes by subway from midtown Manhattan, offers affordable, larger rooms in a setting that's less frenetic and commercialized than most of Manhattan.

If you're interested in booking a room in Long Island City, here are some of the hotels worth considering:

- **Four Points Sheraton**, 27-05 39th Ave, 718-786-8500, www. fourpointslongislandcity.com; just a few blocks from several subway lines and restaurants, this hotel is comfortable and convenient with the amenities that are standard for this reliable chain.
- **The Paper Factory Hotel**, 37-06 36th St, 718-392-7200, www.paperfactory-hotel.com; as its name suggests, this hotel was once a paper factory; now it's an option for visitors looking for trendy, design-savvy rooms at a more affordable price than Manhattan. Near several trains, a popular fair trade coffee shop (Coffeed), and the city's largest rooftop garden, it's a big draw for visitors to nearby Kaufman Astoria Studios.
- **Q4 Hotel**, 29-09 Queens Plaza North, 718-706-7700, www.q4hotel.com; convenient to Queensboro Plaza and the 7, N, and Q trains, as well as Queens Plaza, this hostel gets points for its "price is right" rates; some of its accommodations are as low as $40 a night.

- **Wyndham Garden Long Island City**, 44-29 9th St, 718-906-1900, www.wyndham. com; if you consult the map, you might be dissuaded from staying here; it's a long-ish walk to the nearest subway stations. Consider, however, that the hotel does have a free shuttle that makes regular runs to the trains, and in summer months, the location makes for a perfectly pleasant wander through the neighborhood's streets all the way over to the East River and Gantry Plaza State Park.
- **Z Hotel**, 11-01 43rd Ave, 212-319-7000, www.zhotelny.com; though it may sit in the shadow of some iconic landmarks, including the Queensboro Bridge and the Silvercup Studios sign, this boutique hotel isn't in an ideal location. It's a bit of a hike to the train, though a shuttle offers service to the subway. Still, guests love the modern design and, especially, the trendy rooftop bar with exceptional Manhattan views.

FIRST-CLASS COMMERCIAL OR DELUXE HOTELS

Manhattan is known for its grand and luxurious hotels, a handful of which are legendary: the Pierre, the Plaza, the Carlyle, the Plaza Athénée, the Waldorf Astoria, Four Seasons, and the Peninsula, to name but several—deluxe hotels all. We've chosen to list a few which are perhaps less well-known, on the basis of glamour and singularity as well as fair prices, when they can be found. Discounts and good weekend values in these hotels are generally available only in the summertime. Typically, rates in these hotels will be in the $600+ (some quite considerably +) range, with occasional off-season discounts.

Since rates change often and there are frequent special deals, you should call hotel reservations for rates or look online for special offers. Insiders recommend, in fact, looking up the lowest available price online and then calling the hotel to see if the reservations desk can beat or at least match it. In-room amenities including cable television and mini-bars are typically offered, and most hotels have a concierge and various services available, including afternoon tea, babysitting, massage, and personal shopping

- **Grand Hyatt New York**, 109 E 42nd St at Grand Central Terminal, 212-883-1234, www.grandnewyork.hyatt.com; fast-paced and glitzy, with a terrific lobby, especially when the fountains are splashing, and a dramatic bar cantilevered over 42nd Street. The penthouse health club and other features appeal to business travelers. Weekend specials sometimes available. New York Central Bar and Kitchen, the café-style Market, and The Lounge at New York Central are all on the premises for dining.
- **Mandarin Oriental**, 80 Columbus Circle at 60th St, 212-805-8800 or 866-801-8880, www.mandarinoriental.com; your Frette linens are attended to twice daily in this "most sophisticated" Central Park hotel. Dining includes the best and most expensive European and Asian restaurants in New York City, Per Se and

Masa. Health club on site. Afternoon tea offers a lovely—and truly bird's-eye—view of Columbus Circle and the southwest entrance to Central Park.

- **Michelangelo**, at the Equitable Center, 152 W 51st St at Seventh Ave, 212-765-1900, www.michelangelohotel.com; this is the old Taft Hotel resurrected in Euro-style "neoclassical" elegance to which well-designed rooms and great baths attract a glitzy crowd. Bring the kids. Summer rates are particularly good, and weekend packages may be available.
- **Millenium Hilton**, 55 Church St, 212-693-2001; www.hilton.com; classy and convenient (if you're visiting Wall Street), the Millenium offers stunning views of lower Manhattan, as well as computers and a health club with an attractive pool. Service is also top-notch. Call for rates. All rooms are discounted on weekends.
- **Millennium UN Plaza**, 1 UN Plaza at 44th St, 212-758-1234, www.unplazahotel.com; superior service and sensational views from every room because they begin on the 28th floor. A good-sized pool, health club, tennis court, and free limousine rides to Wall Street make this classically modern hotel unique. Great location.
- **Morgan's**, 237 Madison Ave between 37th and 38th Streets, 212-686-0300, www.morganshotel.com; an upstart on New York's rather traditional hotel scene, this narrow, vertical little place around the corner from the Morgan Library has been redecorated and toned down from its original sleek look to a more muted, design-conscious feel. Small but nicely appointed rooms.
- **Omni Berkshire Place**, 21 E 52nd St at Madison Ave, 212-753-5800, www.omnihotels.com; carefully created bouquets frame the elegant marble lobby and provide a backdrop for the classy tea-and-cocktail area on the far side of the flowers. An accommodating concierge caters to clients with dispatch in this bijou hotel, where the only major drawbacks are smallish rooms. Fitness center on site.
- **Royalton**, 44 W 44th St off Fifth Ave, 212-869-4400, www.royaltonhotel.com; with mahogany beds, Danish faucets, and French and Italian furniture, Ian Schrager has fashioned a swinging silk purse out of a sow's ear. Good location, especially if you love the theater.
- **San Carlos**, 150 E 50th St, between Lexington and Third Aves, 212-755-1800, www.sancarloshotel.com; quiet, small hotel with pleasantly spacious rooms and kitchenettes. Good location.
- **SoHo Grand**, 310 W Broadway between Grand and Canal Sts, 212-965-3000, www.sohogrand.com; one of the neighborhood's first design hotels, SoHo Grand, in-room tech amenities (DVD player and library, iPad and MacBook Pro loans upon request) are matched by cultural events, such as art openings and tech meet-ups, that are as popular among locals as the visitors who are staying there. Located in the midst of the art galleries, boutiques, and cafés that fill the formerly industrial buildings of this landmarked cast-iron district. Check out the Grand Bar & Lounge. Rates vary almost daily.
- **St. Regis**, 2 E 55th St at Fifth Ave, 212-753-4500; www.stregisnewyork.com; this *grande dame* of Fifth Avenue reopened in all her Beaux Arts glory, and then some, after a multi-million-dollar restoration in 1991, and all interiors were

renovated and redesigned again in 2013. If you can't spring for an overnight, do stop in for tea, preferably between Wednesday and Sunday, when a harpist lends even more sophisticated ambiance to the elegant experience
- **W New York Union Square**, 201 Park Ave S, 212 253-9119, www. wnewyorkunionsquare.co; one of several W hotels in NYC, this is one of the most prominent, on Union Square in lower Manhattan. It is really only steps to the city's most popular Greenmarket, where you're likely to rub elbows with famous chefs.

SOME FAVORITES

Small, charming, personal-feeling hotels are not the city's forte, but we list a handful of fairly priced, medium-sized hotels in other Manhattan areas that deserve special mention (the hotels included here reflect a purely personal taste and are not meant to be an all-city catalog of lodgings):

- **Algonquin**, 59 W 44th St, 212-840-6800, www.algonquinhotel.com; This city and literary landmark has long attracted the discerning customer, and its famous lobby bar combines with anachronistic elevators and smallish, genteel rooms to make you feel welcome, secure, and part of a pleasantly elite and talented group. Enjoy cocktails in the Blue Bar or dinner in the on-site restaurant, Round Table. Call for rates and ask about specials, particularly in the summer.
- **DoubleTree Suites**, 1568 Broadway, 212-719-1600, www.doubletree3.hilton. com; overlooking Times Square, DoubleTree rents suites (with sitting room and bedroom) rather than single rooms, at reasonable rates.
- **Hotel Wales**, 1295 Madison Av St, 212-876-6000, www.hotelwalesnyc.com; clean and cheerful hotel, the Wales represents good value in tastefully renovated rooms. Terrific location for Museum Mile along Fifth Ave.
- **Lowell**, 28 E 63rd St, 212-838-1400, www.lowellhotel.com, is a small, 74-room European-style hotel with plenty of amenities, on a quiet Upper East Side street. The more-attractive-than-ever art deco hotel remains intimate and friendly. Great location. Ask about specials.
- **Salisbury**, 123 W 57th St, 212-246-1300, www.nycsalisbury.com; pleasant, pastel rooms in a relatively intimate setting attract a high percentage of women travelers. Large rooms, good prices, and convenient to Central Park.

NEW YORK CITY CRACKLES WITH EVENTS: PARADES, FESTIVALS, CELE-brations, ethnic holidays, shows, feasts, and tournaments. Imperceptible at first, there is, in fact, a rhythm to this endless round of activity; many of these events occur annually at about the same time, and New Yorkers look forward to them. The calendar below lists them by month. Check out the *New York Times*, *New York Magazine*, *Time Out New York*, or the *New Yorker* for specific dates and details. Or stop by the **New York Convention & Visitors Bureau** at 810 Seventh Avenue at 53rd Street, 212-484-1200, to pick up brochures and a complete seasonal calendar of events, or go to their website at www.nycgo.com.

The following is just a fraction of what the Big Apple has to offer.

JANUARY

- **Big Apple Circus**, Lincoln Center, www.bigapplecircus.org
- **Broadway Week**, www.nycgo.com/broadwayweek
- **Hotel Week**, http://www.njfpr.com/hotel-week
- **New York Boat Show,** Jacob Javits Center, www.newyorkboatshow.com
- **Three Kings Day Parade**, www.elmuseo.org
- **Winter Antiques Show,** Park Avenue Armory, www.winterantiquesshow.com
- **Winter Jam**, Central Park, www.nycgovparks.org

FEBRUARY

- **Black History Month**, citywide events
- **Chinese New Year** celebrations, Chinatown and elsewhere
- **Off-Broadway Week**, www.nycgo.com/offbroadwayweek
- **Ringling Brothers & Barnum & Bailey Circus**, Brooklyn, Barclays Center

- **Valentine's Day Wedding Event** at the Empire State Building, www.esbnyc. com
- **Westminster Kennel Club Annual Westminster Dog Show**, Madison Square Garden, www.westminsterkennelclub.org
- **Winter Restaurant Week**, various restaurants in Manhattan, www.nycgo.com/ restaurantweek

MARCH

- **Greek Independence Day Parade**, Fifth Avenue, www.hellenicsocieties.org/ PARADES.html
- **Macy's Flower Show,** http://social.macys.com/flowershow
- **New York City FC and New York Red Bulls** soccer season begins, www.nycfc. com, www.newyorkredbulls.com
- New York International Children's Film Festival, www.gkids.com
- **St. Patrick's Day Parade**, Fifth Avenue, www.nycstpatricksparade.org
- **The Pier Antiques Show**, Manhattan, www.pierantiqueshow.com

APRIL

- **BeFilm: The Underground Film Festival**, www.befilm.net
- **Cherry Blossom Festival** (Sakura Matsuri), Brooklyn Botanic Garden, www. bbg.org
- **Easter Parade**, Fifth Avenue
- **New York International Auto Show**, Manhattan, www.autoshowny.com
- **New York Mets and New York Yankees** baseball season begins**,** http:// newyork.mets.mlb.com, http://newyork.yankees.mlb.com
- **PEN World Voices Festival**, www.worldvoices.pen.org
- **Tribeca Film Festival**, www.tribecafilmfestival.com

MAY

- **9th Avenue International Food Festival**, 42nd to 57th streets**,** www. ninthavenuefoodfestival.com
- **TD Five Boro Bike Tour**, www.bikenewyork.org
- **Book Expo America,** Javits Center, www.bookexpoamerica.com
- **Fleet Week**, Manhattan, www.fleetweeknewyork.com
- **Lower East Side Festival of the Arts**, www.theaterforthenewcity.net
- **Manhattan Cocktail Classic,** www.manhattancocktailclassic.com
- **Outsider Art Fair**, www.outsiderartfair.com
- **Washington Square Outdoor Art Exhibit**, Spring show, on the sidewalks of University Place from East 13th Street south along the side of Washington

Square Park to NYU's Schwartz Plaza (between Bobst Library and Shimkin Hall) and W 3rd St, www.wsoae.org

JUNE

- **Annual Lesbian and Gay Pride March**, www.nycpride.org
- **Belmont Stakes**, Belmont Park, www.belmontstakes.com
- **Bronx Puerto Rican Day Parade**
- **Brooklyn Pride Week**, www.brooklynpride.org
- **Bryant Park Summer Film Festival**, www.bryantpark.org
- **Celebrate Brooklyn!**, Brooklyn, www.bricartsmedia.org
- **Feast of St. Anthony of Padua**, Sullivan Street below Houston, www.stanthonynyc.org
- **Hudson River Park** summer events begin, www.hudsonriverpark.org
- **Mermaid Parade**, Coney Island, Brooklyn, www.coneyisland.com
- **Midsummer Night Swing** at Lincoln Center, www.midsummernightswing.org
- **Museum Mile Festival**, Fifth Avenue, www.museummilefestival.org
- **National Puerto Rican Day Parade**, Fifth Avenue, www.nprdpinc.org
- **Celebrate Israel Parade**, Fifth Avenue, www.celebrateisraelny.org
- **Shakespeare in the Park**, Delacorte Theatre, www.publictheater.org
- **SummerStage** concerts begin, Central Park, www.summerstage.donyc.com

JULY

- **Festa de Giglio**, Brooklyn, www.olmcfeast.com
- **Fringe Festival**, www.fringenyc.org
- **Harlem Week**, Harlem, www.harlemweek.com
- **Lincoln Center Out of Doors Festival**, www.lcoutofdoors.org
- **Macy's 4th of July Fireworks**, Manhattan, http://social.macys.com/fireworks
- **Summer Restaurant Week**, www.nycgo.com/restaurantweek

AUGUST

- **Mostly Mozart Festival**, Lincoln Center, www.mostlymozart.org
- **Summer Streets**, closing of NYC main streets to cars on assorted weekends, www.nyc.gov/summerstreets
- **US Open Tennis Tournament**, Flushing, Queens, www.usopen.org

SEPTEMBER

- **African-American Day Parade**, Adam Clayton Powell Blvd, www.africanamericandayparade.org

- **BAM Next Wave Festival**, Brooklyn, www.bam.org
- **Brooklyn Book Festival**, www.brooklynbookfestival.org
- **Feast of San Gennaro**, Mulberry Street, Little Italy, www.sangennaro.org
- **Labor Day Parade**, Fifth Avenue, 33rd to 72nd Streets
- **Metropolitan Opera** season begins, Lincoln Center, www.metopera.org
- **New York Film Festival**, Lincoln Center, www.filmlinc.com
- **NY Giants** and **NY Jets Football** season opens, New Jersey, www.giants.com, www.newyorkjets.com
- **German-American Steuben Parade**, Fifth Avenue, www.germanparadenyc. org
- **Washington Square Outdoor Art Exhibit,** Fall show, on the sidewalks of University Place from East 13th Street south along the side of Washington Square Park to NYU's Schwartz Plaza (between Bobst Library and Shimkin Hall) and W 3rd St, www.wsoae.org
- **West Indian American Day Carnival**, Brooklyn, www.wiadca.com
- **Wigstock**, Pier 54, 13th Street and Hudson River, www.wigstock.nu

OCTOBER

- **Columbus Day Parade**, Fifth Avenue
- **Feast of St. Francis**, pets and animals from goldfish to horses come to church by the thousands to be blessed, www.stjohndivine.org
- **Village Halloween Parade**, Sixth Avenue, www.halloween-nyc.com
- **Hispanic Day Parade**, Fifth Avenue
- **New York City Wine and Food Festival**, www.nycwff.org
- **New York Rangers** hockey season begins, Madison Square Garden, http://rangers.nhl.com
- **Next Wave Festival**, Brooklyn Academy of Music, www.bam.org
- **Pulaski Day Parade**, Fifth Avenue, www.pulaskiparade.com

NOVEMBER

- **Radio City Christmas Spectacular,** Radio City Music Hall, www.radiocity.com
- **Christmas Tree Lighting**, Rockefeller Center, www.rockefellercenter.com
- **New York City Marathon**, www.tcsnycmarathon.org
- **New York Knicks basketball season begins**, Madison Square Garden, www. nba.com/knicks
- **New York City Ballet**, winter season, Lincoln Center, www.nycballet.com
- **Macy's Thanksgiving Day Parade**, 77th Street to Herald Square, http://social. macys.com/parade
- **Skating Season**, free and fee-based rinks open throughout the city, including www.bryantpark.org, www.wollmanskatingrink.com, www.rockefellercenter.com

- **Veterans Day Parade**, Fifth Avenue, www.americasparade.org

DECEMBER

- **Fireworks**, South Street Seaport; Grand Army Plaza, Brooklyn
- **First Night/New Year's Eve**, events throughout city, www.nycgo.com
- **Lighting of the Hanukkah Menorah**, the world's largest, Grand Army Plaza, Brooklyn
- **New York Road Runners Club Midnight Run**, Central Park, www.nyrrc.org
- **New Year's Eve Celebration**, Times Square, www.balldrop.com
- **New Year's Eve Concert**, New York Philharmonic, Lincoln Center, www.nyphil.org

B ELOW, WE LIST A FEW BOOKS THAT THE NEWCOMER MAY FIND HELPFUL, enlightening, or just entertaining.

GUIDES

- *AIA Guide to New York City* edited by Norval White, Elliot Willensky, and Fran Leadon (Oxford University Press); the guide and reference book for anyone interested in New York City architecture. Includes maps, drawings, and directions to neighborhoods throughout the five boroughs. Encyclopedic and fascinating.
- *Birds of New York City Including Central Park and Long Island* by Randi Minetor (Quick Reference Publishing); map-style guide with plenty of color photos to make identification easier.
- *The Cheap Bastard's Guide to New York City* by Rob Grader (Globe Pequot Press); tips on leading the good life in the city … for pennies.
- *City Walks: New York: 50 Adventures on Foot* by Christina Henry de Tessan (Chronicle); pick a card, any card, and set off on an adventure, propelled by your own two feet.
- *Field Guide to the Natural World of New York City* by Leslie Day (Johns Hopkins University Press); paintings, photos, and maps accompany engaging text that just might convince you New York is much more biologically diverse than you ever imagined.
- *New York Tenants' Rights* by Mary Ann Hallenborg (Nolo Press); though somewhat dated (published in 2002), the author, a landlord-tenant lawyer, provides information that remains useful for new and long-time New Yorkers.

ZAGAT SURVEY GUIDES

- *Zagat Survey: New York City Restaurants*
- *Zagat Survey: New York City Shopping & Food Lover's Guide*

NEW YORK CITY EPHEMERA, ODDITIES, NARRATIVES, AND NICHE INTERESTS

- *Appetite City: A Culinary History of New York* by William Grimes (North Point Press); the *New York Times'* former food critic takes a comprehensive and compelling approach to telling the history of New York's food scene.
- *Here is New York* by E. B. White (Little Bookroom); maybe he's better known for his children's literature, such as *Charlotte's Web*, but E. B. White's slim volume of observations about the city manages to feel both time-bound and timeless, a rare feat.
- *Humans of New York* by Brandon Stanton (St. Martin's Press); the photographer behind the popular blog of the same name collects some of his favorite portraits of New Yorkers, both ordinary and the extraordinary, in this bestselling volume.
- *My First New York: Early Adventures in the Big City (As Remembered by Actors, Artists, Athletes, Chefs, Comedians, Filmmakers, Mayors, Models, Moguls, Porn Stars, Rockers, Writers, and Others)*, compiled by the staff of New York Magazine (Ecco); the lengthy subtitle almost says it all: famous (and a few not so famous) folks' recollections of their earliest adventures in New York.
- *The New York Nobody Knows: Walking 6,000 Miles in the City* by William Helmreich (Princeton University Press); if you were to walk in Helmreich's shoes, you'd traverse nearly every one of the city's streets—6,000 miles in all—meeting the diverse people who make the city what it is. You don't have to walk in his shoes, though; you can just read this book, which is a love letter of sorts to New York.

NEW YORK CITY HISTORY

- *Central Park, An American Masterpiece: a Comprehensive History of the Nation's First Urban Park* by Sara Cedar Miller (Harry N. Abrams)
- *Discovering Black New York: A Guide to the City's Most Important African American Landmarks, Restaurants, Museums, Historical Sites, and More* by Linda Tarrant Reid (Citadel Books); most of the restaurant material is dated, but the history remains a good guide.
- *The Encyclopedia of New York City* edited by Kenneth T. Jackson (Yale University Press); from A&P to Zukofsky, this unwieldy literary monument will delight any Gotham-lover.
- *Gotham: A History of New York City to 1898* by Edwin G. Burrows and Mike Wallace (Oxford University Press); the best and most comprehensive history of early New York.
- *Literary Landmarks of New York: The Book Lover's Guide to the Homes and Haunts of World Famous Writers* by Bill Morgan (Universe; provides a unique look at the city through the city's great scribes, from Poe to Mailer.
- *New York for New Yorkers: A Historical Treasury and Guide to the Buildings and Monuments of Manhattan* by Liza M. Greene (W.W. Norton & Co.); as 21st

century trends grip the city and transform its skyscape, this book seems increasingly important for visual reference to historical styles of "old" New York.

- *New York Streetscapes: Tales of Manhattan's Significant Buildings and Landmarks* by Christopher Gray and Suzanne Braley (Harry N. Abrams); Gray, an architectural historian and *New York Times* columnist, shares the backstories of many of the city's most iconic structures.
- *The WPA Guide to New York City: The Federal Writers' Project Guide to the 1930s New York* by William Whyte—Federal Writers Project (Pantheon Books); the city, mapped, photographed, illustrated, and described in this classic. Among the writers, the young John Cheever.

PARENTS/STUDENTS

- *City Kid New York: The Ultimate Guide for NYC Parents with Kids Ages 4-12* (2010 edition) by Alison Lowenstein (Universe); an indispensable guide to everything from how to fit furniture into your kid's bedroom to how to throw a kid's birthday party in NYC (trust us; you'll need this advice).
- *Frommer's New York City with Kids* (2011 edition) by Alexis Lipsitz Flippin (Frommer's); this useful family-friendly travel guidebook will be especially handy for parents who have just relocated to the city and are keen to discover kid-centric spots.
- *The Manhattan Directory of Private Nursery Schools* (7th edition, 2012) by Victoria Goldman, (Soho Press); it may seem insane (and *is*, in most other parts of the country) that parents need to give so much thought to how they choose a nursery school, but if you plan to have kids in New York, it's never too early to plan for the care and education of your child.

ONCE YOU'VE ESTABLISHED YOURSELF AS NEW YORK'S NEWEST RESI-
dent, you'll want to get to the business of setting up house (or
apartment!) and learning to navigate the city's and state's most essential
services. From decoding the system that governs how and where to park your
car—if you're brave enough to have one here—to figuring out the city's garbage
rules, setting up Internet and cable TV, and if you need it, seeking medical help,
there's a lot to learn when you're resettling in a new city ... especially one as big
and as busy as New York.

What follows is a partial listing of phone numbers and websites that cover a
variety of services, both local and state. Many others are embedded throughout
the book. Check in your section of interest for additional listings.

A great number of city services and agencies are available through two principal conduits: **311** is the city's 24-hour, all-purpose information line, with live
operators prepared to connect you to virtually any city service, from reporting
leaking fire hydrants to finding a towed car; **www.nyc.gov** is the main page for
nearly all of the city's government agencies and services.

ALCOHOL AND DRUG DEPENDENCY

- **Alcoholics Anonymous**, 212-647-1680, www.nyintergroup.org
- **Cocaine Anonymous**, 877-858-8012, www.canewyork.org
- **Narcotics Anonymous, Inc.**, 212-929-6262, www.newyorkna.org
- **National Council on Alcoholism and Drug Dependence,** 212-269-7797,
  www.ncadd.org
- **The Watershed**, 800-861-1768, www.thewatershed.com, a referral service for
  addiction to alcohol and drugs and 24-hour help line

ANIMALS

- **ASPCA**, American Society for the Prevention of Cruelty to Animals, 888-666-2279, 212-876-7700, www.aspca.org
- **Animal Bites**, Bureau of Veterinary Public Health Services, 646-632-6604
- **Animal Medical Center**, 212-838-8100, www.amcny.org; open 24 hours; phone calls 9 a.m. to 11 p.m.
- **Animal Care and Control of NYC,** Manhattan Shelter and Adoption Center, 212-788-4000, www.nycacc.org
- **Animal Rescue Service**, 311

BIRTH/DEATH CERTIFICATES

- **New York City Department of Health**, Vital Records, 311, www.nyc.gov/records

CABLE TELEVISION AND THE DISH

CABLE

MANHATTAN

- **Optimum**, 718-860-3513, www.optimum.net
- **Time Warner Cable**, 800-892-4357, www.timewarnercable.com
- **RCN**, 800-746-4726, www.rcn.com
- **Verizon**, 877-723-8428, www.verizon.com

NEW JERSEY

- **New Jersey**, 866-541-0548, www.cablevision.com
- **Comcast**, 800-934-6489, www.comcast.com

DISH

- **DIRECTV**, 855-854-4388, www.directv.com
- **Dish Network**, 800-823-4929, www.dishnetwork.com

CONSUMER COMPLAINTS AND SERVICES

- **Better Business Bureau**, 212-533-6200, www.bbb.org/new-york-city
- **Federal Trade Commission**, 877-382-4357, www.ftc.gov
- **NJ Attorney General's Consumer Protection Hotline**, 973-504-6200, www.njconsumeraffairs.gov/ocp
- **New York City Department of Consumer Affairs**, 311, www.nyc.gov/dca
- **NY State Attorney General's Consumer Help Line**, 800-771-7755, www.ag.ny.gov
- **NY State Consumer Protection,** 518-474-8583, 800-697-1220, www.dos.ny.gov/consumerprotection

- **NY State Department of Insurance, Consumer Services Bureau**, complaints and inquiries, 212-480-6400, 9 a.m. to 5 p.m., Monday through Friday, www.dfs.ny.gov/consumer/fileacomplaint.htm
- **New York State Department of Transportation**, 518-457-6195, www.dot.ny.gov
- **New York StateConsumer Hotline**, 800-342-3736, www.dfs.ny.gov
- **Public Service Commission's Call Center**, 800-342-3377, www.dps.ny.gov
- **U.S. Consumer Product Safety Commission Hotline**, 800-638-2772, www.cpsc.gov

CRIME/CRISIS

- **Crime in progress**, 911
- **Precinct referrals,** dial 311 or 212-NEW-YORK
- **Suspicious behavior/unattended packages**, 888-NYC-SAFE for MTA

CRISIS HOTLINES

- **Ambulance**, 911
- **Arson Hotline**, 718-722-3600
- **Boys Town National Hotline**, 800-448-3000, www.boystown.org
- **Manhattan District Attorney's Office, Sex Crimes Unit**, 212-335-9373
- **NYPD 24-hour Rape Hotline**, 212-267-7273
- **Safe Horizon, Domestic Violence/Rape/Battered Persons Crisis Center Hotline**, 800-621-4673
- **Samaritans of New York Crisis Response Hotline**, 212-673-3000, www.samaritansnyc.org

CHILD ABUSE & FAMILY VIOLENCE

- **National Center for Missing and Exploited Children**, 800-843-5678, www.missingkids.com
- **New York State Office of Children and Family Services**, Abuse and Maltreatment Report Line, 800-342-3720, www.ocfs.state.ny.us/main/cps
- **NYC Administration for Children's Services**, Emergency Children's Services, 212-966-8000, www.nyc.gov/html/acs
- **Safe Horizon, Domestic Violence Hotline**, 800-621-4673, 24-hour

CULTURAL LIFE

- **Curator's Choice**, http://nymuseums.com

- **New York City & Company**, Convention and Visitors Bureau, 212-484-1200, www.nycgo.com
- *New York Magazine*, www.nymag.com
- *New York Times*, www.nytimes.com
- *New Yorker*, www.newyorker.com
- **NYC-ARTS,** www.nyc-arts.org
- **Telecharge**, 212-239-6200, www.telecharge.com
- **Theatre Development Fund's TKTS Discount Booths**, 212-912-9770, www. tdf.org
- **Ticketmaster**, 800-653-8000, www.ticketmaster.com
- *Time Out New York,* www.timeoutny.com
- **Times Square Alliance**, 212-768-1560, www.timessquarenyc.org; business improvement district
- *Village Voice*, www.villagevoice.com

DISCRIMINATION

- **New Jersey Civil Rights Commission**, 609-292-4605, www.state.nj.us/oag/dcr/commission.html
- **New York City Commission on Human Rights**, 212-306-7560, www.nyc.gov/cchr
- **U.S. Department of Housing and Urban Development**, Fair Housing Complaint Hotline, 800-669-9777, http://portal.hud.gov

EDUCATION

- **New Jersey Department of Education**, 877-900-6960, www.nj.gov/education
- **New York City Department of Education**, 311, http://schools.nyc.gov

ELECTIONS

- **Board of Elections**, 866-VOTE-NYC, TDD 212-487-5496, 9 a.m. to 5 p.m., Monday to Friday, www.vote.nyc.ny.us

EMERGENCY

- **FEMA Disaster Assistance Information**, 800-621-FEMA, TTY 800-427-5593, www.fema.gov
- **Fire, police, medical**, 911
- **Notify NYC Emergency Messaging System**, 311, www1.nyc.gov/nyc-resources/service/2115/notify-nyc-information-and-registration

- **Poison Control Center**, (national) 800-222-1222, TDD 212-689-9014, www. aapcc.org; (NYC) 212-POISONS, www.nyc.gov/html/doh

GOVERNMENT

- **State and local government listings** for all profiled communities are on the net at www.statelocalgov.net.

NEW YORK CITY
- **Bronx Borough President**, 718-590-3500, http://bronxboropres.nyc.gov
- **Brooklyn Borough President**, 718-802-3700, www.brooklyn-usa.org
- **City Council**, 311, www.council.nyc.gov
- **Manhattan Borough President**, 212-669-8300, http://manhattanbp.nyc.gov
- **New York City Mayor's Office/City Hall**, 311, www.nyc.gov
- **Official New York City Website**, www.nyc.gov
- **Public Advocate**, 212-669-7200, www.pubadvocate.nyc.gov
- **Queens Borough President**, 718-286-3000, www.queensbp.org
- **Staten Island Borough President**, 718-816-2000, www.statenislandusa.com

NEW YORK STATE
- **Attorney General**, 800-771-7755, TTY 800-788-9898, www.ag.ny.gov
- **Governor's Office**, 518-474-8390, www.governor.ny.gov
- **State Assembly**, 518-455-4218, www.assembly.state.ny.us
- **State Senate**, www.nysenate.gov

STATE OF NEW JERSEY
- **Attorney General**, 609-292-4925, www.state.nj.us/lps
- **Governor's Office**, 609-292-6000, www.state.nj.us
- **New Jersey Legislature Office of Legislative Services**, 609-847-3905, www. njleg.state.nj.us

FEDERAL
- **Federal Citizen Information Center**, 800-333-4636, www.gsa.gov/fcic
- **Social Security Administration**, 800-772-1213, 7 a.m. to 7 p.m., Monday to Friday, www.ssa.gov

HEALTH AND MEDICAL CARE

- **Ambulance Emergency Number**, 911
- **Dental Emergencies**, New York County Dental Society, 212-573-8500, www. nycdentalsociety.org
- **Lead Poisoning Prevention Program**, 311, www.nyc.gov
- **National Health Information Center** (**NHIC**), U.S. Department of Health and Human Services, 240-453-8280, www.health.gov/nhic

- **NJ State Board of Medical Examiners**, 609-826-7100, www.state.nj.us/lps/ca/medical.htm
- **New York City Department of Health and Mental Hygiene**, 311, www.nyc.gov/html/doh
- **New York County Medical Society (AMA)**, 212-684-4670, www.nycms.org
- **NY State Department of Health** 866-881-2809, www.health.ny.gov
- **New York Public Advocate**, 212-669-7250, www.pubadvocate.nyc.gov
- **Poison Control Center**, (national) 800-222-1222, TDD 212-689-9014, www.aapcc.org; (NYC) 212-POISONS, www.nyc.gov/html/doh
- **U.S. Department of Health and Human Services**, 877-696-6775, www.hhs.gov

HOSPITALS

- **Bellevue Hospital Center**, 212-562-3015, www.nyc.gov/hhc
- **Calvary Hospital**, Bronx, 718-518-2000, www.calvaryhospital.org
- **Coler-Goldwater Hospital**, Roosevelt Island, 212-318-8000, www.nyc.gov/html/hhc/coler-goldwater
- **Columbia University Medical Center**, 212-305-2500, www.cumc.columbia.edu
- **Harlem Hospital Center**, 212-939-1000, www.nyc.gov/hhc
- **Jacobi Medical Center**, Bronx, 718-918-5000, www.nyc.gov/hhc
- **Jamaica Hospital Medical Center**, Queens, 718-206-6000, www.jamaicahospital.org
- **Kings County Hospital Center**, Brooklyn, 718-245-3131, www.nyc.gov/hhc
- **Lenox Hill Hospital**, 212-434-2000, www.lenoxhillhospital.org
- **Manhattan Eye, Ear and Throat Hospital**, 212-838-9200, www.lenoxhillhospital.org
- **Metropolitan Hospital Center**, 212-423-7000, www.nyc.gov/mhc
- **Mount Sinai Beth Israel,** 212-420-2000, www.mountsinaihealth.org
- **Mount Sinai Medical Center,** 212-241-6500, www.mountsinai.org
- **Mount Sinai Roosevelt,** 212-523-4000, www.roosevelthospitalnyc.org
- **New York Eye and Ear Infirmary of Mount Sinai**, 212-979-4000, www.nyee.edu
- **New York-Presbyterian Hospital/Weill Cornell Medical Center**, 212-746-5454, www.nyp.org/facilities/weillcornell.html
- **New York Presbyterian-Lower Manhattan Hospital**, 212-312-5000, www.nyp.org/lowermanhattan
- **New York University Langone Medical Center**, 212-263-7300, www.med.nyu.edu
- **Richmond University Medical Center**, Staten Island, 718-818-1234, www.rumcsi.org
- **Staten Island University Hospital**, Staten Island, 718-226-9140, www.siuh.edu

- **Woodhull Medical and Mental Health Center**, Brooklyn, 718-963-8000, www.nyc.gov/hhc

HOUSING RESOURCES

- **Department of Environmental Protection**, 311, www.nyc.gov/dep
- **Department of Homes and Community Renewal**, 212-480-6700, rent information line 718-739-6400, www.dhcr.state.ny.us
- **Gas or electric service shutoff hotline**, 800-342-3355
- **Housing Authority**, 212-306-3000, www.nyc.gov/nycha
- **Metropolitan Council on Housing**, 212-979-0611, www.metcouncilonhousing.org
- **New Jersey Landlord Tenant Information Service**, 609-292-4174, www.state.nj.us/dca
- **New Jersey Tenants Organization (NJTO)**, 201-342-3775, www.njto.org
- **New York City Loft Board**, www.nyc.gov/html/loft
- **New York City Rent Guidelines Board**, 212-385-2934, www.nycrgb.org
- **NYC Heat Hotline**, 311
- **NYC Urban League**, 212-926-8000, www.nyul.org
- **Office of Rent Administration**, State's Department of Homes and Community Renewal (DHCR), 866-275-3427, www.nyshcr.org
- **Rent Stabilization Association**, 212-214-9200, www.rsanyc.org
- **TenantNet**, www.tenant.net
- **Tenants & Neighbors**, 212-608-4320, www.tenantsandneighbors.org
- **U.S. Department of Housing and Urban Development**, Fair Housing Complaint Hotline, 800-669-9777, http://portal.hud.gov

INFORMATION LINES

- **New York's "311" line** (212-NEW-YORK outside New York City) is the general information line for all city agencies and related services. Operators will transfer calls to appropriate agency departments based on your specific needs.
- **411, 212-555-1212, 718-555-1212**, are general information lines that can be used for locating either commercial businesses or personal phone numbers of anyone or any business listed in the New York City telephone directories. Depending on your phone service provider, you may be charged for directory assistance calls.

INTERNET SERVICE PROVIDERS

- **America Online**, 800-827-6364, www.aol.com
- **AT&T**, 866-861-6075, www.att.com

- **Earthlink**, 888-806-0907, www.earthlink.net
- **NetZero**, 877-665-9995, www.netzero.net
- **RCN**, 800-RING-RCN, www.rcn.com
- **Time Warner Cable**, 800-431-8878, www.timewarnercable.com
- **Verizon**, 800-VERIZON, www.verizon.com

LIBRARIES

See **Literary Life** in the **Cultural Life** chapter for descriptions of **area libraries**. For **branch libraries,** see listings following individual **Neighborhood Profiles**.

- **Bronx Library Center**, 718-579-4244, www.nypl.org
- **Brooklyn Central Library**, 718-623-7100, http://www.bklynlibrary.org/
- **New York Public Library Central Branch**, 212-340-0863, www.nypl.org
- **Queens Library**, 718-990-0728, www.queenslibrary.org
- **Staten Island**, St. George Library, 718-442-8560, www.nypl.org

MARRIAGE LICENSES

- **NYC Marriage Bureau**, 212-669-2400, www.cityclerk.nyc.gov

MOTOR VEHICLES/PARKING

- **American Automobile Association**, 212-757-2000, www.ny.aaa.com
- **Licenses and Registration Information**, New York State Department of Motor Vehicles, 212-645-5550, 8 a.m. to 4 p.m., www.dmv.ny.gov
- **New Jersey Motor Vehicle Commission**, 609-292-6500, www.state.nj.us/mvc
- **NYPD Towing** (towed cars), 311
- **Parking Violations Information**: to locate a car that has been towed and/or to check the status of a parking violation, visit http://nycserv.nyc.gov/NYCServWeb/NYCSERVMain or call 311.
- **State Department of Motor Vehicles**, 212-645-5550, www.dmv.ny.gov

PARKS AND RECREATION

See also **Sports and Recreation** and **Greenspace and Beaches** chapters.

- **General information**, including special events, 888-NY-PARKS, www.nycgovparks.org

POLICE

See **Neighborhoods** chapter for precinct stations.

- **New Jersey State Police**, 609-882-2000, www.njsp.org
- **New York State Police,** NYC, 917-492-7100, www.troopers.ny.gov
- **Police Emergencies**, dial 911

POST OFFICE

- **U.S. Postal Service**, 800-275-8777, www.usps.com

SANITATION AND GARBAGE

- **NYC Department of Sanitation**, dial 311, www.nyc.gov/dsny

SENIORS

- **NYC Department for the Aging**, 311, www.nyc.gov/aging
- **New York Foundation for Senior Citizens**, 212-962-7559, www.nyfsc.org
- **Social Security and Medicare Eligibility Information**, 800-772-1213, TTY 800-325-0778, 7 a.m. to 7 p.m., Monday to Friday, www.ssa.gov

SPORTS

PARTICIPANT SPORTS AND ACTIVITIES
- **Bronx Chief of Recreation**, 718-430-1858
- **Brooklyn Office of the Department of Parks and Recreation**, 718-965-8900
- **Central Park Conservancy**, 212-310-6600, www.centralparknyc.org
- **Gateway National Recreation Area**, 718-338-3799, www.nps.gov/gate
- **Manhattan**, 212-408-0205
- **New York City Department of Parks and Recreation**, 311, www.nycgovparks. org
- **Queens Recreation**, 718-393-7370
- **Staten Island**, 718-390-8000

PROFESSIONAL
- **Brooklyn Nets,** 718-933-3000, www.nba.com/nets
- **New Jersey Devils**, 800-NJ-DEVIL, http://devils.nhl.com
- **New York City Football Club**, www.nycfc.com
- **New York Giants**, 201-935-8222, www.giants.com
- **New York Islanders**, 800-882-ISLES, http://islanders.nhl.com
- **New York Jets**, 800-469-JETS, www.newyorkjets.com
- **New York Knicks**, 212-465-5867, 877-NYK-DUNK, www.nba.com/knicks
- **New York Liberty**, 212-465-6073, www.wnba.com/liberty
- **New York Mets**, 718-507-METS, www.mets.mlb.com

- **New York Rangers**, 212-465-6000, http://rangers.nhl.com
- **New York Red Bulls**, www.newyorkredbulls.com
- **New York Yankees**, 718-293-4300, http://newyork.yankees.mlb.com

STREET MAINTENANCE

- **Potholes**, NYC Bureau of Highways, 311
- **Streetlights**, 311
- **Water mains and sewers**, NYC Department of Environmental Protection, 311

TAXES

CITY
- **NYC Department of Finance**, 311, www.nyc.gov/dof

FEDERAL
- **Internal Revenue Service**, 800-829-4477, www.irs.gov

STATE
- **New Jersey Department of the Treasury,** 609-292-6748, www.state.nj.us/treasury/taxation
- **NYS Department of Taxation and Finance**, 518-485-2889, TTY 800-634-2110, www.tax.ny.gov

TELEPHONE (LAND LINES)

- **AT&T**, 800-222-0300, www.att.com
- **MCI**, 800-444-3333, www.mci.com
- **RCN**, 800-746-4726, www.rcn.com/new-york
- **Sprint**, 866-866-7509, www.sprint.com
- **Verizon**, 800-VERIZON, www.verizon.com

TRANSPORTATION

- **AirTrain**, 800-247-7433, www.panynj.gov
- **NJ State Department of Transportation**, 609-530-2000, www.njdot.nj.gov
- **New York City Department of Transportation**, 311, www.nyc.gov/dot
- **NY State Department of Transportation**, 518-457-6195, 718-482-4594, 800-786-5368, www.dot.ny.gov
- **Port Authority of New York & New Jersey**, 212-564-8484, 800-221-9903, www.panynj.gov
- **U.S. Department of Transportation**, 855-368-4200, www.dot.gov

AIRPORTS

- **John F. Kennedy International**, 718-244-4444 for airport information, 718-244-4225 for lost and found, and 718-244-4168 for parking; www.panynj.gov
- **LaGuardia International Airport**, call 718-533-3400 for airport information; 718-533-3988 for lost and found; and 718-533-3850 for parking; www.panynj.gov
- **Newark Liberty International Airport**, 973-961-6000 for airport information; 908-787-0667 for lost and found; and 888-397-4636, then press 22, to receive parking information; www.panynj.gov
- **Port Authority of New York & New Jersey**, 212-435-7000, 800-221-9903, www.panynj.gov

BUSES

- **Greyhound Lines**, 800-231-2222, www.greyhound.com
- **Peter Pan Bus Lines,** 800-343-9999, www.peterpanbus.com
- **Port Authority Bus Terminal Information**, 212-564-8484, 800-221-9903, www.panynj.gov

FERRIES

- **East River Ferry,** 1-800-53-FERRY, www.eastriverferry.com
- **NY Water Taxi**, 212-742-1969, www.nywatertaxi.com
- **New York Waterway**, 800-53-FERRY, www.nywaterway.com
- **Seastreak**, 800-BOAT-RIDE, www.seastreak.com
- **Staten Island Ferry**, 311, www.nyc.gov/statenislandferry

RAIL

- **Amtrak** (Penn Station), 800-872-7245, www.amtrak.com
- **Long Island Railroad** (Penn Station), 511, 718-217-5477, TTY 718-558-3022, www.mta.info
- **Metro-North,** 511, 212-532-4900, TTY 800-724-3322, www.mta.info
- **New Jersey Transit** (Penn Station), 9730275-5555 www.njtransit.com
- **Staten Island Railway**, 511, www.mta.info/sir

SUBWAYS AND CITY BUSES

- **Lost and Found** (NYC Transit Authority), 511, www.mta.info
- **MTA Customer Service**, 718-330-1234, www.mta.info
- **MetroCard**, 511
- **PATH service to New Jersey**, 800-234-7284, www.panynj.gov
- **Subway and Bus Schedules** (NYC Transit Authority automated system for fares, routes, schedules), 718-330-1234, www.mta.info

TAXIS, LIMOUSINES

- **Taxi and Limousine Commission**, 311, www.nyc.gov/taxi

TOURISM AND TRAVEL

- **National Park Service**, www.nps.gov
- **New Jersey Division of Travel & Tourism**, 800-VISIT-NJ, www.visitnj.org
- **NYC & Company** (NYC's official marketing, tourism, and partnership organization), 212-484-1200, www.nycgo.com, www.nycandcompany.org
- **New York State Travel Information Center**, 800-CALL-NYS, www.iloveny.com
- **New York Passport Agency**, Automated Appointment Number, 877-487-2778, www.travel.state.gov

UTILITY EMERGENCIES

- **Electrical emergencies or gas leaks**, Con Edison, 800-752-6633, www.coned.com
- **Gas or electric service shutoff hotline**, 800-342-3355

ZIP CODE INFORMATION

- **USPS ZIP codes request**, 800-275-8777, www.usps.com

INDEX

JULIE SCHWIETERT COLLAZO IS A NYC-BASED WRITER WHO has lived in the city since 1999. To learn more about her work, visit www.collazoprojects.com.

READER RESPONSE

e would appreciate your comments regarding this twenty-third edition of the *Newcomer's Handbook® for Moving to and Living in New York City.* If you've found any mistakes or omissions or if you would just like to express your opinion about the guide, please let us know. We will consider any suggestions for possible inclusion in our next edition, and if we use your comments, we'll send you a free copy of our next edition. Please e-mail us at readerresponse@firstbooks.com, or mail or fax this response form to:

Reader Response Department
First Books
6750 SW Franklin, Suite A
Portland, OR 97223-2542
Fax: 503.968.6779

Comments: _____

_____

_____

_____

_____

_____

_____

_____

_____

_____

Name: _____

Address: _____

_____

Telephone: ( ) _____

Email: _____

6750 SW Franklin, Suite A
Portland, OR 97223-2542
USA
P: 503.968.6777
www.firstbooks.com

RELOCATION RESOURCES

Utilizing an innovative grid and "static" reusable adhesive sticker format, *Furniture Placement and Room Planning Guide...Moving Made Easy* provides a functional and practical solution to all your space planning and furniture placement needs.

MOVING WITH KIDS?

Look into *The Moving Book: A Kids' Survival Guide*. Divided into three sections (before, during, and after the move), it's a handbook, a journal, and a scrapbook all in one. Includes address book, colorful change-of-address cards, and a useful section for parents.

Children's Book of the Month Club "Featured Selection"; American Bookseller's "Pick of the List"; Winner of the Family Channel's "Seal of Quality" Award

And for your younger children, ease their transition with our brand-new title just for them, *Max's Moving Adventure: A Coloring Book for Kids on the Move*. A complete story book featuring activities as well as pictures that children can color; designed to help children cope with the stresses of small or large moves.

NEWCOMERSWEB.COM

Based on the award-winning *Newcomer's Handbooks*, **NewcomersWeb.com** offers the highest quality neighborhood and community information in a one-of-a-kind searchable online database. The following areas are covered: Atlanta, Austin, Boston, Chicago, Dallas–Fort Worth, Houston, Los Angeles, Minneapolis–St. Paul, New York City, Portland (Oregon), San Francisco, Seattle, Washington DC, and the USA.

NEWCOMER'S HANDBOOKS°

Regularly revised and updated, these popular guides are now available for Atlanta, Boston, Chicago, China, Dallas–Ft. Worth, Houston, London, Los Angeles, Minneapolis–St. Paul, New York City, Portland, San Francisco Bay Area, Seattle, and Washington DC.

"Invaluable ...highly recommended" – *Library Journal*

If you're coming from another country, don't miss the *Newcomer's Handbook® for Moving to and Living in the USA* by Mike Livingston, termed "a fascinating book for newcomers and residents alike" by the *Chicago Tribune*.